Rural Livelihoods and Poverty Reduction Policies

Based on case study research in four low income sub-Saharan African countries – Uganda, Kenya, Tanzania and Malawi – this book brings together the micro-level realities of gaining a living in rural areas with the macro-level policies that seek to secure rapid poverty reduction in line with the United Nations Millennium Development Goal of halving global poverty by the year 2015.

The starting point is the livelihoods approach to poverty reduction that provides a powerful framework within which micro-level experiences of poverty and vulnerability can be connected to the policy contexts that either block or facilitate people's own efforts to escape from poverty. Initial chapters provide evidence concerning the multiple and diverse character of rural livelihoods. The book then goes on to examine the institutional context of livelihoods, including decentralisation, taxation, markets, land tenure and agricultural research. The natural resource dimensions of agriculture, livestock, fisheries, small-scale irrigation and community-based natural resource management policies are then analysed. The concluding chapters consider micro–macro linkages, including linking micro-level poverty traps to Poverty Reduction Strategy Papers; incorporating rural poverty measurement in such strategies; and tracing macro-micro economic links.

This book exposes the gap that occurs between the rhetoric of poverty reduction strategies in capital cities and the practice of public sector delivery in rural areas. It will be essential reading for advanced students and researchers in the fields of rural development, rural livelihoods, poverty reduction strategies and sub-Saharan African development as well as advisors and practitioners in international organisations.

Frank Ellis has a Chair in the School of Development Studies at the University of East Anglia. He works as an agricultural economist in developing countries and has published widely on topics including crop marketing, agricultural policy reform, household economics and diverse rural livelihoods. **H. Ade Freeman** is a Director at the International Livestock Research Institute, Nairobi, Kenya. He has worked as an Economist with the Consultative Group on International Agricultural Research since 1991 and has published extensively on themes related to agricultural and livestock productivity, rural livelihoods and poverty reduction in developing countries.

Routledge studies in development economics

1 **Economic Development in the Middle East**
Rodney Wilson

2 **Monetary and Financial Policies in Developing Countries**
Growth and stabilization
Akhtar Hossain and Anis Chowdhury

3 **New Directions in Development Economics**
Growth, environmental concerns and government in the 1990s
Edited by Mats Lundahl and Benno J. Ndulu

4 **Financial Liberalization and Investment**
Kanhaya L. Gupta and Robert Lensink

5 **Liberalization in the Developing World**
Institutional and economic changes in Latin America, Africa and Asia
Edited by Alex E. Fernández Jilberto and André Mommen

6 **Financial Development and Economic Growth**
Theory and experiences from developing countries
Edited by Niels Hermes and Robert Lensink

7 **The South African Economy**
Macroeconomic prospects for the medium term
Finn Tarp and Peter Brixen

8 **Public Sector Pay and Adjustment**
Lessons from five countries
Edited by Christopher Colclough

9 **Europe and Economic Reform in Africa**
Structural adjustment and economic diplomacy
Obed O. Mailafia

10 **Post-apartheid Southern Africa**
Economic challenges and policies for the future
Edited by Lennart Petersson

11 **Financial Integration and Development**
Liberalization and reform in Sub-Saharan Africa
Ernest Aryeetey and Machiko Nissanke

12 **Regionalization and Globalization in the Modern World Economy**
Perspectives on the Third World and transitional economies
Edited by Alex E. Fernández Jilberto and André Mommen

13 **The African Economy**
Policy, institutions and the future
Steve Kayizzi-Mugerwa

14 **Recovery from Armed Conflict in Developing Countries**
Edited by Geoff Harris

15 **Small Enterprises and Economic Development**
The dynamics of micro and small enterprises
Carl Liedholm and Donald C. Mead

16 **The World Bank**
New agendas in a changing world
Michelle Miller-Adams

17 **Development Policy in the Twenty-First Century**
Beyond the post-Washington consensus
Edited by Ben Fine, Costas Lapavitsas and Jonathan Pincus

18 **State-Owned Enterprises in the Middle East and North Africa**
Privatization, performance and reform
Edited by Merih Celasun

19 **Finance and Competitiveness in Developing Countries**
Edited by José María Fanelli and Rohinton Medhora

20 **Contemporary Issues in Development Economics**
Edited by B.N. Ghosh

21 **Mexico Beyond NAFTA**
Edited by Martín Puchet Anyul and Lionello F. Punzo

22 **Economies in Transition**
A guide to China, Cuba, Mongolia, North Korea and Vietnam at the turn of the twenty-first century
Ian Jeffries

23 **Population, Economic Growth and Agriculture in Less Developed Countries**
Nadia Cuffaro

24 **From Crisis to Growth in Africa?**
Edited by Mats Lundal

25 **The Macroeconomics of Monetary Union**
An analysis of the CFA franc zone
David Fielding

26 **Endogenous Development**
Networking, innovation, institutions and cities
Antonio Vasquez-Barquero

27 **Labour Relations in Development**
Edited by Alex E. Fernández Jilberto and Marieke Riethof

28 **Globalization, Marginalization and Development**
Edited by S. Mansoob Murshed

29 **Programme Aid and Development**
Beyond conditionality
Howard White and Geske Dijkstra

30 **Competitiveness Strategy in Developing Countries**
A manual for policy analysis
Edited by Ganeshan Wignaraja

31 **The African Manufacturing Firm**
An analysis based on firm surveys in sub-Saharan Africa
Dipak Mazumdar and Ata Mazaheri

32 **Trade Policy, Growth and Poverty in Asian Developing Countries**
Edited by Kishor Sharma

33 **International Competitiveness, Investment and Finance**
A case study of India
Edited by A. Ganesh Kumar, Kunal Sen and Rajendra R. Vaidya

34 **The Pattern of Aid Giving**
The impact of good governance on development assistance
Eric Neumayer

35 **New International Poverty Reduction Strategies**
Edited by Jean-Pierre Cling, Mireille Razafindrakoto and François Roubaud

36 **Targeting Development**
Critical perspectives on the Millennium Development Goals
Edited by Richard Black and Howard White

37 **Essays on Balance of Payments Constrained Growth**
Theory and evidence
Edited by J.S.L. McCombie and A.P. Thirlwall

38 **The Private Sector After Communism**
New entrepreneurial firms in transition economies
Jan Winiecki, Vladimir Benacek and Mihaly Laki

39 **Information Technology and Development**
A new paradigm for delivering the internet to rural areas in developing countries
Jeffrey James

40 **The Economics of Palestine**
Economic policy and institutional reform for a viable Palestine state
Edited by David Cobham and Nu'man Kanafani

41 **Development Dilemmas**
The methods and political ethics of growth policy
Melvyn Ayogu and Don Ross

42 **Rural Livelihoods and Poverty Reduction Policies**
Edited by Frank Ellis and H. Ade Freeman

Rural Livelihoods and Poverty Reduction Policies

Edited by Frank Ellis and
H. Ade Freeman

Routledge
Taylor & Francis Group
LONDON AND NEW YORK

First published 2005
by Routledge
2 Park Square, Milton Park, Abingdon, Oxon OX14 4RN

Simultaneously published in the USA and Canada
by Routledge
711 Third Avenue, New York, NY 10017

Routledge is an imprint of the Taylor & Francis Group

First issued in paperback 2011

Typeset in Bembo by Wearset Ltd, Boldon, Tyne and Wear

British Library Cataloguing in Publication Data
A catalogue record for this book is available from the British Library

Library of Congress Cataloging in Publication Data
A catalog record for this book has been requested

ISBN13: 978-0-415-34119-6 (hbk)
ISBN13: 978-0-415-51139-1 (pbk)

Contents

Illustrations

Figures

Tables

Contributors

This list contains details of the first, and, where applicable, second authors of the chapters in this volume where details other than just simple affiliation were made available. In cases where other authors provided details of their organisation only, this information is contained in a footnote at the end of the chapter.

Eddie Allison is a Senior Lecturer in Natural Resources in the School of Development Studies at the University of East Anglia, Norwich, UK. His research interests are in environmental management and development issues in coastal and wetland systems and he conducts policy and management advisory work for a variety of international agencies in this field. Over the past few years he has been studying the adaptive livelihood strategies of small-scale fisherfolk in the African Great Lakes region, which complements his earlier work on the ecology and productivity of these lakes.

Edward Anderson is a Research Officer at the Overseas Development Institute (ODI), London. His main research activity over the past few years has concerned how the integration of people and households into international trade affects poverty and inequality, particularly via the labour market. He has lectured in economics and statistics at the Universities of Keele and Sussex. He has published articles in the European Review of Economic History and Development Policy Review, and produced background papers for the 1999 UNDP Human Development Report and the DFID White Paper on Globalisation.

Steve Ashley is Partner and Principal Consultant with the IDL group, and Director of its parent company In Development Ltd. Steve is an economist who specialises in pro-poor policy, poverty analysis and the facilitation of policy processes. The IDL group works principally at the interface between policy and practice and is a multidisciplinary, permanently-staffed development organisation with skills in poverty and livelihoods analysis, institutional development, economics, political science and social development: www.theIDLgroup.com.

Godfrey Bahiigwa is currently a Senior Research Fellow at the Economic Policy Research Center (EPRC), Kampala, Uganda. He is a full-time researcher and in recent years his research has concentrated on rural livelihoods and poverty reduction, agricultural productivity, agricultural price policy and food security. He is currently the team leader of a rural taxation study in Uganda funded by the Department for International Development (DFID-EA Uganda). He worked closely with the government of Uganda in designing its Plan for Modernisation of Agriculture (PMA), a rural development strategy for poverty eradication. His research and career interests are in agricultural and rural development and poverty reduction.

Chris Barrett is Professor of Applied Economics and Management and co-Director of the African Food Security and Natural Resources Management program at Cornell University. He holds degrees from Princeton, Oxford and the University of Wisconsin–Madison and worked as a staff economist with the Institute for International Finance in Washington, DC in the 1980s. He has published extensively on the themes of poverty reduction, food security, agricultural productivity, individual and market behaviour under risk and uncertainty, and sustainable natural resources management in developing areas. He is co-editor of the American Journal of Agricultural Economics and serves as an associate editor or editorial board member of Environment and Development Economics, the Journal of African Economies and World Development.

Kate Bird is a Research Fellow at the Overseas Development Institute (ODI) in London, and a core team member in the international Chronic Poverty Research Centre where she leads work on investigating the association between remoteness and the chronicity of poverty. Her other recent research includes work on intrahousehold differentiation, trade-poverty linkages, the contribution of governance and poverty failures to food insecurity in southern Africa. She has published on chronic poverty, and issues around rural livelihoods and diversification. She has particular experience in sub-Saharan Africa and India, but has worked elsewhere in Asia and in transitional economies.

Piers Blaikie is a Professorial Fellow at the School of Development Studies, University of East Anglia. He has worked in the hybrid field of Political Ecology for twenty years and the wider fields of the political economy of agrarian change and the environment and environmental policy. The regional focus of his research has been Nepal, India, and more recently, central and southern Africa.

Deborah Fahy Bryceson is a Senior Research Fellow at the Afrika-studiecentrum, Leiden University, the Netherlands. She coordinated a pan-African research programme on deagrarianisation from 1996–2001. She has written extensively on a number of rural and urban development topics. Her published books include: *Women Wielding the Hoe: Lessons from*

Rural Africa for Feminist Theory and Development Practice (Berg Publishers 1995); *Farewell to Farms: Deagrarianization and Employment in Africa* (Ashgate 1997); *Disappearing Peasantries: Rural Labour* in *Africa, Asia and Latin America* (Intermediate Technology Publications 2000); *Livelihoods, Linkages and Policy Paradoxes* (Special Issue of the *Journal of Contemporary African Studies* 19 (1), 2001); *Alcohol in Africa: Mixing Business, Pleasure and Politics* (Heinemann/Greenwood 2002); and *The Transnational Family* (Berg Publishers 2002).

Brian Cooksey is co-founder (in 1988) and director of the Tanzania Development Research Group based in Dar es Salaam (email: tadreg@raha.com). He has conducted research and written on a wide range of topics, including agricultural marketing, corruption and aid. His recent publications include 'Aid and Corruption in Africa' *The Economist Intelligence Unit, Sub-Saharan Africa: Regional Overview*, April 2003; 'Marketing Reform? The Rise and Fall of Agricultural Liberalisation in Tanzania', *Development Policy Review*, 21 (1): 67–90, 2003; and 'The Power and the Vainglory: Anatomy of a Malaysian Independent Power Project in Tanzania', in Jomo, K.S. (ed.) *Ugly Malaysians? South-South Investments Abused*, Centre for Black Research, Durban, South Africa, 2002.

Sholto Cross is an affiliated research fellow of the Overseas Development Group at the University of East Anglia. He has most recently been working on issues of local governance and rural development in east and central Africa, including decentralisation and land reform. He is currently advising on the launch of an independent venture based in civil society to monitor democratic accountability and the institutional effectiveness of the public sector in Africa.

Priya Deshingkar directed the Andhra Pradesh studies for the three-year DFID funded Livelihood Options project and is a Research Associate of the Overseas Development Institute, London. She has a Ph.D. from the Institute of Development Studies, UK, and was formerly on the staff of the Stockholm Environment Institute, Sweden. Her main interests over the last three years have been livelihood diversification, seasonal migration, rural market imperfections, and the social and political dynamics of vulnerability. She has worked and published extensively on questions of poverty, environment and livelihoods in India. Her most recent work is *Policy Windows and Livelihood Futures: Prospects for Poverty Reduction in Rural India* a book that she is co-editing with John Farrington and others.

Catherine Dolan is an Assistant Professor of Anthropology at Northeastern University in Boston, MA, USA. She has taught and researched in Anthropology, Development, African Studies and Gender Analysis at various UK universities, and has held Visiting Fellowships at the Centre of African Studies, SOAS; the Department of Anthropology, University of North Carolina at Chapel Hill; and the International Center for Research on Women in Washington, DC. Her research is focused on the social impacts of globalisation, gender and economic change, and rural livelihoods, particularly in east Africa. She is currently engaged in research on ethical trade, gender and rights in African agriculture.

Frank Ellis is currently director of the Overseas Development Group (ODG) at the University of East Anglia, Norwich, UK, and has a chair in the School of Development Studies. His main research activity over the past few years has concerned rural livelihoods and poverty reduction in Uganda, Kenya, Tanzania and Malawi; and he was team leader of the LADDER research project funded by the Department for International Development (DFID) from 2000 to 2004. He has published widely on the theme of the diversity of rural livelihoods in low income countries, and retains an interest in areas of rural development strategy, household economics and agricultural policies.

H. Ade Freeman is Director, Targeting Research and Development Opportunities Theme at the International Livestock Research Institute, in Nairobi, Kenya. He has worked as an economist with the Consultative Group on International Agricultural Research (CGIAR) since 1991 and has published extensively on themes related to agricultural and livestock productivity, market linkages for smallholder farmers, natural resource management, rural livelihoods and poverty reduction in developing countries. He was the Team Leader of the Kenya component of the LADDER research project. His current research focuses on the impact of agricultural research investments on poverty reduction and food security.

Paul Kimalu is an assistant analyst – Kenya Institute for Public Policy Research and Analysis (KIPPRA) – on secondment from the government of Kenya. He is a senior economist with the Ministry of Planning and National Development. Kimalu has over ten years working experience with the government and also had field experience – having worked as a District Development Officer for a period of three years. He is a graduate of the University of Nairobi, where he earned an MA in Economic Policy Management, and a BA in Economics. His research work has focused on rural welfare, poverty, education, labour market and health modelling and analysis. He has published widely on poverty, education, health and labour issues.

Mwangi Kimenyi holds a Ph.D. in Economics from the Center for Study of Public Choice at George Mason University, USA, and is the Executive Director of the Kenya Institute for Public Policy Research and Analysis (KIPPRA). He has been Assistant Professor of Economics at the University of Mississippi (1986–1991) and University of Connecticut (1991–2003). He is also the vice-president of the African Educational Foundation for Public Policy and Market Process. Professor Kimenyi has authored over 60 referred journal articles and is the co-author of five books. Professor Kimenyi's current research focuses on institutional and economic reforms.

Milton Kutengule is currently Secretary to the Treasury in the Ministry of Finance in Malawi. He was formerly Permanent Secretary of the Ministry of Economic Planning and Development, responsible for monitoring the implementation of Malawi's Poverty Reduction Strategy by various stakeholders including government ministries and departments, the private sector, donor agencies and the civil society. He studied rural livelihood diversification for his doctorate at the University of East Anglia, Norwich, UK, from 1997–2000. He has been involved in the design and management of various social and economic research activities in Malawi, including serving as the Malawi Project Coordinator of the LADDER Research Project from 2000–2002. He also has much experience in the design and management of economic and social development policies and programmes in Malawi. Recently, he has been involved in various reviews of decentralisation and poverty reduction initiatives in southern Africa and in Malawi.

Bruce Lankford is a senior lecturer at the School of Development Studies at the University of East Anglia, Norwich, UK. His main research activity over the past few years concerns irrigation in relation to rural livelihoods, river basin management and dynamic hydrological environments, mainly in Tanzania. He has over twenty years experience in irrigation and water resources management stemming from work in Swaziland, India, Kyrgyzstan, Pakistan, Sudan and Malaysia. Related interests cover water user associations, analysis of efficiency and productivity, and research on intersectoral allocation of water.

Damiano Manda holds a Ph.D. in Economics and is a lecturer in the Department of Economics, University of Nairobi. He is a senior policy analyst at the Kenya Institute for Public Policy Research and Analysis (KIPPRA), and also a researcher at the African Economic Research Consortium (AERC). His research focuses on labour markets and poverty as well as education and health policy issues.

John McDonagh is a lecturer in Natural Resources and Development and a member of the Overseas Development Group (ODG) in the School of Development Studies at the University of East Anglia, Norwich, UK. His research interests revolve around low input resource management in farming systems, particularly soils, with a recent regional focus of southern and eastern Africa. He has more recently been involved in rural livelihoods research in eastern Africa as part of the LADDER project and in separate research looking at options for improving the effectiveness of the agricultural support services in rural Uganda.

Germano Mwabu holds a Ph.D. in economics and is currently the chairman of the Department of Economics, University of Nairobi, Kenya, and a coordinator (jointly with Erik Thorbecke), of the African Economic Research Consortium (AERC) project on poverty, income distribution and labour markets in sub-Saharan Africa. Professor Mwabu has authored a number of referred journal articles and is a co-author of several books His research interests are in areas of rural development, health policy and social provision in Africa.

Nancy Nafula is an assistant analyst in the Social Sector Division. She holds an MA in Economics from the University of Nairobi. At KIPPRA, she is involved in sectoral modelling for education and health and in microsimulation work for poverty analysis and other research activities in the division. She also has experience in working with household data surveys. She has co-authored a number of publications in the areas of poverty, health and education. Her research interests are in the areas of poverty, education, health and labour markets.

Colin Poulton is Research Fellow in the Department of Agricultural Sciences, Imperial College London, Wye campus. His research addresses various aspects of the question: 'how can pro-poor economic growth in rural Africa best be stimulated?' Specific interests include the organisation and performance of African cotton systems, the challenge of providing seasonal finance to agricultural households and the requirements for, and livelihood impacts of, sustainable intensification of smallholder agriculture. He is currently working in Kenya, Tanzania, Zimbabwe and South Africa and is principal researcher for the DFID-funded research project 'Competition and Coordination in Cotton Market Systems in Southern and Eastern Africa', which runs until 2005.

Kunal Sen is a Reader in Economics in the School of Development Studies, University of East Anglia, Norwich, UK. As a part of the LADDER project, he has been researching the linkages between macroeconomic policies and their micro-level outcomes on rural livelihood diversification in sub-Saharan Africa. His other current research interests are growth-poverty linkages, and the impact of international trade on labour markets.

Brent Swallow is a Principal Economist with the World Agroforestry Centre (ICRAF) in Nairobi, Kenya. He currently serves as Theme Leader for Environmental Services, Lead Scientist for Environmental Governance, and focal point for HIV/AIDS. Since 1984 he has been involved in multidisciplinary studies of agriculture and environment across Africa, with major emphasis on rangeland management, trypanosomosis control and watershed management. He has published extensively on collective action and property rights in natural resource management and is a member of the Executive Committee of the Collective Action and Property Rights Programme of the CGIAR. For the last two years he has been working with Chris Barrett to develop and apply the theory of fractal poverty traps.

Foreword

Rural livelihoods entered development discourse a little over a decade ago and is now the preferred term in development literature. This does not mean that earlier terms, such as smallholder, peasant, or farm household, are lacking in their own usefulness for describing important facets of gaining a living in rural areas. Nevertheless, livelihoods invoke a larger landscape of options and opportunities for rural dwellers. The livelihood concept was crystallised in the early 1990s by Robert Chambers and Gordon Conway, the latter currently being president of the Rockefeller Foundation. The livelihood framework shifted focus away from purely income generating activities to access, ownership and management of assets by the household, with changes in asset status being a key determinant of households moving in and out of poverty. The other core feature of the framework was the diversity of strategies to maintain household welfare, often consisting of a mix of agricultural, home processing, marketing and off-farm labour activities together with reciprocity relations with other households. The result was a much richer and more nuanced understanding of households' ability to cope and adapt to difficult economic, social and environmental circumstances, and as such a more informed understanding of poverty and its determinants. The diversification dimension was developed by Frank Ellis in his book *Rural Livelihoods and Diversity in Developing Countries,* and he is both co-editor and contributor in several places to this volume.

The present book develops empirical applications of the rural livelihoods framework in the four sub-Saharan African countries of Uganda, Kenya, Tanzania and Malawi, with a case study from rural India also included. The most interesting aspect of this book is the book's approach of 'embedding' the analysis of the diversity of household and community livelihood strategies within the broader context of rural institutions and government policies. This in turn gives insights into poverty reduction, particularly through such mechanisms as Poverty Reduction Strategy Papers (PRSPs). Early on, the book observes that rural policy and institutions are often 'ineffective and parasitic' rather than being 'effective and facilitating'. That is, resources are extracted from poor households to maintain inefficient rural institutions that do not serve the interests of the rural population. Certainly in Africa an agricultural surplus, whether in the form of labour or commodities, has been at the heart of development policy since the hut taxes of the colonial era. This extractive process did not change with independence, as state marketing boards commanded an even higher percentage of export prices from African farmers. However, major social and political changes have occurred only recently in many parts of the continent. The question is whether under increasing democratisation, market liberalisation, and incipient decentralisation there is the possibility for changing accountability in the flow of funds and building more responsive and efficient rural institutions. If so, then rural Africa is at an historical watershed. This volume suggests that this will not be an easy task, but one must assume that these are necessary pre-conditions to building better delivery of health, education and agricultural services to rural households.

A key to rural poverty alleviation in Africa must be in building more accountable rural institutions and service delivery systems. While the linkage from household analysis to macro policy formulation is important, decentralisation is shifting the focus more to meso-scale issues. This has involved building more participatory processes into district level planning and resource allocation, ensuring market access by smallholders through farmer collective action and institutional innovation by both private sector and civil society organisation, and building more demand responsiveness and quality assessment into rural service delivery. Rural institutional innovation at this meso scale is where the impacts of decentralisation and local level democratisation will be most pronounced. Ameliorating rural poverty in Africa will not be easy, but the sense is of a reversal in the historical balance between the state and the interests and welfare of its rural populations.

Finally, the book also provokes questions about the roles of diversification and specialisation in African rural economies. The extraordinary diversity of rural livelihood strategies may be as much a symptom of poverty, as a means out of it. Rural households in Africa must have the flexibility to source multiple income streams virtually to survive, but their way out of poverty must be, as in Asia and Latin America, through greater specialisation in production, processing and marketing. Diversification clearly provides an interim solution for rural households to the persistent problem of poverty and vulnerability, but does not diversity at some point become a constraint on further increases in household and market productivity and efficiency? A critical example is the very high transaction costs of assembling surpluses from diversified smallholders within heterogeneous agro-ecologies in Africa. Answers to these questions become critical to how a sustainable growth path will be developed in rural African economies. This book provides insights into the complexity of that task.

In summary, the Rockefeller Foundation was pleased to provide support to a conference and a volume that sparks such questions, and moves enquiry on the poor and excluded in Africa further forward.

John K. Lynam
The Rockefeller Foundation
Nairobi, Kenya

Preface

The chapters in this volume arise from two different sources. The first was a four-year rural livelihoods research programme entitled LADDER that conducted research in Uganda, Kenya, Tanzania and Malawi between 2000 and 2003, and produced over thirty working papers on an array of different dimensions of rural livelihoods. The second was an international conference held in Nairobi on 13 and 14 January 2003 on the subject of Rural Livelihoods and Poverty Reduction Policies. This conference brought together roughly one hundred participants, mainly policy makers from those four countries as well as researchers from them, and from Europe, North America and India. These two sources overlap since many, but not all, the conference papers coincided with working papers from the LADDER project, while others were presented by policy makers or researchers who had not been involved in the project.

The main preoccupations and themes of the book are set out in full in the first chapter, however they can be briefly summarised here. At its centre, the book is about the micro-macro connections between the realities of making a living in rural areas of low income countries and the macro level policies that seek to accomplish poverty reduction goals. Perhaps not surprisingly it is found that there is a substantial mismatch between the micro realities and the macro policies. While rural livelihoods are diverse, flexible, mobile, and cross-sectoral, macro policies embodied in Poverty Reduction Strategy Papers (PRSPs) mainly seem to end up as little more than sectoral expenditure plans, albeit fluffed up by a consultative and participatory rhetoric.

However, what is really important are the things that PRSPs fail to address rather than the things to which they end up devoting resources. In particular, they fail to create public sector institutional environments that facilitate rather than hamper people's own efforts to devise pathways out of poverty. A failure which can be severe and pervasive. On close inspection local level institutional contexts often reveal themselves as ineffective and parasitic. They are ineffective because they fail to deliver more than a small fraction of the services that they are mandated to provide. They are parasitic because they tend to treat all local level private activity, whether household or business activity, as 'fair game' for levies and fees and fines and taxes and tithes of every conceivable kind. The relationship between public service and citizen can be more akin to predator and prey than the delivery and accountability guise in which it is typically cloaked.

The chapters of this book provide numerous insights into the micro–macro disconnection. After setting out the stall more completely than is possible here in the first two chapters of the book, a following set of five chapters provide a wealth of evidence concerning the multiple and diverse character of rural livelihoods and the implications of this in terms of supporting flexibility and mobility rather than continued policy thinking along rigid sectoral and sub-sectoral lines. A second set of five chapters examines various dimensions of the institutional context of rural livelihoods, utilising country case studies. These dimensions include decentralisation, taxation, markets, land tenure and agricultural research. A third set of five chapters examines natural resource aspects of livelihoods and their institutional context, including agriculture, livestock, fisheries, small-scale irrigation and community-based natural resource management policies. Finally, a set of three chapters examines various aspects of micro-macro links including linking micro level poverty traps to PRSPs; incorporating rural poverty reduction into PRSPs; and understanding macro-micro economic links.

The scale and scope of the Nairobi conference would not have been possible without generous support from the Rockefeller Foundation in Nairobi in addition to resources that the UK Department for International Development (DFID) made available for this event. The four-year research programme entitled Livelihoods and Diversification Directions Explored by Research (LADDER) was funded predominantly by the Policy Research Programme of the then Rural Livelihoods Department of DFID, with some supplementary funding for work in Kenya provided by the UNDP. Alas, the main DFID bodies concerned have subsequently disappeared in a reorganisation. Nevertheless the authors of this volume would like to express their considerable gratitude to DFID for the opportunities to do innovative research enabled by the LADDER research grant. Thanks are due to Mike Scott and Jim Harvey, with special mention due to Lucy Ambridge who managed the programme on the DFID side with great flexibility and good humour.

As editors of this volume we are grateful to a great number of people who collaborated with us, supported us and assisted us in the preparation of the chapters of the book, as well as the underlying activities that occurred behind them. First of these are the chapter writers themselves who in the main willingly and efficiently revised or prepared materials so that they could be utilised in this form. Second there are the country research teams that organised and conducted the livelihoods research in each of the four countries, and especially Godfrey Bahiigwa in Uganda, Ntengua Mdoe in Tanzania and Milton Kutengule in Malawi. Other country collaborators that deserve mention are Joseph Semboja and Sam Wangwe in Tanzania, and Alfred Nyasulu in Malawi. Third, there are the participants in the Nairobi conference, some of whom belong also in one of the preceding two groups and others who came specially to the conference and helped to make it a success. Finally, there are always unsung heroes behind the scenes of any endeavour like this, and John Mims provided extraordinary research support through most of the LADDER research programme.

Needless to say, the views expressed in the chapters of this book are those of the authors or the editors and in no way reflect official positions of the Department for International Development (DFID), the Rockefeller Foundation, nor any other organisation that supported the research process in different ways.

Frank Ellis and H. Ade Freeman
Norwich, UK and Nairobi, Kenya
April 2004

Part I

Introduction

1 Conceptual framework and overview of themes

Frank Ellis and H. Ade Freeman

Introduction

This book arises from rural livelihoods research conducted in eastern and southern Africa in the period 2000 to 2003. The central theme of the book is the connection that needs to be made between patterns of rural livelihoods as they actually occur and the Poverty Reduction Strategy Papers (PRSPs) that are the centrepiece of government-donor efforts to reduce the incidence of absolute poverty in low income countries. It might be thought that this connection is obvious and hardly requires further elaboration, particularly given the efforts that are made to inform PRSPs by consultative exercises with civil society organisations and participatory poverty assessments.

However, such a presumption would be seriously wide of the mark. The reality is that despite their stated intentions to be innovative and cross-cutting documents, most PRSPs end up looking rather like sectoral expenditure plans, even a bit like those monolithic national development plans that were so popular three or more decades ago. Meanwhile, livelihoods are not like that at all; they are multiple, diverse, adaptive, flexible and cross-sectoral. Evidence provided in the chapters of this book suggests a serious mismatch between macro level poverty reduction strategies and the realities of micro level livelihoods.

This chapter provides an overview of the conceptual framework that informs the approach of many of the later chapters in the book, as well as a synthesis of the themes that bind the chapters together into a mosaic that seeks to shed light upon, and to take forward discussion about, the mismatch alluded to above. The starting point is the livelihoods approach to poverty reduction that provides a powerful framework within which micro-level experiences of poverty and vulnerability can be connected to the policy contexts that either block or facilitate people's own efforts to escape from poverty. It is the livelihoods framework that permits apparently disparate dimensions and entry points into poverty reduction debates to be brought together in a reasonably unified way.

The Livelihoods Framework[1]

The term livelihood attempts to capture not just what people do in order to make a living, but the resources that provide them with the capability to build a satisfactory living, the risk factors that they must consider in managing their resources, and the institutional and policy context that either helps or hinders them in their pursuit of a viable or improving living. The basic livelihoods approach or framework is illustrated in Figure 1.1.

In the livelihoods approach, resources are referred to as 'assets' or 'capitals' and are often categorised between five or more distinct asset types owned or accessed by family members: human capital (skills, education, health), physical capital (produced investment goods), financial capital (money, savings, loan access), natural capital (land, water, trees, grazing etc.) and social capital (networks and associations). These asset categories are admittedly a little contrived, and not all resources that people draw upon in constructing livelihoods fit neatly within them. Nevertheless, they serve a useful purpose in distinguishing asset types that tend to have differing connections to the policy environment. For example, human capital connects to social policies (education and health), while natural capital connects to land use, agricultural and environmental policies.

It is worth mentioning in passing that the category social capital remains somewhat elusive as a guide to improving pro-poor policies despite a decade or so of academic musings about it (Harriss 1997). While it can readily be accepted that the quality of certain types of social connectedness can make a big difference to people's livelihood prospects, this quality factor is difficult to pin down. For example, kinship ties can play roles both as valuable support networks and as demands on resources to meet familial obligations. Likewise, some types of social linkage seem more designed to keep the poor in their

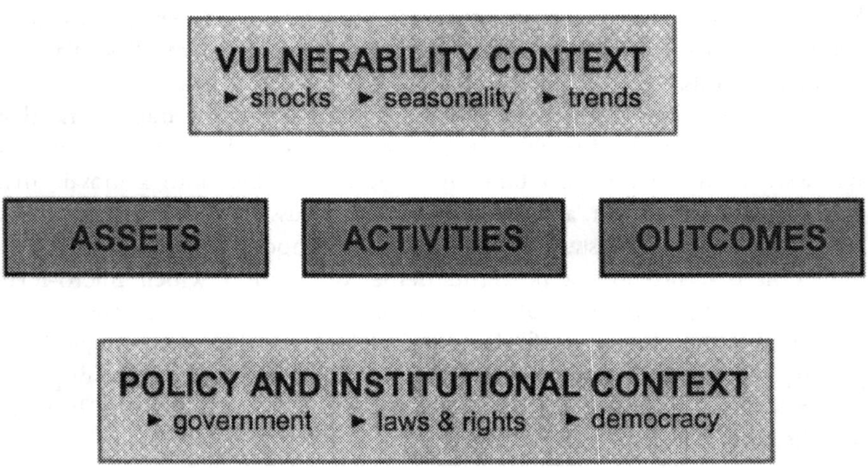

Figure 1.1 The basic livelihoods framework (source: Ellis (2003a, 2003b).)

place than to assist them to overcome their poverty (bonded labour, caste systems and some types of traditional authority are examples).

This caveat aside, the livelihoods framework regards the asset status of poor individuals or households as fundamental to an understanding of the options open to them. One of its basic tenets, therefore, is that poverty policy should be concerned with raising the asset status of the poor, or enabling existing assets that are idle or underemployed to be used productively. The approach looks positively at what is possible rather than negatively at how desperate things are. As articulated concisely by Moser (1998: 1) it seeks 'to identify what the poor have rather than what they do not have' and '[to] strengthen people's own inventive solutions, rather than substitute for, block or undermine them'.

As illustrated in Figure 1.1, the things people do in pursuit of a living are referred to in the livelihood framework as livelihood 'activities'. Activities include remote as well as nearby sources of livelihood for the resident household; thus migration and remittances by family members is considered a category of livelihood activity, as well as crop production, livestock keeping, brick making and so on. The risk factors that surround making a living are summarised as the 'vulnerability context', and the structures and processes associated with government (national and local), authority, laws and rights, democracy and participation are summarised as the 'policy and institutional context'. People's livelihood efforts, conducted within these contexts, result in outcomes: higher or lower material welfare, reduced or raised vulnerability to food insecurity, improving or degrading environmental resources, and so on. Figure 1.1 is consciously devoid of arrows implying causality or feedback. Livelihoods are complex and changing. Although of course they encompass links between cause and effect, as well as cumulative processes, these cannot be captured adequately in such a simplified representation.

The livelihoods approach sets out to be people-centred and holistic, and to provide an integrated view of how people make a living within evolving social, institutional, political, economic and environmental contexts (Carney 1998a; Bebbington 1999). It has proved to have considerable strengths, especially in recognising or discovering:

- the multiple and diverse character of livelihoods (Ellis 1998, 2000);
- the prevalence of institutionalised blockages to improving livelihoods;
- the social as well as economic character of livelihood strategies;
- the principle factors implicated in rising or diminishing vulnerability;
- the micro–macro (or macro–micro) links that connect livelihoods to policies.

Migration and vulnerability as illustrations of the approach

This section provides two interwoven illustrations of how the livelihoods approach can be utilised to gain a clearer understanding of particular development issues. One is migration, understood as a spatial separation between the location of a resident household or family, and one or more livelihood activities engaged in by family members. The other is vulnerability, defined as the proneness of a household or family to acute food insecurity when confronted by a calamitous event like a drought or flood. Different types of migration are one manifestation of the more general phenomenon of livelihood diversification (Ellis 1998, 2000), and many of the arguments that follow about migration apply also to other forms of diversification.

Migration is a central feature of the livelihoods of the majority of households in low income countries. The immediate connections to the livelihoods framework in Figure 1.1 are to human capital (migration involves mobility of labour, together with a person's experience, skills, education level and health status), and to the set of activities that comprise the occupational portfolio of the household. More than this, however, different types of migration play multiple roles in reducing the vulnerability of households, and in potentially enabling virtuous spirals of asset accumulation that can provide families with exit routes from poverty.

It is nowadays well understood that vulnerability is different from poverty. Poverty, certainly as defined by economists, describes a state with respect to an absolute or relative norm (e.g. a poverty line). Vulnerability, by contrast, refers to proneness to a sudden, catastrophic, fall in the level of a variable, usually interpreted as access to enough food for survival. The phrase 'living on the edge' provides a graphic image of the livelihood circumstances that vulnerability tries to convey. This phrase evokes the sense of a small push sending a person or people over the edge, and it is just this knife-edge between ability to survive and thrive, and sudden loss of ability to do so, that the term vulnerability seeks to describe (Ellis 2003b).

Two factors that predispose rural poor people to vulnerability are seasonality and risk. Both these factors can be ameliorated by migration. Seasonality causes what is known as the 'consumption smoothing' problem (Morduch 1995). Income flows, for example from crop production, are uneven relative to the constant needs of food consumption. The migration of household members to take advantage of differing seasonal patterns of farm production elsewhere (rural–rural migration) and of non-farm jobs in the off-season (rural–urban migration) are responses to the seasonality problem, and several case studies of these patterns have been detailed in recent literature (de Haan and Rogaly 2002; Rogaly *et al.* 2002). For food insecure rural households, out-migration of family members in the peak food deficit season may be essential for the survival of the resident group that stays behind by reducing the number of people to feed (Toulmin 1992: 51; Devereux 1993: 53)

Poor rural households in low income countries construct their livelihoods in a risky environment. They are prone to the personal shocks of chronic illness (including HIV/AIDS), accidents, and death as well as confronting natural hazards and market instability. Risks are reduced by diversifying livelihoods. This risk amelioration can, to a limited extent, occur *in situ*, for example by diversifying cropping patterns on farms or by combining farm and non-farm activities in the same location. However, because agriculture-related activities like crop processing or trading collapse when harvests collapse, more effective risk reduction occurs by spreading risk across assets and activities that have different types of risk associated with them. This is where migration comes in, because it provides just such a spread of spatially separated activities with differing risk profiles.

Vulnerability can be portrayed as a risk sequence (Figure 1.2), making it clear how it connects to the livelihoods approach as well as where migration fits into the picture. This also acts as a bridge to poverty reduction aspects of migration. Poor households build their livelihoods in a context of pervasive uncertainty comprising the seasonality and risk factors already described, as well as, quite often, political and governance risks. They are used to this, so they manage risk as best they can, and migration can play a pivotal role in helping them to do this. If a shock occurs (either a personal shock or a widespread shock like rainfall failure), they adopt coping behaviours to reduce the adverse impact of the shock, and, again, migration plays a significant role here. Coping strategies produce outcomes: relative success or failure at dealing with the shock. In the extreme case ('people fleeing drought'), resident livelihoods collapse and entire families go on the move.

Critical to the degree of vulnerability represented by risk management and coping within the sequence illustrated in Figure 1.2 is the asset status of the households and how this is changing over different time periods (see also Chapter 2). In general terms, the higher the level and the more diverse the assets owned by the household, the greater its capacity to manage risk and cope with shocks, i.e. the less vulnerable it is. So far, we have referred to migration principally in terms of one category of asset, namely labour, the mobility of which helps to ameliorate seasonality and risk. However, the asset effects of migration go further than this. The earnings obtained from migrating, and the remittances sent back by migrants to their resident families, are

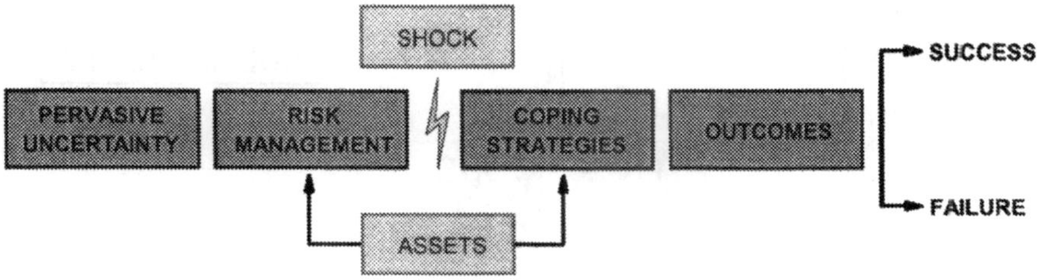

Figure 1.2 Vulnerability as a risk sequence (source: Ellis (2003b).)

critical to maintaining or raising the level of other assets: savings, land, equipment, livestock, education of children and so on. Migration also widens social networks and consequently increases so-called social capital.

In order to move out of poverty, poor households have to increase the assets that they can deploy productively in order to generate higher incomes. Numerous studies have observed that moving out of poverty is a cumulative process, often achieved in tiny increments. Assets are traded up in sequence, for example, chickens to goats, to cattle, to land; or, cash from non-farm income to farm inputs to higher farm income to land or to livestock (Ellis and Mdoe 2003; Chapter 3 this volume). A critical constraint slowing down or preventing such 'virtuous spirals' is the inability to borrow or to generate cash (often discussed under the rubric of credit market failures). For this reason, earnings or remittances from migration can play a pivotal role in initiating and sustaining such cumulative processes. Nor do the cash flows have to be large in order to do this. In the context of so-called dollar-a-day poverty i.e. when the poor are defined as those getting by on under the equivalent of a dollar per day worth of consumption per person, very small amounts of additional cash can make significant differences to the options available to people to get a toehold on ladders out of poverty.

The connections discussed in preceding paragraphs are summarised in Figure 1.3, which displays the fundamental ways that migration and remittances can help to reduce vulnerability and poverty for people trying to put

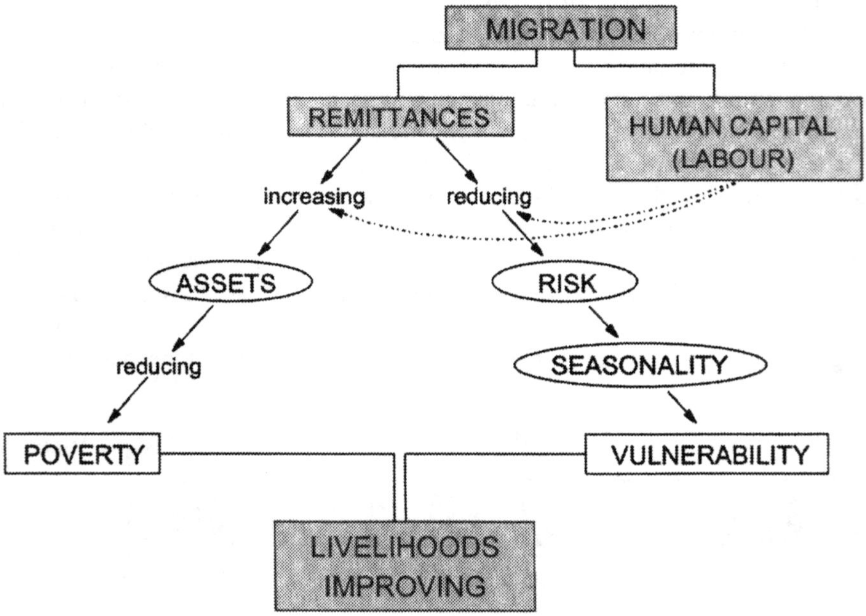

Figure 1.3 Positive links between migration and improving livelihoods. (source: Ellis (2003a).)

together adequate and improving livelihoods. The following list represents some of the positive ways that earnings and remittances from migration can strengthen rural livelihoods:

- investment in land, or land improvements, including reclaiming previously degraded land (Tiffen *et al.* 1994) provided one of the better-known examples of this for Machakos district in Kenya);
- purchase of cash inputs to agriculture (hired labour, disease control etc.), resulting in better cultivation practices and higher yields (Carter 1997);
- investment in agricultural implements or machines (water pumps, ploughs etc.);
- investment in education, resulting in better prospects for the next generation (Francis and Hoddinott 1993; Hoddinott 1994);
- investment in assets permitting local non-farm income to be generated (bicycle taxi, motorbike, milling machine, kiosk etc.).

Migration is typical of the type of cross-cutting phenomenon that PRSPs seem poorly equipped to handle, and it therefore provides a suitable example of the mismatch between micro livelihood priorities and macro policy formulation referred to at the start of this chapter. In a survey of forty-eight PRSPs undertaken in 2003, migration was found not to be mentioned at all in twenty-one of them. Most of the remaining twenty-seven PRSPs referred to migration in negative or pejorative terms. Seventeen, for example, posed internal migration as a problem for development, eight cast migration as a cause of urban poverty, and others pointed to the negative effects of migration in spreading HIV/AIDS and contributing to crime. Eight PRSPs expressed the need for internal migration to be controlled by the state i.e. for rural–urban migration to be reduced (Black *et al.* 2003: 18–19).

An improved policy understanding of many other aspects of rural poverty is facilitated by the livelihoods approach. To provide just one more example, natural resource management institutions, understood as the customs, rules, laws and organisations that determine people's access to different types of natural resource, constitute part of the policy and institutional context of livelihoods (see Figure 1.1 again). Such institutions are also strongly linked to the livelihoods asset category referred to as natural capital (access to land, grazing, water, forests, fisheries and so on), and to the set of natural resource activities that comprise part of the occupational portfolio of the household. Like other dimensions of the policy and institutional context, NRM institutions can hamper or facilitate the ability of poor people to move out of poverty. This book contains numerous examples of the challenges posed for pro-poor policies by NRM regimes (see the chapters in Part IV of the book).

The LADDER Project and its methods[2]

The LADDER Project was a four-year rural livelihoods research programme conducted in Uganda, Kenya, Tanzania and Malawi in the period 2000 to 2003. Since many of the chapters of this book are derived from Working Papers that were produced by this research programme, it is appropriate here to provide a brief summary of the goals of LADDER and the methods used to pursue its objectives. Subsequent chapters that have their origins in one way or another in the LADDER project are Chapters 3, 6–10, 12–18 and 21. Some of these draw directly on quantitative results from household surveys; others on qualitative work done on institutions and specific policy environments.

The main goals of the LADDER project were to

- examine patterns of livelihood diversification, and especially whether the rural poor differed from the rural better-off in respect to the composition of their livelihoods;
- distinguish factors in the policy and institutional environment surrounding poor rural people that hampered rather than facilitated their efforts to construct pathways out of poverty;
- make micro–macro policy links such that national level poverty reduction policies would gain from the micro-level insights provided by the research.

In late 1999, when the LADDER project was devised, PRSPs had only just come into existence.[3] It was therefore not clear at that early stage, although it became so later, quite what sorts of policy arena at the national level would be receptive to micro-level findings of the type that the project set out to discover.

LADDER utilised a combination of quantitative and qualitative research methods to discover people's livelihood patterns and the institutional context within which they evolve. This mixture of qualitative and quantitative data collection has gained credence in the literature on development research methods (Kanbur 2001; White 2002), with qualitative methods seen as more effective in understanding social contexts, while quantitative methods are required in order to make statements about dispersion, prevalence, and cause-and-effect in the details of people's livelihoods (Booth *et al.* 1998).

The project undertook research between early 2001 and mid-2002 in Uganda, Kenya, Tanzania and Malawi. In this period qualitative research was conducted in nine districts and thirty-seven villages across the four countries, and 1,345 households were interviewed using a quantitative and qualitative questionnaire survey. Selection of districts and villages in each country was made on the basis of the twin criteria of, first, representation of rural livelihood patterns in a broad sense and, second, ability to capture the effect of livelihood 'gradients' of various kinds. The critical livelihood gradients that determined village selection were intensive vs extensive farming, small vs large farm size, variations in rainfall and other agro-ecological conditions, variations in extent of livestock keeping, proximity or remoteness from public infrastructure and services, and variations in access to non-farm activities. In addition, in each country one or more community NRM issue was used as a guide to village selection, for example, artisanal fisheries, community forestry or farmer-managed irrigation.

Within each village, a PRA wealth-ranking exercise was conducted, resulting in the identification of three wealth groups that acted as the sampling frame for a stratified random sample. With a list of households in each wealth group, ten households were randomly chosen from each of the well-off and middle categories, and fifteen households from the poor category, resulting in a sample size of thirty-five households for each village. In some instances, this procedure was altered in order to create sub-samples comprising particular categories of village household, for example boat owners, crew members or migrant fishermen in fishing villages.

The effect of the wealth ranking, aside from the perceptions about poverty and wealth gained from the exercise itself, was to ensure that the household sample drawn per village represented the full range of livelihood circumstances to be found in villages, rather than being accidentally clustered around the mode of the range. It is important to note that the procedure described was not designed to make inferences about the larger populations from which the samples were drawn, whether at village, district or country levels. The purposive fieldwork selection procedure from districts, to villages, and to households set out to identify and describe a range of livelihood patterns that were likely to contain within them the experiences of a substantial proportion of rural individuals and households in each country. Statistical analysis undertaken on the resulting dataset reported in Chapter 3, for example, refers only to sample characteristics, and gains its interest from within-sample comparisons of livelihood indicators across different socio-economic groups, not from a claim to represent national patterns.

Much of the effort of qualitative research was directed towards discovering the linkages between what people do and the institutional context they confront. This entailed a considerable amount of probing and triangulation of information around the idea of factors in the policy and institutional context that hamper rather than help people to improve their livelihood prospects. Interestingly, PRA methods as conventionally applied proved fairly poor at achieving this, despite the array of well-tried methods at the disposal of PRA researchers (Pretty *et al.* 1995). Two fairly obvious reasons for this are, first, that in group meetings subordinate members of the group are unlikely to challenge the views articulated by authority figures; and, second, that many institutional behaviours are so much part of the routine of life in villages that they are not considered remarkable enough to comment upon in the presence of outsiders. These, and other flaws of PRA methods, are now fairly widely understood (Cooke and Kothari 2001).

It may be thought that achieving links between the micro-level experiences of trying to construct an improving livelihood at the household level and macro level economic and social policies would be a daunting task due to the complexity attendant on both levels. However, the advent of PRSPs with their specific mandate to advance poverty reduction goals makes the task a lot easier. When following any particular strand discovered as important at the micro level, the question merely has to be asked: does this strand feature in a positive and helpful way in the PRSP? The migration example given above illustrates how mismatches can occur between the preoccupations of PRSPs as strategic documents, and the preoccupations of poor people as they go about constructing their livelihoods. This tracing of strands can, of course, go both ways. Strands in PRSPs that end up as priorities in the sense that resources are put behind the achievement of them, can be traced down to the micro level in order to assess their relevance to the constraints confronted by poor people in trying to improve their livelihoods. Anyone who has delved into a PRSP will be aware that their rhetoric is often not matched by the components of them that eventually emerge as funded priorities.

It is possible that the poverty reduction approach ushered in by PRSPs works best for big expenditures on services where targets are relatively straightforward to specify, the costs of what is intended can be estimated fairly accurately, budgets can be tracked, compliance with accounting procedures can be monitored, and outcomes accurately measured. Education, health and roads comply in varying degrees with these aspects, exemplified by the universal primary education target of the millennium development goals. The elusive 'enabling environment' that is required in order to facilitate pro-poor growth and widen the asset and activity options of the poor is more difficult, as also is the delivery of 'soft' services such as appropriate advice on agricultural technologies to the rural poor. These do not require the same scale of donor funding as education or roads, but without progress happening in them, the outcomes for poverty reduction of the big expenditures may turn out to be a lot less impressive than is currently hoped. These are considerations to which this book returns (Chapter 22) when attempting an overall interpretation of the evidence and ideas collected together in the intervening chapters.

Themes and the structure of the book

Many of the themes with which this book is concerned are apparent from the foregoing discussion. There is an over-arching theme of rural poverty reduction, and a subsidiary theme within that of creating enabling conditions for the poor to construct their own pathways out of poverty. There are themes at the micro-level about the multiple and diverse character of rural livelihoods, the cumulative effects that different livelihood components have upon each other, and the potential to identify virtuous spirals out of poverty. There are themes about the policy and institutional context governing access to resources, and the prevalence of institutionalised blockages to improving livelihoods. There are themes concerning the micro–macro (and macro–micro) links that connect livelihoods to Poverty Reduction Strategy Papers (PRSPs). These themes and the connections between them are illustrated in Figure 1.4 below.

The book is structured to bring out and combine these themes in ways that will hopefully contribute to policy debates about poverty reduction. Chapter 2 proposes an extension to the livelihoods approach in order to recognise more distinctly the resource and access thresholds that result in some families being trapped in persistent poverty ('poverty traps') while others are able to make the leap to relatively stable accumulation strategies that provide pathways away from poverty.

Part II of the book provides micro-level evidence about various characteristics of diverse rural livelihoods, including some of the cumulative features that are already alluded to above. Chapter 3 summarises comparative livelihood features across four African countries as found in the LADDER project. Chapter 4 takes a broader view for sub-Saharan Africa deriving from an earlier multi-country comparative research project (the Deagrarianisation Project) and focuses on the degree to which agriculture is tending to become marginalised by social change in SSA economies. Chapter 5 presents findings on diverse rural livelihoods for case study villages in Andhra Pradesh, India;

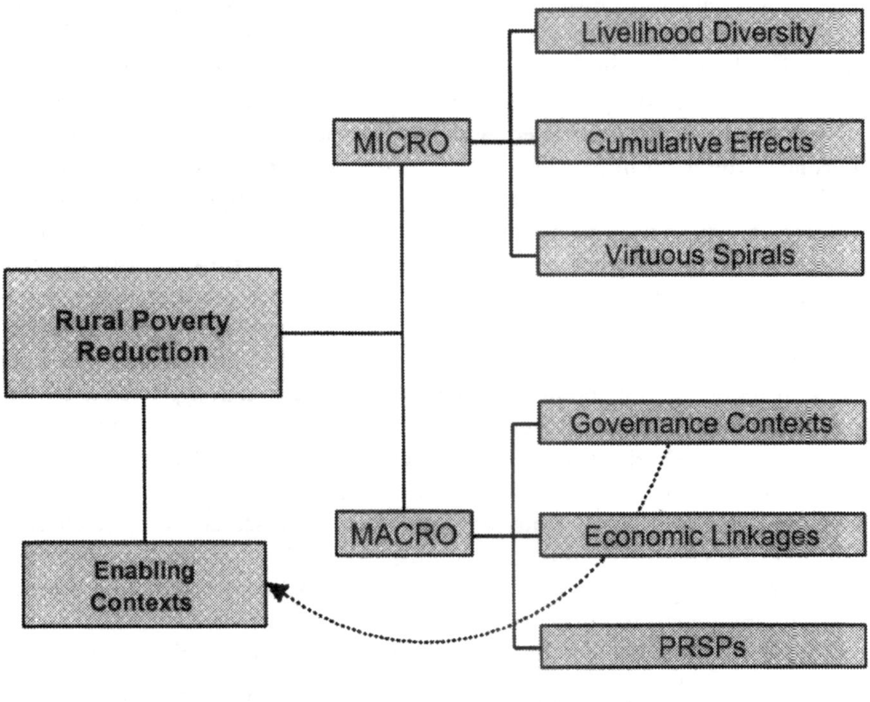

Figure 1.4 Connections between the main themes of the book.

while Chapter 6 examines the gender aspects of diverse rural livelihoods based on findings from the villages studied in Uganda under the LADDER project. Finally, Chapter 7 examines the factors that result in persistent or chronic rural poverty, based on supplementary fieldwork in a sub-set of the LADDER Ugandan villages.

Part III is concerned with the institutional and policy contexts of rural livelihoods, with special attention to evolving institutions, the future working of which will make big differences to people's ability to create spaces to move forwards in their livelihoods. Chapter 8 uses Malawi as a case study to examine the genuine political and organisational difficulties posed by decentralised local government, bringing to the surface critical considerations that tend to be skated over or ignored by enthusiasts for decentralisation. Chapter 9 examines specific issues for poverty reduction raised by methods of rural tax collection in rural Uganda, including anti-poor biases that reside in the way tax rates are set and operate in practice. Chapter 10 demonstrates how agricultural market liberalisation is an incomplete process in a country like Tanzania, with remnants of previous state marketing regimes still in place, or being reinvented in modified forms. Chapter 11 pursues the marketing theme with an examination of market constraints in the cotton sub-sector post-liberalisation, utilising Tanzania as a case study. Chapter 12 provides a comparative overview of land tenure institutions in the four countries, including interpreting the scope and likely impact on land access of different groups of recent land legislation enacted in three of the countries. Finally in Part III, Chapter 13 examines the implications of diverse livelihood strategies for the institutional arrangements whereby agricultural research reaches farmers.

Part IV of the book explores in considerable detail one particular category of institutions; those associated with the management of natural resources. This takes the form in part of a critical examination of the popular community-based natural resource management (CBNRM) approach to achieving sustainable exploitation of natural resources on which the poor (and the not-so-poor) depend for their livelihood strategies. Chapter 14 sets this topic in train by considering crop production performance in Uganda in recent years, and the policy and institutional factors that enable farming to thrive or otherwise. Chapter 15 follows on by tracing through the multiple roles of livestock in reducing vulnerability and facilitating accumulation processes for the rural household. Chapter 16 examines natural resource management in relation to inland fisheries resources in eastern and southern Africa. Chapter 17 pursues similar themes in regard to the management of small farm irrigation schemes, especially in dealing with conflict over scarce water resources. Chapter 18 completes this set of chapters with a critical overview of CBNRM, giving examples from Malawi and Botswana to illustrate purposes, illusions and practical outcomes of community approaches.

Part V of the book switches attention to micro–macro links in several different guises. Chapter 19 considers how village level poverty traps might be portrayed and addressed in Poverty Reduction Strategy Papers. Chapter 20 shows how spatially disaggregated poverty data collected in particular historical periods can be used to make poverty projections useful both at the meso or district level for describing emerging poverty trends in particular places, and at the macro level for informing PRSPs. Chapter 21 considers macro–micro economic links including the exchange rate, inflation rate, and rural–urban terms of trade to describe the ways that the macroeconomic environment is transmitted down to the micro level, with examination of trends in these variables in three countries over the past two decades.

Finally, Chapter 22 of the book provides a brief synthesis of the arguments and findings presented in the preceding chapters, and sets out some policy implications arising from these findings. The focus here is particularly on how PRSPs may in the future evolve towards incorporating a better understanding of the realities of how people go about making a living, and put in place policies and supporting institutions that build on these realities rather than undermining them by ignoring, misunderstanding or blocking them.

Notes

1 This and the following section draw on unpublished reports written by one of the authors (Ellis 2003a, 2003b).

2 Considerably more detail on LADDER background and research methods can be found in Ellis (2001) and LADDER Research Team (2001).

3 The name PRSP was adopted by the WB and IMF in September 1999 and followed closely the adoption of the 'enhanced HIPC initiative' that year, which gave thirty-six highly indebted poor countries a process by which they could become eligible to have their debt cancelled or significantly reduced.

2 Dynamic poverty traps and rural livelihoods*

Christopher Barrett and Brent M. Swallow

Starting points

The concept of poverty traps has achieved some prominence within macro development economics to explain the co-existence of groups of national economies that continually grow, invest and become prosperous with other groups of economies that stagnate, under-invest and remain poor. A parallel concept of livelihood strategies has been developed by a multi-disciplinary group of development researchers and practitioners to explain the interconnections between asset portfolios, multiplex strategies of groups and individuals, and outcomes for the welfare of the rural poor (see Chapter 1 in this volume). This chapter brings together these two concepts and draws out implications for applied research, policy and planning.

Background

At the end of the last decade the global community agreed on the need for concerted action to redress the global problems of poverty, malnutrition, poor health, low education, gender imbalances and environmental degradation. The first of the eight Millennium Development Goals formulated then was to cut by half the percentage of people living on less than $1 per day between the year 1990 and 2015. This goal, which even if achieved would still strand hundreds of millions of people in persistent poverty, is proving very difficult to achieve in many developing countries. Indeed, many countries in Africa have actually experienced increased poverty rates and negative per capita income growth since 1990.

The various agencies involved in development assistance and development policy have shown an increasing, although still highly variable, concentration on the goal of reducing poverty in the world's poorest countries. Macroeconomists are told to focus on pro-poor growth; health agencies are told to give priority to the needs of poor districts; and veterinary scientists are told to develop vaccines that will contribute to pro-poor livestock development. The Future Harvest Centers of the Consultative Group on International Agricultural Research (CGIAR) articulate their goal in terms of food security, poverty reduction and environmental conservation and have begun to explicitly consider poverty reduction in impact assessment studies (e.g. Adato and Meinzen-Dick 2002).

Framing development assistance in terms of poverty reduction requires conceptual frameworks and analytical approaches that truly capture the nature and dimensions of poverty, that distinguish the proximal and distal causes and correlates of poverty, and that integrate across enterprises, sectors and social–spatial scales. Some progress has been made. The World Bank 'Voices of the Poor' studies (Narayan *et al.* 2000a; Narayan *et al.* 2000b; Narayan and Petesch 2002) and its *World Development Report 2000/1* (World Bank 2001a) made a compelling case for the need to consider poverty in terms of low purchasing power, high vulnerability to social, economic and ecological shocks, and lack of voice and accountability (Narayan and Petesch 2002). Improved data, analytical methods and communication techniques have led to greatly improved understanding of the spatial distribution of poor people and environmental resources, the vulnerability of different population groups, the quality of national governance, and the correlates of poverty at different scales (Elbers *et al.* 2001; McCay and Lawon 2003).

Of special interest to those concerned with rural development policy is the analytical focus on livelihood strategies, rather than more specific production or marketing strategies. The sustainable livelihoods framework depicts the five types of capital that rural residents access – physical, social, natural, financial and human – the policies and institutions that define people's options for using that capital, the livelihood strategies that people use to transform assets into income, service and product streams, and the way that income and product streams are translated into welfare outcomes (Scoones 1998; Bebbington 1999; Ellis 2000). The sustainable livelihoods framework informs much of the empirical analysis presented in other chapters of this volume.

We propose that the livelihoods framework can be further strengthened through more explicit conceptual and empirical attention to dynamic poverty traps. The essence of the relation between livelihood strategies and dynamic poverty traps can be distilled into four general points. First, there is often a clear and shared preference ordering among the multiple livelihood strategies that are observed among individuals or households within a particular rural population. Second, specific assets often constrain the level of welfare associated with a livelihood strategy. Third, thresholds in the relationships that transform assets into outcomes mean that households that accumulate higher stocks of assets are sometimes able to generate much higher marginal returns than households that accumulate lower stocks of assets. Fourth, systematic imperfections in rural financial markets mean that individuals, households and communities commonly need to self-finance most capital accumulation. In this chapter we develop these points and discuss the implications for analysis and policy.

Theory and evidence on poverty and livelihoods

The last ten years has witnessed a paradoxical juxtaposition in Africa: worsening poverty trends accompanied by greatly improved understanding of poverty and the livelihoods of the poor. Some of the key findings about poverty can be summarized into the two key points below.

Macro poverty traps are a reality

As first discussed by classic development economists such as Mydral (1957), Young (1928) and Rosenstein-Rodan (1943) in the middle of the last century, there does indeed appear to have been a bifurcation of economic progress among the developing countries of the world. From relatively similar initial conditions, some developing economies have achieved sustained economic progress and accumulation, while others appear to be caught in *poverty traps* of under-investment, low productivity and high poverty. These differences in performance cannot be explained by differences in macro-economic policy and governance alone. Subsequent analysts have postulated different combinations of conditions that can generate such multiple equilibria:

1 increasing returns to scale technologies, often due to externalities at the societal level (Romer 1986; Lucas 1988; Azariadis and Drazen 1990; Durlauf 1996);
2 spatial agglomeration economies and resulting market and technological effects at the regional level (Krugman 1991; Fujita *et al.* 1999);
3 financial market failures combined with either indivisibilities in key investments, such as education or livestock (Loury 1981; Galor and Zeira 1993; Dercon 1998; Mookherjee and Ray 2002);
4 irreversibilities due to subsistence or nutrition thresholds (Dasgupta 1997; Zimmerman and Carter 2003; Dasgupta 1997).

Barrett and Carter (2001) and Easterly (2001) discuss the implications of these macro poverty traps for public policy and development assistance programmes.

There are strong links between household assets, livelihoods and poverty

The availability of new sets of household panel data has stimulated several studies of the determinants of rural poverty and income in African countries. The results from ten of these analyses are summarized in Table 2.1. The results on assets and income are quite consistent and intuitive across the studies. Both livestock assets and agricultural land holdings are strongly and positively correlated with income in almost all studies. Primary education is

Table 2.1 Relations between assets, livelihoods and household incomes: summary of results from previous studies from Africa

Study sample	*Asset and correlation*	*Livelihood and correlation*	*References*
Kenya 1994 (~10,000 households)	primary education (+), land holdings (ns)	agriculture dependence (−)	Geda *et al.* (2001)
Uganda 2000 (315 households in 3 districts)	land holdings (+), livestock (+), productive tools (+)	self employment (+)	Ellis and Bahiigwa (2001)
Zimbabwe 1995 (594 households in 3 semi-arid districts)	oxen (+), scotch carts (+), wheelbarrows (+), education (+)	regular wages (+)	Bird and Shepherd (2003)
South Africa 1998 (1,200 households in KwaZulu Natal)	arable land (+), family members (−)	(not reported)	Carter and May (2001)
South Africa 1999 (number of households not reported)	(not reported)	formal sector employment (+)	Aliber (2003)
Malawi 1998 (12,960 households)	education (+), agricultural land (+), livestock (+), distance to public services (−)	formal sector employment (+), tobacco production (+ in one region, ns in one region)	Mukherjee and Benson (2003)
Ethiopia 1995 and 1996 (2,695 households)	agricultural land (+), livestock (+), primary education (ns), secondary education (na)	(not reported)	Jayne *et al.* (2003)
Kenya 1997 (1,416 households)	agricultural land (+), livestock (+), primary education (+), secondary education (+)	(not reported)	Jayne *et al.* (2003)
Zambia 1999/2000 (6,330 households)	agricultural land (+), livestock (+), primary education (+), secondary education (+)	(not reported)	Jayne *et al.* (2003)
Rwanda 1991 (1,108 households)	agricultural land (+), livestock (+), primary education (+), secondary education (na)	(not reported)	Jayne *et al.* (2003)
Mozambique 1996 (3,851 households)	agricultural land (+), livestock (+), primary education (ns), secondary education (ns)	(not reported)	Jayne *et al.* (2003)

Sources: as given in the right hand column.

Note

*(+) indicates positive impact on household income, (−) indicates a negative impact on household income, (ns) indicates no statistically significant impact on household income, (na) indicates not applicable.

positively correlated with income in all countries except those in which average primary education is very low (e.g. Mozambique and Ethiopia).

The results on livelihood patterns and income levels are not as consistent. Formal sector employment is positively correlated with income in some countries, but is not a viable livelihood option in several other countries. While dependence on agriculture is negatively correlated with income in some countries, this effect is limited by the small size of land holdings in other countries. Jayne *et al.* (2003) argue that small land holdings in many countries limit the viability of agriculture as a livelihood strategy, forcing many small farmers to diversify into less profitable livelihood options.

A more detailed analysis of the links between livelihood strategies and income has been conducted for Rwanda by Barrett *et al.* (2001a). Figure 2.1, which is adapted from that study, depicts the cumulative frequency distributions of total income among 1,079 households in Rwanda, organized into four distinct livelihood strategies. The farm and farm worker (FFW) strategy includes households that only work as unskilled agricultural labourers or farm their own land. The full-time farmer (FTF) strategy represents households that farmed their own land and livestock and had no off-farm employment. The mixed strategy (MIX) includes non-farm employment with farming and unskilled agricultural labour. Finally, the mixed-skilled only (MSO) strategy involves only farming or skilled non-farm labour for a salary or as an entrepreneur. As displayed in Figure 2.1, full-time farming (FTF) and especially

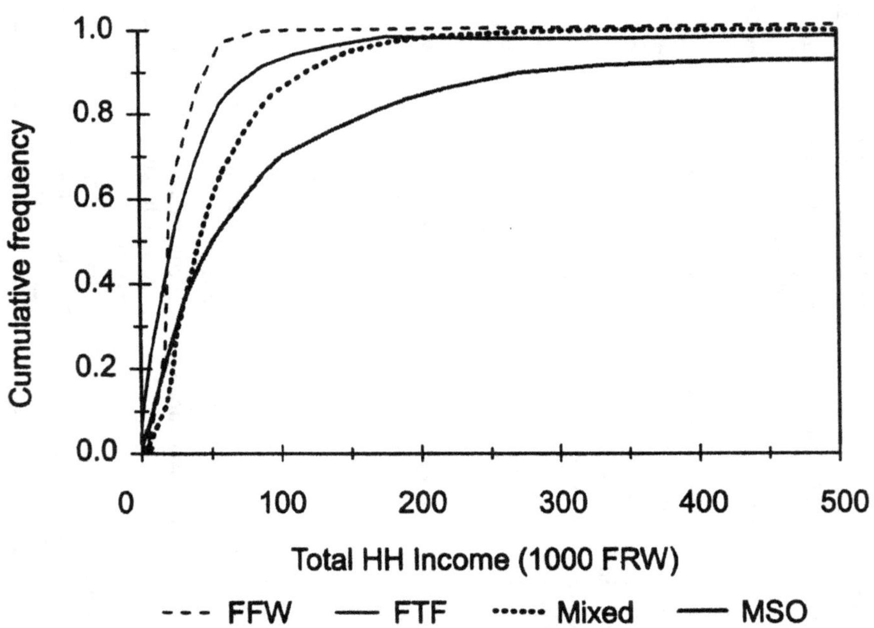

Figure 2.1 Income orderings by livelihood strategy in Rwanda. (source: Barrett *et al.* (2001b).)

farm and farm worker (FFW) livelihood strategies are stochastically dominated by mixed strategies, especially those involving only skilled labour and farming (MSO). No one would choose the FFW strategy if they had access to the MIX or MSO strategies. Barriers to entry into higher return strategies become evident by revealed preference.

Micro-scale poverty traps and livelihoods

Welfare orderings among distinct livelihood strategies, such as those presented in Figure 2.1, appear to be strongly related to barriers to entry that impede access to more remunerative livelihoods by those lacking the necessary financial, human or natural capital to undertake these activities (Dercon and Krishnan 1996; Ellis 2000; Barrett *et al.* 2001b). In the Rwandan example, full-time farming is only an option for those endowed with enough land or livestock to absorb all the adult labour in the household. Skilled nonfarm employment is only available to those with education, particular skills (e.g. blacksmiths, lorry drivers), or the necessary financial capital to start a business.

The general nature of this situation is confirmed by a growing number of studies of livelihood, income and asset dynamics. For example, Barrett *et al.* (2001c) found that among rice farming households in Côte d'Ivoire, households with poor initial asset endowments were unable to access superior livelihood strategies that bestowed considerable income gains following the massive CFA franc exchange rate devaluation of January 1994. Those with poor endowments were less able to respond to attractive emerging on-farm and non-farm opportunities, while *ex ante* richer households reaped considerable gains from devaluation that was promoted as benefiting small farmers. In Ethiopia, Lybbert *et al.* (2004) found that pastoralists whose livestock herds fall below a threshold of 12–15 head of cattle tend to become involuntarily sedentarized because of a minimum necessary scale for successful transhumant migration. Dercon (1998) likewise found that initial assets condition the ability of Tanzanian agro-pastoralists to accumulate wealth and move out of poverty. And Dercon and Krishnan (1996) find that in both Ethiopia and Tanzania, households' initial asset holdings – especially education, marketable skills and capital – are strongly and positively related to the likelihood of following the most remunerative livelihood strategies observed in their samples.

Together this evidence supports a number of parallels between the macro-level poverty traps described above and the micro-level situation of households and individuals in rural Africa. First, initial differences in asset holdings can have lasting effects on farm families' livelihoods. At the macro level of national economies the relevant assets include communication and transportation infrastructure, water storage and electricity generation capacity, the quality of health and education services, the quality of governance and the quality of the labour force. At the micro level of households and individuals, key assets include livestock, land, farm implements, treadle pumps and education of the family members.

Second, asset holdings constrain options available for production and accumulation of more assets. At the macro level, whole industries such as telecommunications, finance or tourism may be essentially ruled out as avenues for growth and tax generation because of low levels of infrastructure or education or due to prohibitively restrictive policies (Romer 1994). At the micro level, we know that those with little or no assets or skills are unlikely to be able to enter into remunerative non-farm activities that lead to higher income, higher consumption and improved production (Dercon and Krishnan 1996; Barrett *et al.* 2001b). Households caught on the wrong end of such traps often end up in a pattern of persistent poverty and steady degradation of the natural resource base on which they depend (Shepherd and Soule 1998; Coomes and Burt 1997; Coomes *et al.* 2000; Barrett *et al.* 2002a). Sufficient conditions for the existence of dynamic poverty traps at the household scale are that they have incomplete access to financial services (credit or insurance) along with:

1 high return production or marketing strategies that exhibit a minimum efficient scale of production that is beyond the means of the credit-constrained poor (Barrett and Swallow 2003) or;
2 risk and subsistence constraints discourage long-term investment in high-return assets among poorer, more credit-constrained households (Zimmerman and Carter 2003).

The most extreme cases of micro-scale poverty traps involve essentially irreversible human capital accumulation failures due to childhood undernutrition, illness and lack of education. Perhaps the most compelling models of poverty traps emerge at this micro scale, where undernutrition and morbidity early in life can lead to permanent reductions in physical stature and health status associated with sharply increased risk of involuntary employment and lower incomes in adulthood (Dasgupta 1997; Strauss and Thomas 1998), and where household-scale financial constraints can cause underinvestment in the education of children – even those with manifestly high natural ability – thereby propagating poverty across generations (Loury 1981).

Implications for livelihood studies

The remainder of this chapter draws out the implications of the presence of dynamic poverty traps for livelihood studies and rural development policies. In this section we explore the need to adjust livelihood studies to better consider asset accumulation, livelihood ladders linked to those assets, transitions between livelihood strategies, and the strategies that farmers take to safeguard their assets against risks.

Asset accumulation and livelihood ladders

The alternative livelihood strategies pursued by rural residents in a particular area will have distinct pathways of accumulation and welfare (i.e. income, expenditures or other measures of well-being) and distinct dynamic equilibria at which the strategy reaches a steady state of asset stocks and welfare. The steady states of distinct livelihood strategies may co-exist if there are asset thresholds that are difficult to surmount through self-finance. For example, the steady state for small-scale poultry production may make it difficult to accumulate enough assets to move into cattle production. Small differences in initial assets or idiosyncratic (i.e. household-specific) asset shocks can mean that some households are able to surmount thresholds and move to livelihoods offering higher welfare, while other households are unable to do so over extended periods. With several possible livelihoods, this could take the appearance of a livelihood ladder that some households are able to climb while others are unable to do so.

For example, Moser and Barrett (2003) show that adoption of SRI (a high-yielding, low-input rice production method) in Madagascar is positively related to regular off-farm salaried employment and to prior adoption of off-season crops (mainly potato, to a lesser degree barley under contract farming arrangements with the national brewery) that produce a harvest just as the labour-intensive field preparation, planting and transplanting season begins for rice, thereby obviating seasonal liquidity constraints that otherwise impede adoption. Floyd *et al.* (2003) found that households in the western hills of Nepal that were more self-sufficient in food were more likely to experiment with and ultimately adopt two or more new agricultural technologies, with adoption rates among all groups highest for the technologies that are based on the existing production system and lowest for technologies based on exotic production systems. The small proportion of households who were able to adopt multiple technologies reported large improvements in welfare.

Analysis of such livelihood ladders requires panel household data on assets, technology adoption, incomes and livelihoods, combined with data from communities and local markets for interpreting patterns among the households. Research needs to combine quantitative and qualitative techniques and to be sensitive to the various ways that households may earn their livelihoods and the key types of capital that are necessary for those livelihoods.

Thresholds and asset transitions

A wide range of thresholds have been identified that affect the livelihoods of rural households in Africa. Here we suggest that these may be grouped as follows:

1 *Thresholds in agricultural production* are consistent with dynamic equilibria in which some farmers engage in high investment–high return enterprises while other farmers do not. Examples are lumpiness of dairy cattle and oxen,

lumpiness of farm implements, increasing economies of scale in agro-pastoral livestock production up to minimum levels of production (Barrett *et al.* 2002b).

2 *Thresholds in non-farm rural employment* are consistent with segmented rural labour markets and bifurcated welfare levels in which some families are able to afford to educate their children for the skilled labour market while other families are unable to do so. In their study in high density areas of western Kenya, Marenya *et al.* (2003) found that households with high levels of education had higher fertilizer application rates, higher probability of owning dairy cattle and tea bushes, had higher maize yields, and earned higher off-farm income per day.

3 *Thresholds in economies of scope among household livelihood strategies* are consistent with the successful coupling of agricultural enterprises, such as coffee and dairy cattle in Kenya, and with high correlations between level of income and particular combinations of income sources. This is different from diversification per se. Other chapters in this volume show that more diverse livelihood strategies are not necessarily associated with higher welfare. For example, rural households with salaried employment are almost always usually able to achieve higher levels of income than rural households that do casual work for their neighbours. Rural households that earn important shares of their livelihood through extraction of natural resources are usually among the poorest in their villages.

4 *Thresholds in processing and marketing* condition entry into higher-return value-adding activities post-harvest for rural households. Financing, scale of operation and infrastructure constraints may limit access to remunerative activities, such as bulk storage, cooling and pasteurization of milk in dairy cooperatives or horticultural products (e.g. fruits, vegetables, cut flowers) subject to costly, strict international grades and standards enforcement. In southwestern Morocco, Lybbert *et al.* (2002) found that access to electricity and finance segmented households between distinct markets that emerged for argan oil, with the high-end export market controlled by non-natives of the argan forest whose superior capital and electricity access enabled them to test, certify and package the oil for European markets in ways beyond the reach of poorer forest dwellers, who were stuck selling only to lower-value local markets.

Asset risk and poverty traps

Standard economic analysis of risk considers the effects of stochastic processes on the payoffs to particular strategies and attitudes toward variation in payoffs. The perspective of dynamic poverty traps adds another dimension to this analysis: reductions in asset stocks below key threshold levels may cause households to shift from higher return to lower return livelihood strategies.

The poor tend to be much more exposed than the rich are to asset risk and thus face a higher probability of being cast below critical thresholds due to adverse shocks caused, for example, by drought, floods, hurricanes, infectious disease or war. This is true at the macro scale. For example, IFRCRCS (2002) reports that more than 98 per cent of the people affected by different types of environmental (e.g. droughts, earthquakes, floods, avalanches) and technological (e.g. industrial or transport accidents) disasters worldwide, between 1992 and 2001, lived in low and medium human development nations. It is also true at the micro scale. For example, Strauss and Thomas (1998) review a range of evidence showing that poorer people consistently suffer more episodes of illness than do the rich. Krishna *et al.* (2003) show that health shocks are by far the most common reason for households falling into poverty in Rajasthan, India, and western Kenya. In the absence of effective safety nets to limit the damage done by asset shocks, people routinely fall not only into poverty, but beyond critical asset thresholds and into poverty traps.

Asset shocks are problematic not only because they occur, destroying personal and family capital by droughts, floods, hurricanes, wars, etc., but also because people follow precautionary strategies in order to try to avoid them. The existence of critical thresholds at which people switch between livelihood strategies heavily affects household risk management. Because households know: (1) that asset shocks occur with positive probability; (2) that this probability is affected by current allocation decisions and; (3) that some asset shocks induce involuntary livelihoods transitions, people adapt their behaviours accordingly. They become more likely to choose activity and asset portfolios that limit asset and income risk, foregoing high-return investments that would demand significant short-term sacrifice beyond what is prudent and safe (Binswanger and Rosenzweig 1993). They willingly destabilize consumption in order to protect assets so as to minimize the probability of suffering irreversible asset shocks in the next period (Zimmerman and Carter 2003; Barrett *et al.* 2003a). The further they move beyond critical asset thresholds, the more they can begin to afford to undertake higher risk and higher return livelihood strategies, leading to locally increasing returns to assets.

Implications for rural development policies

Integration of the concepts of dynamic poverty traps and rural livelihoods raises several important implications for rural development policy as well. We emphasize four in particular.

Agricultural extension for poverty alleviation

Extension services should distinguish client groups on the basis of livelihood strategies and asset portfolios, and consider how new technologies would fit into different strategies and how they might be limited or facilitated by different asset levels. For households that are relatively rich in land and labour, but poor in other assets and income generation potential, extension agents might focus on knowledge-intensive techniques that are not subject to threshold effects. For example, there is evidence from Zambia, Malawi and Kenya that access to information and germplasm are the most important constraints to the adoption of agroforestry approaches to soil fertility enhancement, even among relatively poor households and female-headed households (Place *et al.* 2002; Gladwin *et al.* 2002).

Agricultural technology development

Research on improved technologies typically focuses on expanding the yield frontier or on developing crop and animal varieties that can better resist abiotic or biotic stresses. This is obviously desirable for those farming households that presently appear willing and able to employ frontier technologies. But in many cases, households opt for seemingly inferior, earlier generation technologies, leaving 'improved' seeds, machinery and methods on the shelf. A key insight offered by the dynamic poverty traps approach is that the highest return technologies, at least in terms of welfare improvements among the poor, may come not from expansion of the agricultural production frontier so much as from creating and introducing 'transition technologies' that are feasible and desirable to adopt now, but which naturally lead to accumulation and graduation to still-better technologies. Technologies that increase returns to existing livelihood strategies can thus become avenues to new, more desirable, livelihood strategies that can be adopted in the future.

Rural financial markets

If poorer households could freely draw down cash savings or take out loans at reasonable interest rates or receive insurance payments on extraordinary losses, most problems of persistent poverty would vanish. In poor communities, however, incomplete rural financial markets limit people's ability to make trades across time and across states of nature so as to overcome the financing constraints that underpin poverty traps. Limited access to finance severely limits uptake of improved technologies and investment in productive assets or activities offering high expected rates of return. Furthermore, the poor commonly have trouble weathering shocks, suffering either persistent or catastrophic health problems (Hoddinott and Kinsey 2001) or necessitating distress sales of valuable productive assets. Hence the push to extend microfinance, encompassing both savings and credit products for the poor (Zeller *et al.* 1997), and to provide novel forms of insurance against rainfall and other shocks (Skees 2000).

Safety nets

The threat of uninsured asset loss and the possibility that unforeseen events can knock people into lower-level livelihood strategies underscore that safety nets can play an extremely valuable role in mitigating asset risk, in keeping short-term shocks from leading to chronic poverty through endogenous asset decumulation or low-return production and portfolio strategies. There are examples of safety net schemes that seem to work, perhaps especially those based on public employment guarantees, such as food-for-work programmes, when designed and implemented properly (von Braun 1995; Ravallion 1999; Barrett *et al.* 2003b). Food aid can likewise contribute to better consumption outcomes and anthropometric status and to the protection of crucial productive asset stocks (Quisumbing 2003; Barrett and Maxwell 2004), although it largely fails to help move recipients out of chronic poverty. Rather, food aid prevents decline into deeper destitution.

In sum, rural development policies need to emphasize both opening up pathways out of poverty for those seemingly trapped in chronic poverty – through improved access to transition technologies and to financial products – and to erect and maintain effective safety nets to keep the poor from being undercut by adverse shocks. Extension services play a potentially valuable role in identifying distinct client groups on the basis of livelihood strategies and asset portfolios and thus in helping to target different policy interventions to communities and households with different needs.

Note

* This chapter draws ideas and some material from Barrett and Swallow (2003). We thank Larry Blume, Doug Brown, Michael Carter, Alain de Janvry, Andrew Mude, Ben Okumu, Frank Place and participants at the January 2003 LADDER conference for helpful discussions.

Part II

Evidence from rural livelihoods research

3 Comparative evidence from four African countries*

Frank Ellis and H. Ade Freeman

Introduction

This chapter summarizes the comparative results of research undertaken on rural livelihoods and poverty reduction in Uganda, Kenya, Tanzania and Malawi.[1] There are good reasons for using micro-level research as a reality check on the macro strategic policies currently in vogue. Despite the rhetoric of participation, empowerment and ownership that infuses the discourse on PRSPs, these are nevertheless fundamentally rather centralized processes following blueprints available on World Bank and IMF websites, and connected to central budget support and public expenditure management considerations that are to do with improving governance at high government levels.[2] While all PRSPs contain performance indicators and establish poverty monitoring institutions and instruments, indicators by themselves rarely result in critical examination of the often complicated relationships of cause and effect that produce particular outcomes.

Livelihoods research can also help to bridge the gap between the levers on rural poverty reduction that the PRSPs set out to strengthen, and the intermediating role of district councils or assemblies in the poverty reduction process.[3] The 'institutional context' of rural livelihoods is significantly altered, for better or worse, by decentralization, and livelihoods precepts can help track the effects of these changes on the expansion or contraction of opportunities that permit the poor to build their own pathways out of poverty. The idea of an 'enabling environment' for poverty reduction is often alluded to in poverty documents, including PRSPs, but little attention is given to what this really means, nor to the changed behaviours on the part of the public sector, including the decentralized public sector, that this idea necessitates.

This chapter thus utilizes the framework outlined in Chapter 1 to connect factors inhibiting the achievement of poverty reduction at village and sub-district levels, to revenue collection and service delivery attributes in decentralized district level local authorities, and upwards to priorities articulated in PRSPs. A central notion is that successful poverty reduction may be more to do with creating a local level public sector institutional environment that actively facilitates the multiplication of diverse and dynamic economic activities than to do with the sectoral expenditure targets in areas like education and road building that tend to preoccupy PRSPs. Institutional constraints and blockages are identified by livelihoods research, they reside in the way authority is interpreted in decentralized institutions, and they are addressed sketchily, if at all, in PRSPs as they are currently formulated.

The chapter proceeds as follows. The next section sketches out a broad comparison between the four countries, as a backdrop to the research findings, and also provides an overview of the PRSP process across them. This is followed by a summary of comparative village and household level characteristics that emerged from qualitative and quantitative research undertaken in the four countries in 2001–2003. This focuses on the asset status of rural citizens, the income-generating activities in which they engage, and the institutional environment within which livelihood strategies are adopted and adapted. The chapter concludes by linking the micro-level findings back to macro-level poverty reduction strategies with a view to identifying gaps in these strategies that need to be addressed if real progress in rural poverty reduction is to be achieved.

Comparative overview: four countries and their PRSPs

The four countries under consideration here have distinct political histories post-independence, yet turn out to have much in common in terms of the social and economic circumstances that prevail within them at the start of the twenty-first century.[4] They are all previous British colonies, and all attained independence between 1961 and 1964.[5] Kenya, Uganda and Tanzania were grouped together as East Africa for a number of administrative and infrastructural purposes during the colonial era, and this evolved after independence into the customs union of the East African Community which disintegrated in the 1970s and was revived a quarter of a century later in the late-1990s.[6] Malawi, formerly Nyasaland, was part of the colonial federation that included modern day Zimbabwe and Zambia. None of the countries have yet achieved sustained economic growth for a sufficient duration to lift them from the low income and high poverty incidence that have characterized them for the past forty years; although among them Uganda has been making notable gains from a low base since the late 1980s.

In the current era, three of the four countries have a constitution allowing for multi-party democracy and elections every five years, with elected Presidents only permitted two terms in office. Uganda is an exception, with political competition allowed within the broad-based Movement party that emerged from civil war in the 1980s, but not between separate parties.[7] However, in Uganda too, a constitutional amendment permits the President only two terms in office. In two cases, Kenya and Uganda, incumbent Presidents had already been in power before the two terms rule was introduced, so that by the end of his period in office in December 2002 President Moi in

Kenya had been in power for twenty-four years, while in Uganda the continuing presidency of Yoweri Museveni had lasted seventeen years as of 2003.

The convergence in political systems across the region is of recent origin, dating from the mid-1990s. For most of the post-independence period, each country followed very much its own political trajectory and the ostensible philosophies pursued differed markedly between them. Under Nyerere, Tanzania was explicitly socialist in its approach to development, involving the relocation of the scattered rural population into nuclear villages, state ownership of enterprises across the sectors, and parastatal control of crop marketing. Under Kenyatta, then Moi, Kenya pursued an apparently private enterprise and market-oriented approach to development. Malawi, under 'President for Life' Dr Hastings Kamuzu Banda, differed yet again, with a bias towards land and wealth accumulation by a small minority, and reliance on labour migration to South Africa to provide remittance income to the low income rural customary sector. Until the late 1980s, Uganda had the most unstable post-independence political history, characterized by volatile electoral politics in some periods, the dictatorship of Idi Amin, and civil war.[8]

Past divergencies in political ideas tend to exaggerate true differences in the interplay of politics and economics in the four countries. In reality, quite a lot of important things were approached in much the same way everywhere, for example the marketing of strategic export and food crops was undertaken in all countries by monopoly marketing boards and parastatals. All countries have been beset by a central problem of political power and public office coming to represent leverage over private wealth, a problem exacerbated in the 1980s by steep declines in the real level of public sector salaries.[9] The side effects of the failure to maintain a separation between public office and private income generation are widely apparent: poor discharge of public functions; demotivation of lower level government employees; declining delivery of public services including utilities and infrastructure; and a difficult and unpredictable, even sometimes hostile, public sector disposition towards those private sector enterprises not owned or part-owned by politicians and civil servants.

Some basic current economic and social comparisons between the four countries are summarized in Table 3.1. Their per capita income in the year 2000 ranged from US$190 (Malawi) to US$360 (Kenya). Kenya remains, as it always has been, the best-off country in this region, although the per capita income gap between Kenya and Uganda is narrowing fast due to zero growth in this indicator in Kenya compared with a sustained increase of nearly 4 per cent per year in Uganda. While three of the countries still obtain more than 40 per cent of their GDP from agriculture, in Kenya this proportion has fallen to 20 per cent due to the significance of services, tourism and industry in that economy.

All four countries still have relatively high rates of population growth, varying between 2.4 (Kenya) and 3.0 (Uganda) per cent during the 1990s,

Table 3.1 Basic economic and social indicators 2000

Category	*Units*	*Kenya*	*Uganda*	*Tanzania*	*Malawi*
Economic data 2000					
GNI per capita	US$	360	310	280	170
Rank	Rank	172	176	184	200
Growth rate 1988–2000	% p.a.	0.0	3.7	0.5	0.6
Agriculture GDP share	%	19.9	42.5	45.1	41.6
Population 2000					
Total population	million	30.1	22.2	33.7	10.3
Growth rate 1990–2000	% p.a.	2.4	3.0	2.8	2.6
Rural	% total	66.6	85.8	67.7	85.3
Urban	% total	33.4	14.2	32.3	14.7
Social indicators 2000					
HDI index	index	0.513	0.444	0.440	0.400
Rank	rank	134	150	151	163
Life expectancy	years	47.0	42.1	44.4	38.8
Infant mortality	per '000	77.7	83.0	92.8	102.8
Adult literacy	%	82.4	67.1	75.1	60.1
Official aid flows 2000					
Total aid	US$m	512.3	819.4	1,044.6	445.3
Share of GDP	%	4.9	13.3	11.6	26.2
Aid per capita	US$	17.0	36.9	31.0	43.2

Sources: UNDP (2002a); World Bank (2002a); World Bank (2002b); World Bank (2002c).

though this has come down from higher rates that prevailed in the 1970s and 1980s. The share of the population living in rural areas is estimated at around 85 per cent in Malawi and Uganda, and 67 per cent in Tanzania and Kenya.[10] The countries fall within a fairly narrow band with respect to human development indicators, being ranked between 134th (Kenya) and 163rd (Malawi) amongst countries for which the Human Development Index is compiled (UNDP 2002). Life expectancy at birth, ranging between 39 and 47 years, has been falling in the region due to the impact of the spread of HIV/AIDS and declining standards of public health in some countries. The high reliance of three out of the four countries on foreign aid is notable, net aid flows per capita ranging from US$31 for Tanzania to US$43 for Malawi, and corresponding to more than a quarter of GDP in Malawi.

Estimates of the prevalence of absolute poverty in the four countries come from household income and expenditure surveys that are national in scope, and aim to be representative of the country as a whole (Table 3.2). Malawi has by far the greatest proportion of its population living in poverty, with 65 per cent of the total population estimated to be in poverty, and a poverty incidence of 67 per cent in rural areas and 55 per cent in urban areas. Kenya, despite its highest per capita income level in this group of countries, has the next highest poverty proportions, estimated as 52 per cent overall, 53 per cent rural and 49 per cent urban. Tanzania and Uganda display fairly similar

Table 3.2 Poverty estimates in the four countries (headcount %)

Year	*Kenya 1997*	*Uganda 1999–2000*	*Tanzania 2000–2001*	*Malawi 1997–1998*
Total	52.3	35.2	35.7	65.3
Rural	52.9	39.1	38.7	66.5
Urban	49.2	10.3	17.6/25.8*	54.9

Sources: Appleton (2001a); Kenya (2001a); Malawi (2000a); Tanzania (2002a).

Note

*The two poverty percentages given here refer to Dar es Salaam on its own, and all other urban areas, respectively.

poverty profiles according to recent evidence, both with 35 per cent of their total population designated as poor, 39 per cent poverty incidence in rural areas in both cases, and between 26 per cent (Tanzania) and 10 per cent (Uganda) poverty incidence in urban areas.

The differences between the comparative poverty profiles of each country and their comparative per capita GDP levels reflect, of course, income distribution considerations. Uganda and Tanzania have less unequal income distributions than Kenya or Malawi.[11] Poverty trends, where these are available, are also indicative of the success or failure of past policies and patterns of economic growth for reducing poverty. For Uganda, it has been estimated that overall poverty declined from 56 per cent in 1992 to 44 per cent in 1997 and 35 per cent in 2000 (Appleton 2001a). This is quite an achievement. The estimated incidence of rural poverty fell by 20 percentage points, from 59 per cent to 39 per cent, in this eight-year period.

For Tanzania, small gains in reducing poverty between 1991/1992 and 2000/2001 are estimated, from 39 to 36 per cent of the total population and 41 to 39 per cent of the rural population (Tanzania 2002a). For Kenya the incidence of poverty appears to have increased, between 1992 and 1997, from 46 to 52 per cent of the rural population, and 29 to 49 per cent of the urban population (World Bank 1995; Kenya 2001a). For Malawi, a lack of comparable data across time periods means that the direction of poverty trends cannot be verified, it seems likely, however, from indirect indicators, that poverty increased there during the 1990s.

All four countries considered in this chapter have Poverty Reduction Strategy Papers (PRSPs) or their equivalent. The Uganda PRSP is called the Poverty Eradication Action Plan (PEAP). In all countries the first moves towards an integrated approach to poverty occurred during the mid-1990s,[12] but it was the establishment of the PRSP framework as part of the Enhanced Highly Indebted Poor Countries initiative (HIPC), and as a replacement for structural adjustment lending by the IMF and World Bank that precipitated the preparation of interim and final PRSP documents.[13] The publication dates of first round PRSPs were March 2000 (Uganda), October 2000 (Tanzania), June 2001 (Kenya) and April 2002 (Malawi). Uganda and Tanzania reached the 'completion point' for enhanced HIPC debt relief in May 2000 and November 2001 respectively, while Malawi achieved 'decision point' in December 2000, and Kenya has yet to start the HIPC sequence.[14] A special feature of the Uganda approach is the so-called Plan for the Modernization of Agriculture (PMA), which is closely integrated to the PEAP, and seeks amongst other things to implement radical change in the delivery of services to farmers (Uganda 2000a).

PRSPs contain many strands and themes in common, and are similar, too, in that some elements of them are elaborated and costed in great detail, while others fall back on generic statements of intent. Their goals typically include sustainable growth, macroeconomic stability, good governance, human capital development, improving the quality of life of the poor, and increasing the ability of the poor to raise their own incomes, or, as stated in the Malawi PRSP 'to create the conditions whereby the poor can reduce their own poverty' (Malawi 2002: 1). This last objective is amongst the least well articulated in all PRSPs. While components such as school building targets, or safety net supports, are often quite precisely specified and costed, the changes in public roles and modes of conduct required in order to facilitate the poor to construct their own routes out of poverty are barely considered.

It is possible that the poverty reduction approach ushered in by PRSPs works best for big expenditures on services where targets are relatively straightforward to specify, the costs of what is intended can be estimated fairly accurately, budgets can be tracked, compliance with accounting procedures can be monitored, and outcomes accurately measured. Education, health and roads comply in varying degrees with these aspects, exemplified by the universal primary education target of the Millennium Development Goals. The elusive 'enabling environment' that is required in order to facilitate pro-poor growth and widen the asset and activity options of the poor is more difficult, as also is the delivery of 'soft' services such as appropriate advice on agricultural technologies to the rural poor. These do not require the same scale of donor funding as education or roads, but without progress happening in them, the outcomes for poverty reduction of the big expenditures may turn out to be a lot less impressive than is currently hoped. These are the policy considerations to which this chapter returns after looking at the micro level of rural livelihoods and poverty in the four countries.

Comparative evidence on livelihood patterns, assets and activities across different income groups

The findings described here arise from qualitative and quantitative field research undertaken with 1,345 households and thirty-seven villages across the four countries in 2001–2003. The research methods used and details of the fieldwork locations and research sites are provided in other sources (LADDER Research Team 2001; Ellis and Freeman 2004).

Wealth ranking exercises conducted in the thirty-seven research villages revealed many patterns in common across countries in the attributes that are considered by villagers themselves to define relative poverty and wealth. Households that are considered 'well-off' are typically defined by owning more than two to three hectares of land, more than five goats, more than two cattle (for pastoralist peoples, a lot more), a house with brick walls and a corrugated iron roof. Further, they are food secure all year round, hire labour seasonally, are educated up to primary level or higher, and engage in diverse non-farm activities (trading, milling, shopkeeping, brick making, lodgings and bars) in addition to farming.

A middle category of households are defined by owning less of most or all these assets. Towards the lower wealth end of this category, households tend to be net sellers rather than buyers of labour, they are seasonally food insecure in most years, and they engage in few or no non-farm activities.

Households regarded as poor tend to have less than 0.5 hectares of land or do not own land at all, do not own cattle or goats, have houses in poor repair constructed of mud and thatch, are food insecure for much of the year, and depend on selling labour or on safety net supports for survival. Social groups that are typically assigned to the poor category in wealth ranking exercises are the elderly whose families live away from the village, divorced or widowed women, those with chronic health problems, the disabled, and those not possessing land.

The poor as thus defined by qualitative methods are a sub-set of the poor as would be defined by the consumption criterion used by economists to measure poverty. For villagers, poverty is defined mainly by reference to attributes of social exclusion (hence, elderly, divorced, widowed, disabled), while for the economist it is defined by failure to reach a minimum acceptable consumption level of food and basic needs.[15] In the circumstances that prevail in rural Malawi, for example, a substantially larger proportion of rural households would be defined as poor according to the economic measure than by reference to the qualitative perceptions articulated during wealth ranking in villages.

Distinctions of rural assets status are explored further here by reference to household level data collected in nine districts across the four countries. Taking land as an asset first, Table 3.3 shows how mean land ownership

Table 3.3 Mean land ownership by income quartile, by country

Sample		*Income quartile*				*Total n = 1,295*
		I	*II*	*III*	*IV*	
Land owned (ha)						
Uganda	(n = 315)	0.59	1.05	1.96	2.15	1.43
Tanzania	(n = 350)	0.94	1.39	1.70	2.13	1.54
Malawi	(n = 280)	1.34	1.32	1.22	1.69	1.39
Kenya	(n = 350)	1.43	1.81	2.02	2.16	1.86

Source: sample surveys carried out in 37 villages, 2001–2002.

changes across different household income levels, divided into quartiles from the lowest income 25 per cent up to the highest income 25 per cent of sample households. The typical pattern, as expected, is for a steady rise in mean land owned across the income quartiles, i.e. more land is associated with greater income; however, in the Malawi sample this effect does not kick in until the highest income quartile.

A reason for this finding is discovered by comparing the proportion of sample households that own land of varying amounts, across the country samples (Table 3.4). In both the Uganda and Tanzania samples, most of those with low income had little or no land. In the Malawi and Kenya samples, by contrast, almost everyone was found to own some land, and therefore variations in income levels within the lower income groups are more strongly to do with factors other than area of land owned. A notable feature shown in Table 3.4 is that in all countries except Kenya, about three-quarters of sample households owned less than two hectares of land.

Similar findings occur with respect to livestock holdings across different income levels, as shown in Tables 3.5 and 3.6. For this purpose, all livestock

Table 3.4 Land ownership distribution across sample households

Proportion of sample households owning	*Uganda n = 315 %*	*Tanzania n = 350 %*	*Malawi n = 280 %*	*Kenya n = 350 %*
No land	23.2	22.3	2.1	1.1
Less than 0.5 ha.	41.3	33.4	11.0	19.4
Less than 2 ha.	76.9	74.0	79.9	67.7
Between 2 and 5 ha.	17.7	19.4	19.4	26.9
More than 5 ha.	5.4	6.6	0.7	5.4
Total	100.0	100.0	100.0	100.0

Source: sample surveys carried out in 37 villages, 2001–2002.

Table 3.5 Mean livestock ownership by income quartile, by country

Sample	*Income quartile*				*Total*
	I	*II*	*III*	*IV*	*n = 1,295*
Livestock CEUs*					
Uganda (n = 315)	0.77	1.92	2.01	3.15	1.96
Tanzania (n = 350)	0.28	0.94	0.48	1.92	0.89
Malawi (n = 280)	0.28	0.24	0.54	0.93	0.50
Kenya (n = 350)	2.85	4.31	5.16	5.95	4.57

Source: sample surveys carried out in 37 villages, 2001–2002.

Note

*Cattle Equivalent Units (CEUs) add up household livestock holdings by counting each head of cattle as one and other livestock according to their market price level compared to cattle; for example, if goats are worth 1/6th the value of cattle, then a goat would count as 0.17 CEU.

Table 3.6 Proportions of sample households lacking livestock assets

Proportion of sample households owning	*Uganda* *n = 315* %	*Tanzania* *n = 350* %	*Malawi* *n = 280* %	*Kenya* *n = 350* %
No cattle	71.1	94.8	93.2	28.3
No goats	55.6	84.6	74.3	52.6
No chickens	35.2	47.4	39.3	19.7

Source: sample surveys carried out in 37 villages, 2001–2002.

possessed by households was aggregated into the single measure of cattle equivalent units (CEUs). In this instance there are only minor inter-country departures from the general trend that livestock ownership increases steadily across the income ranges (Table 3.5). The trend is steepest for Tanzania and Uganda, and is less marked, although for differing reasons, in the Malawi and Kenya samples. Again, information on extent of ownership of different types of livestock can help to explain variations in these findings (Table 3.6). In the Tanzania and Malawi samples most households possess neither cattle nor goats, Uganda lies in an intermediate position, and ownership of these livestock types is most widespread in the Kenya sample.

In addition to land and livestock, the key assets of rural families in the case study countries are their own labour (active adults in the household), their educational attainment (measured here by years of education accomplished), and their ownership of productive implements and tools (measured as the aggregate value owned). The mean levels of all five of these assets as found in the country samples are shown in Table 3.7.

Figure 3.1 takes just one of these cases, the Uganda sample, and displays the comparative level of holdings of the five assets, or asset categories, for the whole sample divided into per capita income terciles, in the form of a radial graph. The interesting features revealed by this graph are, first, that the top and middle income thirds of households do not differ hugely in their average possession of the five key assets; and second, that the lowest third of households are shown to be deficit particularly with respect to land, livestock and

Table 3.7 Mean level of selected assets in country samples

Asset variable	*Units*	*Uganda* *n = 315*	*Tanzania* *n = 350*	*Malawi* *n = 280*	*Kenya* *n = 350*
Labour	EAAs	1.92	2.08	2.03	2.06
Land	ha	1.43	1.47	1.39	1.86
Tools	value	10.31	12.72	4.12	6.75
Education	years	9.62	9.60	8.13	14.59
Livestock	CEUs	1.96	0.89	0.50	4.57

Source: sample surveys carried out in 37 villages, 2001–2002.

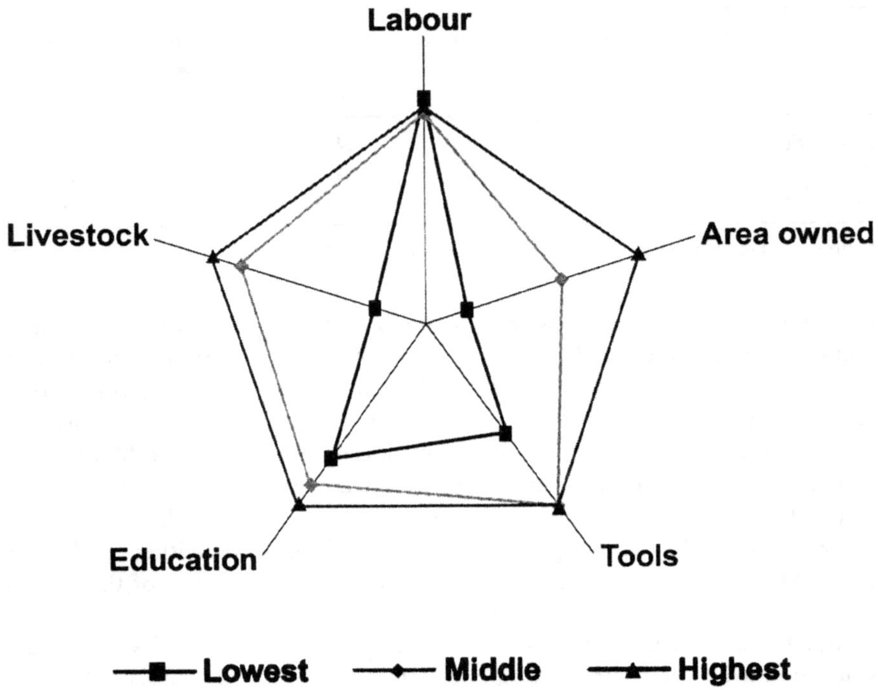

Figure 3.1 Selected assets by income tercile, Uganda sample (source: sample survey carried out in nine villages, January to March 2001.)

'tools of the trade' and much less so with respect to human capital, i.e. number of working adults and their average level of education.

This basic pattern recurs across countries, although with minor variations between them (Ellis and Mdoe 2003; Ellis *et al.* 2003). The lower one-third of the income distribution is invariably both livestock and land poor compared to all other households, but the position with respect to other assets is narrower and less clear cut. At the same time, the level of livestock holdings in all cases sharply distinguishes the top income one-third of households from other households. It is interesting that education levels reached by household members do not display these marked differences between income groups, despite education being identified in a number of studies as a critical variable explaining rural income differences (World Bank 2001a). It is also worth noting that in lakeside villages where fishing is combined with farming, the ownership level of fishing assets was found to be an additional factor clearly distinguishing the top income one-third of households (Allison and Mvula 2002; Ellis and Bahiigwa 2003).

The multiple roles of livestock in contributing to successful livelihood strategies emerges clearly from the country studies. High livestock ownership not only denotes high wealth associated with livestock as a store of value, but also implies high income, always placing livestock owners in the upper per capita income ranges. Notably, however, it is not livestock itself that is the major contributor to these higher incomes. As is shown later in this analysis, the income composition of the top income quartile is dominated by non-farm self-employment income in all countries. This illustrates the interlocking nature of relative livelihood success in rural areas. Livestock is a substitutable asset that can be sold in order to invest in land or small businesses, and vice versa, non-farm income can be used to build up herds; the ordering of these sequences depends on the personal and market opportunities that prevail in different time periods.

Moving now to activities and specifically to farming and livestock activities, data for agricultural land use by sample households across the nine case study villages emphasizes the dominant position of maize within farming systems in the region. The mean proportion of maize in total land use was 44 per cent, while in Malawi this rose to 70 per cent. Only in Uganda, where cooking bananas (*matooke*) are the staple food crop in the case study districts, does maize fall in significance, although even there maize and maize mixtures remained the largest single land use category. Rice is also a popular crop in those places with sufficient water for it cultivation, corresponding to 12 and 14 per cent of sample land use in Tanzania and Malawi respectively.

Qualitative research revealed significant changes in patterns of crop production during the ten years preceding the research, in many study locations. A repeated finding was the decline of traditional cash crops like coffee and cotton and the rise of new ones. For example, in the Tanzania study sites, cotton, coffee, sunflower and castor disappeared during the 1990s from villages that formerly grew them as significant cash crops. This was attributed by villagers to the disintegration or dissolution of the cooperatives and parastatals that formerly supported those crops. As sources of cash income they had been replaced by rice, playing a dual role as food and cash crop, and also by sesame seeds, tomatoes and vegetables.[16]

The overall monetization of the agrarian economy is a feature pertinent to poverty reduction efforts. If markets are working well, and trade and exchange are flourishing, then this increases the cash in circulation in rural areas and gives individuals broader opportunities to construct pathways out of poverty. Table 3.8 provides sample data by country on the output share of principal crops consumed by the household rather than sold in the market. The continued reliance within livelihood strategies on subsistence consumption for household food security is revealed. In Uganda, 73 per cent of the food staple, *matooke*, was retained for home consumption amongst sample households. In Kenya, Tanzania and Malawi the share of the maize harvest consumed by sample households was 90, 78 and 97 per cent respectively. As will be discussed in due course, one reason for this is a trading environment where market risk is artificially increased by multiple taxation and rent-seeking by public agencies and officials.

The role of subsistence in rural livelihoods is further examined by reference to the overall share of own consumption by value in household

Table 3.8 Output share consumed by households, selected crops and livestock

Subsistence share %	*Kenya* *n = 350*	*Uganda* *n = 315*	*Tanzania* *n = 350*	*Malawi* *n = 280*
Crops				
Bananas	–	73.2	–	–
Maize	90.0	57.9	77.8	96.8
Rice	–	–	60.5	48.2
Millet	95.1	82.4	–	–
Sorghum	89.1	–	60.1	–
Beans	81.8	65.7	59.2	79.2
Groundnuts	–	68.1	–	88.0
Cassava	–	87.4	59.5	–
Sweet potatoes	–	95.5	–	89.9
Irish potatoes	–	59.1	–	57.4
Livestock				
Milk	75.3	50.6	–	–
Chickens	65.6	62.9	53.2	75.3
Goats	17.5	27.2	11.9	44.4

Source: sample surveys carried out in 37 villages, 2001–2002.

income across different income levels.[17] The relevant data is shown in Table 3.9. In general, reliance on subsistence falls steadily across the income quartiles, the rate of this decline varying across the country samples. Thus in Uganda, the decline is from 33 per cent to 23 per cent between the bottom and top income quartile; while in Kenya it is from 47 per cent to 9 per cent. Differences in the pattern of these shares between villages within each study location suggest that relative remoteness from markets and services tends to be associated with continued high reliance on self-provisioning, even at higher income levels overall. In particular, proximity to an urban area such as a district capital both lowers this subsistence share in general, and results in its steep decline towards the upper end of the income distribution. Richer rural folk own businesses in nearby towns.

The composition of household total incomes provides relevant insights into the way that asset differences result in different patterns of income

Table 3.9 Share of subsistence consumption in total income, by income quartile

Country	*Income quartile*				*Total*
	I	*II*	*III*	*IV*	
Uganda (n = 315)	33.4	32.6	29.4	23.2	25.9
Tanzania (n = 350)	39.1	28.7	22.1	14.0	18.5
Malawi (n = 280)	44.4	47.5	30.3	18.4	25.3
Kenya (n = 350)	47.0	31.3	19.2	8.8	15.1

Source: sample surveys carried out in 37 villages, 2001–2002.

earning across income levels. Overall, in the research, it was found that household total income divided almost equally between farm activities (crop and livestock production) and non-farm activities (wages, self-employment and remittances). The Tanzania sample, used here as an illustration (Table 3.10), fits this division exactly. The basic pattern reproduced in all country samples is for farming to decline in importance as incomes rise while non-farm activity rises. However, within these aggregate categories important subsidiary patterns are revealed. In the Tanzania case, crop income falls across the quartiles, but livestock income rises sharply for the top income quartile. In the non-farm category both wages and transfers fall as income rises; while non-farm self-employment rises dramatically, from 11 per cent to 44 per cent of total income between the bottom and top income quartile.

Becoming less reliant on agriculture is part of the process of climbing out of poverty in Tanzania, as well as elsewhere, but this is not the end of the story. A further notable feature is that land productivity also increases steeply with rising income, as shown for all countries in Table 3.11. This is measured

Table 3.10 Income portfolios by income quartile, Tanzania sample

Income sources	*Composition of Household incomes %* *Income quartile*				*Total* *n = 344*
	I *n = 87*	*II* *n = 88*	*III* *n = 88*	*IV* *n = 81*	
Maize	27.1	21.5	15.1	7.9	12.4
Rice	12.3	14.2	10.3	8.8	10.0
Other crops	23.3	19.9	23.8	11.8	16.3
Livestock	5.0	7.7	6.5	14.1	11.0
Sub-total agric	67.7	63.3	55.7	42.6	49.7
Wages	14.6	8.9	9.3	11.0	10.5
Non-farm	11.5	23.7	29.3	44.0	36.1
Transfers	6.3	4.2	5.7	2.5	3.7
Total	100.0	100.0	100.0	100.0	100.0

Source: sample survey conducted in 10 sub-villages, May–August 2001.

Table 3.11 Net agricultural output per hectare (ha.), by income quartile (US$/ha.)

Country	*Income quartile*				*Ratio IV:I*
	I	*II*	*III*	*IV*	
Uganda	131	215	295	487	3.7
Tanzania	81	108	156	381	4.7
Malawi	18	44	84	109	6.0
Kenya	135	266	358	430	3.2

Source: sample surveys carried out in 37 villages, 2001–2002.

by mean net agricultural output per hectare in each income class, converted in Table 3.11 to US$ at the exchange rates prevailing at the time the research was conducted.[18] This finding reinforces the cumulative nature of becoming better-off in rural areas of the case study countries, a process that has been identified by many other researchers.[19] The direction of causality is that non-farm income enables the household to hire labour to undertake timely cultivation practices, and helps to fund the purchase of farm cash inputs; conversely, hiring out labour by poor households causes their own farm productivity to stagnate or fall. Livestock ownership plays a reinforcing role in virtuous spirals of accumulation, just as its absence contributes to the inability of poorer households to climb onto the first rung of the 'ladder' leading out of poverty.

Institutions and rural livelihoods

The term institutions is used in this book to describe customs, rules, regulations, laws, public agencies, and the way these habitually, and from precedence, go about doing what they do. Institutions as so defined change much more slowly than the structures in which they are contained (North 1990). The creation of structures ushering in democratic decentralization does not in practice quickly change habitual relationships between public officials and rural citizens (Crook and Manor 1998).

Qualitative research conducted in thirty-seven villages provided useful insights into the institutional context within which individuals and households attempt to construct viable livelihood strategies. It was found that this institutional environment rarely actively fosters the flourishing of diverse activities that are required in order to achieve rapid poverty reduction in rural areas (see Chapters 5, 6, 7 and 8 in the next section; also Francis and James 2003; Ellis and Freeman 2004). The norm tends to be in an opposing direction; with access to enterprise and opportunity being discouraged or blocked by formal and informal gatekeepers including 'gratifications' to traditional leaders, onerous licensing requirements, multiple taxes on crops and livestock, official and unofficial roadblocks and so on. A small minority of individuals with the requisite personal networks and contacts in the local or national public sector are able to avoid or rise above the legal or informal restrictions with which most rural citizens must comply.

Summary and conclusions

This chapter set out to make the links between macro-level endeavours to develop a comprehensive approach to poverty reduction in Uganda, Kenya, Tanzania and Malawi and a micro-level understanding of the circumstances and prospects of the rural poor. At the macro level, approaches to poverty reduction are set out in Poverty Reduction Strategy Papers or equivalent documents written between 1999 and 2001, and the question that needs to be posed is whether these documents formulate the poverty reduction problem in a way that addresses the real patterns of people's livelihoods, and the barriers that rural citizens confront in their efforts to construct pathways out of poverty. At the micro level, the livelihoods framework outlined in Chapter 1 was utilized to gain a more accurate picture of the asset and activity patterns that characterize the poor in particular, and the institutional context that either blocks or enables rural citizens in their pursuit of more secure livelihoods over time.

The research described in this chapter emphasizes features of rural poverty that are commonplace throughout the region. These features include small and declining farm sizes, lack of livestock as a substitutable asset, prevalence even in normal years of food deficit from own production, low monetization of the local economy, and consequently little cash in circulation to act as a stimulus to multiplying rural activities. In addition, in some locations, deteriorating civil security in villages adds to the difficulties of improving household asset status.

Moreover, individuals and households confront numerous institutional gatekeepers and blockages that paralyse all but the most energetic from taking additional risks or exploring new avenues for gaining a viable livelihood. These blockages reside primarily in the way district level licensing and taxation systems work, although they can also be associated with traditional authority systems at sub-district level, and with 'invisible' levies and tithes and permissions that are haphazard in their incidence, and variable in the discouragement they represent. These blockages to improving livelihoods are described in several later chapters of this book.

At the level of the family or household, securing better living standards is a cumulative process that requires an ability to build assets and diversify across farm and non-farm activities. In this process, cash generation is critical, since it confers the capability to invest either in improved farm practices or in non-farm assets, or some combination of both, according to the options that arise to reduce risk and increase income generation. Multiple legal and illegal taxes and blockages at village level suppress cash generation at the very point where it can make the most difference to the livelihoods of the poor. More than this, the uneven, haphazard and often personal rent-seeking character of behaviours adds to risk, and therefore further inhibits the multiplication of economic activities in rural areas.

Notes

* This chapter is an abridged and edited version of a paper published in *The Journal of Development Studies* (Ellis and Freeman 2004).

1 The research programme was entitled LADDER, standing for Livelihoods and Diversification Directions Explored by Research, an acronym devised to evoke the notion of 'climbing out of poverty'. The programme was funded principally by the Policy Research Programme of the UK Department for International Development (DFID), with a contribution to work in Kenya made by the United

Nations Development Program (UNDP). The findings and views expressed here are solely the responsibility of the authors and are not attributable to DFID or UNDP. This cross-country overview draws on and synthesises material published in individual country papers (Ellis and Bahiigwa 2003; Ellis and Mdoe 2003; Ellis *et al.* 2003; Freeman *et al.* 2004).

2 The World Bank defines PRSPs as follows:

> Poverty Reduction Strategy Papers (PRSP) describe a country's macroeconomic, structural and social policies and programs to promote growth and reduce poverty, as well as associated external financing needs. PRSPs are prepared by governments through a participatory process involving civil society and development partners, including the World Bank and the International Monetary Fund.

This as well as other details of the PRSP approach can be found on the World Bank website at: http://www.worldbank.org/poverty/strategies.

3 See Norton and Foster (2000) for a useful discussion of the links between livelihoods approaches and PRSPs.

4 The similarities in rural livelihood circumstances found across these four countries as detailed later in this paper is in itself an interesting finding of the research, given their disparate political and economic strategy histories post-independence.

5 The independence dates of the four countries were Tanzania (1961), Uganda (1962), Kenya (1963), Malawi (1964).

6 The original East African Community lasted from 1967 to 1977, but with decreasing effectiveness through that period. The Community was re-established by the heads of state of the three countries in November 1999.

7 A national referendum was held in Uganda in 2000 to determine whether to move to multi-party politics, and this option was rejected by the majority of voters.

8 These are brief generalisations, and there exists, of course, an enormous literature on the post-independence politics and economics of each of these four countries.

9 For perceptive accounts of politics and the state in post-colonial African countries see Sandbrook (1986, 2000) and also Cross and Kutengule (2001). The decline in real public sector salaries is detailed in Jamal and Weeks (1993).

10 The proportion of the population defined as rural is notoriously sensitive to the cut off point at which larger settlements are treated as urban areas, so these inter-country differences may be somewhat artificial.

11 Available income distribution estimates are somewhat fragmentary, but Kenya had an estimated Gini coefficient of 0.445 in 1994 compared to Uganda (0.374 in 1996) and Tanzania (0.382 in 1993) (World Bank 2002c). In one World Bank source Malawi is cited as exhibiting a Gini coefficient of 0.620 (World Bank 1998).

12 The first draft of Uganda's PEAP was published in 1997; Tanzania's National Poverty Eradication Strategy (NPES) in 1998 (Tanzania 1998); Malawi's Poverty Action Plan (PAP) in 1997.

13 A useful account of PRSP background and processes is provided in Warnock (2002). For the PRSPs of the four countries see Tanzania (2000a), Uganda (2001a), Malawi (2002), Kenya (2001a).

14 Debt relief under HIPC has a number of sequential stages, involving, *inter alia*, endorsement of the PRSP by the IMF and World Bank (decision point) and evidence of one year's successful implementation before the agreed amount of debt is cancelled (completion point). Kenya has so far engaged minimally in the HIPC process in part due to having a per capita income that places it just above the ceiling range of the priority HIPC countries, but possibly more relevantly due to policy lapses as viewed by donors (World Bank 2000b).

15 The economic definition of the poverty line is the level of per capita consumption that just permits the individual to satisfy basic nutritional requirements expressed in calories, given the measured share of food in the per capita expenditure of the poor (Lipton and Ravallion 1995).

16 The longer term impact of these changes on rural incomes depends on factors that fell outside the scope of this research. These include world price trends of the traditional export commodities replaced by new cash crops, exchange rates, and the character of private trading systems that replaced former parastatal marketing bodies.

17 For this purpose, subsistence consumption of crops and livestock products is valued at the average farmgate prices cited in the completed household survey forms.

18 Net agricultural output refers to gross output (quantities produced multiplied by farmgate sales prices) minus purchased inputs into the production process, where hired labour is treated as a purchased input, but family labour is not costed in the calculation. The exchange rates prevailing at the time of the research in each country were (local currency per US$): Uganda (1,772.5 Ushs), Kenya (78.93 Kshs), Tanzania (890.18 Tshs), Malawi (68.12 Mk).

19 For example, World Bank (2001a), IFAD (2001) and Barrett *et al.* (2001d), publications that themselves draw on considerable bodies of poverty research. For similar findings on rising farm productivity across income levels see Evans and Ngau (1991).

4 Rural livelihoods and agrarian change in sub-Saharan Africa

Processes and policies*

Deborah Fahy Bryceson

Introduction

The existence of livelihoods analysis is testimony to the now general acknowledgement that rural areas are: changing very rapidly; no longer necessarily agrarian; no longer bounded by the village and that there are many categories of economic actors in rural areas. Livelihoods analysis focuses on the context of people's livelihood decision-making, but not the causes of the changed context. There is a need for historical study to establish chains of causation revealing not just immediate proximate causes, but also ultimate causations.

Perhaps the best way to come to grips with history is to juxtapose the current "scramble *in* Africa," with the "scramble for Africa," in the late nineteenth century involving Europe's major powers of the day annexing large tracts of the African continent (Pakenham 1991). The colonial economies that followed represented a fundamental re-ordering of land and labor usage, shaping the agricultural peasant, settler farms, plantations and mining sectors with which the continent is identified to the present. In development theory, the African continent has long been associated with agrarian modes of livelihood and an underlying assumption that its abundance of land and relative shortage of labor, especially skilled labor, provides it with a comparative advantage in agricultural production (Boserup 1990).

Recently, however, the World Bank (2000b) has revised this assumption, labeling Africa's agriculture as backward and unproductive.[1] This view appears in the wake of two decades of World Bank-instigated structural adjustment policies pointedly aimed at stimulating smallholder agriculture, reducing urban bias and getting the prices right. IFAD (2001) has taken issue with what is perceived as international financial agencies' complacency about rural poverty. Donor positions aside, African rural smallholders have responded to prevailing circumstances by edging away from traditional export crop production over the past two decades. Amidst high levels of material uncertainty and risk, African rural populations have engaged in widespread occupational experimentation. A century after the scramble for Africa, a "scramble *in* Africa," has been unleashed with profound ramifications for the continent.

A growing body of literature has examined the economic impact of structural adjustment and market liberalization on African peasant agriculture (e.g. Bigsten and Kayizzi-Mugerula 1995; Ponte 1998a, 2002b; Barrett 1998). My concern in this chapter extends to a consideration of these policies' effects on African smallholder peasantries per se. Certainly, the importance of the non-economic sphere has not been lost on policy-makers. International financial institutions (IFIs) and donors have turned their program efforts to "democratization," and "good governance," and the institutional dynamics of an "enabling environment." Most recently, they have directed enquiry into "social capital" networks. Nonetheless, there has been a reluctance to consider how neo-liberal policies impact on African rural social structures. The tendency has been to see African social institutions, especially those associated with rural peasant societies, as constraints on the implementation of economic policies, inferring that vested interests and traditional conservatism cannot rise to the market challenge. This chapter argues the opposite: African peasant societies have been extremely responsive to neo-liberalism with far-reaching and as yet unclear implications for the social and economic fabric of African countries.

Reviewing the qualitative and quantitative findings from village studies undertaken by multi-disciplinary teams of African researchers between 1996 and 1998 in different parts of the continent under the auspices of the Deagrarianization and Rural Employment (DARE) research program,[2] the following sections provide a broad comparative overview of trends and changing patterns in a variety of smallholder rural settlements. The first section begins with a schematic consideration of agricultural trends as a prelude to a more detailed examination of recent rural livelihood patterns. The next section considers some of the structural changes taking place in African peasantries' social institutions. The final section argues that the uncertainty and wasted energy embedded in trial-and-error income earning efforts could be alleviated with a more directional policy approach taking account of rural producers' pressing current aims and long-term occupational futures.

Sub-Saharan Africa's declining agrarian fortunes

Ethiopia, Nigeria, Tanzania, Malawi, Zimbabwe and South Africa, the six countries covered in the DARE research program, represent a striking range of variation in population size, levels of urbanization, and agriculture's contribution to the national economy. Nonetheless, all are undergoing "deagrarianization" and, more specifically, "depeasantization."

Deagrarianization is defined as a long-term process of occupational adjustment, income-earning reorientation, social identification and spatial relocation of rural dwellers away from strictly agricultural-based modes of livelihood (Bryceson 1996). This is a global process prompted by the industrial revolution of the early nineteenth century that accelerated in the twentieth century but has been characterized by great geographical unevenness. Less than half of the world's population now lives in rural areas, and most are peasants. Somewhat paradoxically, deagrarianization in Europe and North America was accompanied by peasant formation in many parts of the non-industrialized world colonized by the early industrial nation states.

The European colonial intrusion in sub-Saharan Africa engendered processes of peasantization that facilitated colonial governments' agricultural commodity export aims. African peasantries have varied in social composition and economic structures, but they have four main characteristics in common, as identified by Shanin (1976). First, they share the pursuit of an agricultural livelihood combining subsistence and commodity production. Second, their internal social organization revolves around the family as the primary unit of production, consumption, reproduction, socialization, welfare and risk-spreading. Third, they are externally subordinated to state authorities and regional or international markets that involve class differentiation and transfers of tax and profit. Fourth, they reside in rural settlements, be they widely dispersed or nuclear villages, and they are often identified with a traditional conformist attitudinal outlook relative to more urbanized populations.

Spurred by colonial taxation, African agrarian producers increasingly produced agricultural commodities in conjunction with their subsistence production, or alternatively exported male labor on the basis of circular migration. Following the Second World War, as nationalism and the Third World gained ascendancy, the emerging African nations were identified as primarily agrarian countries with large peasantries that were developing towards a more modernized, industrial production base. In this context, African post-colonial governments and the international donor community pursued policies aimed at extending, capitalizing and modernizing peasant production to raise peasant productivity and living standards as a foundation for their industrialization efforts (Bryceson *et al.* 2000; Bryceson and Bank 2001).

After a century of colonial and post-colonial peasant formation, depeasantization is currently underway, representing a specific form of deagrarianization in which peasantries lose their economic capacity and social coherence, and shrink in demographic size relative to non-peasant populations.

While government policies were vital for fostering peasant commodity production, they are now instrumental in their undermining. By altering a peasantry's access to essential means of production, be it land, labor or capital, peasant producers' conditions of existence can be detrimentally affected. Certain policy amalgams could be termed "turning-point" policies because they chip away at peasantries' economic viability, social coherence and class position. Naturally, such turning-point policies, be they intentional or unintentional in their destructive impact on peasants, do not eliminate peasantries with a single blow. Far from it, peasantries, as historically rooted societies, are part of an on-going malleable labor process adapting to changing conditions of climate, local resource variation, or demography, as well as to external stimuli such as markets, taxation, and other forms of state intervention. Peasants' enigmatic status as subsistence and commodity producers provides staying power. Their commodity production may be continually eroding while elements of their subsistence production linger on.

Tanzania, Malawi and Zimbabwe have experienced recent turning points. The imposition of structural adjustment programs (SAP) from the mid-1980s to the mid-1990s amounted to a drastic undermining of most peasants' capitalized production through the removal of subsidies on improved inputs like fertilizers, seeds and pesticides. These countries were not equally affected by the enforcement of SAP and market liberalization since their implementation varied in degree and timing. Furthermore, each country represented a different vulnerability in terms of the degree to which its peasantries were involved in agricultural commodity production.

SAP policies largely dismantled African marketing boards and parastatals that had serviced peasants' input requirements, enforced commodity standards, and provided single-channel marketing facilities and controlled prices. The private traders who replaced them varied in performance through time and space, but mounting evidence suggests that they have not lived up to the hopes vested in them by the IFIs. Farmers were faced with a more uncertain market environment, producer prices were subject to wide fluctuations, input prices skyrocketed and supply became tenuous as most traders did not have the rural outreach of the parastatals they replaced (e.g. Bryceson 1993; Jambiya 1998; Mung'ong'o 1998; Madulu 1998; Meagher 2000, 2001). Traders avoided farmers in areas off the main road where transport costs were too high and many did not enforce adequate quality control checks. African export crops lost further market share as importers came to expect below-standard products and Asia's modernized plantations started exporting traditional African crops like cocoa and palm oil (Raikes and Gibbon 2000).

Increased market uncertainty and peasant farmers' reduced access to agrarian subsidies generated a switch to crops with quick or regular year-round returns. Preference was given to "fast crops" like tomatoes, potatoes and bananas with lower fertilizer demands (Ponte 1998a and 2002b; Yunusa 1999). Crops such as year-round harvested cocoa were adopted in areas that had hitherto not produced them (Mung'ong'o 1998; Mwamfupe 1998). Larger-scale farmers became prominent in the production of traditional export crops that smaller-scale farmers found hard to finance (Berkvens 1997; Iliya and Swindell 1997; Meagher 2001). In some areas, smaller-scale farmers attempted to carry on producing crops with reduced inputs, but their yields became disappointingly low. Some reverted to traditional varieties of staple food crops rather than the high-yielding improved varieties requiring expensive inputs (Mung'ong'o 1998; Yunusa 1999). Agricultural income dropped. Mung'ong'o (1998) cites a decline of 71 percent in annual mean household income from agriculture between 1979 and 1992. Not surprisingly, he also notes land being taken out of cultivation.

The countryside is aging. In various case study areas, the older generation was found remarking on youths' lack of interest in commercial farming (Jambiya 1998; Mwamfupe 1998; Mung'ong'o 1998). Yunusa (1999) notes that agricultural production in his Nigerian Middle Belt village was concentrated among an older cohort of people between forty-six and sixty-five years of age. Mustapha (1999), also in Nigeria, records advanced ages for farming heads of households and the tendency for youth to be engaged in activities outside agriculture.

Evidence suggests that peasant adjustments prompted by increasing capital costs led to a reallocation of land and labor away from commercial agriculture. A broad spectrum of poor and middle-income peasants, particularly younger peasants, were deterred by the lack of economic returns from growing Africa's traditional export crops. These crops were subject to deteriorating world prices, reflected in their countries' declining net barter terms of trade, external competition in staple food crop production, and private traders' patchy marketing services. IFIs called for export diversification into non-traditional crops like horticulture but their highly demanding production and marketing requirements made production on a sustainable basis by widely geographically-dispersed, under-capitalized African peasants relatively unlikely. African peasant agricultural commodity production was increasingly losing its place in the world division of labor.

The ensuing scramble for income

Pressing cash requirements

While returns from peasants' commercial agriculture were becoming less certain, daily cash requirements increased under the economic stringency of SAP. In addition to the removal of agricultural subsidies, bankrupt African governments removed subsidies on educational and health services. School fees and user fees at health centers became a high priority in peasant household budgets. Price inflation reached rural consumers through rising import costs of agricultural inputs, and enticing consumer goods that private traders brought to village markets. Market liberalization, from the perspective of the rural consumer, tended to expand choice but at arm's length, for much of the tantalizing merchandize came with unaffordable prices. Meanwhile, peasants continued to shoulder the normal expenses of living in their agrarian communities. Such costs, depending on local circumstances, included agricultural inputs and equipment, community-centered gift-giving, and food purchases.

Farmers increasingly faced agricultural bottlenecks due to rising farm input costs. In those areas where ploughs or mechanized, as opposed to hoe, agriculture is practiced, there are heavy annual capital costs associated with the purchase and maintenance of equipment, or alternatively equipment rental and labor costs. The proliferation and frequent escalation of costs that peasants of all economic strata faced gave rise to far more continuous, year-round cash expenditure requirements, whereas agricultural income was generally characterized by lump-sum payments after harvests. Peasants had to find ways to meet these year-round costs, exacerbated by the declining levels of income derived from flagging commercial agricultural production.

Rising incidence of non-agricultural income diversification

The recent DARE surveys and others suggest that the tendency for declining agricultural commodity production combined with expanding participation in non-agricultural activities gathered momentum during the 1990s (Francis 2000; Kinsey 2000; Ponte 2002b). Mustapha (1999) has the benefit of time series data for his Nigerian cocoa-producing area study site showing a remarkable rise in household participation in non-farm activities from an average of 33 percent in the mid 1980s to 57 percent at the time of the DARE survey in 1997. Sixty-seven percent of household dependants' involvement in non-farm activity in Doma, Nigeria, was initiated during the last 15 years. Forty-three percent had no previous economic activity before setting up (Yunusa 1999). In Madulu's (1998) Mwanza region study in Tanzania, over 50 percent of existing non-agricultural activity started in 1990 or thereafter and another third in the 1980s with only 16 percent of respondents involved in non-agricultural activity in the past. In Jambiya's (1998) study of Tanga Region, Tanzania, non-agricultural activities started in the 1980s.

It seems more than coincidental that the survey findings of the DARE studies report a surge in non-agricultural income sources over the past fifteen years of SAP implementation. This is a perverse outcome for a set of policies that was originally implemented in the name of correcting urban bias and "getting the prices right" for Africa's peasant farmers. To come to grips with this unpredicted twist, it is useful to contextualize it within traditional and more African farming systems.

The growing body of African income-diversification literature has a strong affinity to studies of survival strategies in drought-prone rural areas. In the era of structural adjustment, the concept of household coping strategies was applied to economic as well as climatic shocks and income diversification became aligned with agricultural producers' more generalized experience of risk.

Ellis (1998) distinguishes rational risk-management from default coping strategies. "Risk management" is perceived to be voluntary decision-making that avoids production failure by varying income sources and spreading them over time to reduce co-variate risk and to ensure consumption smoothing, i.e. the continuous realization of the household's basic purchase needs year-round. "Coping strategies," on the other hand, are defined as an "involuntary response to disaster or unanticipated failure in major sources of survival" (Ellis 1998: 13). "Adaptation" is a more reasoned response to changing circumstances of vulnerability and income-earning (Ellis 1998: 14). These distinctions are difficult to disentangle in the field given researchers' reliance on retrospective interviewing. Rather than being qualitatively different approaches to risk, they can form a sequential trial-and-error learning curve in which rural farmers are thrown into coping in the first year or two of a disaster, before managing the risk and in so doing, eventually adapting.

Peasant farmers' responses to sustained change in liberalized rural commodity markets would be likely to unfold in this manner, as opposed to more knee-jerk survival strategies in the wake of sudden natural disaster. Imprecision in understanding risk management seems to arise from the failure to distinguish climatic risk from market risk in the income-diversification literature of the 1990s. The surge in African rural households' income diversification over the last fifteen years cannot be correlated with a flush of bad weather on the continent. While market imperfections are often cited as a cause of small-holders' risk-averse behavior, most of the IFI literature (e.g. World Bank 2000b) side-steps the ubiquitous evidence of SAP and market liberalization's profound risk-enhancing effect on African peasants' agricultural commodity markets.

Certainly there are many forces influencing peasants' selection of income-diversifying activities, but it is nonetheless important to ask *why* such searches are *now* so generalized across the various agro-ecological zones of sub-Saharan Africa. Neo-liberal hype about the benefits of market liberalization for peasants' agricultural production clouded recognition and realistic assessment of peasants' income diversification, risk-averse and labor allocative behavior.

In view of rural households' increasing reliance on non-agricultural income, are such earnings alleviating risk and achieving consumption smoothing? What costs are borne by households in taking this route? In Mwanza Region in Tanzania and Sokoto State in Nigeria, respondents mentioned that involvement in such activities is considered as a somewhat shameful admission of a household's failure to adequately provision household needs within the gamut of agricultural production. The state's withdrawal from provisioning necessary infrastructural support for agriculture was also cited as a reason for initiating non-agricultural activities (Madulu 1998; Iliya 1999). Most case studies, however, document a rural process already well advanced that is now considered normal and certainly not shameful.

Several authors cite the welfare benefits experienced by those households most actively involved in non-agricultural production. In Malawi, households involved in non-agricultural activities averaged 225 percent more annual cash income as opposed to those without (Tellegen 1997: 152). In Zimbabwe, households with incomes from more than one kind of employment, especially if they had formal employment, were less likely to apply for food aid (Berkvens 1997: 12).

The social dimensions of the scramble

Proliferation of income earners within the rural household

Non-agricultural income diversification not only refers to the fact that households are diversifying into non-agricultural activities but that they are often pursuing more than one, sometimes several, different non-agricultural activities simultaneously or at different times throughout the year. Most of the activities are highly opportunistic in nature, involving quick responses to market demand and supply. However, changing labor-force participation patterns are apparent. As more household members are entering non-agricultural production, the male household head's dominant role as family cash-earner – an ideologically ingrained feature of African peasant commodity production – is eroding.

Donor agencies throughout the 1970s and 1980s (Boserup 1970; Rogers 1980) generally assumed African rural women's lack of involvement in cash-earning. Income diversification's pervasive expansion has overturned this assumption. Rural women are earning cash, although their work is generally less remunerative work than men's because women remain largely restricted to income-earning activities based on their home-making skills. Sales of prepared snacks, beer, hair plaiting, petty retailing, prostitution, knitting, tailoring, and soap making, are a few of the many services they sell. In non-Muslim study sites, beer brewing and sales of prepared food were usually women's major income earners, especially for female heads of households who faced major labor constraints due to the relatively small size of their household and lack of male assistance for various tasks (Berkvens 1997; Mulat Demeke 1997; Tellegen 1997; Mung'ong'o 1998). In Malawi, the sale of food snacks and beer brewing accounted for 76 percent of female heads of households' non-agricultural activities.

In Tanzania, village women often referred to their new income-earning role in terms of it having been thrust upon them by worsening economic circumstances (Bryceson 1999). What is apparent is that rural men have generally accepted that their wives and daughters need to work outside the home to earn money. Changes in male attitudes appear to have taken place rapidly and under duress. In Lushoto District, Sender and Smith (1990) observed that male interests were directed at protecting women from having to work outside the home during the mid 1980s. Ten years later, women were emphatic that their menfolk were actively encouraging them to earn an income (Jambiya 1998).

In the Middle Belt and northern parts of Nigeria, the combined influence of plough agriculture and Islam has historically limited women's involvement in agriculture, although in the drier parts of the area they do farm and have a more public presence. Yunusa (1999) found only 22 percent of male household heads derived income from non-agricultural activities compared to 89 percent of their wives and 48 percent of their dependants. Well before SAP, women in these areas were active in food vending and petty retail trade. They tend to rely on the labor of their children to retail their merchandize, so as to conform to purdah restrictions. The starting capital for petty trade is low, hence its popularity as a major avenue for women's income-earning. The attraction for women is that the earnings they generate from non-agricultural activities are theirs as opposed to earnings from farming which belong to the family (Meagher 2000; Yunusa 1999).

Iliya (1999), writing about semi-arid Sokoto State, offers other rationales for women's participation in non-agricultural activities, which relate to the experience of income decline in polygamous family structures. Polygamous wives felt that their husbands could no longer support all their dependants; there was economic rivalry between wives; and women strove to give reciprocal gifts to one another as a form of mutual support and future investment. Although women were allowed to farm in this area, the small size of their agricultural plots and the high capital costs of agricultural input purchases led them to prefer non-agricultural activities. This was borne out by the exceptionally large range of non-agricultural activities they pursued. Iliya counted eighty-nine different female-operated non-agricultural activities compared with seventy-nine for men. Their presence was overly weighted in the low and medium-earning activities. Of all the sampled women 23 percent had received government loans to help finance their enterprises.

However, virtually all the DARE case studies indicated that women have not relinquished their more traditional role in household domestic labor and subsistence regardless of their level of involvement in non-agricultural income diversification. In Igboland, although the gender division of labor in farming is blurred and there is barely any difference between the percentage of total income women derived from non-agriculture (79 percent) and that of men (81 percent), women are more likely to farm than men (Chukwuezi 1999). It is only in Muslim areas that women are not the key producers of subsistence food needs.

Like women, youth, teenagers and young unmarried adults, have actively sought non-agricultural activity involvement. Their presence is especially noted in trade. In Tanzania, the rush into trade has been remarkable. Madulu (1998) notes that Mwanza youth are specializing in medium and long-distance trade, taking advantage of the freedom of movement associated with being unencumbered by family responsibilities. In Mbeya Region, given the proximity of the Malawi and Zambia borders, the East African rift zone's wide variation in complementary agro-ecological zones and the influence of economic liberalization, trading has become a youthful passion (Mwamfupe 1998). In Nigeria's Middle Belt, Yunusa (1999) states that youth dominate non-farm activities, citing an 18 percent increase in family and child non-agricultural activity since 1992. Similarly, in Nigeria's southwestern cocoa-producing area youth of all income strata are far less attracted to farming than their parents and are diversifying into a number of trading and service activities (Mustapha 1999).

The youthful wave of non-agricultural practitioners has early recruits. Several researchers note the growing incidence of children as non-agricultural labor, often at the expense of school attendance (Madulu 1998; Iliya 1999). Mwamfupe (1998: 14) quotes a village elder in the Mbeya region of Tanzania: "school children used to assist in farm work after school hours, but today they dislike agriculture and are increasingly drawn into trading activities."

One of the defining characteristics of peasantries is the strength of family ties. Extended family structures dominate, as they are compatible with labor demands of agrarian production (Wolf 1966). Colonial and post-colonial policies shaped agrarian systems that integrated family subsistence production *and* commodity production. The formation of patriarchal family structures in which senior males as heads of households were accorded the role of liaising with government and co-opted into cash-crop production was encouraged. The male cash-crop/female subsistence spheres date from this period.

Declining African agricultural commodity production over the last twenty years has differentially impacted on men and women. Men's labor time and economic returns from cashcropping have diminished and undermined their role as family provisioners. The decline has been so rapid and forceful that virtually all able-bodied adults as well as many children have sought to earn incomes to prevent impoverishment. The individualization of economic activity and the increasing tendency to engage in non-agricultural income earning have had a dissolving effect on long-standing agrarian divisions of labor as well as economic rights and responsibilities within peasant households (Francis 1998). Pooling of income within the domestic unit is weakening as categories of people who formerly were not expected to earn an income assert a moral right to determine how their income is spent. This assertion is given added emphasis because of a decline, if not a cessation, in income and material goods distribution from the domestic units' erstwhile primary earners; male heads of households.

Increasing economic differentiation

The decline of peasant agricultural commodity production has been differentially experienced by peasant farmers. Broadly speaking, larger-scale farmers and those located in areas close to centers of food demand have managed to retain or even expand agricultural production. Economic liberalization has militated for the spatial contraction of production to those areas that afford higher yields due to favorable agro-climatic conditions or low transport costs (Poulton *et al.* 1999). Within these areas, it is the better-off farmers producing with economies of scale who can purchase the input packages and maintain their yield levels.

In many areas, these forces have engendered a process of land consolidation. The formation of landless agrarian classes is underway in some areas, especially those with high population densities where farmers are cultivating small, fragmented plots (Jambiya 1998). Before actual landlessness appears, poor families experience difficulties in mobilizing resources to farm their small unviable plots. This is especially apparent in areas utilizing plough agriculture, where poor families do not have ready access to the necessary equipment and draught power. The Zimbabwean case study illustrates this dilemma. Poor farmers rent these resources from well-to-do farmers or sharecrop, but invariably they do so at sub-optimal times, since the equipment-owning farmers use the equipment on their own fields at peak times.

For a number of years the non-farm literature has been asking whether non-agricultural activities fuel or alleviate rural poverty. The sub-Saharan African and Asian literatures are often juxtaposed. The Asian case study material tends to suggest that rural non-agricultural activities lessen class differentiation by providing alternative economic livelihoods for the rural poor with limited or no access to land (Saith 1992). Conversely, the African case study material presents a more ambiguous picture. Non-agricultural income diversification can reinforce class stratification as higher-income earners redirect portions of their agricultural capital to more lucrative non-agricultural activities. These activities have high levels of starting capital that preclude the entry of farmers with more modest means (Berkvens 1997; Iliya 1999; Meagher 2001; Mustapha 1999). Tellegen (1997) argues that non-agricultural activity provides the "road to rural wealth." The proportion of total household income derived from non-agricultural sources rose with income suggesting that there are agrarian elites capable of making a success of combined commercial farming and non-agricultural pursuits, relying on commercial agriculture more than any other group. In the cocoa-producing area of Nigeria, 100 percent of upper-income heads of households listed their main occupation as farming as opposed to only 89 and 62 percent in the middle and lower strata (Mustapha 1999). However, these high-income farming heads of households were earning 2.5 times more than middle-income heads and ten times more than lower-income heads from non-farm activities.

On the other hand, DARE survey data show that middle and low-income groups, who are not able to pursue the highest non-agricultural income-earning activities, are nonetheless vitally dependent on non-agricultural sources for their livelihood. This is especially true for heavily populated areas experiencing land scarcity. The Ethiopian and northern Nigerian Sahelian (Sokoto State) study sites both exhibited these characteristics (Mulat Demeke 1997). In Sokoto State, those with low incomes were the most heavily reliant on non-agricultural incomes (Iliya 1999). In the Nigerian Middle Belt, household earnings were inversely correlated with landholdings, with non-agricultural earnings forming 74 percent of the earnings of the landless as opposed to 20 percent for households holding the most abundant land resources (Yunusa 1999). All of these case studies reflected areas of growing land constraint and even landlessness, similar to rural Asian conditions. These too are areas with pronounced wage labor markets. Iliya (1999) and Jambiya (1998) record extensive reliance on local casual wage labor. In Sokoto State, labor is replacing dependence on family labor (Iliya 1999). These case studies suggest that as rural populations expand and land availability contracts in sub-Saharan Africa, non-agricultural activities are becoming increasingly important to rural poverty alleviation. Even in areas which have not experienced generalized land shortages such as in Njombe, Tanzania, young households with restricted land access have become more dependent on non-agricultural economic activities or are resorting to migrant labor (Mung'ong'o 1998).

The DARE research findings suggest that wealth and poverty are increasingly measurable in access to non-agrarian resources and consumption goods rather than land holdings.

Heading for the future

The future of African rural dwellers lies increasingly in labor force participation outside rural agriculture. They need literacy, numeracy, knowledge of the national language, and various occupational and computer skills to give them the means to command sufficient income for themselves and their families, as well as to raise the overall level of labor productivity in their respective countries.

The first and most pressing need for the future, therefore, is to establish a strong foundation to improve rural skills. This entails the resuscitation of primary education that slumped in sub-Saharan Africa during the budgetary cutbacks and economic stringency of the SAP era (Watkins 1999). Besides formal educational opportunities, rural children need extra-curricular clubs and learning programs to expand their informal education, giving them a firmer grasp of practical skills, mathematics, basic science and reading, to take into their adult lives. Secondary school places also need to be expanded. For those who do not receive a secondary education as well as those seeking post-secondary technical training, innovative on-the-job training schemes are required.

In this period of extremely rapid change, targeting youth and children, rather than adults, will have long term poverty reduction benefits. In addition, realistic assessments of rural dwellers agrarian and non-agrarian prospects vis-à-vis local and national markets are vital. Village non-agricultural opportunities and specializations need to be identified and gender stereotyping avoided. Rural communities or groups of communities can potentially provide a social context and platform for mobilizing skills training, marketing, and provide infrastructure for economic activities.

Rural land tenure policy is a vital issue linked to the question of geographical comparative advantage. Many rural areas in Africa languish in confusion about land tenure. Communal tenure arrangements reach the limits of their utility as traditional rural leadership disappears, rural populations become more ethnically and economically diverse, and women gain some degree of economic power but remain constrained by male-biased traditional land inheritance and allocation practices. Rural land tenure policy is fraught with historically-ingrained equity issues that have to be carefully weighed against productivity concerns. Support for non-agricultural activities should not be seen as a way of avoiding having to address land tenure quagmires. However, as rural labor is absorbed into non-agricultural pursuits, political demands for land access may ease, albeit unevenly in different places.

Bringing the town to the countryside is a practical rather than impossible orientation for development policy. Provisioning villages with water-supply systems, good road access and electrification need not be expensive if carried out with labor-intensive techniques. One of the main obstacles blocking such efforts is the entrenched bias towards capital-intensive construction methods of Western-trained engineers (Howe and Bantje 1995). Local infrastructural building through public works programs can increase local purchasing power and provide vital building and maintenance skills to local people, in addition to providing them with better physical amenities. Much can be done to improve local-level means of transport and the introduction of appropriate transport technology can expand local employment as well as improve rural people's mobility.

Conclusion

Roughly a century after the scramble for Africa that set in train the formation of peasantries over vast areas of rural Africa, structural adjustment and market liberalization policies have triggered a widespread erosion of local peasant economies and social communities. African depeasantization raises many pressing challenges and threats to people's economic welfare and political stability, but it can be harnessed to good effect with sensitive national and local-level policies. Parastatal marketing and blanket subsidized agricultural inputs are past history that cannot be resurrected (World Bank 2000b). Mkandiriwe and Soludo (1999) stress the importance of future development policy spearheaded by African countries. Ellis's (2000) emphasis on income diversification indicates the direction in which much African experimentation has so far taken place. Now, rural policies are needed offering positive future-oriented, coordinated strategies that lay the foundation for occupational diversification *and* specialization. In the absence of labor specialization, individuals' and households' non-agricultural diversification will face the rapid onset of diminishing returns, growing social demoralization and the increasing likelihood of political instability.

Notes

* This chapter is an abridged and edited version of a paper published in *World Development* (Bryceson 2002). Material is reproduced here with permission of Elsevier.

1 "Centuries of poor policies and institutional failures are the primary cause of Africa's undercapitalized and uncompetitive agriculture" (World Bank 2000b: 170).

2 For more detailed findings and information on the methodologies employed in the studies see the Afrika-Studiecentrum DARE Working Papers: On Ethiopia: Mulat Demeke (1997); On Nigeria: Chukwuezi (1999); Iliya (1999); Meagher (2001); Mustapha (1999); Yunusa (1999); On Tanzania: Jambiya (1998); Madulu (1998); Mung'ong'o (1998); Mwamfupe (1998); van Vuuren (2000); On Zimbabwe: Berkvens (1997); On South Africa: Bank and Qambata (1999); Manona (1999); McAllister (1999) as well as Tellegen's (1997) book on Malawi. The DARE program was made up of a network of researchers engaged in local-level studies of livelihood practices funded by the Netherlands Ministry of Foreign Affairs. I served as the coordinator based at the Afrika-Studiecentrum, Leiden collaborating with the following agencies: the Organization of Social Science Research for Eastern

Africa (OSSREA), Addis Ababa, Ethiopia; the Center for Research and Documentation (CRD), Kano, Nigeria; the Institute of Resource Assessment (IRA), University of Dar es Salaam, Tanzania and the Institute of Social and Economic Research (IZER), Rhodes University, Grahamstown, South Africa. In addition, other Netherlands-based researchers, not funded by the program, have contributed to the publications of the DARE program.

5 Livelihood diversification in rural Andhra Pradesh, India*

Edward Anderson and Priya Deshingkar

Introduction

It is now well known that poor households in rural areas in developing countries often rely on a diverse set of income-generating activities to meet their consumption needs. This diversity can be of considerable importance to the household, in terms of providing security against adverse external shocks, coping with seasonality, and generating additional income. For this reason, the removal of constraints to, or the expansion of opportunities for, livelihood diversification is considered an increasingly important aim for rural development policy (Ellis 1998).

It is also recognised that some aspects of rural livelihood strategies, although of considerable importance in providing short-term security, can be detrimental to longer-term growth in households' living conditions. For example, households that cultivate low-risk crops, or hold a high proportion of assets in relatively liquid form, may reduce their vulnerability to shocks but may also miss out on opportunities offered by the cultivation of higher-risk (although higher-return) crops, or by investment in less-liquid (although more productive) assets (Morduch 1994). Similarly, to the extent that there are gains from the specialisation of labour, the need to maintain a diversified livelihood portfolio may entail a significant reduction in the overall level of household income in an average year (Roumasset *et al.* 1979). For these reasons, the provision of cheaper and more effective forms of insurance to rural households can generate dynamic gains in incomes and productivity as well as short-term gains in household welfare (World Bank 2001a).

This chapter contributes to our understanding of these issues by examining recent case study evidence from rural India. We analyse the causes and consequences of livelihood diversification in a sample of six villages in the state of Andhra Pradesh. We begin by measuring the level of diversity in households' and individuals' sources of earned income. We then undertake two sets of empirical analysis. First, we relate the diversity of household incomes to observed household characteristics, including farm and non-farm assets, membership of local credit/savings groups, receipt of government benefits or migrant remittances, and household size. Our hypotheses are that income diversity is higher in households which:

- own moderate amounts of income-generating assets (e.g. land, livestock, machinery) relative to their labour supply, and;
- have fewer alternative mechanisms for insuring themselves against risk.

Second, we relate individuals' earned income to the diversity of their own income and that of the household in which they live. Our hypothesis here is that diversification reduces individuals' earned income, controlling for other influences on income. This would be the case if the need to maintain a diversified set of income sources, for insurance purposes, prevents some individuals from specialising in the activities in which the average return to their labour is highest.

Our results are as follows: first, we find that levels of diversification in the six sample villages are in fact quite low, in comparison with recent estimates based on similar surveys in Africa. This finding should be treated with caution, as there are certain limitations in the way incomes are measured in our dataset, and in the way different income categories are defined. However, there are also significant differences in the average level of diversification between each village in our sample, which are much less likely to be caused by differences in survey design. We attribute these differences to differences between villages both in *opportunities* for diversification – as proxied by the diversity of the local economy – and in the *demand* for diversification as a form of insurance – as proxied by average village income.

Second, we find an 'inverse-U' shaped relationship between the amount of assets a household owns per adult member and its diversification, and a negative relationship between a household's receipt of migrant remittances and other unearned incomes and its diversification. The former finding is consistent with the hypothesis that income diversity is higher in households which own moderate amounts of income-generating assets, while the latter is consistent with the hypothesis that diversification of earned income sources is used by households as a form of insurance (and that the existence of other unearned income sources reduces the demand for that form of insurance).

Third, we do find evidence that diversification at the household-level has an adverse effect on individual income, but that the magnitude of this effect is small (this contrasts greatly with the findings for Africa described in Chapter 3). Instead, individuals' reported incomes are influenced much more by the *type* of livelihood activities that they are engaged in, rather than by the diversity of those incomes. For example, we estimate that a change from one single source of household income to two equal income sources reduces the income of individuals within the household by a maximum of approximately 15 per cent. By contrast, we estimate that the average earnings of contract labourers is approximately 35 per cent higher than that of casual farm labourers, while the average earnings of industrial labourers is approximately 92 per cent higher.

The implication is that policies designed to help households *upgrade* their livelihood portfolios – from lower to higher average-return activities – are likely to lift more people out of poverty in this region than those designed to help households become more specialised within their *existing* portfolios.

This remainder of the chapter proceeds as follows. The next section presents background information about the state of Andhra Pradesh, and the six villages in the state selected for study. We then outline our chosen measure of income diversification, and present estimates of the amount of income diversification at both the household and individual level, by village, caste group and per capita income quintile. The next section presents the estimates of the determinants of diversification at the household level, followed by a section that presents the estimates of the effect of household- and individual-level diversification on individual income. A final section concludes.

Background

Andhra Pradesh (AP) has an area of roughly 275,000 sq km and a population of 75.7 million in 2001, almost 8 per cent of India's total population. Three-quarters of its population, or 55.2 million people, live in the rural areas, while nearly one-third of its GDP is derived from agriculture. It receives a southwest monsoon from June to September, and the southern parts of the state also receive short winter rains. The rest of the year is dry with the hottest season being April–May. There are twenty-three districts in the state, each of which is divided into mandals, with each mandal covering twenty to thirty villages.

Field work was conducted in three districts of AP, one from each of the state's three main regions; Telangana, Rayalseema and Coastal Andhra. Each region differs in their historical, political and agro-ecological conditions, and display distinct patterns of livelihood evolution and diversification. Telangana is a semi-arid region, with relatively poor levels of infrastructure development, educational facilities and advancement of women. It contains the state capital Hyderabad, which provides urban employment to many rural migrants, but is still home to some of the poorest people in AP. Rayalseema has some of the harshest environmental conditions in the state, and perhaps even the country. Average rainfall is 700 mm, and the proportion of total area which is cultivated is only 38 per cent. Once a prosperous industrial and farming centre, this region is now severely affected by drought: in some parts of the region, 2001 was the fifth consecutive year of drought. Coastal Andhra includes the coastal delta areas of AP which are similar to 'green revolution' parts of Punjab, Western UP, Gujarat and Maharashtra. The region has developed more rapidly than other parts of AP in recent decades, with significant improvements in female literacy, incomes, infrastructure development and infant mortality rates. Agriculture is based on the intensive cultivation of paddy and sugarcane on canal-irrigated lands, and draws in large inflows of seasonal migrant labour.

The three districts chosen, after discussion with key informants, were Medak, Chittoor and Krishna. Within each district, two contrasting villages were selected for detailed household-level study. The selection of villages was guided by various criteria, including proximity to urban areas, roads and markets as well as social and economic indicators of development.

The two villages studied in Medak district, in the Telangana region, are Madhwar (MD) and Gummadidala (GU). MD is a remote village in the dry, backward, north-eastern part of the district. Income levels are low, and a large proportion of the working population migrates on a seasonal basis to high agricultural productivity zones, and to Hyderabad. However, land ownership is relatively equitable, with only 20 per cent of all households owning no land at all. GU, by contrast, lies within an industrial belt in the south of Medak district, and is situated only 40 km from Hyderabad. A significant proportion of total income in this village is derived from industrial labour, and there are many more landless households than in MD. Partly as a result, GU has the largest gaps between the living standards of the rich and poor of all the six villages studied. Poorer households in the village use the nearby reserved forest to collect firewood, *tendu* leaves (used for making country cigars), leaf plates and broom straw.

The two villages studied in Krishna district, in the Coastal Andhra region, are Kosuru (KO) and Kamalapuram (KA). KO is a large, well-connected village with canal irrigation, typical of the better-off villages of the delta zone. The average household per capita income is higher here than in any of the other surveyed villages, although landholdings are highly skewed (65 per cent of households are landless), which explains why KO is also more unequal than the other villages, with the exception of GU (as measured by the ratio of the 90th to the 10th per centile of household per capita income). Assured irrigation enables farmers to harvest two paddy crops each year, and the village is the destination for seasonal immigrant labourers who come for up to between three and four months a year to harvest the paddy. Historically marginalised caste groups – particularly the Yadava, Gowda, Mala and Madiga – have been able to acquire small plots of land in KO over the years; at the same time, richer households and caste groups have diversified into high profit, non-farm occupations. KA is another prosperous village with assured canal irrigation, but is smaller and more remote than KO, with lower average incomes. KA has more small, semi-medium and medium-sized farms than KO. Many richer households have emigrated permanently to nearby urban locations, including Vijaywada, Machlipatanam and Hyderabad, so that population growth in the village has been slow.

The two villages studied in Chittoor district of Rayalseema are Voolapadu (VP) and Oteripalli (OP). VP is in the particularly dry, western part of the district, and has suffered from drought conditions for the last four years. However, it is less remote than OP in terms of labour market linkages: roughly one-quarter of working adults spend part of the year outside the village in seasonal migration, particularly on construction sites in nearby urban centres. Sericulture is a major occupation in the village, which expanded rapidly during the 1990s, but is now under threat from cheap Chinese silk imports. OP village lies in the eastern part of Chittoor district, close to the border with Tamil Nadu. It has also been affected by serious drought during the past five years, and is now officially classified as drought-prone. Many farmers, particularly those traditionally involved in groundnut cultivation, now leave their lands fallow rather than taking the risk of farming with uncertain outcomes. Several poor households have diversified into service sector jobs, catering to establishments in the nearby town of Chittoor. Collecting and selling of non-timber forest products (NTFPs) is a significant source of income for poorer households, particularly during the lean work season.

Information was collected from every household in each of the six villages on the ownership of assets, membership of local associations and credit groups, receipt of government assistance, extent of debts, receipt of migrant remittances and caste group. Information was also collected from every individual in each household in each village on age, gender, marital status, education level, their primary and secondary occupations (if working), the income obtained from each of those occupations and whether or not they spent part of the year outside the village through seasonal migration. Twenty-six different income categories were specified in the census questionnaire, as specified in Table 5.1.

We also aggregated these twenty-six activity groups into ten broader groups, as shown in Table 5.2

Some basic statistical information about each of the villages derived from the household census is presented in Table 5.3.

Table 5.1 Income categories specified in the census questionnaire

Income categories		
1 Cultivation	10 Barber	19 Government service
2 Agricultural labour	11 Washerman	20 Cattle herding
3 Contract labour	12 Leather worker	21 Sheep herding
4 Carpentry	13 Potter	22 Goat rearing
5 Weaving	14 Trader/middleman	23 Sericulture
6 Blacksmith	15 NTFP sale	24 Industrial labour
7 Goldsmith	16 Forest labour	25 Poultry
8 Basket making	17 Small scale industry	26 Other
9 Mat weaving	18 Private sector	

Table 5.2 Broad activity groups used in data analysis

Income groups			
i	Cultivation (1)	vi	Livestock (20–22, 25)
ii	Agricultural labour (2, 3)	vii	Services (18, 19)
iii	Traditional occupations (4–13)	viii	Sericulture (23)
iv	CPR related (15–16)	ix	Industrial labour (24)
v	Trade/self-employed (14, 17)	x	Other (26)

Table 5.3 Statistical information regarding the six villages

	Madhwar	*Gummadidala*	*Kosuru*	*Kamalapuram*	*Voolapadu*	*Otiripalli*
Income shares (% of village total)						
Own cultivation	0.17	0.16	0.35	0.50	0.31	0.34
Agricultural wage labour	0.73	0.31	0.27	0.35	0.41	0.27
Traditional occupations	0.01	0.03	0.02	0.01	0.00	0.03
CPR related	0.00	0.00	0.00	0.00	0.00	0.00
Trade/self-employed	0.00	0.09	0.05	0.02	0.02	0.07
Livestock	0.01	0.01	0.02	0.00	0.02	0.02
Services	0.03	0.15	0.18	0.08	0.03	0.15
Sericulture	0.00	0.00	0.00	0.00	0.17	0.00
Industrial labour	0.02	0.23	0.00	0.00	0.00	0.00
Other	0.04	0.03	0.11	0.03	0.04	0.11
Seasonal migration (% of working individuals)	66.00	3.00	8.00	11.00	24.00	4.00
Household per capita income (rupees per year)						
Mean	2,326	4,497	7,433	5,045	4,137	4,238
10th percentile	719	833	2,000	1,541	1,667	1,200
50th percentile (median)	1,900	3,000	4,500	3,870	3,250	3,000
90th percentile	4,173	9,573	15,000	9,550	7,000	7,243
Landholdings (% of households)*						
Landless	20.7	71.4	64.9	44.8	21.5	35.9
Sub-marginal	14.5	2.3	1.3	0.8	19.3	6.0
Semi-marginal	23.0	5.8	7.6	6.8	18.8	14.4
Marginal	20.4	6.9	8.1	9.2	18.0	20.5
Small	16.0	5.9	7.8	14.6	15.1	14.9
Semi-medium	3.0	4.0	5.8	11.8	3.6	6.0
Medium	1.6	2.8	3.4	10.1	2.7	1.4
Large	0.4	0.5	0.6	1.5	0.7	0.4
Number of households	427	1,560	1,429	464	553	214

Source: sample surveys carried out in six villages, 2001–2002.

Note

*Sub-marginal farmers own less than 0.5 hectares of land, semi-marginal farmers between 0.5 and 1.25 hectares, marginal farmers between 1.25 and 2.5 hectares, small farmers between 2.5 and 5 hectares, semi-medium farmers between 5 and 10 hectares, medium farmers between 10 and 25 hectares, and large farmers over 25 hectares.

Measures of diversification

Methodology

We calculate livelihood diversification at the household level using the 'inverse Herfindahl-Hirschman diversity index' (labeled IHHD), equal to:

$$IHHD_i = \left[\frac{1}{\Sigma a_j^2} \right]_i \tag{1}$$

where each a_j represents the proportional contribution of each livelihood activity j to household i's overall income. The maximum possible value of this index is the total number of different income sources, which is attained if total income is distributed equally between each source (Ellis 2000). The minimum possible value is one, attained when all income is obtained from one source only. We calculate the index for each household in the census, on the basis of their earned income only. (In other words, we do not include any income received from national/state government, or via migrant remittances, or any other sources of unearned income, in the calculation). In doing so we use the twenty-six different categories of earned income listed in the previous section.[1]

Household diversification can arise because each individual within the household has a diverse income portfolio, or because individuals within the household are specialised in different activities. We use the same measure to calculate how diversified individuals are *within* the household. In other words, we calculate the inverse Herfindahl-Hirschman diversity index for each individual in the village censuses, where each a_j in this case represents the proportional contribution of livelihood activity j to overall individual income.

The data used to calculate these measures of diversification are limited, for three reasons. First, information was collected on individuals' income from their primary and secondary occupations only, and not from any others they may have. To the extent that individuals do receive income from more than two sources during the year, our results will under-estimate the true amount of income diversification at both the household and individual level. Second, our estimates refer to the diversity of household and individual incomes over the course of the whole year. Some income diversity may reflect the fact that households and individuals are engaged in different activities during different seasons, rather than in different activities within any one particular season, but we are unable to say exactly how much.[2] Third, individual diversification is underestimated by the data because people who report their occupation as agricultural labourer, or 'kuli', in fact do all kinds of labouring work, depending on the seasonal availability of employment and raw materials such as coconut leaves, bamboo, wild vegetables and seeds.

Results

Table 5.4 shows means and standard deviations of household-level and individual-level activity diversification in each of the six villages. We also show results by caste group and by quintiles of household per capita income. The average household-level activity IHHD index across all households is 1.28, while the average across the poorest 20 per cent of households is 1.16. The standard deviation of each diversity index in each group is shown in parentheses.

Levels of diversification differ by village, most notably in the cases of Gummadidala and Madhwar, where households are more specialised (less diversified) than the other villages, at both the household and individual level. It is interesting to note that, in the case of Madhwar, the village as a whole is also highly specialised, with 73 per cent of total income coming from agricultural labour (Table 5.3). Gummadidala, by contrast, is the most highly diversified village – the highest share of any one activity in total village income is 31 per cent (agricultural labour) – even though households and individuals *within* the village are among the most specialised. A plausible explanation is that households tend to be more specialised in Madhwar

Table 5.4 Livelihood diversity by village, caste and income

	IHHD index (household, by activity)	*IHHD index (individual, by activity)*
All	1.28 (0.43)	1.09 (0.25)
by village:		
Otiripalli	1.38 (0.48)	1.14 (0.29)
Voolapadu	1.37 (0.47)	1.17 (0.32)
Kosuru	1.36 (0.46)	1.15 (0.31)
Kamalapuram	1.30 (0.43)	1.10 (0.27)
Gummadidala	1.16 (0.35)	1.01 (0.10)
Madhwar	1.23 (0.43)	1.01 (0.09)
by caste category:		
Scheduled tribe	1.28 (0.45)	1.04 (0.16)
Scheduled caste	1.26 (0.41)	1.10 (0.26)
Backward caste	1.31 (0.45)	1.09 (0.24)
General category	1.23 (0.40)	1.08 (0.24)
by household income quintile:*		
1 (poorest 20%)	1.16 (0.35)	1.04 (0.18)
2	1.23 (0.40)	1.07 (0.23)
3	1.33 (0.46)	1.09 (0.26)
4	1.37 (0.47)	1.12 (0.30)
5 (richest 20%)	1.31 (0.44)	1.12 (0.27)

Source: sample surveys carried out in six villages, 2001–2002.

Note

*Defined as total household income (excluding remittances and government benefits), divided by the number of household members of all ages.

because they have fewer opportunities to diversify out of agricultural labour, while households tend to be more specialised in Gummadidala because they have less need to diversify (earnings in individual occupations being higher on average and more predictable over time).

There are few clear differences in mean diversification levels across caste groups, except that diversification at the individual-level is clearly lower in the scheduled tribe group than in others. This latter result does not extend to household-level diversification, however, indicating that the scheduled tribes are relatively good at combining individual-level specialisation with household-level diversification (perhaps because household sizes are larger). In terms of differences in mean diversification by income, we note that diversification at both the household and individual level first increases through the first four quintiles, and then either declines or stabilises in the fifth (richest) quintile.

There is quite a lot of variation around these averages, as is evidenced by the values of the standard deviation of each diversity index. Even within villages, and within caste and income groups, some households maintain a more diversified income portfolio than others. In the next section we investigate some of the reasons why this might be the case. Nevertheless, it is worth pointing out that the average levels of diversification shown in Table 5.4 are low, in comparison with studies of other areas. Ellis (2000), for example, reports household-level IHHD indices in the range of 2.2–2.8 for three villages in the Hai District of northern Tanzania. This may simply reflect differences in survey design, and in the definition of income categories, but it may also reflect underlying economic and/or social characteristics of these villages of Andhra Pradesh which make households more specialised than elsewhere. We are unable to say any more about this in this paper, but it may provide a motivation for further research.

Causes of household diversification

In this section we investigate in more detail why some households maintain a more diversified income portfolio than others. There are of course many reasons, both economic and social, why households diversify, and we do not attempt to provide a full accounting of each of these different potential explanations. Our more limited aim in this section is to assess the extent to which *asset-based* and *insurance-based* theories of diversification can explain differences in observed levels of income diversity between households in our sample of six villages in Andhra Pradesh.

According to an assets-based view, the amount of diversity in a household's income portfolio reflects the amount of diversity in the assets (or factors of production) it owns or has access to. For example, households which own lots of land relative to their labour power specialise in cultivation, while households which own very little or no land relative to their labour power specialise in wage labour. Households which possess some land, but not enough to fully employ the household's labour supply, derive their income both from own cultivation and wage labour.[3] According to this view, we would expect there to be an 'inverse-U' shaped relationship between the amount of land per person owned by a household, and the amount of diversification of its income portfolio. A similar argument can be extended to the ownership of other income-generating assets, such as livestock. Households which own some livestock, but not enough to fully employ the household's labour supply, derive their income both from livestock-related activities and wage labour.

According to an insurance-based view, diversification is used by the household as a way of insuring against income shocks.[4] If this is the case, we would expect the amount of diversification to vary across households according to their demand for this particular form of insurance, and its cost. The demand for diversification as a form of insurance will depend positively on how risk-averse the household is, and on how much income volatility it is subject to, and negatively on the extent to which it has other ways of insuring against or coping with risk, such as owning liquid assets (food stocks, cash, livestock), access to communal credit/loan groups, crop insurance, state safety nets, or migrant remittances. The cost of diversification is the amount of income the household sacrifices, in an average year, in maintaining a diversified set of income sources. This will depend (positively) on the extent to which its 'optimal' livelihood strategy – as dictated by the combination of assets it owns – is to specialise. It will also depend on the range of activities which the household has access to, which will in turn depend on the household's asset base, including human capital, the amount of discrimination its members face in local factor markets, and on the diversity of the local economy as a whole.[5]

Data and methodology

In order to test these hypotheses, we estimate the following econometric model:

$$hhdv_i = b_0 + b_1(assetspc)_i + b_2(assetspc)_i^2 + b_3(adults)_i + b_4(remitpc)_i + b_5(incomepc)_i + b_6(sprotect)_i + b_7(credit)_i + b_8(location)_i + b_9(caste)_i + e_i \qquad (2)$$

where each i indicates a separate household. The definition of each variable is given in Table 5.5. According to asset-based theories of diversification, we would expect the coefficient b_1 to be positive and b_2 to be negative (yielding an inverse U-shaped curve). According to insurance-based theories, we would expect the coefficients b_1, b_4, b_5, b_6 and b_7 to be negative. According to both sets of theories, we would expect the coefficient b_3 to be positive. This may be because diversification in small households requires more diversification at the individual level, which can be costly in terms of lost opportunities for productivity gains associated with specialisation, or because

Table 5.5 Variables included in household diversification regression

Variable name	*Variable description*
Hhdv	Household diversification index, as measured by the inverse Hirschman-Herfindhal index (IHHD).
Assetspc	Value of assets per adult. Four different types of assets distinguished: land, livestock (bullocks, cows, buffalo, goats, sheep, pigs, poultry, ducks), agricultural (tractors, threshers, oil/electric motors, bullock carts), and non-agricultural (TV, radio, vehicles, phone, cooking gas). Measured in logs.
Adults	Number of adults in household. Measured in logs.
Remitpc	Value of migrant remittances to the household per adult. Measured in logs.
Sprotect	Receipt of national/state government support (1 = yes, 0 = no). Two different types of support are distinguished: social security (including old age pensions, widow pensions, national family benefit, and national maternity benefit), and subsidised food (the PDS system).
Incomepc	Other sources of unearned income received by the household per adult. Measured in logs.
Credit	Membership of DWRCA thrift and credit group (1 = yes, 0 = no).
Location	Qualitative variables for five different villages: Voolapadu, Kosuru, Kamalapuram, Gummadidala, and Madhwar. Oteripalli is the reference location.
Caste	Qualitative variables for three different caste groups: Scheduled Tribe (ST), Scheduled Caste (SC), and Backward Caste (BC). General Category is the reference caste group.

small households are less likely to possess skills and experience in a wide range of livelihood activities.

The coefficients b_8 and b_9 tell us whether the amount of diversification at the household level differs by village or by caste, controlling for the other explanatory variables, and if so by how much. We have no a priori expectations regarding the sign of these coefficients. One the one hand, the more marginalised caste groups – the so-called 'backward castes', 'scheduled castes', and 'scheduled tribes' – may tend to be less diversified, if they face discrimination in accessing some livelihood activities, but may on the other hand be more diversified if their incomes are lower and their demand for insurance is as a result higher. Similarly, households in villages with higher average incomes – Kosuru and Kamalapuram – may tend to be less diversified, because demand for insurance is lower, but may also tend to be more diversified, as the range of livelihood activities to which they have access is higher.

Note we do not include the household's earned income in this regression. Although we would expect households with higher earned incomes to have less diversified income portfolios, on the basis that they are less risk-averse than poorer households, we also expect households with more diversified income portfolios to be poorer, on the basis that they are prevented in specialising in their most remunerative activity. In econometric terms, earned income is an endogenous variable the inclusion of which would violate the assumptions of the method of ordinary least squares (OLS) used to estimate equation (2).

Results

The results of estimating equation (2) by ordinary least squares (OLS) are presented in Table 5.6. The first point to make is that we have only limited success in explaining differences in the amount of income diversification across households, using the set of explanatory variables in Table 5.5. We are only able to explain 16 per cent of the total variation in the IHHD index. Nevertheless, we do find that our explanatory variables are, in most cases, related to diversification in the ways suggested by theory.

First, we find evidence of an inverse U-shaped relationship between the assets a household owns, per adult member, and its diversification. This is illustrated by the negative coefficients on the value of land, agricultural assets and non-agricultural assets owned by the household, per adult member, and the positive coefficients on the square of these variables. In the majority of

Table 5.6 Regression results, household diversification

Variable	*Coefficient*	*t-statistic*
Constant	0.961	26.0
Land value per adult, log	0.024	3.9
Livestock value per adult, log	−0.004	−0.6
Agricultural asset value per adult, log	0.010	1.2
Non-agricultural asset value per adult, log	0.017	3.2
Land value per adult squared	−0.001	−2.1
Livestock value per adult squared	0.002	2.7
Agricultural asset value per adult squared	−0.002	−1.9
Non-agricultural asset value per adult squared	−0.002	−2.7
Log number of adults in household	0.142	7.0
Years of schooling in household	0.002	1.3
Log remittances per person	−0.014	−2.7
Log unearned income per person	−0.005	−0.9
Membership in DWCRA	0.048	3.1
Social Security	0.044	2.0
Food security	0.057	4.3
Voolapadu	−0.003	−0.1
Kosuru	0.085	2.7
Kamalapuram	−0.015	−0.4
Gummadidala	−0.093	−3.0
Madhwar	−0.164	−4.7
Scheduled Tribes	0.123	3.5
Scheduled Caste	0.045	2.3
Backward Castes	0.097	6.5
N	4,477	
R2	0.157	

cases, these results are statistically significant at the 5 per cent level (as indicated by a t-statistic greater than two, in absolute terms). This finding is supportive of the view of diversification as resulting from the particular combination of assets owned by households. The one exception is the value of livestock owned by the household, which has a consistently positive effect on the amount of diversification. This finding, statistically significant at the 5 per cent level, contradicts both the insurance and asset-based views of diversification. One possible explanation is that income diversification is only a partial form of insurance against income risk, so that risk-averse households who tend to hold more diversified income portfolios also tend to hold a larger proportion of their assets in relatively liquid form, such as livestock (e.g. Jalan and Ravallion 2001; Dercon 1998).

Second, we find that the amount of migrant remittances, and other unearned incomes, have a negative effect on household diversification. In the case of migrant remittances, the effect is statistically significant at the 5 per cent level. This finding is consistent with the hypothesis that diversification (of earned income sources) is used by households as a form of insurance, and that the existence of other (unearned) sources of income reduces the need (or the demand) for that insurance. However, we find that membership of a local credit association, and receipt of benefits from national or state-level governments, both have a positive effect on diversification, which is contrary to expectation. One possible explanation is reverse causation: poorer households are both more likely to be members of local credit associations or receive government benefits, and have more diversified incomes.

Third, we find that our qualitative variables for the five different villages in the region and the different major caste groups have, in the majority of cases, significant effects on diversification. Controlling for the other variables in Table 5.5, the average household IHHD index is highest in Kosuru (0.09 points above Oteripalli) and lowest in Gummadidala and Madhwar (0.09 and 0.16 points below Oteripalli). There are no significant differences (statistically speaking) between the average household IHHD index in Voolapadu, Kamalapuram, and Oteripalli. The average IHHD index is highest among scheduled tribes (0.12 points above the general category), followed by the backward castes (0.10 points above) and the scheduled castes (0.05 points above), again controlling for all other variables in Table 5.5.

Effects of diversification

In this section we investigate the effects of income diversification. The hypothesis we test is that diversification has an adverse effect on individuals' earned income. This will be the case if the need to maintain a diversified set of income sources, at either the household or individual level, for insurance purposes, prevents some individuals from specialising fully in the highest-paid activity they are qualified to carry out. This is one of the channels through which ex-ante household responses to risk can be a cause of income poverty.

Other channels include the choice of traditional crops over riskier but more profitable varieties (e.g. Dercon 1996), and the holding of assets in relatively liquid but unproductive form (e.g. Jalan and Ravallion 2001).

A simple example is useful to illustrate our argument. We imagine two households, A and B, each containing two individuals, 1 and 2, who have access to two alternative income sources, F and NF, one of which (F) is assumed to generate higher returns in an average year. Both income sources are subject to fluctuations over time, but they are less than perfectly covariant. Household A is assumed risk-averse, and in the absence of alternative insurance arrangements maintains a diversified income portfolio, in which person 1 works in activity F and person 2 works in activity NF. Household B is assumed risk-neutral, and so both individuals work in activity F. Resulting levels of earnings and household-level diversification are shown in Table 5.7. In this case, earnings of individuals in the more diversified household are on average 25 per cent lower than those in the more specialised household.

Our interest lies in measuring how much income individuals do sacrifice in this way, on average, in our sample of six villages in Andhra Pradesh. If the amount is large, one could inform policy-makers that household strategies to reduce risk come at a high economic cost, and that the provision of alternative forms of insurance would have a high economic pay-off. Of course, the amount may well be small, if diversification is in fact the close to 'optimal' livelihood strategy for most households, given the combination of assets they own. It may even be positive, if there are significant complementarities between different income-generating activities.[6]

Data and methodology

Our empirical approach is to estimate the following econometric model:

$$\begin{aligned} income_i = {} & a_0 + a_1(age)_i + a_2(age^2)_i + a_3(schyrs)_i + a_4(gender)_i + a_5(mainocc)_i \\ & + a_6(ptime)_i + a_7(inddv)_i + a_8(hhassets)_i + a_9(hhschyrs)_i + a_{10}(hhadults)_i \\ & + a_{11}(hhdv)_i + a_{12}(location)_i + a_{13}(caste)_i + u_i \end{aligned} \quad (3)$$

where each i indicates a separate individual. The definition of each variable is shown in Table 5.8. Our main interest lies in the sign and magnitude of the coefficients a_7 and a_{11}. Following the above discussion, we expect these

Table 5.7 Individual earnings and household level diversification: a simple example

Household	*Individual*	*Activity*	*Individual earnings*	*Household-level diversification index*
A	1	F	100	2
A	2	NF	50	2
B	1	F	100	1
B	2	F	100	1

Table 5.8 Variables included in individual income regression

Variable name	*Variable description*
Income	Total individual income, imputed in the case of own cultivation. Measured in logs.
Age	Age of individual, in years.
Schyrs	Years of schooling of individual. Estimated from underlying education attainment data in survey.
Gender	Qualitative variable equal to 1 if individual is female, 0 otherwise.
Mwocc	Main occupation of individual. Defined as occupation which generates the largest proportion of individual's income. Twenty-six separate categories, listed in Table 5.1, are distinguished. Agricultural labour (2) is the reference category.
Ptime	Qualitative variable equal to 1 if individual's secondary occupation is working (one of occupation codes 1–26), but primary occupation is not; zero otherwise.
Inddv	Individual diversification index, measured either by IHHD or DV75.
Hhassets	Value of assets owned by household. Three different types of assets distinguished: land, livestock (bullocks, cows, buffalo, goats, sheep, pigs, poultry, ducks), and agricultural (tractors, threshers, oil/electric motors, bullock carts). Measured in logs.
Hhschyrs	Years of schooling of other household members.
Hhadults	Number of adults in household, defined as persons aged 14 or over. Measured in logs.
Hhdv	As Table 5.5
Location	As Table 5.5
Caste	As Table 5.5

coefficients to be negative, and their absolute magnitude to indicate exactly how much income individuals sacrifice, on average, in maintaining a diversified income portfolio, at either the household-level (a_{11}) or at the individual-level (a_7). We expect the coefficient a_7 to be larger (in absolute value) than a_{11}, on the basis that diversification at the individual level is likely to be particularly costly in terms of lost opportunities for productivity gains associated with specialisation in one activity.

We specify a number of other variables which we expect to influence individuals' earnings. These include, at the individual-level, age, age squared, education level, gender, whether the main occupation involves work outside the household, and the main occupation itself. We expect, following the results of several other studies, schooling years to have a positive effect on earnings ($a_3 > 0$), the relationship between age and earnings to show a 'U-shaped' profile ($a_1 > 0$, $a_2 < 0$), and men to have higher average earnings than women ($a_4 < 0$). We also expect that individuals who report working mainly on household activities earn less than others ($a_6 < 0$), mainly because they are likely to spend fewer hours in paid employment. We also include, at the household-level, the value of land, livestock, agricultural assets, and schooling years per adult member of the household, and qualitative variables for caste group and village. We expect individuals in households with more land, livestock or agricultural assets per adult to have higher earnings ($a_8 > 0$, $a_9 > 0$, $a_{10} < 0$), as the marginal product of their labour in own-cultivation will be higher.

The coefficients associated with qualitative variables for the 26 occupation codes (a_5) are of major interest. They tell us the extent to which the average income of each occupation differs from the average income of agricultural labourers, controlling for the other variables. If the coefficient associated with a particular occupation is positive and large in size, the implication is that there are barriers to entry to that occupation, and that improving poor people's access to those occupations would reduce poverty. Such barriers may take on numerous forms, including a lack of training and experience, lack of access to information, unfavourable geographical location, an inability to take on risk, or discrimination. We do not make any attempt in this paper to determine which barriers are most serious for which occupations, which is instead left for further work.

There are three main limitations with this approach. First, much household income is earned jointly, rather than individually, and in particular that from own cultivation. In this case, we cannot be sure what proportion of the income from cultivation reported by the household is generated by each family member. To avoid this problem, we impute each individual's earnings from own cultivation, by calculating total household income from own cultivation, and dividing it by the number of adults in the household stating own cultivation as their primary or secondary occupation.[7] Second, we have no information regarding the amount of time worked by each individual during the course of the year, which is clearly an important influence on total earned income.[8] Third, a negative relationship between household-level diversification and individual income may partly reflect reverse causation, in that households with higher earned incomes may well be less risk-averse, and therefore less diversified, than poorer households. This means that our estimates of the effect of diversification on income should be regarded as an upper-level estimate: the true effect is likely to be lower.

Results

The results of estimating equation (3) are shown in Table 5.9. The sample is restricted to all those aged between 14 and 60 inclusive with positive earnings (including imputed vales), and estimation is by OLS. We have more success explaining differences in earnings across individuals than we do differences in diversification across households. Using the set of explanatory variables in Table 5.8 we can explain approximately 40 per cent of the total variation in income across individuals in the six villages. We also find that our explanatory variables are, in most cases, related to income in the ways suggested by theory.

First, as expected, individuals' years of schooling and age have a positive effect on earnings, while age squared, being female, and being part-time have

Table 5.9 Regression results, individual earnings

Variable	*Coefficient*	*t-statistic*
(Constant)	7.654	86.8
Sex	−0.427	−25.9
Age	0.032	8.8
Age squared	−0.0004	−7.2
Schyrs	0.016	8.1
Ptime	−0.460	−7.6
Own-cultivation	0.245	11.1
Contract labour	0.309	5.0
Carpenter	0.053	0.5
Weaving	0.013	0.0
Blacksmith	0.152	0.9
Goldsmith	0.197	0.6
Basket making	−0.340	−1.9
Mat weaving	0.693	1.5
Barber	0.081	0.8
Washerman	0.123	1.5
Leather worker	1.159	4.3
Potter	0.226	1.7
Trader/middleman	0.586	11.5
MFP sale	0.258	0.9
Forest labour	0.908	2.4
Small scale industry	0.598	7.5
Private	0.817	17.4
Government service	1.448	26.7
Cattle herding	−0.020	−0.2
Sheep herding	0.874	3.2
Goat rearing	0.716	4.9
Sericulture	0.991	13.0
Industrial labour	0.653	17.4
Poultry	0.547	3.5
Others	0.240	5.8
Scheduled Tribes	−0.075	−1.8
Scheduled Caste	−0.129	−5.4
Backward Castes	−0.059	−3.0
Voolapadu	0.202	5.5
Kosuru	0.381	11.2
Kamalapuram	0.435	11.0
Gummadidala	0.154	4.5
Madhwar	−0.044	−1.1
Female-headed household dummy	0.009	0.3
Household years of schooling	0.003	5.7
Value of land, log	0.003	1.9
Value of livestock, log	−0.005	−2.5
Value of agricultural assets, log	0.014	6.2
Log number of adults in household	−0.154	−7.7
Inddv	0.458	14.1
Hhdv	−0.142	−8.0
N	8,950	
R^2	0.42	

a negative effect. Individuals based in households which own more land or agricultural assets, or have less adult members, also have higher earnings, controlling for other factors. The one unexpected result is the negative effect of the value of livestock owned by the household on the earnings of household members. This finding might reflect reverse causation; in particular, it could be that poorer households tend to hold a higher proportion of their assets in relatively liquid form, such as livestock, than richer households, as has been found in other studies (Jalan and Ravallion 2001; Dercon 1998).

Second, there is some support for the hypothesis that diversification reduces income. In particular, the coefficient on the household-level diversification measure is negative and statistically significant at the 5 per cent level. In other words, individuals based in households with more diversified incomes have lower overall incomes than individuals based in more specialised households. Our interpretation is that this illustrates one of the costs of diversification. We also find, however, that diversification at the individual level has no such cost; it is in fact associated with higher overall earnings. This result is contrary to our initial expectation. One possible explanation is that individuals with two occupations simply work more hours during the year than those with only one. (Unfortunately, we are unable to test this hypothesis, as we lack information on time worked). Another possibility is that some people report an occupation as being their own when in fact someone else in the household is doing it.

How large is the cost of diversification? According to these estimates, an increase in the household IHHD index of one unit – corresponding, for example, to a change from one single source of household income to two equal income sources – reduces the income of individuals within the household by 15 per cent.[9] Although this amount is clearly not negligible, other explanatory variables have larger effects. In particular, there are some very large differences between the average earnings of individuals in different occupations, even controlling for differences in age, schooling, assets and so on. For instance, earnings of contract labourers are estimated to be approximately 35 per cent higher than those of casual agricultural labourers, while earnings of industrial labourers are 92 per cent higher. Similarly, earnings of own-cultivators are on average 28 per cent higher than those of agricultural labourers, while those of individuals engaged in sericulture are 170 per cent higher. In other words, it appears that the *type* of livelihood activities that individuals and households are engaged in is a more important determinant of their income (and in turn, their welfare and ability to meet basic needs) than the *diversity* of those activities.

Conclusions

This chapter analyses the causes and consequences of livelihood diversification in a sample of six villages in the Indian state of Andhra Pradesh. Our main findings are threefold. First, average levels of income diversification at the household level appear to be quite low, in comparison with studies of other regions and countries. Second, differences in the amount of diversification between households reflect differences in the combinations of assets owned by households, and differences in the demand for diversification as a form of insurance against income shocks, as suggested by theory. Third, although we find that greater diversification at the household level is associated with a reduction in individual (and therefore household) income, the size of the effect is small. Other explanatory variables, particularly those relating to the type of activities in which individuals and households are engaged, have much larger effects on income. Policies which help households *upgrade* their income portfolios from lower to higher average-return activities are likely to lift more people out of poverty in this region than those designed to help households become more specialised within their *existing* portfolios. Understanding the specific barriers which households face in accessing higher-return activities is an important task for further research.

Notes

* Work for this chapter was carried out as part of the ODI Livelihood Options Study, funded by the UK Department for International Development. We are grateful to Dirk Bezemer and John Farrington for comments, and to Sreenivas Rao, Usha Kulkarni, and Laxman Rao for invaluable assistance with the data.

1 The results were in fact very similar when using the ten broader groups, indicating that there is little diversification within households within these broader groups.

2 More detailed information regarding household livelihood strategies for a sample of households from each village was also collected, in each of the two different seasons of the year (Kharif and Rabi). Analysis of this information, which will complement that contained in the present chapter, will be contained in a separate paper, (Deshingkar *et al.* 2004).

3 According to this view, unanticipated shocks to a household's assets – a collapse in the productivity of its land for example – may cause the household to diversify, as is emphasised in views of diversification as an involuntary but necessary strategy for coping with crisis (e.g. Davies 1996).

4 In particular, when different income-generating activities are subject to shocks which are less than perfectly covariant over time, income generated by a diversified livelihood portfolio will vary less over time than that generated by a more specialised portfolio. This view of diversification as a deliberate *ex ante* household strategy for reducing risk has been emphasised by Townsend (1995) and Morduch (1995).

5 Locations with larger markets, or better access to larger markets, can typically support a wider range of different income-generating activities. Rising farm productivity can therefore facilitate household diversification, by raising local incomes and the size of local markets, as emphasised by the 'rural growth linkages' approach (Ellis 1998).

6 A large body of research suggests that *crop* diversification by farm households in developing countries typically reflects various complementarities between crops, and as such entails little loss in, or indeed increases, total farm income (Ellis 1998). Our paper does not consider diversification between different crops, but the underlying argument – that there may be complementarities between different livelihood activities – is the same.

7 A further, although less serious problem, is that some individuals refused to state their income. These people are excluded from the analysis.
8 This introduces the possibility that individuals with more diversified income sources may in fact be observed to have higher earnings than others, simply because they spend more time in paid employment during the year.
9 The coefficients in Table 5.9, which are measured in log points, can be converted into percentages according to the following formula: [exp(coefficient)-1]*100.

6 Household composition and rural livelihoods in Uganda*

Catherine S. Dolan

Introduction

There is now a sizeable body of literature documenting the complexity of rural livelihoods in developing countries.[1] Recent development literature has generally depicted such diversification favourably, associating it with poverty reduction, employment generation and enhanced market linkages for rural households. While the multidimensionality of rural livelihoods is now taken for granted, the role that gender plays in enabling or disabling livelihood choices has received comparatively little attention. Yet a number of well-known gender-related constraints circumscribe the extent to which households are willing, or able, to increase their output. Female household heads, in particular, can face distinct constraints stemming from their sole responsibility for income generation and reproductive work, fewer endowments, and a higher dependency burden than male household heads (Rosenhouse 1989). Specifically, female headed households' (FHHs) differential access to productive resources often limits their access to livelihood strategies that are more lucrative or impedes their capacity to overcome the difficult circumstances in which they find themselves.

This chapter seeks to contribute a gender perspective to the analysis of rural livelihoods in Uganda, where households have grown ever more dependent on a broad range of economic undertakings, including agriculture, petty trade and wage employment. It aims to document the differences between male- and female-headed households and the ways in which household headship might influence their livelihood choices. Although the focal point of the chapter is economic activity, it draws mainly on anthropological and sociological insights to explain rural livelihoods. The chapter is structured as follows. The next section discusses why household headship is important to an analysis of rural livelihoods. Then a description of the districts under study is provided and an outline of the main features of household livelihood portfolios. The following section examines how participation in particular economic undertakings is influenced by the nature of household headship. Next, gender-based constraints to livelihood diversification are examined, followed by the conclusion.

Gender and rural livelihoods

Livelihood strategies are shaped by a broad range of economic, political and social factors, and vary markedly between economic necessity (responding to shocks, vulnerability and poverty) and choice (as a way to further investment, savings and accumulation) (Kabeer and Anh 2000). However, while various external factors – resource endowments, accessibility to markets and the capacity to mobilise social networks – mediate livelihood options, the choice to pursue various strategies is also shaped by the composition and internal dynamics of households. For example, it is within the context of the household that social divisions such as gender and kinship operationalise systems of labour obligation, resource allocation and income distribution giving rise to well-documented inequalities. For women, in particular, the position they occupy within households often directly determines their asset endowments – especially land, livestock and labour – and hence the types of livelihood opportunities that are open to them.

From a gender perspective, the fact that households are differentiated by individuals with varying degrees of agency, entitlement and mobility, is fundamental to an analysis of livelihood diversification. One way of gauging gender differences in poverty levels and livelihood options is to compare the circumstances of female- and male-headed households. Over the last decade a number of empirical studies have concluded that FHHs warrant specific policy attention due to their triple burden of disadvantage. This burden stems from three stylised features of FHHs:

1. the head is frequently the single (or primary) earner of the household;
2. as a woman, the single earner faces gender-based discrimination in the labour market and in other productive activities (such as access to credit);
3. the female head faces unique time constraints stemming from her role as both the main economic earner and provider of reproductive labour (domestic work and child care) (Fuwa 2000).

Several economists[2] have wrestled with the question of whether these factors lead FHHs to be disproportionately represented among the poor, while other studies[3] have questioned whether the category of 'female headship' is an appropriate tool for targeting policy interventions. Although the conclusions have been inconsistent, pointing to the tenuous and highly contextual nature of the relationship between female headship and poverty, they have nevertheless reinforced the need for fuller understandings of household composition. While poor female-headed households are not a proxy for poor women, headship nevertheless provides insights into two important dimensions of rural livelihoods. First, it helps to illuminate the role that gender plays in shaping the capabilities, entitlements and subsequent opportunities of households (Fuwa 2000). And, second, it allows us to pinpoint more clearly the barriers and constraints to livelihood diversification, and the extent to which they are linked to gender.

District and household descriptions

This chapter is based on qualitative research conducted with 315 households across three districts in central and eastern Uganda: Mubende, Kamuli and Mbale. Three villages were selected in each district, with a series of Participatory Rural Appraisal (PRA) and wealth ranking activities undertaken to ensure that the households drawn from each village represented, as broadly as possible, the full range of livelihood activities including farming (crop and livestock production), off-farm and fisheries-based activities experienced by rural individuals and households in Uganda (Table 6.1).[4]

While Mubende, Kamuli and Mbale are generally classified as belonging to the banana/coffee, maize/cotton and montane/banana farming systems respectively, there is considerable variation between and within the districts. For example, the more remote areas of Mubende district, located in the Central Region, are relatively land abundant due to the depopulation arising from years of civil war. In contrast, Mbale district is an area of extreme land shortages with an average population density more than three times the national average.[5] Land scarcity is a significant factor underlying the choice of livelihoods in the region as customary inheritance practices diminish the viability of farming for each generation. Kamuli district, bordering Lake Kyoga in the north, differs from Mbale and Mubende due to the importance of fishing to community livelihood strategies. This is particularly

Table 6.1 Main livelihood features of sample districts

	Mbale	*Mubende*	*Kamuli*
Crop production	Banana, beans, maize, millet, sweet potatoes, coffee, cotton, horticulture	Bananas, beans, cassava, Irish potatoes, maize, ground-nuts, sweet potatoes, coffee	Cassava, maize, millet, sweet potatoes, cotton
Livestock and fish	Dairy cattle, pigs, goats, chickens	Cattle (milk and meat), chickens and goats	Cattle (meat), goats, chickens and ducks, Nile Perch, *mukene*, Tilapia, Lung fish
Off-farm	Sale of labour, petty trade	Sale of labour (farm), petty trade, food processing, shop keeping, transport, construction, government employment, tailoring, hunting	Fish trading, fish carrying, sale of labour, transport (bicycles and boats) shop keeping, firewood, brewing

Source: qualitative research conducted in nine Ugandan villages, January–April 2001.

important from a gender perspective as Kamuli has a high number of *de jure* female household heads, who have migrated to the area to capitalise on the *mukene*[6] trade.

Household portfolios

In Uganda, the circumstances under which women become household heads, and the options and constraints this engenders, is particularly relevant. Evidence suggests that between 20 per cent and 30 per cent of all households in the country are female-headed, and that FHHs may be among the most vulnerable of the country's population (Elson and Evers 1997; Goetz *et al.* 1994). In this study, female-headed households were similarly prevalent, constituting 20 per cent, 20 per cent and 15 per cent of sample households in Mbale, Kamuli and Mubende respectively. Between 15 per cent and 30 per cent of these households were de facto female-headed, with the spouse reported as mostly or permanently away.[7]

In the three districts the mean household size of sampled FHHs is smaller than male-headed households (MHHs), with 73 per cent of sample FHHs containing one or fewer economically active adults (EAAs) in contrast to 17 per cent of MHHs (see Table 6.2). This was expected and is consistent with other studies documenting the smaller size of FHHs (e.g. Fuwa 2000; IFAD 2002). The disparity in household size reflects, in part, widespread rural–urban migration among men. Such migration is especially widespread in Mbale, where over one-third of all FHHs (both *de jure* and de facto) reported at least one household member living away. In the majority of these cases, migration is undertaken by adult sons, who travel outside the districts in search of agricultural work. Women's mobility (and capacity to migrate) is curtailed both by familial and/or childcare responsibilities, as well as cultural norms that stigmatise their free movement in rural areas.

Though income is only one dimension of poverty, if income is used as a proxy for economic welfare then FHHs are disadvantaged relative to their male counterparts. The proportion of FHHs situated in the lowest income quartile is higher in all three districts, with the disparity particularly notable in the agriculturally-based regions of Mbale and Mubende.[8] This is further reinforced by the finding that mean per capita income is lower for FHHs than for MHHs in all three districts.[9] In both cases, this reflects an inability of FHHs' to diversify into higher return activities. As Table 6.2 indicates, FHHs possess lower asset endowments than MHHs, which combined with less labour to diversify, either impede diversification or compels them to diversify into less profitable undertakings.[10] For example, a number of female heads claimed that scarce endowments of land and inputs hindered their ability to raise farm output, or expand into higher return crops. Poor endowments of land or livestock often lay beneath their choice to hire themselves out to work as low wage agricultural workers.

However, within FHHs, widows, particularly older widows, fare much

Table 6.2 Selected household assets by gender of household head

	All		*Mbale*		*Kamuli*		*Mubende*	
	Male $n = 263$	*Female* $n = 52$	*Male* $n = 86$	*Female* $n = 19$	*Male* $n = 86$	*Female* $n = 19$	*Male* $n = 91$	*Female* $n = 14$
Mean no. of years in education per EAA[a] per HH	4.8	3.1	5.7	2.6	4.6	3.1	4.2	3.9
Total no. of years in education (resident EAAs)	10.5	5.2	12.0	3.7	10.2	4.8	9.4	7.8
No. of years in education – household head	5.6	3.7	6.4	3.2	5.7	3.7	4.8	4.5
HH Size (actual – resident)	5.8	4.0	6.0	4.0	5.9	3.8	5.5	4.1
HH Size (actual – non-resident)	0.9	1.7	1.2	2.3	0.9	1.3	0.6	1.4
AEUs: residents	3.9	2.7	4.1	2.6	3.9	2.6	3.8	2.8
AEUs: non-residents	0.7	1.4	0.9	2.1	0.6	0.9	0.5	1.3
AEUs: homestead	4.6	4.1	5.0	4.8	4.6	3.5	4.3	4.1
No. of resident EAAs	2.1	1.3	1.9	0.9	2.2	1.3	2.1	1.6
No. of non-resident EAAs	0.6	1.5	0.9	2.3	0.5	0.8	0.5	1.4
Percent with migrant household members	11.8	23.1	18.6	36.8	8.1	15.8	8.8	14.3
Percent receives remittances	9.9	44.2	10.5	63.2	10.5	31.6	8.8	35.7
Area owned (ha.)	1.6	0.8	1.6	1.2	0.8	0.3	2.2	1.1
Area farmed (ha.)	1.4	0.8	1.6	1.2	0.9	0.2	1.6	1.0
Livestock holding in CEUs[b]	2.2	0.5	1.4	0.7	2.9	0.2	2.4	0.6
Tools[c]	10.8	7.8	15.5	7.1	3.2	0.9	13.6	18.0
Boat assets[d]	15.5	9.7	–	–	15.5	9.7	–	–
Fishing gear assets	14.6	7.8	–	–	14.6	7.8	–	–
Age of household head	40.4	50.1	42.1	55.4	38.3	45.8	41.0	48.6

Source: sample survey conducted in nine villages, January–April 2001.

Notes

a EAA = Economically active adults (individuals aged 15–60 inclusive, except those in education).
b Livestock holding in CEUs (see note to Table 3.5 above).
c Tools is a value based index for ownership of axes, hoes, machetes and sewing machines.
d Boat assets is a value based index for ownership of boats and fishing gears (nets etc.).

worse than either de facto female heads or divorced women in terms of economic welfare, a finding observed in other studies (Dréze and Srinivasan 1997; Appleton 1996). Widows typically expressed higher levels of income vulnerability and impoverishment, suggesting that widow-headed households may be worse off, both among all sample households as well as within the category of FHHs.

Household livelihood activities and incomes

In all three districts, household income is derived from varying combinations of own farm (crop and animal) production, skilled and unskilled employment, and trade and commerce, each of which provides different returns. While female- and male-headed households (as well as the men and women within them) share many of the same economic undertakings, their reliance on particular activities differs (Table 6.3). The following fleshes these strategies out in greater detail, looking at the main income earning strategies of households and how they differ according to headship.

Agriculture: crop-based activities

In Uganda, agrarian-based activities are critical to the livelihood strategies of rural households; 90 per cent of rural women and 53 per cent of rural men are engaged in agricultural production, with women responsible for 80 per cent of food crop and more than half of all cash crop production (Elson and Evers 1997; Kasente *et al.* 2000). In Mbale and Mubende, reliance on agriculture is similarly predominant, with a broad range of food and cash crops grown including bananas (both cooking and eating), maize, beans, sweet potatoes, coffee, cotton, millet and horticulture. Agriculture is particularly significant for FHHs in these districts, who derive 61 per cent and 51 per cent of all household income from farm-based activities in Mbale and Mubende respectively (Table 6.3). In Kamuli, farming activities comprise a much smaller proportion of livelihood activities, with fishing and fishing-related employment the primary source of income. However, across districts, the significance of particular crops to overall household income, varies between female- and male-headed households. For example, 28 per cent of total household income in female-headed households is derived from a single crop – cooking bananas (matooke) – in contrast to 20 per cent of income in male-headed households. Further, cooking bananas alone comprise 73 per cent of all crop income in FHHs, a strong indication of their vulnerability to market or climatic failures.

Agriculture: livestock activities

Livestock rearing plays a relatively small part in the economic portfolio of sample households. Overall, reliance on livestock as an income earning

Table 6.3 Aggregated income portfolios[a] by gender of household head, all cases and by district sample[b]

All cases	*All HHs*		*Mbale*		*Kamuli*		*Mubende*	
	Male n = 263 % of total income	*Female n = 52 % of total income*	*Male n = 86 % of total income*	*Female n = 19 % of total income*	*Male n = 86 % of total income*	*Female n = 19 % of total income*	*Male n = 91 % of total income*	*Female n = 14 % of total income*
Bananas	20.1	28.1	34.4	47.2	0.0	0.0	29.0	34.9
Other food crops	11.7	10.2	9.4	13.4	6.6	2.6	24.4	13.8
Cash crops	0.6	0.1	1.0	0.2	0.0	0.0	1.0	0.1
Livestock	6.0	1.2	4.7	0.2	3.3	1.1	12.6	2.3
Total agriculture	38.5	39.6	49.5	61.0	9.9	3.7	67.1	51.1
Wages	10.8	9.4	14.1	8.7	6.1	11.2	13.0	8.5
Self-employment[c]	26.7	31.1	34.7	13.2	23.3	46.3	18.3	34.1
Fish	22.8	8.2	0.0	0.0	60.1	26.2	0.0	0.0
Transfers	1.2	11.8	1.6	17.1	0.6	12.6	1.7	6.3
Total non-farm	61.5	60.4	50.5	39.0	90.1	96.3	32.9	48.9

Source: sample survey conducted in nine villages, January–April 2001.

Notes

a Income shares for incomes summed across all households in each category.

b n gives the number of observations in each district and gender sub-sample.

c Refers to non-farm private enterprises.

strategy is considerably less among FHHs which only derive one per cent of their total household income from livestock. According to some female heads, this is both a cause and a consequence of capital scarcity with most lacking the resources to purchase large stock. However, ownership of small stock (chickens, goats and pigs) remains important to women in FHHs, whose smaller labour reserves provide fewer alternative options in times of economic shortfall. Several female heads said that livestock was an asset that could be quickly liquidated in the event of market and climatic shocks, or for lumpy expenditures such as medical care, school fees or to pay a dowry. Livestock rearing was also viewed as an investment strategy that allowed them to augment existing income or diversify into something new. As one female head in Mbale described, 'I have more farming activities now because I bought a cow and two goats a couple of years ago. I wanted to invest my money in order to be able to pay my granddaughter's school fees when she starts school. I also wanted to get cow dung to fertilise my bananas, and I milk too.'

Non-farm income activities

While agriculture is an important constituent of household livelihood strategies, over the last decade new avenues for income generation have emerged. Across Uganda there is increasing evidence that households are diversifying in response to poverty push factors, as well as pull factors related to the fast growing economy. In Mbale, Mubende and Kamuli households seldom specialise in one income-earning activity but rather are sustained through a range of income generation and labour allocation strategies, in large part due to declining soil fertility, crop and livestock diseases, increased land fragmentation, and climate change in recent years (Ellis and Bahiigwa 2003). The interlocking nature of these strategies was captured by one female head who said, 'I was only involved in farming until five years ago. I sell my labour now, because at least I can get food to feed the children with. I grow more bananas because even if it is the dry season, we can still get some food from them. I keep chickens too, because they are easy to look after and I can sell some when I don't have any money.' Among FHHs, income from non-farm sources represents 39 per cent, 96 per cent and 49 per cent of total household income in Mbale, Kamuli and Mubende respectively (Table 6.3).[11] The impact of non-farm activities on overall household income level is significant; 64 per cent of FHHs with no access to off-farm income fall into the lowest income tercile in contrast to 26 per cent of MHHs. This corroborates Newman and Canagarajah's study (2000), which showed that the poverty levels of FHHs participating in non-farm activities experienced a steeper decline than those reliant on agriculture alone. Diversification would therefore appear to be strongly linked to economic welfare. However, livelihood diversification strategies are heterogeneous and do not offer similar returns. Whether or not they contribute to poverty reduction (broadly defined) depends upon the nature and type of diversification, an issue to which I now turn.

Self-employment and trade

The majority of sample households are characterised by extensive participation in self-employment and trade-related activities (Table 6.4). Most of these activities exhibit strong gender differentiation, with women (in both male- and female-headed households) predominantly selling cooked or processed food, alcohol (beer and waragi[12]) and charcoal, and men involved in brick making and fish processing. FHHs specifically are highly dependent on self-employment activities, with a greater proportion of their income derived from self-employment activities compared to their male counterparts. In fact, while mean household income is higher among MHHs across the sample as a whole, income derived from businesses is considerably greater among FHHs than MHHs (1,329,807 to 927,246 Ushs or USD 751.30 to 523.87).[11] This difference is most pronounced in Kamuli, where 43 per cent of FHHs in contrast to 13 per cent of MHHs are engaged in self-employment activities, largely due to the dominance of mukene trading among women. For FHHs in Kamuli, who both own less land and have less land under cultivation, income from the mukene trade is extremely important. As one female head said, 'I rely more on trading in dry fish now because I get money for survival and can afford to buy food, paraffin and soap'. For others, trade in mukene provides the capital to invest in other small business activities.

While diversification into self-employment activities is widespread, several factors inhibit it as a path to upward income mobility. First, while there is a positive relationship between diversification and income levels across case study districts, this relationship is less favourable for self-employed FHHs. Roughly one-half of FHHs engaged in self-employment fall into the lowest per capita income tercile. Second, while participation in self-employment enables women (in both MHH and FHH) to balance income earning with domestic responsibilities, trade is also an area in which gender segregation and differential remuneration are apparent. In sample households, women in FHHs tend to be concentrated in low wage activities such as selling cooked food, alcohol, juice and handicrafts on the local market. In Mubende, for example, women trade in parchment beans at the farm gate (due to a lack of capital to engage in coffee processing) while men sell processed coffee at market centres. Further, women tend to participate in businesses that have few entry barriers and low start-up costs, with the income derived from these activities markedly less than the income generated through men's trading activities. And, as was shown above, FHHs have less access to, or potential to acquire the financial capital to embark on more remunerative trading activities. Third, it is important to distinguish between diversification activities that are adopted to reduce risk and avert crises from those that facilitate accumulation (Reardon 1997). For most FHHs, particularly those in Mbale and Mubende, participation in self-employment reflects the paucity of alternative options. As one female head claimed, '[Non-farm activities] are the only sources of livelihood where I get money to feed my family, buy clothes and

Table 6.4 Per cent of households with non-farm income by gender of household head, by district (%)

	All		*Mbale*		*Kamuli*		*Mubende*	
	Male $n = 263$	*Female* $n = 52$	*Male* $n = 86$	*Female* $n = 19$	*Male* $n = 86$	*Female* $n = 19$	*Male* $n = 91$	*Female* $n = 14$
None	16.0	26.9	23.3	47.4	1.2	5.3	23.1	28.6
Wages	24.7	15.4	29.1	21.1	12.8	15.7	31.9	7.1
Salary	1.9		3.5				2.2	
Self-employment	30.0	32.7	32.6	26.3	24.4	31.6	33.0	42.9
Fishing	7.2	1.9			22.1	5.3		
Multiple	0.4				1.2			
Wages and self-employment	8.0	15.4	10.5	5.3	3.5	21.1	9.9	21.4
Salary and self-employment	0.4	1.9	1.2			5.3		
Fishing and wages	0.8				2.3			
Fishing and self-employment	10.6	5.8			32.6	15.8		
Total	100.0	100.0	100.0	100.0	100.0	100.0	100.0	100.0

Source: sample survey conducted in nine villages, January–April 2001.

pay school fees'. Another said, 'I would prefer to plant more maize and beans but I don't have enough money to hire cows to plough the land. I need to sell local brew, which gets enough income to supplement what I get from farming.' This suggests that households may be compelled to diversify, choosing self-employment in the face of deteriorating economic options.

Wage employment

A second avenue for livelihood diversification is wage employment. While both men and women are engaged in seasonal employment on nearby farms, more men are engaged in regular wage employment than women (14 per cent of all men in contrast to 3 per cent of all women). This partly explains the choice of households to place men rather than women on the labour market, since they not only have greater mobility but also tend to have more options and earning power when they do migrate.

While wage employment constitutes a lower proportion of household income in FHHs (7 per cent in contrast to 11 per cent), there is some intra-district variation. Wage employment figures less in the income portfolios of FHHs in Mbale (2 per cent), where crop-based activities are prominent, and more strongly in Kamuli (7 per cent), where agricultural activities have become less viable. Again, this suggests that women do not participate in wage employment, either because they prefer to stay on farm or engage in trade or because they are constrained by a lack of skills or cultural norms that limit their mobility.

But there is the broader question of whether diversification into wage employment ultimately contributes to the enhanced economic welfare and well-being of households. This depends on a number of factors, including the composition of the household and the nature of headship. For example, in situations where male household members migrate for employment, female heads typically assume full responsibility for reproductive activities, which can lead to greater time poverty (lower consumption of leisure time), and reduce options for participating in other income generating activities. On the other hand, these adverse consequences may be offset by remittances, enabling FHHs to hire labour, a situation documented for some FHHs.

When employment is undertaken by female heads themselves, it raises a different set of issues. Chant's (1997) research on FHHs in Mexico suggests a positive correlation between female labour force participation and the welfare of FHHs, which was somewhat supported by this Uganda data. In contrast to self-employment, the majority of FHHs that participate in wage employment fall within the middle income tercile, suggesting a positive correlation between employment and household income, and enhanced options for diversification and investment. This was echoed by a female head from Mbale: 'I earn at least 1,000 shillings per day by selling my labour and I have bought a cow. I am even able to look after my children better than when I was with my husband, who was a dictator in the house.' However, as noted above, it is more often men within FHHs that obtain wage employment that is regular and/or salaried, whereas women are more typically in seasonal employment.

There is, however, a need to exercise caution in viewing employment that is casual or seasonal in nature as a positive diversification strategy. First, as Evans' (1992) work in Uganda illustrates, women often seek employment in response to crises or 'distress' conditions. In this study, such 'distress sales' were recorded among several sample FHHs whereby the same circumstances that led to female headship (separation, divorce and widowhood) also precipitated their entry into wage employment. However, in such cases women often sell their labour well below the market rate (Whitehead 2001: 38). Second, wage inequalities stemming from gender-based discrimination in labour markets can mean that women are locked into low productivity occupations. In Uganda, specifically, women's wages average 40 per cent below men's with half of that difference attributable to discrimination (Appleton 1995). As other studies in Africa have demonstrated, the returns to education and scarce skills are typically much higher than are returns to unskilled labour (Barrett *et al.* 2001c), and casual and seasonal labour are characterised by low and irregular wages, insecurity and often poor employment conditions (Dolan 2004). Hence, although FHHs are diversifying, for women within them, a lack of assets (especially skills) may confine them to poor quality employment with low returns.

Remittances

As Table 6.3 indicated, FHHs have less diversified income sources than MHHs, reflecting lower endowment stocks as well as greater opportunities for mobility among men. The constraint on female mobility is also suggested by the differential reliance that male- and female-headed households have on remittances. While remittances and other transfers scarcely register in the livelihood portfolios of MHHs, they are a critical source of income for FHHs. As Table 6.2 indicates, 44 per cent of FHHs (in contrast to 10 per cent of MHHs) receive remittances. FHHs also draw a greater share of household income from remittances (12 per cent) than do MHHs (1 per cent). This is particularly marked in Mbale where transfers and remittances comprise 17 per cent of income in FHHs in contrast to 2 per cent in MHHs, and where the remittance income of FHHs is double that of MHHs. While this study did not collect information on how remittances might affect the expenditures of households, several FHHs mentioned that remittances ensured subsistence and enabled them to educate and feed their children. According to one female head, 'My husband earns a monthly payment now and sends me money three times a year, which I use to buy seedlings like millet and maize, and to look after the household. When the children are sick he sends me more remittances.' However, whether remittances contribute to broader investment in either agriculture and/or trade, as concluded in Appelton's (1996) study, is unclear.

Gender-based constraints to livelihood diversification

Understanding why households diversify (whether to mitigate risk, seize income earning opportunities, or accumulate capital for investment), and why they might choose less desirable livelihood strategies is crucial to successful policy intervention. Among the sampled FHHs the most probable explanation for FHHs participation in less favourable livelihood activities is the constraints that they face in terms of asset endowments – particularly land, labour and capital. The remainder of the chapter focuses on these constraints, and some of their impacts on FHHs in Mubende, Mbale and Kamuli.

Labour

In sub-Saharan Africa, women's access to labour or to the capital to mobilise labour are often considered more central to well being than having access to land (Whitehead 2001). Because of this, understanding the livelihood strategies of households requires considering the inter-relationship of 'market' and 'non-market' spheres that underpins women's potential to engage in or diversify their productive activities. It has been argued that women's double day (combined productive and reproductive work) is particularly adverse for FHHs, who face greater time poverty due to their sole responsibility for income generation and reproductive work. Among sample FHHs, the 'time poverty' associated with the inelasticity of female labour obligations was exacerbated by the small pool of resident EAAs, placing pressure on women's food cultivation and preventing them from re-allocating their labour time to crops that might be more commercially lucrative, or to labour market opportunities more generally. As one female head in Mubende said, '[There is] no flexibility [in labour]. If the wife is sick the children cook and someone is hired to dig. [Men do] not do any home chores.'

A second labour-related constraint registered among sample households was old age and illness, which were identified as major factors leading to a decline in livelihood choices in all three districts. This was particularly notable in Mubende, where AIDS has led to the impoverishment of several households. Among widow-headed households, specifically, the debilitation of old age exacerbated the gender disadvantages faced by labour, land and other resource-based constraints, leading to circumstances of severe vulnerability.

Land

Despite the importance of labour in all three districts, the paucity and fragility of women's land rights were considered the main source of women's vulnerability, and a significant constraint on household livelihood options. Access to, and control over, land has direct implications for the productivity of women's labour, their willingness to invest in land, their capacity to influence land use priorities, as well as for the nature of livelihood activities they are likely to undertake. Access to land thus has a strong knock-on effect with empirical analyses from Uganda observing that untitled land holders have poorer access to chemical inputs, improved seeds and other productive assets (Bruce and Migot-Adholla 1994).

While women in both male- and female-headed households consider themselves land-poor, the total amount of land owned by FHHs was less than that of MHHs in all three sample districts. Sixty-two per cent of female-headed households had land holdings of under 0.5 hectares in contrast to 37 per cent of MHHs, with FHHs owning an average of 0.8 hectares in comparison to 1.6 hectares among MHHs. These figures echo Appleton's (1996) study of FHHs in Uganda, which indicated that FHHs were less likely to claim cultivable land among their assets than male-headed households. Customary inheritance practices that compel a man to divide land among his sons are particularly inimical for female heads who lose access to the land they have been granted to farm as wives upon divorce or separation or widowhood. For example, in Kamuli 40 per cent of sample FHHs were widows, and half of them had lost access to their husband's land upon his death. Either their father-in-law had expropriated the land, or it had been passed down to their sons. Similar occurrences were recorded in Mbale, where one interviewee said, 'My land was taken away by my sons when my husband died and now I have to sell my labour to get money for survival'. In another case, a woman's husband had sold off their land before his death in order to pay for medical costs.

However, even where FHHs may own land, this may not confer ownership or access rights to individual women within those households. While women are legally entitled to own land, in practice their access to land remains contingent on social relations, with kinship and conjugal norms generally taking precedence over statutory rights.[13] As a result, in the bulk of cases, women's rights hinge on the benevolence of their male kin, placing them in a position of ongoing dependency.

For those women who lack ownership and/or access rights to land, renting in land is common. This is particularly significant in Kamuli, where renting land from inshore villages is widespread. However, for some households the cost of renting land is prohibitive. As one female head said, 'There is no land to cultivate crops. In the past we used to cultivate freely, but now you have to hire land which is impossible for us . . . I don't have a husband to hire for me land for agriculture.' In fact, the cost of renting land was a key factor underlying the shift toward non-farm activities.[14]

Financial capital

The third type of endowment constraint confronted by sample FHHs is 'investment poverty' – a paucity of resources to direct toward income generation or production activities (Reardon 1997). Several FHHs claimed that they would prefer to specialise in agriculture but lacked the money to purchase land, inputs (seeds, fertilisers, pesticides), or to hire the labour to assist them. As one female head claimed, 'I would like to plant more bananas but I'm prevented from doing it by a lack of money to hire labour'. Capital constraints also contributed to gender differences in the capacity of male- and female-headed households to participate in non farm activities. For example, most FHHs claimed that their inability to finance initial start-up costs prevented them from investing in more lucrative businesses and trade activities. This leaves FHHs confined to trading activities characterised by low returns, limiting their prospects of generating a surplus for reinvestment in agriculture or other off-farm endeavours.

One way that capital constraints can be alleviated is through the provision of credit, which is often considered a promising route out of poverty for the rural poor. Most sample FHHs identified credit as the main resource that would enable them to broaden their livelihood options, whether it be agriculture, trade or other non-farm entrepreneurial activities. However gender-based institutional barriers that exclude women from formal credit have been widely documented in Uganda (Goetz 1995), and were evident in sample districts. As a result, most women resort to informal credit systems such as the female-dominated rotating savings and credit associations (*kamatuli*) found in both Mbale and Mubende.

In both male- and female-headed households, *kamatuli* were seen as a valuable source of savings and economic betterment, providing women with the ability to hire land and labour, and pay for medical costs and school fees. However, the associations generally represent a narrow segment of women in the middle income tercile, and tend to marginalise poorer women who are unable to mobilise the funds required to meet the regular repayments. Similarly, the loans provided by the well-known financial institution, Foundation for Credit and Community Assistance (FOCCAS), were best placed to assist better-off women, particularly those who had businesses or stable trading activities, and could meet the weekly repayment schedule. This effectively excluded many FHHs, who have less liquidity. For example, one female head from Mbale said, 'I no longer dig as I used to, because I don't have enough money to employ labour. Even the cassava and soya beans I used to grow have declined due to disease, and I sold my cow in order to pay back the loan I got from FOCASS.'

Conclusion

The general picture emerging from the above review is that the livelihood portfolios in Mbale, Kamuli and Mubende districts vary substantially between male- and female-headed households. In all three districts, household assets and endowments, which are important determinants of income and welfare, are differentiated between male- and female-headed households, with the latter disadvantaged relative to their male counterparts.

Similarly, the potential for diversification is differentially experienced by male- and female-headed households. While the importance of livelihood diversification for poverty reduction has been well-documented, this analysis suggests that the benefits of diversification are often contingent upon the kinds of off-farm activities in which households are likely to engage. Because the number and type of off-farm opportunities available to FHHs are more circumscribed than they are for MHHs, the former are more likely to participate in self-employment activities that have low barriers to entry and generate lower returns. Overall, diversification into self-employment has not provided a route out of poverty, and the majority of FHHs participating in self-employment remain in the lowest income tercile. Hence, self-employment and trade are more strongly correlated with sustaining or augmenting existing livelihood activities rather than diversifying out of them entirely. In contrast, wage employment is more positively associated with higher income levels among FHHs. However, the nature of that employment and its implications for gender equity are less clear. First, a large part of employment in FHHs is comprised of men who have out-migrated, leaving the burden of reproductive responsibilities to women. Second, in cases where female heads themselves are employed, the outcome depends on the quality and security of the employment, and the extent to which employment encroaches on the time available for other productive and reproductive responsibilities. Finally, this chapter has pointed to differences in the nature of constraints that female- and male-headed households face, which tend to circumscribe their capacity to stabilise and/or broaden their livelihood portfolios. Although livelihood activities vary between the three districts, common to each location is that FHHs experience limited endowment stocks, particularly land, labour and capital. This not only acts as a constraint for women facing economic difficulties, but highlights the gendered nature of livelihood opportunities themselves and how gender continues to shape poverty and well-being in Uganda.

Notes

* This chapter is a shortened version of LADDER Working Paper No. 10 (Dolan 2002). The author is indebted to the LADDER Team and to John Mims for assistance with data analysis. All errors remain the author's responsibility.

1 See Carney (1998), Chambers (1989), Chambers and Conway (1992), Ellis (1998, 2000), Gonzalez de la Rocha (2000), Hussein and Nelson (1998), Ranis and Stewart (1993), Reardon (1997), Scoones (1998), Singh and Gilman (1999) and Yunez-Naude and Taylor (2001).

2 See Appleton (1996), Bruce and Lloyd (1997), Fuwa (2000) and Handa (1994).

3 See Buvinic and Gupta (1997) and Chant (1997).

4 The research did not attempt to reproduce the national representativeness of the large-scale household surveys that form the basis of poverty comparisons in Uganda nor was the research designed to make inferences about the larger populations from which the samples were drawn (Ellis and Bahigwa 2003).

5 The average population density is 284 persons per sq km (James *et al.* 2001).

6 *Mukene* refer to a shoaling fish found in freshwater lakes in the region.

7 Numerous studies have demonstrated that the concept of headship applied in the research process influences the type of policy inferences or empirical conclusions drawn. In this study FHHs included:

a *de jure* FHHs where a woman was declared a household head with no legal male partner (e.g. widows, unmarried or divorced women). There were sixteen, ten and fourteen FHHs in the sample of Kamuli, Mubende and Mbale respectively;
b de facto FHHs where a woman was entered as 'wife' but there was either no resident husband or the husband or male household head was listed as permanently or mostly away. There were three, four and five de facto FHHs in the sample of Kamuli, Mubende and Mbale respectively.

8 In Mbale and Mubende, the proportion of FHHs in the lowest income quartile is 37 per cent and 36 per cent in contrast to 22 per cent and 23 per cent for MHHs.
9 Per capita income was Ush 562,315 (USD 320) among MHHs in contrast to Ush 388,306 (USD 221) among FHHs.
10 However, the effect of the smaller household size is two-way. One the one hand, it limits diversification, however, on the other hand, it lowers the dependency burden.
11 These figures are consistent with Reardon's (1997) review of twenty-three studies in SSA, which calculated over 45 per cent of rural household income based on non-farm activities.
12 An alcohol distilled from cassava.
13 All three districts in this study are characterised by patrilineal kinship systems, where land is inherited agnatically from father to son.
14 In Bukhasusa, Mbale, renting land for cultivation averages approximately sh.50,000/- per acre for one production season.

7 Chronic poverty in rural Uganda

Harsh realities and constrained choices*

Kate Bird and Isaac Shinyekwa

Introduction

This chapter presents findings from research on chronic poverty in rural Uganda. The analysis builds on the qualitative and quantitative livelihoods research undertaken in three districts in Uganda by the LADDER project (see Chapter 1). We explore multi-dimensional chronic poverty through focus group discussions and in-depth life history interviews with the heads of twenty-eight households in three of the LADDER villages: Buwapuwa in Mbale district; Kiribairya in Kamuli district; and Kalangaalo in Mubende district.

Our findings provide a starting point for understanding the trajectories into and out of poverty that individuals and households follow, and identify some possible entry points for constructive policy change.

Chronic poverty

The distinguishing feature of chronic poverty is its extended duration. The chronically poor are poor for much of their life, and may 'pass on' their poverty to subsequent generations (Hulme and Shepherd 2003). How long someone has to remain poor before they are considered to be chronically poor is open to debate, but Hulme and Shepherd (2003: 405) argue for a five-year threshold. This is because five years is perceived to be a significant period of time, in terms of an individual's lifecourse, in most cultures. In addition, people who stay poor for five years or more are highly likely to remain poor for the rest of their lives.

Chronic poverty may be hard to spot. Poverty data is rarely disaggregated by severity, let alone by duration. The chronically poor tend to be amongst the most marginalised in any society. Because chronic poverty can be ascribed (e.g. you are poor because of who you are – older, mentally or physically impaired, living with AIDS, from an ethnic minority, etc.) it may be intensified by socially constructed norms and intrahousehold differentiation. Chronically poor people can be found within non-poor households. So, 'while all members of a household may experience poverty in similar ways over similar periods of time, this should never be assumed' (Hulme and Shepherd 2003: 405). Later in this chapter we show that events within households can have a significant, differential and long-term impact on individual household members.

Poverty and chronic poverty in Uganda

Table 7.1 summarises trends in poverty data by region arising from a series of household income and expenditure surveys. Uganda has experienced sustained economic growth over the last decade and has outperformed many other countries in sub-Saharan Africa in terms of poverty reduction. There is widespread confirmation that poverty was reduced by a third or more during the 1990s (Appleton 1998, 2001a, 2001b; Okidi and Mugambe 2002), reaching 35 per cent by 2000 (Appleton 2001a). However, experience has been uneven, with some parts of the country lagging behind others. This is particularly true of the Northern Region, which continues to be conflict affected (Table 7.1). The poor are disproportionately rural (39 per cent in aggregate), and improvements have been slower for non-coffee growing households and amongst the unemployed (Appleton 2001a), with government employees, traders and cash crop farmers those most likely to have gained.

The analysis of poverty data from 1992 and 1996 undertaken by Okidi and Mugambe (2002) shows a varied picture. Some households moved out of poverty, others became poor and a third group were poor during both periods (54 per cent of the poor for the country as a whole; 61 per cent in

Table 7.1 Poverty in Uganda between 1992 and 2000, by region

	1992/ 1993	*1993/ 1994*	*1994/ 1995*	*1995/ 1996*	*1997/ 1998*	*1999/ 2000*
National	55.5	52.2	50.1	48.5	44.0	35.1
Rural	59.4	56.7	54.0	53.0	48.2	39.0
Urban	28.2	20.6	22.3	19.5	16.3	10.1
Central	45.5	35.6	30.5	30.1	27.7	20.1
Eastern	59.2	58.0	64.9	57.5	54.3	37.3
Western	52.8	56.0	50.4	46.7	42.0	28.0
Northern	71.3	69.2	63.5	68.0	58.8	64.8
Central rural	52.8	43.4	35.9	37.1	34.3	25.6
Central urban	21.5	14.2	14.6	14.5	11.5	7.0
Eastern rural	61.1	60.2	66.8	59.4	56.8	39.2
Eastern urban	40.6	30.5	41.5	31.8	24.8	17.4
Western rural	53.8	57.4	51.6	48.3	43.2	29.4
Western urban	29.7	24.9	25.4	16.2	19.9	5.6
Northern rural	72.2	70.9	65.1	70.3	60.7	66.7
Northern urban	52.6	46.2	39.8	39.6	32.6	30.6

Source: Okidi and Mugambe (2002); based on Appleton (1999); Appleton (2001a).

rural areas), indicating that they were probably chronically poor. Unsurprisingly, the severely poor (those in the lowest income quintile) were found to be more than twice as likely to be trapped in poverty than those just below the poverty line. The majority of the chronically poor[1] (79 per cent) work in the agricultural sector. Nearly two-thirds of them are children, over half of them live in large households with between six and nine people, and elderly women are disproportionately represented (Okidi and Mugambe 2002: 14).

Nearly two-thirds (63 per cent) of the total expenditure of the chronically poor is on food. Although nearly all (95 per cent) owned the house they lived in, it was of poor quality with 46 per cent living in huts. Human capital is low, with over half (51 per cent) of the rural chronically poor illiterate (Okidi and Mugambe 2002: 14). Deininger and Okidi (2002) found that while good access to public and merit goods (e.g. health care and both road and power infrastructure) are strongly associated with poverty reduction, outcomes are affected by households' initial health status and asset endowments. Poor households possessing sufficient human and physical capital assets were able to move out of poverty between 1992 and 1996, but households with health problems and large families[2] in 1992 were found to have fallen into deeper poverty by 2000.

Methodology

The overall methodology of the LADDER studies is described briefly in Chapter 3 of this volume, and in several published sources (e.g. Ellis and Bahiigwa 2003; Ellis and Mdoe 2003). For the three villages in which additional field work was conducted, key informant interviews and focus group discussions were used to supplement an average of nine in-depth life histories (oral testimonies) in each village. Life history interviewees were selected randomly from the sampling frame represented by the LADDER wealth ranking exercises. We interviewed predominantly from poorest groups with some interviewees from the less poor groups to cross-check that the experiences associated with the severely poor were unique, or at least more common, within that wealth strata. We hypothesised that the majority of the chronically poor would be found amongst the most severely poor, but wanted to test this hypothesis as well as identifying the key drivers, maintainers and interrupters of chronic poverty (Hulme and Shepherd 2003).

Life histories were collected during semi-structured interviews which traced an individual's life from their earliest childhood to the present day, including key life-changing events. By talking also to the non-poor we hoped to identify some of the advantages which protected them from falling into poverty, and to show in what way the experiences of the severely and persistently poor differed from those of the transitory poor. By talking to a person about their life, rather than taking a thematic approach, we hoped to identify path-determination in individuals' lives and to pinpoint key moments of choice, or the absence of choice.

Information gathered through the life history interviews allowed us to plot the trajectories followed by the individual and their household as they declined into poverty or moved out of poverty. It also enabled us to identify the most common covariant and idiosyncratic shocks which triggered a decline into poverty (drivers) and the constraints which prevented accumulation, investment and movement out of poverty (maintainers).[3]

The interlocking problems of the chronically poor

Downwards trajectories

The field work revealed the predominance of downward movement. Talking to older people illustrated how much more prosperous they had been, in general, during their early lives than they were now. This could be seen as simply reflecting the positive gloss that many of us like to put on the past, however, the examples that individuals gave to support their stories made it clear that there was more to it than this. A number of older people, both men and women, recounted childhoods in compounds where there was a plentiful food supply and where land and livestock was abundant. The often sharp declines in their fortunes since the 1930s–1950s illustrated the devastating impact of conflicts which followed the mismanagement and repression of the Obote I and II and Amin regimes. Despite the sustained economic growth of the last decade, this growth has occurred from a very low base and is yet to bring households and individuals back to the levels of basic food security and well-being that were enjoyed in the first half of the twentieth century.

If this is the context within which these life stories were told, then the individual life histories presented below thematically illustrate the way in which covariant shocks combine with the idiosyncratic to drive people into both severe and chronic poverty.

Differential well-being in the study sites

Data from the LADDER household survey shows per capita incomes to be low in all three study villages, particularly in Kiribairya, which has the lowest per capita income and smallest standard deviation, indicating widespread poverty and low differentiation within the community (Table 7.2).

Household wealth ranks were correlated with a number of variables (education of household head, household education, land ownership, livestock ownership [in CEUs[4]], household assets, ownership of tools, migration, the household's dependency ratio, receipt of transfers and the livelihood diversity index). The strength of correlation varied amongst the villages and the only variables important in all of the three villages were land ownership and household assets. Education and the ownership of livestock and tools were important in some but not all of the villages. Looking at the dataset for all

Table 7.2 Average annual per capita income, by village (Ugandan Shillings)

	N	*Mean*	*s.d.*	*Median*
Bukhasusa	35	329,867	333,559	271,130
Buwopuwa	35	310,300	325,654	220,839
Bunabuso	35	1,007,127	1,114,872	640,469
Iyingo	35	885,526	1,545,029	501,999
Kinamwanga	35	425,122	1,216,684	189,801
Kiribairya	35	192,194	159,098	150,963
Kabbo	35	395,763	283,444	330,237
Kansambya	35	268,493	215,489	205,408
Kalangaalo	35	439,910	325,195	383,730

Source: sample survey conducted in nine villages, January–April 2001.

nine LADDER villages we found a significant difference (at the 0.01 level) between rich and poor households in terms of the ownership of land, livestock, tools and household assets. There was a significant difference also (at the 0.05 level) in terms of the education level of the household head and reliance on own production for subsistence.[5] Which way causality runs for each of these variables is difficult to determine.

Membership of a non-poor family provides an individual with a number of positive and mutually reinforcing advantages: good diet; access to education; access to health care; higher status; a network of friends and patrons in and outside the village; access to travel outside the village, and therefore exposure to ideas; more land or livestock to inherit and more likelihood of marrying well.

Perceptions of the causes of poverty

The emphasis given by elite women and men to the causes of poverty differed. Focus group discussions with non-poor women and men in Buwapuwa, Mbale generated some interesting observations (Boxes 7.1 and 7.2). We see from the summaries below that men emphasised meso-level problems, external to the household, while women emphasised those within the household. By combining these different perspectives we probably get nearer to the full picture. Women highlight alcohol as a direct cause of poverty and a contributory factor to many others. (see p. 110)

Land ownership

Land ownership in the study villages is closely related to wealth grouping. The poor have marginal holdings, and in Kiribairya only the rich own any land at all. Local inheritance practice (whereby all sons receive a portion of their father's land on marriage, rather than primogeniture where only the oldest son inherits) results in land fragmentation. Many holdings are marginal,

Box 7.1 Male perceptions of the causes of poverty: Buwapuwa

Men discussed mostly meso-level causes of poverty. The market was seen as being a source of problems. Richer farmers can no longer afford to employ casual labourers due to the monetisation of labour. So, less land is cultivated. 'In the past you could cultivate a lot of land by using community labour. People would come and dig and you just fed them. Now its cash.' This problem has been compounded by devastating livestock diseases which have reduced cattle stocks and animal traction. Poor access to markets limits livelihood opportunities and makes life hard. 'The absence of an adequate feeder road network in the sub-county limits connectivity and forces people to either take long detours or to cut across the bush with head loads or on a bicycle.'

Local markets do no function well enough for farm-households to benefit from liberalisation.

Inadequate service delivery also has a negative impact. Poor local education standards prevent local children's access to good secondary schools. The cost of medical treatment is something that can push people into poverty, as is the loss of labour associated with long-term illness.

Theft was cited as a serious problem, not just as an irritant but actually limiting investment and accumulation. In Buwapuwa there is petty theft of crops, but also armed robberies by thieves from outside the community who club together with villagers with inside knowledge. They pinpoint individuals with household assets or money from a recent sale of livestock or grain. As a result young people with some money would rather invest it in towns which are more secure. The community has no faith in the police, who are seen as utterly corrupt. This has led to the community taking the law into their own hands and lynching nine robbers in the last five years.

Problems at the household level included land fragmentation due to population pressure. This has affected some families where 'the land is divided first amongst four sons, then ten grandsons'. This is particularly a problem in polygamous households, and polygamy was identified as a cause of poverty.

Source: Focus group discussion with three older elite men in Buwapuwa, Mbale, October 2002.

leading to un- and underemployment, particularly amongst the youth, reduced levels of aggregate and individual well-being and increased differentiation. Differentiation is driven by the distress sale of land by households attempting to meet contingencies or clear debts, and is leading to the proletarianisation of some peasant households and the accumulation of capital by others.

Vulnerable groups

Despite flaws in the use of the term 'vulnerable groups' as an identifier, principally to do with spatial and temporal variations in vulnerability, the term is used here to describe certain categories of the chronically poor that

Box 7.2 Female perceptions of the causes of poverty: Buwapuwa

'Poor people have no land, no money. All they can do is casual work.' The women listed the key causes of poverty. These were:

- Ignorance: defined as a lack of knowledge; doing things which are not helpful, and an inability to communicate the necessary information (e.g. to husband or to wife). As a result do not use their assets well (e.g. their land).
- Laziness: defined as people who do not want to work. They are able, they have the knowledge, they aren't stupid, but they don't want to work (e.g. someone who has land, but instead of cultivating it, rents it to obtain money for alcohol or despite having their own land they do casual work to get quick money for alcohol).
- Drinking: 'some people just get up to drink'.
- Poor soil fertility: leading to low yields. Farm fragmentation/small holdings mean that people cannot fallow their land, but cultivate it continuously with food crops, leading to reduced matooke*, potato and cassava yields.
- Theft: of animals was blamed on 'people who drink at any time of day'; of crops occurs when people steal bunches of matooke from the trees; armed theft from shops – outsiders bring guns and work with locals who identify premises. Villagers cannot afford to 'raise security' themselves to defend their property and the police are ineffective.
- Animal diseases: these have impoverished people, in particular those affecting cattle and pigs.
- Decline in farm-gate prices.
- Lack of cooperation within families. The problem is mainly men 'stealing' stored household maize to sell, although sometimes women do this too. Men use the money to go and drink whereas women buy soap, salt and other necessities for the family. An example of how little men contributed to their families was given by a former nurse's aid who said that only one man in fifty will pay for their children's medical treatment – this is left to women. Fathers pay school fees, but mothers must find money for everything else – soap, salt etc. When asked what the scale of the problem was, the women estimated that two-thirds of households in the village suffered from a lack of internal cooperation.
- Men curtail their wives' movements. When women start a self-help group their husbands stop them going to meetings and make them withdraw their savings. This was explained as men fearing women using meetings as an excuse for other activities. One of the interviewees tried to start a self-help group to help women save to buy livestock, but the members' husbands put a stop to it.
- Polygamy is seen as a problem. Women are tricked into becoming second or third wives. The husband may have had a disagreement with his first wife and sends her away, then finds another wife, by the time his first wife has returned the new wife may be pregnant, or is trapped in the situation. Some in monogamous marriages might be poor because they don't have enough land or money to hire labour/oxen, but some men in polygamous marriages do not

care for their wives and will not allocate enough land. The husbands won't hire oxen to plough the land. One respondent is a first wife. She has three children. Her husband has a second wife with four children, a third wife with seven children, and a fourth wife with six children. The last two wives are still producing children. She says that all his resources are concentrated on the younger two wives and their children.

- Education. 'Most of the youth do not have skills so they spend their day drinking and then gang up to break into homes.' The women link the lack of education to polygamy as the husbands concentrate on one wife and her children and the others are neglected and not educated. The girls are 'sentenced to marriage'. 'No more school fees for you. Go and get married!'
- Variable climate: Drought causes problems as does too much rain – unseasonal or too heavy – which can cause seeds to rote in the soil rather than germinate.
- Sale of household assets by husbands. Husbands (including those in polygamous marriages) will sell his wife's goats to spend the money on a mistress or prostitute. The husbands feel that they can do anything they like. 'If a wife complains she is told to go back to her parent's house. I am too old to want to do this, so I keep quiet to maintain the status quo.'
- Sickness: (HIV) 'During the first phase of the illness, people think that they have been bewitched and sell a lot of goats and chickens to consult traditional healers. During the second phase they discover that they are sick with HIV. They become weak and cannot work hard. They have lower income and spend a lot of money on treatment. The problem of HIV is just in its beginning phase here in Buwapuwa. Most who suffer from AIDS have been migrant workers (e.g. in Kenya), and come home when they are already sick. Sometimes they 'have relations' with people in the village. When it becomes known that they have AIDS the people that they have had sex with will keep it a secret – so HIV is spread through the community.' The respondents are scared that HIV is going to take its toll in the village. 'Sexual morals in the village are very poor. In Uganda it is taboo to have sex with a cousin, and yet this taboo is ignored. Also if a prostitute comes to the village all the men who drink in the village centre will rush to sleep with her. Men don't use condoms. They can be bought in the trading centre, but a tiny minority bother. They might use them if they were free.' (Malaria and diarrhoea) can be very costly – especially if children become sick. Some people have to have blood transfusions because they are anaemic – this is very expensive also.

Source: Focus group discussion with three elite women in Buwapuwa, Mbale, October 2002.

Note
*Matooke is the savoury green banana grown in the central belt of Uganda as the staple food crop, where it is strongly preferred over maize.

are regularly identified as vulnerable in poverty discourse in Uganda. Vulnerable groups are commonly identified as including children (particularly orphans), the sick, people with physical and mental impairments, widows and widowers, the elderly and the landless (Babirye 1999; Mijumbi and Okidi 2001). While findings on some vulnerable groups in Uganda are contradictory a strong picture emerges that very high proportions of children

(Uganda 2000b) and disabled people fall within the vulnerable category (Mijumbi and Okidi 2001).

The chronic poverty research conducted in three villages identified widows (Box 7.3), orphans, children of second, third or unfavoured wives (Box 7.4), older people, HIV/AIDS affected households and the long-term ill and physically impaired, as belonging to definable vulnerable groups. The character of the vulnerability experienced by these groups becomes clearer when we come to consider the drivers and maintainers of chronic poverty in the next section.

Box 7.3 Displaced, widowed and vulnerable

Grace was widowed shortly after she and her husband escaped brutal inter-tribal violence which took place in Uganda in the mid to late 1980s. They escaped from Teso across Lake Kyoga to Kamuli District with a little money, but lost almost all their accumulated assets. With the sound of bullets coming closer they had to make stark choices between saving a cooking pot or a child.

Once in Kamuli District, her husband spent the little money they had to buy some land, but soon after he was murdered by the land's original owners. She was driven away, and settled in Kiribairya, an internally displaced people's camp on the shore of Lake Kyoga. She has now been there for over 10 years, but twice a refugee, Grace has been able to re-accumulate very little. She lives in a simple one-roomed thatch hut, which is her only asset. She owns no land and 'even the hoes I had have been stolen'.

Grace has limited support from others. Although she had thirteen children, only five lived beyond early childhood. Of the surviving children, the youngest daughter died some time ago of AIDS leaving three children. Two of these children died and Grace is now bringing up the third, a girl. She feels that she has no-one else to go to for help in the village, as there are no clan leaders or members of her tribe in the camp, and although her three surviving daughters and her son are all in the camp they rarely give her any food or other support. When she is ill it is difficult for her to go to the clinic, as 'you have to go with your brother', meaning that you have to take a bribe for the doctor. She does not have anyone who will give her the money. Nevertheless she is not entirely without a support network. A young man lent her a small patch of land during the last agricultural season, on which her children helped her cultivate sweet potatoes. An old man built her a granary next to her house, where she planned to store the potatoes. Unfortunately pests destroyed the crop, leaving her no better off than before. She does not expect to be offered land again 'you are given only once, and if you are unfortunate, that is it'.

Source: Life history interview conducted by Kate Bird and Isaac Shinyekwa in Kiribairya, Kamuli District, 2002.

Box 7.4 The long-term impact of marital conflict

Laurant is 22. The story of his life illustrates the potentially long-term impact of conflict within the household. His father is an alcoholic and regularly beats his mother. Laurant has tried to intervene, but feels unable to protect his mother, Agatha, from his father's drunken rages. Their poor relationship affected him as a child, and has strongly influenced the way his life has turned out, influencing his diet as a child, his access to education, the amount of land he now has to farm and his choice of wife.

Laurant's father is relatively wealthy by village standards. He had five acres of land, a range of productive and household assets[a] and a better quality house than many, with internal walls separating the living space into separate rooms. The household had two granaries, and they used to have a number of cattle and goats. He was respected in the community and was the elected village head[b] until 18 months ago. Nevertheless Laurant is poor.

Laurant's father had two wives. His mother, Agatha, was the first wife, but it was the second wife who was favoured. When Laurant was a child, his father gave his stepmother meat to cook for herself and her children, but only vegetables to his mother. When Laurant was only a few months old his father lost his Kampala-based job in a hotel. He chased Agatha away and sold off household assets in an attempt to maintain consumption levels for his second wife. Agatha left her children behind[c], but Laurant's 'stepmother' refused to feed them. His father claimed that Laurant was illegitimate and singled him out for harsh treatment. When Agatha found out what was happening, she collected her children and took them to live with her at their grandfather's house. But she had difficulty supporting them as a single mother, resulting in the children being shuttled between their father's and their grandfather's house. She kept Laurant with her, to protect him and eventually, when Laurant was two years old, decided to go back to her husband. This seemed to be the only way to ensure that everyone had enough to eat. She and her husband had several more children, but by the time he was six the marriage had broken down again. She left, but returned *again* when he was fourteen to ensure that her sons were given some of their father's land when they got married.

Laurant knew that with his family's history of problems it would be difficult to find a woman prepared to marry him, but two years ago he was introduced to a secondary school drop-out who was eight weeks pregnant. He is delighted with his wife, has adopted her daughter, and they have had a son together. There is little now left of the family's former wealth for Laurant and his five brothers to inherit, and Laurant received only one-eighth acre from his father when he got married. They depend on brick building and casual work in order to have enough to eat.

What is clear is that Laurant's poverty is not simply due to the erosion of family assets. It is also the long-term outcome of strife between his parents, the systematically unequal distribution of resources within the household, and the damage to his family's reputation made by his father's alcoholism and his parent's erratic relationship.

Source: Life history interview conducted by Kate Bird and Isaac Shinyekwa in Buwapuwa, Mbale District, 2002.

Notes

a Including nine hoes, a panga, an axe, five saucepans, a bicycle and a radio.

b LC1 Chairman.

c This is entirely normal in a Ugandan setting. Men do not pay maintenance for ex-wives and children, so leaving your children with your husband is often the only way of ensuring that they will get fed.

Poverty dynamics in rural Uganda: drivers and maintainers

Domestic conflict, separation and divorce

Domestic conflict, separation and divorce emerged as a recurrent theme in our work in the study villages. Both women and men would end marriages and well over a third of interviewees had personal experience of abandonment, separation and divorce. Some of our interviewees (both men and women) were on their third marriage and many on their second.

Domestic violence was reportedly widespread, with women commonly suffering years of persistent and severe beatings to avoid the consequences of breaking up the family. This indicates that many tolerate a violent marriage rather than risk intensified poverty and food insecurity following the likely loss of access to productive resources. Women might seek arbitration by clan leadership but others were 'reluctant to interfere in the business between a husband and wife'. Violence was strongly associated with husbands' heavy alcohol consumption (see p. 110), but was also linked to a 'lack of co-operation within the household'. Women explained that where marital relationships were poor, husbands would take livestock and 'steal' from household granaries and fields, to sell, using the cash to support heavy alcohol consumption and expenditure on mistresses and prostitutes. However, women would also steal from household granaries. They claimed to use the money for household necessities (e.g. salt and soap), but men complained that women spent money on frivolous things, were silly and lazy.

Patrilocal marriages and the low status of women meant that women lived their lives as a visitor in their husband's house. All stocks and assets were seen as the property of the husband, who might dispute his wife's right to anything by pointing out that 'the food and livestock come from *my* father's land'. Women feared that their attempts to curb their husbands' behaviour might result in savage beatings and expulsion from the household.

It was common for adults who had experienced downward mobility to trace the start of their misfortunes to the breakdown of their parent's marriage. In many cases it was having an impact on their lives decades later (Box 7.4). As with widowhood, families commonly break down on the separation of parents. If the mother did not rapidly remarry she would rarely be able to access adequate land to 'dig' and feed the family. As a result she would leave children with her former husband or take them to live with maternal relatives. A second husband rarely accepts another man's children into his house and mothers were found to commonly leave children with relatives or on re-marriage establish a separate household with the children from her previous marriage(s) (and then any additional children). Widows commonly marry into polygamous households, which can complicate family arrangements and lead to children being treated unequally, having limited access to education, poorer quality food and clothing and a greater burden of productive or reproductive work. It could also cause tension between wives (see *Polygamy*, below). In addition, if sons do not leave their current homes to return to their father's village they lose their land rights.

Polygamy

Nuclear families had higher mean incomes than non-nuclear households in most of the nine LADDER villages and in each of the three study villages. Non-nuclear households were larger than nuclear households in all villages except for Kiribairya, which may be explained by survivors from ethnic cleansing re-marrying to form (smaller) polygamous households.

There were divergent field study findings on the impact of polygamous marriages. They were sometimes advantageous to both wives and their children (if the children were from the current husband, and the wives lived on one compound). Women more rarely saw polygamy as beneficial, commenting that if men took a second or third wife they tended to divert resources unfairly to her and her children – to the point of not feeding and clothing their other children. In some life histories polygamy emerged as a serious source of conflict, contributing to increased domestic violence and eventual family break-up. However, some of the children of polygamous marriages stated that they had enjoyed having a number of 'step-mothers' to turn to, and lots of children their own age to play with.

Alcohol[6]

The social and economic cost of heavy alcohol consumption was a recurrent theme in many of our life history interviews and focus group discussions. We found that alcohol consumption was not just a case of a cheery beer on a Friday afternoon. In all three study villages men would congregate in the centre of the village and in compounds around the village and start drinking millet beer from early in the morning. Addiction to *waragi* (local 'gin' – in fact a raw and powerful rum distilled from cane juice or molasses) had blighted the lives of several respondents. UPPAP II (the second Uganda Participatory Poverty Assessment) confirms this, by singling out alcohol as a key cause of poverty, second only to ill-health (Uganda 2003a).

In our study villages, women drank far less often than men, probably due to cultural norms. Male drinking was common and associated by women with the squandering of household resources; domestic violence and family breakdown; male promiscuity and a failure to contribute to the household. Men countered the women's accusations by pointing out that it gave them access to information that they would not get access to if they stayed at home. They added that drinking took them out of the house, getting them out from under their wives' feet and preventing them from picking fights with them. Because of the reportedly strong two-way link between heavy drinking and poverty (drinking to forget and further impoverishment), we have developed this area as a major theme in this chapter.

Crisis levels of alcoholism are now found in rural Uganda, with a high proportion (50–70 per cent) of households profoundly negatively affected (focus group discussions, own research). We argue that this is due to socio-economic shifts which have introduced new alcoholic beverages and altered the population's relationship with alcohol. Historically, locally brewed alcohol was cloudy and had a reasonably high nutritional and low alcoholic content, ranging from 2–11 per cent proof (Willis 2002). It was used to mobilise work parties and to mark traditional ceremonies. Community values and norms were constructed around alcohol consumption to moderate negative impacts. From the 1950s to mid-1970s alcohol consumption was regulated. Sale was only permitted through regulated bars, during specific opening hours. Individuals would brew alcohol privately for home consumption and celebrations but regulations appeared to contain excess. Underage youths were not allowed into bars and women rarely stayed in them for long. Since the 1980s the norms around hosting beer parties have changed.

The monetisation of the economy means that people are less willing to work for food and beer, which is now more commonly brewed for sale in bars and from people's homes. This coincided with the relaxation of regulation following the fall of Amin, and has resulted in the proliferation of alcohol manufacture and retailing. Alcohol producers have innovated, producing stronger beers and distilling *waragi*. All of this has made alcohol consumption more difficult to regulate and has contributed to the development of a culture of regular 'binge' drinking. But there is also a positive impact on the supply side. Alcohol production is a source of employment and provides important local agro-processing value-addition. It is a significant and central source of revenue for many households, particularly for those led by widows and divorced women, who can no longer access land. Nevertheless the social costs of over-consumption are considerable. Policy-makers need to explore a suitable entry-point for tackling this problem, be it through health promotion, education or the development of credible local 'women's courts', designed to tackle the fall-out from marriage-breakdown and domestic violence.

Conflict and internally displaced people

Conflict emerged as an important theme in this study. This may, in part, be due to the villages that we selected but is also evidence of the surprisingly long-run impact of the ethnic and political conflict and mass-killings which marked the decline of the Amin and Obote II eras (ending in the mid-1980s). Mubende district was known to have been a locus of intense conflict, and we selected Kalangala village because it was understood to have been highly affected. However, in Kiribairya (Kamuli district) conflict emerged unexpectedly as a major source of ill-being and we use the experiences of this village to illustrate the impact of conflict in driving chronic poverty and the failure of effective public policy responses to overcome it.

A failure to recover from conflict in Kiribairya

The village of Kiribairya developed into its current form in 1986 when internally displaced people (IDPs) settled in the area having crossed Lake Kyoga to escape ethnic cleansing of Bantu speaking peoples from Teso. Ethnic tensions heightened following Museveni's ascension to power in 1986, when a Bantu president replaced the incumbent, Obote, a non-Bantu. These inter-ethnic tensions were exacerbated by seemingly co-ordinated cattle raids by the Karamajong who swept south and east into Teso lands, looted and left with the majority of the Teso herd. The Karamajong were regarded by some as having been encouraged to raid the Teso in order to impoverish them and undermine their attempts to raise an opposition force to Museveni. The Bakenya ethnic group were seen by the Teso as having collective guilt for aiding the Karamajong. The Teso retaliated brutally, burning and looting houses, raping women, hounding people from their homes and killing the men, women and children who failed to flee in time. Those who escaped across Lake Kyoga were pursued and the Teso raided Kiribairya and other IDP camps in an attempt to eradicate the Bakenya. NRM militia were assigned to protect the lake shore villages and raids were rebuffed.

The Bakenya fled to the Kiribairya area because their kin had settled in the area over the preceding decades. Many residents in the area took the IDPs into their households providing them with food and shelter for up to two years. A local land owner agreed to loan the IDPs land to build a camp, on the condition that it was temporary. Small huts were built crowded together on the lake shore and they are still there. There are few 'permanent houses' partly due to poverty and partly because the villagers do not own the land they live on.

In the immediate aftermath of the crisis the Government and the International Red Cross provided support, but this appears to have been limited to emergency feeding and the distribution of household items (jerry cans, saucepans and blankets). There was no relief-to-development phase, and the destitute and assetless remain largely that. District officials and the staff of a well-known international NGO claimed not to know that there was still an internally displaced population in the district, commenting 'oh, haven't they gone back?' (i.e. returned to Teso).

Many of the IDPs arrived in Kiribairya with literally only the clothes they stood up in, others escaped with cash and resources. The difference between these two groups has largely determined where they are now. Those with resources have been able to move on, and have bought land or established enterprises, usually elsewhere. Grace's story above (Box 7.3) illustrates that 'in-comers' face risks, so that buying land does not guarantee security. But those who arrived destitute have had many fewer choices and have found it very difficult to accumulate and leave the village. Those living in Kiribairya now are either fisherfolk or are IDPs who are too poor to move on. This population subsists cultivating small parcels of rented land and working as casual labourers fishing the lake. A few have been able to accumulate and acquire boats and nets. Few have returned to Teso as some of those who tried have been murdered or driven out again. Despite this continued tension, some of the poorest in Kiribairya travel across the lake to find casual agricultural work, but they refuse to stay after dusk, explaining that 'there are too many bushes over there'. On probing it emerged that the Teso whisper to them that they will 'kill them like chickens' if given the chance.

Conclusion

Many of the chronically poor in the three field sites were found to be low in capabilities and functionings (Sen 1996), with low and in many cases declining asset bases (social, human, natural, physical and financial). There were surprising levels of downward mobility, with many of the poorest interviewees having come from non-poor families. This highlighted that despite nearly seventeen years of post-conflict reconstruction and a sustained period of economic growth, Uganda is still in a process of recovery. Levels of well-being appear to be commonly lower than those enjoyed in rural areas in the 1950s. A recurrent finding from the in-depth interviews, undertaken for this research, was that the poorest had suffered recurrent and composite shocks and personal tragedies. Those who had retained their non-poor status had simply managed to avoid personal disaster, allowing them to retain their assets and sometimes continue to accumulate.

Conflict and dislocation, ill-health, abandonment in old age, death of the head of household, alcohol abuse and household disputes and breakdown appeared to be some of the most serious and widespread causes of declines in well-being. The depth and multidimensionality of the problems facing individuals and households means that positive change is extremely difficult to secure. For many, their ability to reduce their own poverty, themselves, and without external support is constrained by an absence of opportunities. Government programmes are not reaching the poorest in ways that alter their lives for the better. NGOs are not active in any of the study areas, and local village-level institutions do not appear to be helpful to the poor, although charity from neighbours keeps the destitute alive. This provides policy makers and development practitioners with a real challenge. What can be done to assist those not reached by current policies and programmes?

Designing effective government interventions to target the chronically poor throughout Uganda is a challenge. It must start with a robust understanding of the key drivers, maintainers and interrupters of chronic poverty. In other words what causes people to be chronically poor, what are the day-to-day experiences of chronically poor people and what are the things that they can do – or that government or others can do – to help them to move out of chronic poverty. As we have seen in this chapter, people's responses to adversity and opportunity are complex and varied, and range from optimistic and risk-taking entrepreneurialism to passive fatalism and self-destructive alcohol addiction. Faced with this diversity, identifying entry points and deciding how to sequence interventions is a challenge, but it appears that it is not a challenge that the government of Uganda and local and international NGOs active in Uganda have even begun to address in a serious manner.

Substantial investments in rural roads over the last decade have had a considerable impact on reducing distance from markets, now complementary interventions are needed which create an enabling environment for rural enterprise, employment generation and economic growth. However, these interventions are necessary but not sufficient for sustainable reductions in chronic poverty in Uganda. Changes must be made at the household level which will provide the chronically poor with the tools to benefit from opportunities in their improved environment. So, while improving road access is important, improving household characteristics (e.g. number of literate household members, size and quality of household workforce and size and quality of household land holdings) is more so (Okidi 1999). In order to achieve these positive changes at household level, Uganda must refocus efforts to improve local level service delivery.

There is also a clear need for Ugandan policy makers to reconsider social protection, and to provide a strong lead to district administrations on how and when to intervene. With the poorest 20 per cent not benefiting from the past decade of sustained growth we cannot continue to wait for trickle down to work. There are patchy interventions for orphans and people living with HIV/AIDS, commonly implemented by NGOs, and these should now be evaluated and the best used as the model for scaling up interventions and providing extended coverage. These should include pensions for the poorest abandoned elderly and targeted support to orphans, widows and the disabled. Legal innovations are needed to strengthen the rights of divorced women, widows and wives in polygamous marriages, to ensure that women and their children are protected.

In the absence of legal reform, improved public service provision and some form of targeted social protection it is difficult to see how the short-term well-being of the poorest can be improved to allow for the long-term investments in asset development that will allow for their permanent escape from poverty. Without efforts to generate the political will and the public (or elite) acceptance of this as a central issue in Uganda's poverty reduction agenda, the country will continue to fail to extend the benefits of growth to the poorest.

Notes

* Many thanks to Frank Ellis and others in the LADDER team for sharing their dataset and qualitative data with Chronic Poverty Research Centre (CPRC) researchers. Thanks also to John Mims for his input into the re-analysis of the LADDER data set, and for constructive comments on an earlier draft from Bob Baulch, David Hulme and Ade Freeman. This chapter can also be found under the title Multiple Shocks and Downward Mobility: Learning from the Life Histories of

Rural Ugandans as *CPRC Working Paper*, No. 36, downloadable from the website: http://www.chronicpoverty.org.

1 Taken by Okidi and Mugambe to be synonymous with the severely poor in the lowest 20 per cent. They justify this by showing that *very few* of the severely poor moved out of poverty between 1992 and 1996.

2 Confirmed by Uganda (2000b) which states that in each of the four regions and in both rural and urban areas, large families (an average of more than five persons) are likely to be poorer than smaller ones.

3 In this first round of collecting life histories we interviewed only household heads who had been interviewed during the LADDER survey. This enabled us to move straight into the life history interview, without having to spend time collecting basic household asset, income and livelihood data. Due to the large number of female-headed households this did not lead to an absence of women's stories, but may have biased our findings in other ways (e.g. inadequate attention to 'youth', women within male-headed households, the situation of co-wives, the chronic poverty of children and so on). In subsequent research we plan to systematically interview other household members to explore intrahousehold differentiation (see Bolt and Bird 2003 for an outline of the method that we hope to use) and other issues.

4 Cattle Equivalent Units.

5 Using a version of Dunn's test given in Siegel and Castellan (1988: 213–214).

6 This section draws on Shinyekwa (2002).

Part III

Institutions and policy contexts of rural livelihoods

8 Decentralization and rural livelihoods in Malawi*

Sholto Cross and Milton Kutengule

Introduction

This chapter sets out to examine decentralization in Malawi from the point of view of its possible beneficial contributions towards efforts to enhance the livelihoods of the rural poor. Currently much attention is being devoted to institutional reform of the public sector, and the installation of local government which lies at the centre of such efforts. Detailed plans and schedules have been announced, planning handbooks devised, numerous workshops and conferences held. Local elections have taken place. Donor funding and advice promoting this cause have been generous. Yet after a decade of gestation very little of practical consequence has emerged.

The argument here is that much of the activity of reform is apparent rather than real. The pursuit of decentralization by Malawi's political leaders, on the evidence of what has in practice been achieved, has been at best half-hearted. There are a variety of reasons for this. A primary difficulty is that the building of political and administrative decentralization has been an externally induced rather than an organically generated process, and as such it faces inherent contradictions. The inducements for continued efforts are largely provided by donors who control the pipeline supplying aid and all the associated perquisites, rather than by popular pressure for political accountability, or local demands for further subsidiarity in administration.

More fundamentally, the prescriptions of decentralization offer solutions to the perceived inadequacy of the public sector to deliver that are implicitly based on a model of Western-type polity. The Malawian state is far from being such. Political parties do not operate from the bottom up, agglomerating and channelling demands, but rather from the top down. The administrative structure is that of the weak state, with scant capacity; it is deferential and hierarchical, not consultative and interactive with civil society. Key elements for successful decentralization, namely the effective articulation of demand at the local level, and a strong, impartial administrative ethos supported by several levels of capabilities, do not exist. More training courses are an inadequate response.

This chapter presents the view that decentralization, as currently undertaken, is unlikely to succeed because it is misconceived. Current policies seek to 'reform' public sector institutions based on a notion that the African state is failing because the political class has been insufficiently diligent in pursuing the construction of Western-style multi-party democracy (Chabal 1997). A more fruitful line of approach is to see the Malawian polity as a neo-patrimonial state engaged in a crisis of modernity (where modernization does not imply becoming increasingly Western, any more so than it does for many Asian countries which have moved out of poverty), rather than as a failing neo-liberal state. Neo-patrimonialism denotes the dominance of patrimonial practices within an officially legal rational bureaucratic framework. This perspective has the advantage that it does not require the recommendation of yet more improbable levels of reformism. It may also help to explore what room to manoeuvre plausibly exists at the local level.

The patrimonial state

> Nothing is not my business in this country: everything is my business, everything. The state of education, the state of our economy, the state of our agriculture, the state of our transport, everything is my business.

This declaration by Dr Hastings Banda (cited in Alan 1999), prime minister and then life president of Malawi 1964–1993, may be taken as an exemplification of African patrimonialism. He might have added that a significant part of this country – particularly newly privatized land and retail and agricultural marketing services – was indeed his business, in a strictly personal sense. It is fashionable to dismiss Dr Banda as a self-regarding and self-rewarding tyrant, yet it is hard to overestimate the impact of his rule. The single party regime which he fashioned was a classic example of the neo-patrimonial African state, made more distinctive by the absence of military coups and threats and an ultimate peaceful transition to what has been described as the era of 'multi-partyism and democratization', by way of referendum.

The inadequacies which eventuated from his rule from the point of view of socio-economic development were notable, the most particular outcome being not so much the degree of immiseration of the populace as the inherently weak state it created. It is this contemporary Malawian state which may be depicted as a case of a failing or transitional neo-patrimonial state, rather than as an incipient parliamentary democracy (Bratton and Van De Walle 1994). The classic hallmarks that indicate this are seen in the norms and expectations of officialdom, the mode of operation of political parties, and the state of civil society.

From the perspective of development policies that rely on public sector channels for their implementation, it is perhaps the economic rather than the administrative aspects of neo-patrimonialism which are the most significant. The key point is that the end goal of economic policy within this system is to retain the power to control the patrimony. This may involve 'development', but that is not its fundamental purpose, which is why sustainability is rare. It may even result in 'rural development' – that is, the application of funds to individuals and communities that are locationally specific to a particular community or potential resource – the purpose of which is not popular mobilization for self-help (the terminology used in the Banda era), but rather the reverse – handouts as rewards for loyalty expressed through passive acquiescence.

In this system, formal distinctions between public and private wealth are constantly undermined by the need for patrons to maintain their client networks through due reward: indeed, democracy and regional development within the patrimonial system are essentially constituted by ensuring that national, regional and local networks are properly taken into account when the cake is shared out. Investment is inherently low, because the demands for consumption by clients are so high. The canalization of funds to private ends also has the self-reinforcing effects of weakening the currency, capital flight and the consequent shortage of funds for what local investment there is, most notably public infrastructure (Sandbrook 1985). The indebtedness which ensues weakens the state yet further, and intensifies the struggle to maintain the networks of loyalties which sustain power. In resource-rich countries, this may lead either to the complete collapse of the formal state into a number of warring entities, where disorder becomes a functional political instrument (Chabal 1997) or even to the emergence of what has been termed 'the felonious state' (Bayart *et al.* 1999), where the inter-penetration of organized crime with the organs of state is more or less complete.

In resource-poor countries, the more common outcome has been the propensity for individuals to seek public office – as civil servants, party officials, politicians – primarily in order to acquire personal wealth and status. Receivable salary is rarely enough: public office grants access to a number of sources of rents and petty corruption, which are viewed as an entitlement of office. The effort in capturing these resources is not of course then dissipated in the fulfilment of tasks for which no clear loyalty network is thereby being maintained (Bayart 1993). The world of donor aid falls ready prey to these propensities, indeed encourages them, and it might be argued displays some of the same characteristics. This was particularly notable in the case of Malawi in the early 1990s, where donors scrambled to establish their programmes with the onset of political respectability in one of Africa's poorest countries. Competition for access to key cadres through their incorporation into the world of daily subsistence allowances, study abroad, and the endless conference round validated neo-patrimonial practices, buffered as they were within the lofty rhetoric of democracy and development.

With these considerations as a background, an assessment of the prospects of a beneficial relationship between decentralization and local level development in Malawi requires the examination of a number of elements. These are:

1 an understanding of the case for decentralized government, which takes into account not only the principles on which this is based, but also the systemic context within which it is being implemented;

2 the background of local government in Malawi and the persistence of 'traditionalism';
3 administrative developments during the one-party era;
4 an understanding of the dynamics of the reform era.

The case for decentralized government

The case for decentralization is primarily a political one. The promotion of decentralization has the virtue that it allows its external proponents to appear as non-political, concerned with good governance but not interfering in internal politics. It is unsurprising therefore that the major developmental agencies should have adopted the promotion of decentralization as a central plank in the political reforms which they wished to see pursued in developing countries. The Governance and Civil Service Reform Program adopted by the World Bank in the early 1990s explicitly saw decentralization as a primary means of tackling those public bureaucracies 'which are by and large "patrimonialized" by ruling elites' (World Bank 1994). Malawi was included as a pilot country case study as part of the institutional assessment for this program.

Other arguments advanced in favour of decentralization are that it promotes better service delivery and more efficient government; promotes political stability; and assists in inter-jurisdictional and other forms of equity. In theory, yes. But the prerequisites are that local government is both more capable and more constrained in its patrimonial instincts than central government; that the promotion of local political party bases is not viewed as a threat by the centre; and that imbalances at both the meso- (rich districts subsidizing poorer ones) and micro-levels (affirmative action for women) are genuinely addressed. These pose major difficulties. As was concluded in a major recent study on public administration in Africa (Adamolekun 1999a): 'although local governments are covered under the public administration reform efforts in most sub-Saharan African countries, there are no real success stories as far as improved development performance at the local level is concerned'.

The evolution of decentralization policy

It would be a mistake to regard the adoption of decentralization in Malawi as simply a recent development. The move towards decentralization in Malawi is part of an unfolding process in that country that goes to the heart of its political economy. A comprehension of its many twists and turns, and likely future trajectory, requires the identification and tracing of a number of strands, and the investigation of some major areas of conflict and disagreement.

Pre-independence and the role of chiefs

The assessment of village-level political and administrative structures commences with the role of the chiefs. Under the administrative system established after the declaration of Nyasaland as a British protectorate in 1891 chiefs had a role in collecting hut tax from the beginning, and were formally established as part of the local administrative structure by the Native Authority Ordinance of 1912. Rather than the decline in power of traditional authorities which often accompanied the growth of the colonial state, circumstances in Nyasaland progressed otherwise. Indeed the position of chiefs was strengthened in 1933 when their role as raisers of revenue for the purposes of development was extended beyond poll taxes, fees and fines to include land rents, ivory sales and small grants-in-aid.

In sharp distinction to neighbouring Mozambique, where chiefs were absorbed into a highly commandist system of local prefectures, chiefs and headmen in Malawi enjoyed a high degree of legitimate authority throughout the colonial period. Chiefs were included as council members in six District Councils first established by the colonial District Councils Act of 1953. Over subsequent years more DCs were established, providing a comprehensive coverage of twenty-four districts, with elected councillors gradually introduced. Both chiefs and councils were popular with local communities as they were seen to be delivering a wide range of services – graded roads, local produce markets, bridges, schools, boreholes – with a supportive central ministry (Local Government and Rural Development, MLGRUD) (Graham-Jolly 1995).

Much of this success derived from the fact that at their height in the late 1960s, the councils had a diversified revenue base, with income exceeding expenditure. There were three main sources of revenue: self-financing services such as education, forestry, veterinary and postal services; direct government grants; and income from poll taxes, fees, rates, licences and land rentals. They were able to retain the services of able civil servants, with training and support through MLGRUD. There was no difficulty in recruiting voluntary labour for self-help projects (for which they provided 60 per cent of costs).

The incorporation of the chiefs into the colonial local administrative system, and the introduction of the participatory principle through the elected councillors, thus provided a remarkable boost to the longevity of traditional authority. It is a notable feature of contemporary rural Malawi that chiefs still retain considerable authority, and continue to exercise important functions concerning the allocation of land under customary tenure and the validation of the place of the individual within the community. However in terms of their sense of political identity and capacity for concerted political action, rural Malawians were constructed as subjects rather than as citizens. Local government, although it came to be both effective and popular towards the end of the colonial period, was not engaged in a democratic dialogue with its populace. The growth of such an engagement might well have been pursued in the post-colonial period, but the aims of the first generation of 'liberation' leaders proved to be in an entirely different direction.

The era of party–state hegemony

The accession to power of Dr Banda, and the installation of the one-party state under the Malawi Congress Party, sounded the death knell for participatory local government. It is instructive to examine the reasons for this. Many aspirant politicians had commenced their careers in the local councils, and they were the training grounds for the first generation of civil servants. However, the inherent dynamic of the one party system required the dismantling of local government because it was based on the centralization of power in the office and person of the president; the encadrement of all public officials in a commandist structure; and the canalization of revenue flows into a single stream.

The jealous displacement of local councils commenced in 1967 with the establishment of District Development Committees (DDCs), coordinated through the Office of the President by administrative fiat, with a similar mandate to that of the councils. The DDCs were linked in a hierarchical relationship with Area and Village Development Committees (ADCs, VDCs) all staffed by party cadres, with no community involvement in decision-making. The aim was to ensure party control over all institutions from village level to the centre of government.

In terms of resources, this was easily accomplished. The lion's share of government resources and all donor funding was channelled away from the councils to the DDCs, which were staffed exclusively by party functionaries. The attitude of DDC personnel to the councils and their assets was one of plunder:

> Party officials slept in Council rest houses free, and used Council vehicles as and when they wanted without paying for them. Party officials refused to pay rates and fees, for either party functions or personal use. Since the Party was supreme and no one could challenge its functionaries, Council resources were plundered.
>
> (Apthorpe *et al.* 1995)

In this process, MLGRUD systematically sidelined the councils, reduced their autonomy and fund-raising powers, and removed their control over the appointment and management of human resources. There was a consequent massive exodus of skilled personnel. The collection of local taxes was centralized, and most development functions with their attendant revenue streams were transferred to centralized sectoral ministries. By the early 1970s, the golden age of popular local government in Malawi was at an end.

The patrimonial authority of chiefs was incorporated within the new hegemonic form of party power, yet they appear to have retained their legitimacy within the community. Chiefs came to occupy an intermediary role: their hereditary mode of appointment and incorporation within a top-down chain of command fitted well with the new ethos of elite control of the political process. Yet they also had to maintain a certain distance in order to maintain credibility and legitimacy. Their continuing role in controlling land allocations, and in ritual offices such as burial proved to be resilient. The response at village level to these developments was one of increasing apathy and withdrawal from participation in community activities.

The destruction of democratic local structures of government was accompanied by the installation of new forms of extraction from rural communities. These were essentially concerned with the processes of accumulation by party officials, bureaucrats and politicians through which Dr Banda sought to underpin his regime. Agricultural workers on land held by customary tenure were forbidden to grow the main cash crop available to them, namely burley tobacco, which became the prerogative of commercial growers and tenant farmers. The ruling regime encouraged its senior members to engage, with the connivance of chiefs, in the transfer of land from customary to private tenure, for cash-cropping purposes. These *obwera* or *akudza* (Chewa: interlopers, strangers) as they are known, are widely resented, and provide one of the important issues in the current debate on land reform (Ahene 2000).

The control of the land vested in the president was also widely used to build Banda's client base: large amounts of state land were simply handed over to the private control of important individuals. The scale of this land alienation was considerable. In the early 1970s there were some 229 estates covering 255,800 hectares with an average size of some 1,000 hectares each, representing the historic pattern of commercial settlement in forestry, tea, sugar, coffee, maize and tobacco. By the end of the Banda period in 1993, this had risen to 23,000 estates occupying 1.2m hectares, with an average size of some fifty hectares, largely consisting of the new client class of tobacco growers (FAO 1995a). By way of contrast, the same period saw a decline in plot size in the customary sector from over two hectares for 70 per cent of producers (1969) to less than 15 per cent having more than one hectare (1995).

The reform wave: 1993–1998

> There is a need ... to change the terms of the political discourse which creates the expectation of material gain in return for political allegiances ... Inappropriate incentive structures have been identified as the fundamental cause of low productivity and poor work ethic, particularly in the civil service ... These include low salaries, poor monitoring, no punishment for poor performance, and opportunities for fraud and corruption.
>
> (Mathews Chikaonda, Minister of Finance 2001)[1]

The referendum of May 1993 which ushered in the era of democratization and multi-partyism was a decisive defeat for Banda. Concepts of 'good governance' joined with the contemporary understanding of the importance of popular participation to provide a new impetus for the resuscitation of local government.

However many of the key actors – politicians and officials – continued in prominent positions. The expectation that public office was a reliable road ahead for acquisition of material wealth was heightened by the opening up of new opportunities, and the politics of patrimonialism were reinforced, rather than the reverse. The extent of seriously large corruption was briefly revealed in 1997/8 by the exposure of a massive fraud at ministerial level, eventuating in a cabinet reshuffle and the sacking of three prominent politicians. The Public Service Act of 1994 sought to affirm the non-partisan, professional nature of the civil service. There was also a necessary slimming down of this corps (which had expanded from 10,000 at independence to 110,000 in 1995). While civil service salaries saw significant erosion and decreasing wage compression (salary ratios from 1:42 in 1982 to 1:20 in 1995), politicians were awarded huge increases in salaries and allowances in 1994 and 1997 (Adamolekun and Mvula 1999). The process of restructuring parastatal organizations was initiated, but proved slow and partial in implementation. While some sixteen political parties sprang up, only three currently have representation in Parliament. Early amendments to the new constitution included the abolition of a proposed Senate, and the removal of a clause enabling constituents to recall their MP on the grounds of ineffectiveness.

The first measures towards decentralization followed a number of situational analyses on poverty undertaken in the early 1990s. The lead role was taken by the UNDP supported by other bilateral and multilateral funders. A key report was commissioned in 1995 (Apthorpe *et al.* 1995), the recommendations of which formed the essential base for a new policy on decentralization. This study was followed by a number of others, culminating in an approval in principle by cabinet in January 1996, the establishment of a Decentralization Secretariat within the Office of the President, and the passing of a comprehensive Local Government Act in 1998 (Malawi 1998a). The centrepiece of this new policy is the establishment of the District Assembly (DA), with the object 'to further the constitutional order based on democratic principles, accountability, transparency and participation of the people in decision-making and development processes'.[2]

Membership of the DA consists of traditional authorities and MPs within the area as ex officio but non-voting members, one elected member for each ward, and five persons to be appointed by the elected members to cater for special interest groups. The executive functions are to be carried out by the District Executive Committee (DEC), which presides over a number of sectoral sub-committees. It was decreed that the chairperson of the DEC would not, however, be elected by the DA as envisaged in the Act, but would be the DC. This has the effect of making the DEC potentially little different from the old DDC, which still continues as an interim arrangement in most districts. The aim is that over a transitional period – originally anticipated to run for two to three years, but increasingly being extended as the magnitude of the tasks becomes apparent – the DA would gradually take on its own staffing and employment functions, generate its own revenue, and operate as a fully fledged form of local government.

There are a number of intrinsic difficulties in the way this is being implemented. These may be considered in terms of function, capacity, and structure. Such is the nature of the contemporary Malawian state that the key ministries are essentially setting their own pace. Some ministries have been at the forefront of promoting decentralization (e.g. Environment), others have been less enthusiastic (e.g. Agriculture). The consequence of this is that the decentralization process is being rolled out on a sector by sector basis, rather than district by district.[3] This poses major problems of function for the fledgling DAs: lacking control over the ministries and without their own specialist staff, the key development planning functions are likely to remain under the control of the remnant party–state structure, the DDC.

The current picture is therefore one where massive problems of coordination and capacity overshadow all.[4] By capacity is meant not only the managerial and technical skills of DA members, but also their attitudes and expectations, the formal and informal levels of authority which they may acquire, and the level and type of resources they may be able to deploy in fulfilling their functions of promoting people-centred development.

Research in one district, Dedza,[5] highlighted these difficulties. Decentralization in Dedza was kicked off by the local government election of November 2000. Turnout was some 14 per cent. This was attributed not so much to poor publicity as to cynicism and apathy. Despite the fact that Dedza was traditionally an MCP stronghold (John Tembo's[6] constituency is Dedza Central), most counsellors stood as United Democratic Front (UDF) members, or joined the UDF soon after gaining office. The expectation that supporting the ruling party was the quickest way ahead was clear.

One counsellor, a young recently married man with two children, had resigned his job with a private enterprise to stand for the DA, but subsequently rather regretted his decision. Offices had not been designated, no proper allowances and stipend were forthcoming, and he was having to make ends meet by doubling up his counselling role by trading in maize, beans and tobacco. He was unaware that any formal meetings of the DA had been held, and had little grasp of the training seminars he had attended. Other members of the DA had similar stories, although the chairman showed an appreciation of the need for popular interaction in order to get development projects moving. However, there was also a widespread perception that council members would have little more than a cosmetic role to play, and would be easily out-manoeuvred by ex officio DA members. Real power, it was argued, lay with MPs and chiefs, who between them had a greater ability to manipulate the levers of power.

Striking by its absence in discussions with DA members was any reference to the nature of structures whereby participation in development activities could be taken to the sub-district level. While general concerns were expressed with growing poverty (and in particular with the worsening crime statistics), there was no sense of councillors role as potential mobilizers of village-level initiatives. In terms of function, the making of linkages through which to attain the objective of community participation in development is seen in the Local Government Act as a central *raison d'être* for the DA, but little attention in practice appears to have been given as to how this will be implemented.

Yet there is a long, if complex, tradition of collective action in Malawian rural society. This has been subjected over time to powerfully distorting pressures but may be rescuable. A few examples of how this might occur are provided by certain development agencies. The Malawi Social Action Fund (MASAF) is singled out for mention. MASAF was established in 1995 (with a World Bank loan of $56m), with a further similar tranche of funding in 1998, and a third phase agreed in June 2001. The design principles are those which have been tried and tested in a number of developing countries, and indeed are the basis for some of the most successful community based development projects elsewhere in southern Africa.[7] These are that communities should retain 'ownership' of the process, by being involved from the beginning in the identification of development activities, and making financial or equivalent contributions (20 per cent generally, 5 per cent for the more capital intensive projects such as water). The establishment of a Project Management Committee (PMC) democratically elected by the community, with a deliberate attempt at gender balance, supported by facilitation for the management of bank accounts, administration, dispute resolution and similar functions was central to making this work.

MASAF has of course been criticized. It has been attacked variously for being insufficiently politically accountable, too focused on infrastructural projects, and tending towards top-down management practices. Referring specifically to the Safety Nets programme, an independent evaluation team found that there was limited sense of community ownership, and gender bias against women because of the predominance of labour-intensive road-building projects, although the community-based project committees 'won the respect of the communities in all project areas because of their leadership skills, moral support ... and above everything else their unfailing efforts in presenting their grievances and other concerns to the District Teams (DTs)'. The 'attitudinal problems' of the DTs – the DC, district clerk, and sectoral ministry technical advisors – were singled out for sharp criticism (poor standards of reporting, delays in making payments, grumbles over lack of perquisites) (Zvogu *et al.* 1998). These criticisms are revealing. Some interesting insights also emerged from a further evaluation study (Chilowa *et al.* 2001):

> The general feeling among the study respondents was that there is a lot of political pressure on the MASAF development initiative. The majority

> of community members observed that they would rather work with chiefs than politicians in implementing the grassroots development interventions. Their rationale was that politicians either from the government or opposition side are often partisan in administering development interventions . . . The study has further established that MASAF . . . interventions have somewhat been a success because of the pivotal role of PMCs. They, in the absence of a regularized system of extension, serve as a direct link between MASAF and the target communities.

The conclusion from a review of decentralization prospects in Dedza district was that there are large needs and a high level of responsiveness by communities, but little prospect for mechanisms being put in place to articulate these via the decentralization process as currently being implemented. There are also some major questions over the degree to which chiefs and headmen are valid representatives of community interests. On the other hand, organizations with a degree of independence and delinkage from the state, and a professional ethos and experience of grassroots development, are in great demand. A key difference between MASAF and development NGOs on the one hand, and the DA on the other, is of course that of access to resources. Currently the local revenue base for district development in Dedza is a slender one, consisting mainly of market and clinic fees, liquor licences and forest sales. It is interesting to note that community contributions to MASAF programmes have averaged between twice and sevenfold the revenue generated by districts on their own account (Malawi 1998b; the Schroeder Report).

The prospects for fiscal decentralization

Finance has proved generally to be the most critical issue for decentralization, and in the African experience inter-governmental transfers the most critical stumbling block (Adamolekun 1999b). Malawi has proved no exception. The recent history of the agrarian economy in Malawi has been marked by a shrinking availability of land to householders, declining soil fertility and the rapid degradation of the environment. Population growth (combined in certain areas such as Dedza with the influx of refugees) and high levels of endemic disease have added to general immiseration and the proportion of the rural population in a highly vulnerable state. It is not surprising therefore that the local revenue base available to district councils has provided less than five per cent of their expenditures. Moreover, as the Schroeder report concluded:

> The many years of disregard of local councils, particularly district councils, have left them essentially moribund and has created a number of issues. The capacities of councils have been allowed to deteriorate, there is considerable uncertainty concerning what the councils and councillors

are expected to do, and, as importantly, central government ministries have a general negative attitude towards local government.

There has been a flurry of studies proposing the design of new systems for the management of revenue generating systems and inter-governmental transfers.[8] Taken together, these propose a wholesale re-engineering of local government. This will entail a rebuilding of capacity from the bottom up, to enable all enterprises and assets (including land) within the purview of councils to be measured and rated, entered on a database, and subjected to effective collection procedures. It has likewise been recommended to central government that the whole system of rating and taxation[9] be thoroughly overhauled, and the transfer of funds to districts subjected to a rational formula taking account of population and development status. These have included proposals on the re-allocation of funds currently going to sectoral ministry headquarters (e.g. Health and Education Funds) to be placed under the control of the district. It has also been proposed that donor funding, which comprises some 80 per cent of the development budget, also be made available to district level authorities and development agencies. Without at least the majority of these recommendations being put into effect, decentralization will remain an empty shell. Yet the consequences of such a restructuring for the Malawi polity would be traumatic. It would require the toppling of the powerful baronies of interests situated in the sectoral ministries and parastatals, and require the reorientation of political parties from their concerns with ensuring access at the centre, to the difficult and uncertain waters of being held accountable at the local level. Effective fiscal decentralization requires the revolutionary transformation of government of an order significantly greater than that experienced during the transition from one-party to multi-party rule.

Likely outcomes and conclusion

There are then converging arguments and indicators which suggest that the most likely outcome of the decentralization process will not be fundamental change. Rather it will simply twist the kaleidoscope of neo-patrimonialism to produce a variant pattern, where local elites have larger opportunities to capture assets and extract wealth. The poor will remain passive and suspicious, lacking effective channels to make political demands. Immiseration will express itself through growing levels of insecurity and short-term survivalist strategies which will continue to intensify the pressure on the natural resource base.

Experience elsewhere in the developing world suggests that valuable benefits of decentralization can possibly be gained even in the face of seemingly overwhelming odds, if certain pre-conditions can be established. These, in essence, represent the best hopes of dissolving the patrimonial system from below. The central tenet in the literature is that subjects should be empowered as citizens through the acquisition of effective political rights, commencing with the establishment of accountability running through all levels of the political and administrative systems. Manor (1999) in his study of sixty country case studies, concluded that three factors are essential if decentralization is to lead to the promotion of sustainable livelihoods for the poor: elected local bodies with sufficient funding, adequate powers and reliable mechanisms to ensure two kinds of accountability – the accountability of elected representatives to citizens, and of bureaucrats to representatives.

The signal lack of enthusiasm shown by the Malawian electorate in the local government elections of 2000 does not bode well for the prospect that political accountability may be enhanced through the decentralization process. Yet the empowerment of communities – what Ribot (1999) has referred to as their enfranchisement – is a priority. Paradoxically, it may be the case that in Malawi decentralization is being attempted too swiftly rather than too slowly, in that the organic base of an actively engaged citizenry does not exist: cautious and suspicious subjects are unable to fulfil the necessary functions of demand and recall. There is an absence of effective structures at sub-district level within the currently conceived plans for decentralization for any real political engagement, and the prospects for the neo-patrimonial bureaucratization of what may emerge are strong.

Yet the makings of such a transition are there. It is difficult to argue for a delinkage between the reform of the state apparatus and socio-economic development interventions at the same time as one proposes enhanced grass-roots politicization through this very same process. But it is in this complex space that some room for manoeuvre would appear to exist. A parallel form of development intervention is required. This means that the central target (for the poverty agenda of external agencies, as well as for a genuinely concerned internal leadership) should be the enhancement of the model of the community-based project management committee. Ideally this should be delinked from the formal administrative and political process, running perhaps in parallel with ongoing attempts to breathe life into local government. Once such community structures are well established, a possible area of linkage with formal decentralization may be to equip them with the management capacity, authority and resources to buy in extension services and sectoral support from the ministries, through the DA. Such an approach would require a clear understanding and commitment by the donor community to their own internal coordination: difficult as this would be to achieve, it may be the lesser task compared with driving top-down decentralization through the reluctant centre.

In summary, if decentralization in Malawi is viewed simply as a techno-rational process, then the plans, training courses and handbooks seen as essential to driving forward the capacity to implement it are likely to do little more than inflate a carapace over the patrimonial body corporate. The state certainly has to establish an enabling environment, through the reform of laws and institutions which currently constrain the economic freedoms of rural households and place power which is increasingly being abused in the hands of local elites. But a parallel process of community enablement is required, which can assist in the achievement of an effective political voice for the poor, and assist them to pursue their interests as critically engaged citizens rather than as passive and dependent subjects at the bottom end of the patrimonial foodchain.

Actions which create more space for community-based structures, and economic choices by individuals, are uncertain in outcome. They may be less welcome than the formal agenda of the promotion of good governance, in that they pose a long-term threat to the dominance of elite interests. It is the contention of this chapter however that the creation of an enfranchised citizenry capable of articulating political demands is the only basis on which effective local government can be built.

Notes

* This is an abridged and updated version of LADDER Working Paper No. 4 that first appeared in October 2001 (Cross 2001).

1 Chikaonda, M., Budget Speech, 22 June 2001 as reported in Malawi News, 23 June 2001.

2 Malawi (1998a) Clause 3.

3 At the time of writing, research is being conducted by OXFAM in a number of districts on issues of sectoral coordination.

4 It is apparent from a number of interviews with senior personnel in the Decentralization Secretariat that these are by no means unknown or underestimated.

5 Interviews were conducted with the District Commissioner, District Development Officer, the Chairman of the District Assembly and two members of the DA (June 2001).

6 Tembo, number two to Banda, was, until a recent – and disputed – court order, leader of the MCP, the official opposition party.

7 The Community Employment Programme of the Independent Development Trust (1993–1998) pioneered this approach during the political transition in South Africa to great effect. The Mvula Water and Sanitation Trust has continued this approach. Both approaches worked closely with government policy objectives but were independently funded and autonomous in management. Direct community ownership of assets and resources, with contributions in the 5–10 per cent range, were sine qua non of project design.

8 In addition to the Shroeder report, there have been the Kampanje Report (Malawi 1999a), the Kelly Report (Kelly 2001) and the Boex Report (Malawi 2001a).

9 The Kelly Report states bluntly that 'the primary obstacle to enhanced revenues is weak administration and political will for enforcement . . . Tax registers do not exist or are incomplete and out of date' (Kelly 2001: 2). In June 2001, the Malawi Revenue Authority (MRA), having failed for 18 months to receive a response from the Malawi Broadcasting Authority (MBA) as to why PAYE collected from its large payroll by its directors had not been handed over, sealed the premises and assets of the MBA. The MBA then called in the police riot squad to break the seals. At the time of writing it was not clear whether the MRA had received the PAYE funds in question.

9 Rural taxation and poverty reduction in Uganda*

Godfrey Bahiigwa

Introduction

Rural taxation has received a lot of attention in Uganda since the late 1990s. A number of studies have highlighted rural taxation regimes as a hindrance to achieving expressed objectives in the government's poverty reduction programmes. In a study on rural livelihoods in nine villages of rural Uganda, Ellis and Bahiigwa (2003) found that the existing taxation regimes were not compatible with achieving poverty reduction and agricultural commercialisation objectives identified in the national framework for poverty reduction, the Poverty Eradication Action Plan (PEAP) and the Plan for Modernisation of Agriculture (PMA). The debate surrounding rural taxation started with the PEAP in 1997 (Uganda 1997). This document highlighted the graduated tax[1] (G-tax) as an unpopular tax. The first Uganda Participatory Poverty Assessment Project, (UPPAP I), conducted across thirty-six communities in twelve districts in 1999 also found the G-tax to be unpopular in rural areas. The manner in which the tax was assessed was perceived to be unfair, methods of enforcing collection included arrests, and its poor timing of collection was not consistent with the seasonal nature of rural incomes.

The PEAP 2000 (Uganda 2001a) highlighted the need for reform in local tax systems, especially the G-tax. It identified two major problems with G-tax. First, it appeared to be regressive. Given that most rural residents pay a flat tax rate, the burden of the tax is proportionally larger on the incomes of the poor than on the incomes of the rich. Second, it was costly to collect. Some districts reported that the annual salaries of sub-county chiefs were larger than the amount raised from G-tax. While these local officials have other duties, tax collection is one of their major responsibilities. The cost of imprisoning and maintaining G-tax defaulters is high, in terms of public expenditure as well as to the defaulters and their families (Uganda 2000c: 81). The PEAP identified the need to develop better forms of local taxation based on studies by the Local Government Finance Commission (LGFC).

The problem of rural taxation in Uganda goes beyond the G-tax. Ellis and Bahiigwa (2003) noted that rural Ugandans pay a bewildering array of taxes. Such taxes included business licences, crop taxes, livestock taxes, fish taxes and market dues – both formal and informal. The levels and incidences of these taxes are discussed in more detail in section four. The Poverty Status Report (PSR) 2003 (Uganda 2003b) also highlighted the problem of rural taxes and the potential negative impact on the poor and rural economic activities. The PSR urged government to review local tax policies to ensure that the burden of local taxation on rural taxpayers is appropriate and methods of collection are efficient and equitable.

The purpose of this chapter is not to paint a grim picture of local taxation. Indeed, local tax revenues are expected to provide several benefits for rural households. The underlying principle is that elected district and sub-county councils have to deliver services in rural areas, and that a proportion of these budgets should be raised locally so that taxpayers can make a connection between council performance in the delivery of services and taxes paid (Ellis and Freeman 2004). On the other hand, tax levels and methods of collection, need to take into account the severity of tax incidence on the rural poor and avoid the creation of an environment that is not conducive for economic activities to prosper. Local taxation should not be overly regressive, the rich should pay a higher proportion of their income than the poor. At the same time, the financing needs of local governments should be taken into account. Indeed the government recognises that reforms in local taxation should generate sufficient revenue to provide decentralised administrations with a degree of budgetary autonomy (Uganda 2003b: 32). However, local revenue generation should not be at the expense of rural economic growth and transformation.

The 2002 Poverty Reduction Strategy Paper (PRSP) progress report (Uganda 2002a) identified two important challenges:

1 the need for local governments to raise more revenue without hurting the poor, yet the tax base is narrow and there is growing need to provide services;
2 the co-financing required by a number of government programs and most donor projects.

Local governments are required to co-finance up to 10 per cent of the value of the grant for some development initiatives such as the Local Government Development Program (LGDP) and the PMA Non-Sectoral Conditional Grant (NSCG). Without adequate ability to generate local revenue, districts find it difficult to meet their co-financing obligations, yet they need the development funds to deliver services to the people.

The foregoing exposition indicates that rural taxpayers perceive local taxation as a burden to them and this has been reflected in a number of studies. Taxpayers also do not see a connection between the taxes they pay and the services delivered to them by local governments. Government documents acknowledge the problems afflicting local taxation and do recognise need for reforms. However, for policy change to happen it is important to demonstrate the tax burden and regressive nature of taxes paid by rural households, especially the poor. It is equally important to demonstrate how the revenue collected locally is utilised as a justification for tax collection. This chapter concentrates on the taxpayer rather than on revenue collection and utilisation of rural taxes. Its objective is to examine the nature and burden of taxes within the institutional context in which rural households pursue a range of livelihood strategies as pathways out of poverty. The analysis is based on household data collected in three districts and nine villages of rural Uganda between January and April 2001.[2] In addition to quantitative survey data, further insights are gained from qualitative data collected from focus group discussions and key informants in each of the nine villages as well as secondary data from districts and sub-counties. The village and districts in the LADDER study are presented in Table 9.1.

Uganda's poverty agenda

This section reviews Uganda's main poverty reduction strategies, the objective being to relate the policy objective to the manner in which rural taxation is handled by local governments. The review helps examine whether poverty reduction can be achieved in rural areas under the current taxation system.

The Poverty Eradication Action Plan (PEAP)

The government of Uganda formulated a poverty strategy in 1997, known as the Poverty Eradication Action Plan (PEAP). The PEAP target is to reduce absolute poverty to 10 per cent of the population by 2017 (Uganda 2001a; Uganda 2002a). When the PEAP was designed in 1997, its target was based on a twenty-year time horizon (1997–2017). The PEAP emerged out of consultations among government, civil society, academics, researchers and development partners. However, with increasing need to involve the poor and

Table 9.1 LADDER villages in Uganda

No.	*Village*	*Livelihood system*	*Sub-county*	*District*
1	Bukhasusa	upland coffee–banana	Butiru	Mbale
2	Buwopuwa	lowland maize–cotton	Butiru	
3	Bunabuso	upland coffee–banana	Bududa	
4	Iyingo	fishing and farming	Kagulu	Kamuli
5	Kinamwanga	fishing and farming	Kidera	
6	Kiribairya	fishing and farming	Buyende	
7	Kabbo	banana–maize, livestock	Kasambya	Mubende
8	Kansambya	coffee–banana, livestock	Madudu	
9	Kalangaalo	coffee–banana, livestock	Bulera	

Source: Mims and Mathieu (2002).

have their voices heard and their concerns addressed both at policy and budget level, the government launched the Uganda Participatory Poverty Assessment Process (UPPAP) in 1998. The intention was to bring the voices of the poor at the forefront of policy debate and formulation. The PEAP was revised in 2000 in an attempt to include the lessons learned from UPPAP. In 2002, a second round of the PPA was conducted. Both PPAs highlighted rural taxation as a problem, especially G-tax.

The PEAP (2000) has four specific goals, under which sectoral plans and programmes for poverty eradication have been developed. These goals are:

1 creating an enabling environment for rapid and sustainable economic growth and structural transformation. The main objectives of this goal are to maintain macroeconomic stability and provision of macroeconomic incentives for private sector development; and equitable and efficient use of public resources;
2 ensuring good governance and security – this covers decentralisation, law and order, increased transparency, accountability for public expenditure, and public information;
3 increasing the ability of the poor to raise their incomes. Under this goal, the main areas of focus are investments in feeder roads, agriculture – particularly extension services, small-scale enterprises, vocational education and energy for the poor;
4 improving the quality of life of the poor. This goal is aimed at improved provision of basic social services such as primary health care, water and sanitation, primary education and adult literacy.

It is from these four goals that the line ministries derive their mandate to develop comprehensive development programs that are expected to meet the overall national development objectives. Several sectoral programs and plans have been developed to implement the PEAP, among them the PMA. The reference to the PEAP goals in relation to rural taxation is important in order to make a connection between national level policy objectives and local level outcomes. The goals on economic growth, good governance and increased incomes of the poor can only be attained if a conducive environment exists in rural areas.

The Plan for Modernisation of Agriculture (PMA)

In response to the rural poverty concerns and also to operationalise the PEAP objective of increasing the ability of the poor to raise their incomes, the government designed the Plan for Modernisation of Agriculture (PMA) in 2000. The PMA is a poverty-focused rural development framework focusing on agriculture, perceived to be the main activity of the poor. The main objectives of the PMA are to:

1 increase incomes and improve the quality of life of poor subsistence farmers through increased agricultural productivity and increased share of marketed production;
2 improve household food security through the market rather than emphasising self-sufficiency;
3 provide gainful employment through the secondary benefits of PMA implementation such as agro-processing factories and services;
4 promote sustainable use and management of natural resources by developing a land use and management policy and promotion of environmentally friendly technologies (Uganda 2000d).

Seven intervention areas were identified to achieve these objectives. These are: research and technology development; agricultural advisory services; rural finance; agro-processing and marketing; agricultural education; supportive infrastructure; and, sustainable natural resource use and management. An additional intervention is the Non-Sectoral Conditional Grant (NSCG) to local governments to implement rural poverty reduction programs that have been identified and prioritised by the local communities through their planning process. Again the review of the PMA objectives, especially the one on increase market participation has direct relevance to the rural taxation question. It assumes that the existing tax regime is conducive for increased marketing of agricultural products in rural areas.

Implementation of the PEAP, the PMA and other sectoral plans at the grassroots level is through the decentralised system of government. Local governments (districts and sub-counties) are required to have development plans that provide input into central level planning. These plans are also a requirement for releasing funds from the centre to local governments for implementation of PEAP priorities as well as other sectoral and local priorities. Decentralisation offers an opportunity to accelerate rural development as it brings services closer to the people. However, it also presents challenges because not all districts have the capacity to cope with the demanding challenges of decentralisation. Rural taxation is one of those challenges facing local governments from different angles. On the one hand local governments have to raise local revenue to fund expenses that cannot be met by grants from central government. On the other hand, they have to support economic growth in rural areas although this is usually not revealed by the manner in which rural taxation operates.

Institutional context of rural taxation

This section describes the institutional context within which rural taxation takes place. Uganda has a decentralised system of government that was passed into law with the 1995 Constitution and the Local Governments Act, 1997. This legal framework devolved political and administrative powers from the centre to local governments. There are five layers of local government referred to as local councils (LCs), ranging from LC1 (village level) to LC5 (district level). At the intermediate levels are parish level (LC2), sub-county level (LC3) and county level (LC4). The sub-county (LC3) and district (LC5) are the most important with regard to service delivery. Under the 1995 Constitution and the Local Governments Act, 1997, the LC5 and LC3 have full responsibility for the provision of most public services. They receive funds from the central government and donors to finance recurrent and development expenditures contained in their three-year development plans.

Central government transfers and donor funds account for over 90 per cent of most local government budgets. Less than 10 per cent of total budget is collected from local revenue sources. The central government, therefore, recognises that local government revenue mobilisation is vital for improving service delivery in a decentralised system. Although local revenues account for less than 10 per cent of total funds available to local governments, the central government contends that the potential for increase is substantial and within reach. G-tax, property tax, licenses, market and other fees, and a rural development charge are examples cited by government (Uganda 2002a: 23). Studies under the LGFC reveal several constraints to local revenue mobilisation, including limited capacity, the need to clarify the purposes of local revenue and political interference at local level that tends to undermine local revenue enhancement efforts.

Local tax collection distinguishes between collection of G-tax and other taxes. G-tax is collected by the sub-county chief, who serves as the accounting officer at that level, assisted by the parish chief at the parish level. In contrast, collection of the other taxes (market dues, business licences, park fees etc.) has been privatised in most local governments. The district sets base value for markets, parks and landing sites and invites tenders from interested companies or individuals. Evidence from a village census conducted in the same communities as the PPA2, indicated that in most cases tax collection by private individuals resulted in an increase in revenue collection. However, while most districts had data on their revenues, they had little idea on how much money was actually collected by the tender holder (Crommelynck 2002). The tender holders are in this business to make a profit and therefore have strong incentives to maximise the difference between actual collections and the reserve price that they need to remit to the local government revenue office. Most districts do not have reliable mechanisms for tracking how much tax revenue is actually collected. Ellis and Bahiigwa (2003) argue that the system is open to abuse. Collusion between members of the tender board and private collectors can result in low tax targets (hence a low reserve price for the market or landing site), and division of surpluses collected between the parties involved. Brown (2002) also noted the possibility of collusion in the tendering process in the fisheries sector.

In addition to these formal channels of local tax collection, rural households are subject to other forms of tax collection, especially informal fees and taxes. For example, in the fishing villages of Kamuli district, besides the private tender holder of the landing site, there is the *gabunga* (traditional caretaker of the landing site) to whom a daily informal tax has to be paid by all fishermen landing fish at the site. This can be cash payment or in kind (an agreed amount of fish). Then there is the fish guard, an employee of the Department of Fisheries Resources in the Ministry of Agriculture, Animal Industry and Fisheries (MAAIF). The fish guard collects a daily informal tax on fishermen. Failure to pay this tax may result in confiscation or destruction of fishing gear. The LADDER research findings on the institutional context of livelihoods showed that fishermen characterised government institutions such as the fisheries department as unhelpful in pursuit of their efforts to get out of poverty.

Rural taxes

There are three main categories of formal rural taxes: business taxes (licenses and fees), commodity taxes (market dues) and G-tax. Each category comprises several taxes depending on the type and size of business, type of commodity, location of the transaction, and the level of income of the taxpayer. There are other informal taxes particularly in the fishing communities of Kamuli district. Table 9.2 gives detailed information on the taxes that were encountered during interviews with the focus group discussion in the nine LADDER villages during the survey in 2001. G-tax is paid exclusively to the sub-county chief, assisted in collection by the parish chief. G-tax is a tax payable by all able males that are eighteen years and older as well as females that are gainfully employed or own a business. Unemployed adult women do not pay G-tax. As discussed earlier, G-tax has been found to be an unpopular tax by the taxpayers because it is regressive, costly to collect and difficult to assess. In Kidera sub-county, Kamuli district, it was reported that there has not been any assessment of G-tax assessment for over five years. The sub-county chief simply applied a percentage on the original assessment value to assess the tax levied on taxpayers. Given the dynamic nature of poverty in rural areas, it is likely that individuals who have become poorer over time would bear a higher tax burden with a percentage-based type of assessment than they would pay if regular and accurate assessment were carried out. Irregular and unfair G-tax assessments are some of the complaints made by taxpayers against this tax.

Virtually all economic activities in rural areas that involve monetary exchange are taxed. Non-farm business enterprises have to pay an annual license fee and sometimes daily, weekly or monthly fee to the tender holder of the market or landing site. This depends on whether the business owner sells in a fixed location such as a retail shop or a vendor that sells in various markets. Retail shop owners pay a fixed annual business license but do not pay daily fees. However, market vendors pay an annual licence equivalent to the retail shop business licence, however, in addition they have to pay market dues every time they sell in any market. All trading of crops and livestock

Table 9.2 Taxes and fees paid in rural Uganda in 2001

Category of tax	*Amount to pay*	*Comment or description*
Business licenses		*annual license fees paid to the sub-county chief or the parish tenderer*
shop	10,000–15,000/-	annual license fees are often supplemented by varying charges on throughput e.g. 200/- per customer, per guest, per day etc.
restaurant	8,000–13,000/-	
bar/drinking joint	5,000–11,000/-	
butchery	11,000–21,000/-	
lodging	20,000/-	
fishing boat	10,000/-	
fisheries dept levy	4,500/-	for application and painting license no. on boats (to fisheries dept)
fish smoking unit	5,000–20,000/-	varies according to size of unit
fish mongering	12,000/-	
distilling Waragi	6,000–15,000/-	plus 200/- per jerrican
drug shop	100,000/-	annual license
hair salon	5,500/-	annual license, plus 500/- per day to tender
Crop taxes		*collected by tenderer*
maize per 100 kg bag	500–1,000/-	varying rules on sales, purchase and market place taxes
millet per 100 kg bag	1,500–2,000/-	
tomatoes per box	500/-	
trading in markets	200–500/-	market fees per day (small amounts)
trading not in markets	100–200/-	roadside petty trading per day

Livestock taxes		*collected by tenderer unless otherwise specified*
market taxes per cow	2,000–3,000/-	varying split, seller and buyer
slaughter tax per cow	1,000–2,000/-	levied on person slaughtering
movement letter	1,000–2,000/-	levied by LC1 chair
movement permit	2,000–3,000/-	levied by the veterinary officer
market taxes per goat	200–500/-	varying split, seller and buyer
slaughter tax per goat	500/-	levied on person slaughtering
movement letter	200–500/-	levied by LC1 chair
movement permit	1,000/-	levied by the veterinary officer
Fish taxes		*collected by tenderer unless otherwise specified*
Formal		
fishermen per day	100–500/-	daily fishing tax, unrelated to catch
sales tax per bag	500–2,000/-	tax on dried *mukene*
market tax per bag	500–1,000/-	tax on dried *mukene*
fish guard monthly	4,000/-	paid by fish traders to fish guard for quality inspection
Informal		
gabunga levy per day	200–500/-	traditional payment to *gabunga*
fish guard daily	500/-	unofficial payment to fish guard

Source: Ellis and Bahiigwa (2003).

attracts taxes and fees, some of which are multiple and cumulative in their incidence on a single transaction (Ellis and Bahiigwa 2003).

Effects of rural taxation

Table 9.3 provides further insights into the effects of rural taxes on the poor by computing the ratio of market dues collected by tender holders to the respective market prices for crops, livestock and poultry. The table clearly illustrates the regressive nature of rural taxes on crops and livestock. The data show that larger quantities of crops (e.g. a bag) attract a proportionately lower tax that smaller quantities (e.g. a tin), even for the same commodity. For example, the market due on a bag of dry maize represents 3.33 per cent of the market price, compared to 7.50 per cent on a tin of dry maize. Similarly, the tax on a bag of sweet potatoes is 4.58 per cent of the market price while the tax on a tin of sweet potatoes is nearly 19 per cent. Such taxation is regressive because smaller quantities of products attract proportionately higher taxes than larger quantities of the same product. More importantly, poor producers with limited land are unlikely to produce and sell in large quantities, while better-off taxpayers are able to produce and sell larger volumes since they are not limited by land (Ellis and Bahiigwa 2003). Therefore, the taxation system hurts the poor more than the better-off taxpayers because the former can only produce and sell smaller volumes given their resource constraints.

The situation for livestock is similar to that for crops. As shown in the lower panel of Table 9.3, the larger and higher priced livestock, a cow, attracts just over 1 per cent in taxes (market dues), while smaller livestock,

Table 9.3 Crop and livestock market dues in Kamuli, 2001

Crops	*Unit*	*Tax*	*Price*	*Tax as % of price*
Beans	Bag	1,000	38,300	2.61
Cassava	Bag	500	16,250	3.08
Maize (dry)	Bag	500	15,000	3.33
Potatoes	Bag	500	10,912	4.58
Millet	Tin	300	5,750	5.22
Groundnuts (unshelled)	Bag	1,000	18,000	5.56
Millet	Bag	1,000	14,000	7.14
Maize (dry)	Tin	200	2,667	7.50
Groundnuts (unshelled)	Tin	500	5,000	10.00
Potatoes	Tin	300	1,617	18.55
Livestock				
Cow	Animal	2,000	180,000	1.11
Pig	Animal	1,000	24,750	4.04
Goat	Animal	1,000	18,500	5.41
Duck	Bird	300	3,090	9.71
Chicken	Bird	300	2,526	11.88

Source: Finance Department, Kamuli District Local Government Offices, 2001.

such as a goat, attracts 5.4 per cent of its market price. The smallest and lowest priced poultry, a chicken, attracts almost 12 per cent of its market price in taxes. Again, the poor households are the most likely to sell chicken because they have the least amount of livestock (Ellis and Bahiigwa 2003). Market dues for livestock and poultry are also regressive and are more inequitable when compared to crops when one considers the tax rate differential between small and large livestock.

Unlike crops, larger livestock (cattle, goats and pigs) attract other fees besides market dues. These include movement permits issued by the LC1 chairperson, certifying ownership of the animal and another issued by the veterinary officer, certifying origin of the animal. The magnitude of these taxes and their incidence is illustrated using data collected from Kiribairya village in Kamuli District (Table 9.4). The incidence of taxation is similar to that in Table 9.3 when other livestock taxes are included. Still, cows attract a lower proportion of tax than the smaller livestock such as goats and chicken that are more likely to be owned by poor farmers in rural areas.

In Kiribairya, a fishing village, market dues were collected for two types of fish, the larger Nile Perch (sold by the kilogram) and the smaller Tilapia (sold as heaps of between two and five fish depending on size). Similar to livestock and crops, the larger fish attracted a proportionately lower tax than the smaller fish. This also has poverty implications because the nets for catching Nile Perch are more expensive and therefore owned by richer individuals. Yet, larger fish caught attracts a lower tax than for the poorer individuals that can only afford the nets for the smaller Tilapia fish.

Besides the poverty effects of these taxes, they are also distortionary in nature and may affect resource allocation by farmers, especially regarding crop choice and ultimately land, labour and other productive resources. For example, in Table 9.3, both cassava and potatoes are fresh perishable

Table 9.4 Livestock, crop and fish taxes in Kiribairya village

Livestock	*Unit*	*Price (Sh)*	*LC1 permit*	*Veterinary permit*	*Market dues*	*Total taxes*	*Tax share (%)*
Cattle	Animal	150,000	1,000	2,000	1,000	4,000	2.7
Pig	Animal	35,000	1,000	1,000	None	2,000	5.7
Chicken	Bird	3,000	None	None	200	200	6.7
Goat	Animal	20,000	500	1,000	500	2,000	10.0
Crops							
Millet	Bag	50,000	None	None	2,000	2,000	4.0
Maize (dry)	Bag	25,000	None	None	1,000	1,000	4.0
Tomatoes	Box	6,500	None	None	300	300	4.6
Fish							
Nile Perch	Kg	1,400	None	None	50	50	3.6
Tilapia	Bundle	1,000	None	None	50	50	5.0

Source: Rural Taxation Survey, March 2003.

foodstuffs, yet a bag of fresh cassava attracts a tax of about 3 per cent while a bag of fresh potatoes is charged about 4.6 per cent. If such a tax rate differential persists over time, farmers may opt to produce more cassava (which attracts a lower tax) than potatoes, yet consumers may demand more potatoes. The end result is loss of welfare to society. Such distortionary characteristics of the existing tax regime ought to be avoided.

These findings for crops, livestock and fish are not compatible with the objectives of the PMA to promote increased market participation of the poor small-scale farmers and fishermen. Embedded within the current rural taxation system are hidden disincentives to production and market participation, particularly for smaller producers. Well-functioning markets ought to send positive signals to producers of commodities that are traded. It is conceivable that current participation in markets by small-scale farmers and fishermen may be the result of distress sales due to the need for cash to meet pressing household expenses rather than a response to incentives created by marketing institutions or government policy. The PMA seeks to re-orient subsistence farmers from producing predominantly for household consumption to producing for the market (Uganda 2000d). This means that the PMA has to create an environment that makes the re-orientation possible. Certainly, a rural taxation system that is regressive and hurts more the poor scale producers (the target of the PMA), does not constitute an appropriate environment that would bring about the desired transformation from subsistence to market-oriented agriculture.

An assessment of the G-tax for Kamuli district also reveals the regressive nature of this tax. In August 2001, the Minister of Local Government issued the G-tax schedule with twenty-two income brackets with their respective levels of G-tax for taxpayers falling within that income bracket. Local governments are supposed to simply implement this without changing the number of income brackets and the associated G-tax level. The responsibility of local governments is to assess the income of taxpayers in order to determine who falls within what income bracket, and the resulting level of G-tax to be paid. Table 9.5 shows the share of G-tax in per capita income reveals the regressive nature of G-tax. The lowest decile of tax payers paid almost 9 per cent of per capita income while the highest decile paid about 5 per cent of their per capita income. Again the incidence of taxation falls more heavily on low-income earners than better off individuals. A progressive system of G-tax would be one in which richer individuals pay a proportionately higher share of their income than poorer taxpayers.

The LADDER household data for the three districts (Mbale, Kamuli and Mubende) were used to assess the impact of G-tax on the taxpayer. The regressive nature of G-tax is further demonstrated in Figure 9.1. The U-shaped curve is consistent for all the three districts. In all the three districts, the taxpayers in the lowest quintile paid a higher proportion of their per capita income in G-tax (6.8 to 7.3 per cent) while, for the highest quintile, the share ranges from 5.2 per cent to 5.9 per cent of per capita income. Here

Table 9.5 Per capita income and graduated taxes for Kamuli, 2001

Decile	*Per capita income (Sh)*	*Average G-tax (Sh)*	*G-tax share (%)*
1	46,557	3,454	8.63
2	97,680	5,917	6.05
3	142,887	7,467	5.24
4	197,874	8,846	4.48
5	279,217	11,750	4.22
6	345,683	15,000	4.34
7	434,563	18,400	4.24
8	558,296	28,182	5.04
9	851,744	50,000	5.81
10	3,124,791	91,538	4.79

Sources: Finance Department, Kamuli District Local Government Offices, 2001; Mims and Mathieu (2002).

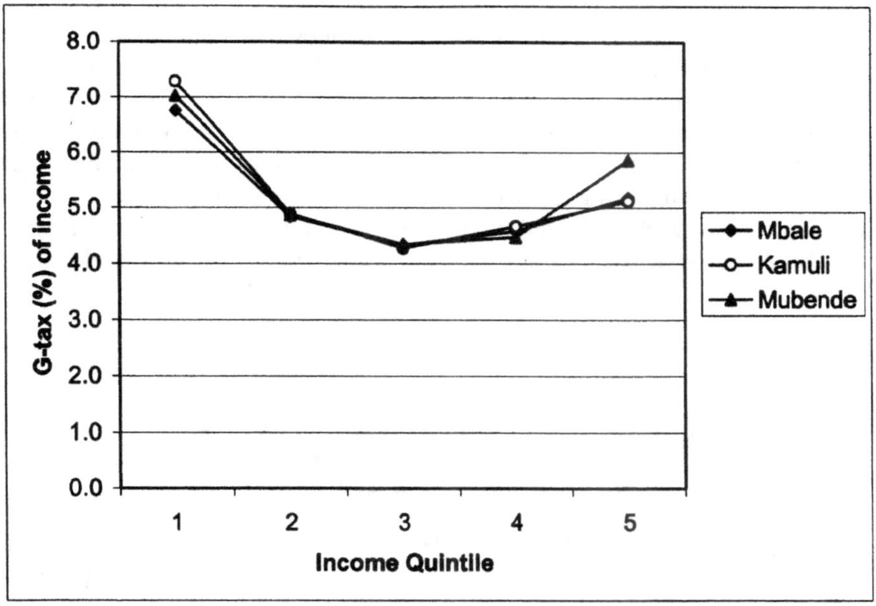

Figure 9.1 Share of G-tax in per capita income (source: sample survey carried out in nine villages, January to March 2001; Uganda (2001b).)

also the incidence of taxation is lower for the better-off individuals. However, the taxpayers in the third quintile pay proportionately lower G-tax (4.3 per cent for all three districts) than the lowest and highest quintiles, hence giving the curves an approximate U-shape.

In fact, the G-tax schedule from the Ministry of Local Government in August 2001 itself reflects the regressiveness and is U-shaped as Figure 9.2 illustrates.

In March 2002, the Ministry of Local Government issued a more progressive G-tax schedule (Figure 9.2) with seventeen tax bands, down from twenty-two in August 2001. However, in practice, it is regressive because after the 2001 presidential elections, most taxpayers opted to pay the minimum Ush 3,000 arguing that the president had already assessment them. For example in Butiru sub-county (Mbale district), almost all taxpayers in 2002/2003 fiscal year paid a flat rate of Ush 3,000. Using the G-tax schedule, this translates in 5 per cent for the lowest income bracket but only 0.25 of the highest (rich) income bracket.

Another aspect of local taxation that is briefly discussed is the local government–citizen relationship. It is common for taxpayers to complain about levels of taxes, but one would expect effective and efficient service delivery in return for taxes paid. Given the decentralised nature of government in Uganda, taxpayers ought to see the benefits of paying taxes reflected in the manner in which the local governments address the needs that are identified by the community and reflected in local government plans. The lowest local government, the village council (LC1), is supposed to get 25 per cent of locally generated revenue that is retained at the sub-county level (LC3), while the sub-county level itself retains 65 per cent of locally generated revenue.[3] Citizens within an LC1 should, therefore, be able to visibly see the benefits of their taxes in the form of service provision or investments made by their LC1 council in accordance with community needs. However, available evidence suggests a mixed picture, with some local governments receiving the 25 per cent without any problem while others find it difficult to get

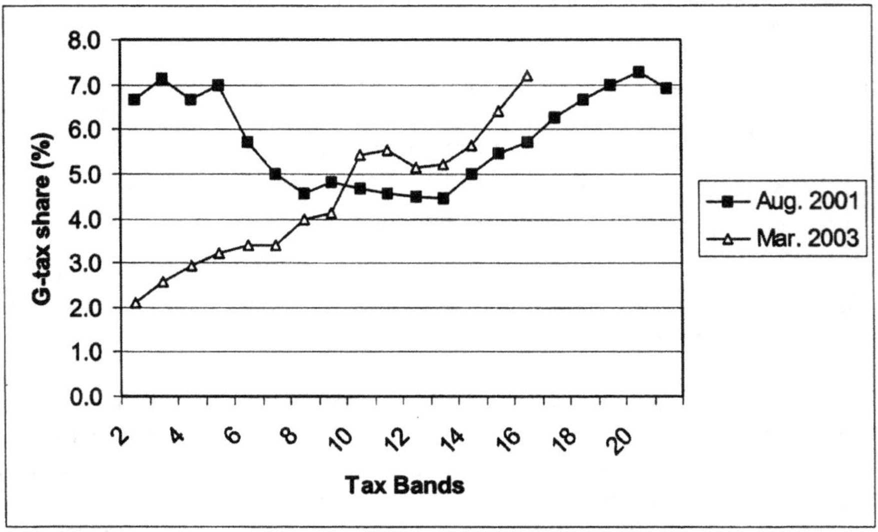

Figure 9.2 G-tax schedule for August 2001 and March 2002 (source: Uganda (2001b, 2002b).)

their share from the sub-counties. This is a subject that needs further analysis that is beyond the scope of this chapter.

Policy implications of rural taxation

This chapter has clearly demonstrated that the current tax system comprising G-tax, licenses and market dues hurts the poor more than it does the better-off individuals. The revenue generated from local revenue collection accounts for less than 10 per cent of the total district revenue, yet such taxation could stifle growth of small business enterprises and agricultural production. It seems that local governments, through the private tender system, exert a lot of undue pressure on rural economic activities, especially the small-scale producers. It is quite understandable that local governments must raise their own revenue and increasingly become less dependent on central government transfers. However, this implies that a balance has to be struck between the need to generate revenue and the responsibility of government to create an enabling environment for productive activities and small business enterprises to flourish. While government policy documents (e.g. PEAP and PMA) state that the role of government is to create an enabling policy environment, in practice this does not seem to be the case with the existing local taxation system. Stimulating economic growth should be an explicit objective of local governments, for without economic growth, tax revenue cannot grow either.

Locally generated revenue forms a small proportion of the total district budget. The pressure exerted on local taxpayers, especially on small businesses and agricultural products could be eased without substantially affecting the operations of the districts. It should be possible to exempt taxation on certain businesses, especially the very small ones and those at the start-up stage, to allow them grow into more vibrant businesses that would yield greater revenue in the future. The same principle could be applied to taxation of agricultural products brought for sale in markets. Otherwise, growth in rural enterprises will be stifled and the benefits that could accrue from growth (e.g. employment and higher future tax revenue) will not be realised. The debate, therefore, should focus on the trade-off between foregoing current revenue generation and fulfilling the government's role of creating an enabling policy environment for poor people to create and accumulate wealth.

Notes

* This chapter reflects LADDER research as well as the DFID-funded Uganda Rural Taxation study undertaken by a team led by the author in 2003.

1 The Local Governments Act, 1997 (Fifth Schedule, Article 2 (1)) provides that every district or urban local council shall levy an annual tax to be known as graduated tax:

a on every male person of, or above the apparent age of 18 years...;
b on female persons of or above the apparent age of 18 years engaged in any gainful employment or business (Uganda 2001c).

2 The data were collected under the Livelihoods and Diversification Directions Explored by Research (LADDER) project. LADDER was funded by DFID and the objective was to identify alternative routes by which the rural poor can climb out of poverty. LADDER worked in thirty-seven villages and 1,345 households in Uganda, Tanzania, Malawi and Kenya. The Ugandan component was a collaborative effort between the Overseas Development Group (ODG) of the University of East Anglia (UK) and the Economic Policy Research Center (EPRC), Kampala, Uganda.

3 The Local Governments Act, 1997 (Fifth Schedule, Article 15 (c)) provides that of the 65 per cent of the local revenue retained at the sub-county, 25 per cent of the 65 per cent shall be distributed amongst the village councils (LC1) (Uganda 2001c).

10 Marketing reform?

The rise and fall of agricultural liberalisation in Tanzania*

Brian Cooksey

Introduction

This chapter offers a critical interpretation of the dominant narrative of the liberalisation of Tanzanian agriculture over the last decade and a half. This narrative seriously exaggerates the extent to which market liberalisation has been implemented for Tanzania's main export crops, fails to recognise the powerful anti-liberalisation forces within Tanzanian society, and has yet to acknowledge the recent recrudescence of statist legislation, policies and practices. On the other hand there has been a significant and sustained liberalisation of the markets for maize and other grains and internal markets for these crops and other locally consumed foodstuffs are relatively efficient and competitive.

The chapter briefly describes the nature of market liberalisation using the examples of maize and coffee, and includes an analysis of the liberalisation of trade in fertiliser. In the case of coffee, an initial surge in private sector input supply and crop buying after 1993–1994 was followed by the partial recovery of cooperative unions, and the re-emergence of crop boards as major actors in the market place.

The present official policy discourse is of a shared neo-liberal vision, based on strong local ownership and joint funding of a set of pro-poor policies and programmes, linked to long-term debt relief. Past failures of structural adjustment have been the rule in Africa, of course, but currently Tanzania is being touted as a star performer in the Poverty Reduction Strategy stakes, having reached the Heavily Indebted Poor Country (HIPC) 'completion point' ahead of the field, and remaining well 'on track' for most of the key indicators of success.

Yet the 'second generation' reforms for export crop liberalisation in particular, have been hotly resisted by significant players in 'the system' who feel that there has been enough externally-driven liberalisation and are determined to revert to a more interventionist model of public policy.[1] Examples of this trend include:

1 the re-empowerment of export crop boards that tax traders and exports (and therefore farmers) and regulate markets in which they are active commercial players;

2 the arbitrary and sometimes oppressive treatment of farmers by local government authorities, *inter alia*, through taxation;
3 the proliferation of sector policies and strategies that privilege the state as initiators rather than facilitators at central and local levels, notably through the vehicle of foreign aid-funded projects;[2]
4 the continued practice of state-guaranteed bank lending to certain cooperative unions. These neo-statist trends are the main focus of this chapter.

Currently, there is a growing gap between the market-friendly rhetoric of official government policy statements and the market unfriendly behaviour (official and unofficial) of key state functionaries and the political class. I argue that state failure – defined as the limited capacity of central and local governments, as a result of patronage, cronyism and related inefficiencies, to implement coherent policies that are in the public interest – contributes much more than is currently acknowledged in the literature to the lack of dynamism and accumulation in the agricultural sector.

Lastly, the chapter is not an apologia for 'more and better' market liberalisation, let alone deregulation, but a critique of the view that liberalisation has taken root in both local and export markets, and that the consolidation of the market economy is just a matter of time. The re-empowerment of state agencies described below does not protect the poor against the depredations of corporate capitalism: on the contrary, it threatens to disempower and impoverish them even further.

The following section summarises the trajectory of Tanzanian agricultural liberalisation to date. I describe the declining fortunes of cooperative unions and concurrent changes in the organisation of input and output markets, taking maize, coffee and tobacco as examples. I then discuss the form and function of the emerging marketing boards in export crops, with examples from coffee, tobacco and sugar. The final section deals with the nature of the aid relationship, and the tension between the old-style conditionality approach to sector support and the current 'post-conditionality' (Ponte 2002a) aid regime based on local ownership.

Market liberalisation in theory and practice

Tanzania's capitulation to structural adjustment after a protracted stand-off with the Bretton Woods institutions in the early 1980s is usually seen as the end of President Julius Nyerere's socialist experiment and the beginning of a gradual and still incomplete transition to a market economy. In the last fifteen years, Tanzania has indeed taken a number of steps towards a market, that is, capitalist, economy, as summarised below. Over such a short period, it would be surprising indeed if anything like a full transition to a market economy could be achieved. Yet both government and donor discourses see the transition as largely complete.

The post-1985 economic reform measures notched up a number of major achievements. Devaluation removed the downward pressure on farm incomes caused by an overvalued exchange rate. Import liberalisation made basic consumer goods available after years of shortages. The monopoly of state trading companies and cooperative unions was broken for both export crops and maize, and most agricultural markets now involve significant local and international players, with varying degrees of competition. Broadly, denationalised banks now decide what to do with their money (some provide crop finance) rather than take orders from the government. Partly as a result of the above, inflation has been reduced from over 30 per cent a year up to the early 1990s to single digit levels since 1999 (Tanzania 2001a).

The gradual liberalisation of Tanzanian agricultural input and output markets brought to an end two decades of state control that had seen the successful growth of the internal maize market, large falls in traditional export crop production and a consequent increase in subsistence and rural poverty. The 'deconfinement' of domestic food crop marketing after 1986 saw the successful replacement of the National Milling Corporation monopoly by private traders and the end of 'pan-territorial' pricing. Gradually, all crops were liberalised and the role of parastatal crop authorities reduced, although the process was patchy and incomplete, as shown below. From 1991, fertiliser subsidies were phased out and markets were opened to private traders.

To illustrate the above themes, I present brief case studies of market liberalisation for maize and coffee. The importance of fertiliser liberalisation is highlighted for maize.

Maize and fertiliser

Maize has been one of the success stories of agricultural liberalisation in Tanzania. The withdrawal of subsidies from basic staples such as maize can spark off riots among the urban poor. The liberalisation of maize markets in Tanzania did not have this effect: in general the availability of maize has kept pace with demand.[3] Bad years reflect the failure of rains, not markets, and there has not been a major famine, or tendency to rely on food aid. This 'success story' is generally explained by the de facto liberalisation of grain supplies in the pre-reform period. In effect, the monopoly grain purchasing parastatal the National Milling Corporation had been gradually supplemented, even surpassed, by the private sector in the pre-liberalisation period. 'Liberalisation' simply legalised the existing 'parallel' grain trade.

Although maize production has continued to expand steadily, returns to farmers have been badly hit by the increased price of farm inputs (discussed below) and a fall in prices since the early 1990s. Also, the removal of pan-territorial prices led to a decline in marketed production in three of the main maize growing regions (Mbeya, Ruvuma and Rukwa) and an increase in Iringa, which is nearer Dar es Salaam (Delgado and Minot 2000: 53).

The liberalisation of maize markets needs to be seen in relation to the liberalisation of farm inputs, the most important of which is chemical fertiliser.

The dominant 'liberalisation' narrative contrasts a period of relatively successful fertiliser supply to 'smallholders' with a subsequent period of 'market failure' as a result of liberalisation and the removal of subsidies. This chapter argues that the majority of subsidised fertiliser users were probably 'large', not smallholders, and that in all events the use of fertiliser was probably so inefficient that it had a relatively minor impact on yields. Even in a context of efficient markets (which were never put in place) the mass of small farmers would not have profited from systematic inorganic fertiliser use.

Prior to the mid-1990s, fertiliser importation and distribution was in the hands of the Tanzania Fertiliser Company, financed by state-owned banks. Most fertiliser was supplied as commodity aid. The dominant narrative argues that, although supplies were erratic and insufficient and distribution costly and inefficient, state agencies still managed to deliver subsidised fertiliser to smallholders and, through pan-territorial transport pricing regimes, even smallholders in relatively remote areas could afford to grow crops, particularly maize, for urban markets.

The dominant narrative also maintains that, with the removal of state monopolies and the arrival of private-sector input distributors, including multinational seed/food companies, fertiliser procurement and distribution became more efficient, but the removal of subsidies led to a large increase in the relative price of fertiliser (and other inputs) and many farmers were driven back towards subsistence, or alternative crops (Delgado and Minot 2000: Chapter 2)

This mainstream narrative obscures as much as it explains. First, at the height of fertiliser importation, only one Tanzanian farmer in seven was using imported fertiliser.[4] It is likely that a disproportionate amount of fertiliser was consumed by a relatively small group of 'rich' farmers. This group is the main loser from liberalisation. Second, of course, fertiliser is used on a relatively narrow range of crops and locations – principally, maize (Southern Highlands), coffee (Kilimanjaro) and tobacco (Tabora). So we should be careful not to put all farmers in the same geographical baskets. Also, there is evidence that the supply of inputs on credit through cooperative unions was under stress before the liberalisation of fertiliser took place. In the late 1980s the Cooperative and Rural Development Bank was withdrawing credit from cooperatives that were not paying back their loans.[5]

One source estimates that fertiliser use accounted for half a million tonnes of cereals in the early 1990s (Utne *et al.* 1994: 3). The end of subsidies saw fertiliser consumption fall by 50 per cent. The impact on maize production and sales should therefore have been significant. Yet the most thorough quantitative study to date concludes that 'the impact on national maize production [of declining fertiliser use] has been modest (less than 5 per cent)'. This can be explained in terms of:

> a) low initial use of fertiliser on food crops in a national context; b) calculations using the physical response of maize to fertiliser, c) the absence

> of measurable reductions in maize yields, and d) the statistical insignificance of fertiliser price in econometric estimation of maize supply.
>
> (Delgado and Minot 2000)

Confirmation that the fertiliser issue has been overblown lies in the continued relatively robust supply of maize on local markets. Despite the removal of subsidies and falling producer prices after 1993, there was no leap in urban consumer prices of maize or shortfall in supply. The IFPRI (Delgado and Minot 2000) conclusion is that the effective demand for maize (relatively income inelastic) is a bigger constraint than the costs of production.

It is most probable that the majority of Tanzanian maize farmers could not profitably use chemical fertilisers, even if they were available in the right quantities at the right time, if they had to pay 'market' prices for them.

Fertiliser subsidies were gradually removed from 1990 onwards. As prices rose, consumption fell. The Ministry of Agriculture introduced a fund for private companies to supply fertiliser.

> In 1993–4, the subsidy was made available to private importers, resulting in a massive over-supply of fertiliser. Eight importers, some of them with little experience and no storage facilities, imported a total of 227,000 tons, equivalent to a 2–3 year's supply. This . . . resulted in unsold stocks, large losses, and reduced orders in subsequent years.
>
> (Delgado and Minot 2000: 39)

'Senior Government officials and parliamentarians who borrowed over three billion shillings from the Agriculture Trust Fund have defaulted in paying back the loans, hampering smooth operation of the Fund' (Mwondoshah 1998). Furthermore: 'Out of Shs 5.5 billion outstanding [in the Agriculture Trust Fund] an amount of Shs 737 million only has been repaid. A total balance of Shs 4.8 billion (US$5.3) is still outstanding' (Mwakalebela 2001). Indeed: 'This serious laxity will defeat achieving the objectives of the [fund]' (Tanzania 2001a: 175).

The apparent fixation with fertiliser probably has more to do with supplier and large farm pressures bearing a 'modern farming' ideology than with any objective 'needs' of Tanzanian farmers and farming systems.[6] Organic products enjoy a significant price premium in international markets, and the advantages of low-cost, low-input farming for most tropical small-holders are relatively clear. Yet the government's draft fertiliser policy is designed: '[T]o ensure that fertilisers are available to all farmers, particularly smallholders, to the required quantity as well as product-mix at a time needed, and at a reasonable price.' Importation and marketing systems are to be 'streamlined, competitive and efficient' in order to assure fertiliser supplies 'in all villages of the country'.[7]

Export crops and coffee

The various export crops are characterised by different (and changing) private-cooperative arrangements and generalisations on the 'impact of liberalisation' need to be qualified. Liberalisation has led to a sometimes drastic fall in the role of cooperatives in input and output markets. Cashew nut marketing, for example, is 90 per cent privately run (Chachage and Nyoni 2001).

The liberalisation of coffee marketing offers one example of liberalisation in practice. After market liberalisation, both Arusha Cooperative Union (ACU) and Kilimanjaro Native Cooperative Union (KNCU) lost market share to private traders. Liberalisation has spawned a number of new marketing arrangements, some potentially advantageous to producers, some favouring the trade. For example, in Arusha mini coffee auctions at primary society premises force unions and private buyers to compete. When coffee prices are high, private buyers buy more than the union, and vice versa when prices are low. Some new societies ('development groups') take their members' coffee direct to the Moshi coffee auction, thereby cutting out the middleman. As a result 50 per cent better prices have been recorded.

Despite these improvements, the collapse of coffee prices on the international market make coffee a relatively uncompetitive crop: farmers have seen prices fall from Shs 1,000 in 1995 to Shs 200 in 2000. In this context, the old cooperatives provide some protection to producers as 'buyer of last resort'. Competition should make unions more efficient, but 'the old structures are hard to change. MPs and union leaders are strong people and wish to remain that way', as commented in a focus group (Chambo and Cooksey 2000).

In Kagera, with market liberalisation, a number of trading companies were registered to buy coffee from primary societies. As in Kilimanjaro and Arusha, the initial response of farmers was to sell to these private traders. In 1998, all private trading licences were withdrawn and KCU was re-awarded a monopoly buying role. But, with no cash, prices slumped to Shs 200 per kilo, and farmers were given promissory notes rather than cash. Farmers either left their coffee untended or sold to smugglers, thus boosting the Ugandan coffee market.

KCU has long been the victim of factionalism and the use of state power to prevent the break-up of the union. In one well documented union election, the cooperative committee (the governing body) was only re-elected with the presence of the regional police chief and the Field Force Unit (who were mobilised outside the meeting venue) to prevent their ouster by members and an alternative leadership who were campaigning against years of politically sanctioned corruption and mismanagement by the union leadership.[8]

When new major players enter a previously controlled market, conflicts are inevitable. When the new players are foreign multinationals or their agents, and the markets they enter were previously controlled by crop marketing boards and cooperatives, the conflicts are likely to be intense. The advantages of the old system – relative producer price stability, the supply of inputs on credit – were sustained by the insolvency of cooperatives and boards, ultimately underwritten by the tax payer and inflationary banking practices. Take away these props, and the producer becomes vulnerable to both the vagaries of the market[9] and the continued operation of boards and cooperative unions seeking new ways of surviving. Add the enhanced revenue collection powers enjoyed by local government authorities under decentralisation policy, and the result is a three-way squeeze on the producer. The market is not so much liberalised as chaotic.

Although liberalisation is supposed to lead to healthy competition between crop purchasers to the benefit of farmers, in practice, cooperative unions have been fighting a rearguard action to survive as they have been exposed to the rigours of an incipient market economy, for which they were ill-equipped.

For more than a decade, cooperative policy has been based on the principles of voluntary membership and economic viability. Official policy is 'to encourage liberalisation of the cooperatives in line with the current state of affairs'(Tanzania 2001b: 6). Initial attempts by some farmers to operate independently outside the union structure often led to hostile responses from the unions – both new and old – who fall back on the old system of political patronage, including presidential interventions, to force recalcitrant farmers back into line.

Why did marketing reforms succeed for maize, but produced mixed but overall unimpressive results for export crops? An obvious explanation is that the price of maize – the food staple of the urban poor – is too important politically to be left to the mercies of marketing board and cooperative lobbyists. This political imperative does not apply to export crops, where national-local patronage politics and systematic rent-seeking can be more easily accommodated.[10]

The 'new' form and function of state marketing boards

In theory, marketing boards have been stripped of their former powers as 'crop authorities'. Prior to formal liberalisation in the early 1990s, crop authorities oversaw the production, marketing and export of Tanzania's main export crops. These authorities have been replaced by crop boards with radically reduced mandates. In theory, they are responsible for market regulation, including issuing trading licences to private crop buyers and assuring competition and quality control, but not for crop financing or marketing. In practice, the picture is much less clear. Crucially, boards continue to be players as well as regulators, and enjoy formal powers over producers and middlemen that far exceed simple regulatory functions.

In 2001, Bills were presented to the National Assembly to establish the Tanzania Coffee Board and Tanzania Tobacco Board (Lumbanga 2001a, 2001b). A Sugar Bill was also passed during the June 2001 budget session. For coffee: 'The object[ive] of this Bill is to review the law governing the coffee sector . . . so as to provide for the liberalisation of trade in the coffee industry' (Lumbanga 2001a). The boards for the three sectors are responsible for registering and licensing growers, buyers and exporters, as well as for regulation:

> The Board may, subject to approval of the Minister [of Agriculture and Food Security] on specified terms and conditions [,] *perform any commercial activity or hold interest in any undertaking, enterprise or project associated with the coffee industry.*
>
> (Lumbanga 2001a: 6, emphasis added)

According to PART III of the Acts, it is illegal for a farmer or group of farmers to grow coffee, tobacco or sugar (as outgrowers) without the permission of the Boards. Boards will keep and update a register of all growers. All seeds, plants and varieties require prior approval by the relevant director of the Ministry. Penalties for contravening these conditions range from one hundred thousand shillings ($107) for coffee to one million shillings ($1,060) for tobacco and ten million shillings ($10,695) for sugar or prison sentences of up to two years in all cases, or both. For tobacco: 'Any seeds or plants imported, bred or multiplied without the authority of the Director shall be destroyed by the Board at the expense of the offender.' (Lumbanga 2001b: 73). The registration of a new tobacco processing factory (section 14) has a total of eighteen conditions.

Boards are to be funded from (a) money voted by parliament; (b) loans, donations or grants; (c) cess or levy 'imposed under the provision of this Act'; (d) 'any loan or subsidy granted to the Board by the Government or any other person'; (e) other money or property 'which may become payable . . .' Lumbanga 2001b: 79–80.

An industry development fund will be created, financed by a levy 'determined by the Minister for this purpose', to pay for research and development, extension, technology, consultancy and other activities. The Board of Directors of the Coffee Board consists of seven members, four of whom are direct appointees of the Minister. Similar changes to those for coffee and tobacco are proposed for the sugar industry (Lumbanga 2001a, b, c).

It appears that these unbelievably restrictive pieces of legislation and others to follow empower the Minister of Agriculture to make the boards do essentially what he wants them to. The Bills draw no distinction between the boards' regulatory role and the right to enter the market as a commercial actor. Rather than facilitating private initiative, the state sets out with a disposition to control almost all aspects of crop development, with the criminalisation of unauthorised activities as the ultimate sanction. The Boards are funded through virtual taxes in the shape of export levies and annually renewable crop purchasing fees payable by buyers and passed on to farmers. Finally, the composition of the boards is so structured as to give a majority of voting rights to government appointees as opposed to representatives of producers or commercial interests.

The unambiguous statist thrust in the three Bills reflects a consensus among the political class that market liberalisation is no longer a viable policy option. If different degrees of competition have been introduced in export crop markets, it might be that they have been bought via conditionality rather than promoted by strategically placed reformists inside the system. Certainly a $200 million agricultural sectoral adjustment loan in 1990 might have bought a certain degree of market liberalisation, helped on by the virtual withdrawal of the banking sector from agricultural finance (Robert 2002).

We may contrast the Bills summarised above with the proposed policy regarding crop boards. According to the Agricultural Sector Development Strategy (Tanzania 2001d: 51):

> *(d) Providing Legal Empowerment for Stakeholders to Control Commodity Boards*
> Currently the commodity boards are owned and controlled by the Government. Autonomous commodity boards, controlled by the stakeholders, will exert more accountability to members (sic) to produce quality outputs and to adhere to the use and recommended technologies and practices. The Ministry of Cooperatives and Marketing (MCM) will accordingly restructure the commodity boards in close consultation with the stakeholders. The boards will be responsible for self-regulating the industries under their jurisdiction, while Government will enforce the legislation.

The 'real politics' of agriculture make this proposed 'restructuring' unlikely. For example:

> there seem to be very few agents of change within the Government . . . In fact, conservative voices are likely to come back as indicated by the unexpected reshuffle of the crop boards . . . More politicised boards with limited private sector participation are likely to exercise greater control over the sector rather than promote its liberalisation.[11]

This move was linked to the October 2000 presidential and parliamentary elections, which brought back President Mkapa for a second term with a large majority of parliamentary seats.

There are some local private sector actors who are privileged by 'the system', provided they play according to the rules of patronage, including political patronage. Local and foreign companies who attempt to distance themselves from institutions of patronage and cronyism may find it difficult to survive: some withdraw from the market, others are thrown out by the existing boards. To be sure, there are enough examples of private middlemen setting up buying cartels, cheating with weighing and grading, avoiding paying taxes and so on, to lend credence to the argument that 'greedy' and 'unscrupulous' businessmen need to be closely regulated in the interest of farmers. The problem, of course, is that the boards are no strangers to the same 'greed' and lack of scruple that typify the private sector in the official (statist) discourse.

Different constellations of actors characterise different crops. Liberalisation opened opportunities for both local traders and agro-processors (mostly Asian companies) and foreign investors. For example, the country's main sugar estates were recently taken over by South African investors. In 2000, the Minister of Industry and Trade granted import licences for large amounts of 'industrial' sugar (which pays zero import duty), little of which was for industrial purposes. The estates consequently ended up with huge stockpiles of unsold sugar. The minister was forced to resign as a result of the ensuing scandal. The granting of import licences is now in the hands of the Minister of Agriculture and Food Security.

On the other hand, the 'gunny bag' saga described by Chachage demonstrates how an influential local company can manipulate policy to its own advantage. Mohamed Enterprises own a sisal bag factory in Morogoro and, in late 1999, just as the cashew buying season was about to begin, the Cashewnut Board ordered that all cashew nuts were to be packed in sisal bags rather than the (much cheaper) jute bags from Bangladesh. Although the announcement was illegal (and was finally reversed by the Minister of Agriculture), duty on jute bags was increased by an amendment of the relevant act of parliament.[12]

Although formally the government claims that its role is regulatory rather than commercial, it fails to make the distinction in practice. To cite one example of the official confusion of regulatory and commercial roles, under 'support for the rural sector' the PRSP Progress Report 2000/2001 contains the following list of government achievements:

> facilitation of crop credit, intensified search for export markets, revival of agro-processing plants, rationalisation of local government taxation of crops and livestock, further liberalisation of internal and cross-border agricultural trade, and distribution of disease-resistant seedlings.
>
> (Tanzania 2001c: 12)

A more comprehensive political economy of the agricultural sector in Tanzania would need to include the incidence and impact of local taxation. As well as being squeezed by rising input costs and low output market prices, farmers are also at the mercy of local governments' revenue raising strategies.[13] Fiscal decentralisation is intended to enhance local councils' capacity to finance development activities not funded through transfers from Dar es Salaam. In practice, local revenue collection is unfair, inefficient, misused by councils, leads to evasion and bribery and constitutes a disincentive to commercial enterprise (Kobb 2001).

Donor aid to agriculture in Tanzania

With their continued proliferation of projects, and total current commitments of US$500 million in agriculture and related fields, aid donors are major, yet understated, players in Tanzanian agriculture. More than half the current agricultural aid portfolio consists of loans from the World Bank and IFAD. In the past, aid projects failed to provide significant and sustained benefits to farmers. Without major changes in aid modalities, it is debatable whether current projects will fare any better than their predecessors (Cooksey 2001). Aid helps justify the continued deployment of cadres that have consistently failed to deliver significant benefits to farmers. Many activities – research, extension, irrigation, livestock trade, food security – have been 'projectised' over many years. They still function poorly (or not at all), suggesting that donors aid delivery processes are failing to address key issues and are not assimilating lessons from past failures. Two issues are of particular interest: the effectiveness of projects as an aid modality and the effectiveness of conditionality as a means of leveraging reform.

Projects versus programme aid

Under PRSP, overall aid to Tanzania is negotiated within a framework emphasising local ownership of an agreed programme, with enhanced reporting and coordination of donor activities. There is pressure from certain donor agencies, supported by the government, to move away from the project mode towards 'sector-wide' approaches involving basket budgetary support.

The World Bank group's investment portfolio is based on the Country Assistance Strategy (CAS) (World Bank 2000c). The current strategy (2001–2003) mentions donor coordination as a area in which 'the Bank can help remove inefficiencies of fragmented and parallel aid delivery systems by encouraging other donors to assist the government in its efforts to increase selectivity, coherence, and harmonisation of donor resources' (ibid: 21). Bilaterals and international NGOs often tend to see the World Bank as pushing its own agenda at the expense of coordination and selectivity. This was one of the criticisms of the Bank's proposed SOFRAIP, mentioned below.

Strategy proliferation

Critics have frequently commented on the proliferation of uncoordinated projects in various sectors (Therkildsen 2000). The proliferation of sector strategies is a more recent phenomenon, so far without a critical literature. A jointly agreed programme of support to the agricultural sector is currently in preparation. The Agriculture Sector Development Strategy (ASDS) covers agriculture and (up to a point) livestock issues, but ministerial responsibilities for these and related sectors are fragmented, requiring further coordination.

After his re-election in 2000, President Mkapa split the Ministry of Agriculture and Cooperatives, creating a new Ministry of Agriculture and Food Security and a new Ministry of Cooperatives and Marketing. Separating marketing responsibilities from agriculture can hardly be seen as a particularly useful move for pushing ahead with market liberalisation.

As well as ASDS, a Rural Development Strategy (RDS) was recently drafted that focuses largely on social service delivery and infrastructural development. Further coordination issues arise here.[14] As well as the ASDS and RDS, strategies also exist for cooperatives, the environment/natural resources, livestock and water.[15]

All the sector policies and strategies have to be integrated into agreed macro-economic policies and budgetary processes, including the Poverty Reduction Strategy, the Public Expenditure Review, and the Medium-Term Expenditure Framework.

The sector strategies listed above assume prioritisation, coordination and implementation capacities by both government and donors that have never been demonstrated in practice. The aid agencies are jointly responsible with government for this proliferation of sector strategies, usually providing both finance and technical support in their preparation.[16] More importantly, strategies are widely assumed to be a justification for continued donor support.[17] An earlier agricultural strategy contained a short situation analysis followed by a long list of projects that donors would be invited to support. The ASDS contains much more analysis, but the ASDP ('P' is for 'Programme') that is being prepared on the basis of the ASDS also consists of projects to be run by central ministries and financed by donors.

With or without strategies, and in spite of the move towards a sector-wide approach, the principal donors continue to formulate and implement projects. Examples are the World Bank, IFAD and the African Development Bank, all of whom provide soft loans. Bilateral donors and NGOs see this continued strong project orientation as undermining attempts at crafting a sector-wide approach. A recent example, where the 'market failure' in fertiliser supply described above was to be remedied through a large World Bank project (SOFRAIP) managed by local governments and coordinated by the Ministry of Agriculture, was considered so risky that it was sent back to the drawing board, largely because of internal criticism within the Bank.

Donor support to agriculture and related sectors is substantial, accounting for the lion's share of the relevant ministries' development budgets. One critical view of the donor role is that it continues to endorse an essentially statist concept of agricultural development, including continued support for state functions that could arguably be better supplied by the private sector, or simply (and regrettably) abandoned as 'state failures'. For example, research and extension are frequently referred to as public goods that have to be provided by the state (market failure). Yet decades of state and donor support for research and extension have failed to spread these public goods in ways that provide palpable benefits to smallholders (state failure). This challenges the recurrent claim by the state that services have been undermined by budgetary austerity and falling salaries, which implies that more resources, not different institutions, are the solution. For better or for worse, liberalisation raises the question of the role of the private sector (especially multinational corporations) in research and extension, including controversial issues such as genetically modified seeds and the chemical package approach to agricultural intensification (TADREG 2001). These and other similar issues need to be addressed at the highest policy level. There is little evidence that this is happening.

The failure of conditionality

The above discussion leads to the conclusion that the formal liberalisation discourse tends to ignore the reality of aid – support for government and central ministries – just as it ignores, or trivialises, the reality of local politics. While it is the business of donors to support government, there is strong evidence that aid substitutes for foreign investment, and provides perverse incentives to governments *not* to implement agreed reforms. Recent research demonstrates that conditionality can be effective in certain conjunctures, for example, in providing support to a pro-reform group in government at the beginning of the reform process, but can be counterproductive at other times. Space precludes a full treatment of conditionality in agricultural reform, but from the issues raised above it appears that 'policy reversal' characterises the Tanzanian case better than 'stalled reform'. There is indeed strong local ownership of reforms in agriculture, but the reforms currently being implemented are the antithesis of those formally agreed with external development agencies.

Donors have held out against government pressures to enter into joint sector support for agriculture similar to that already in place for health, education and roads. But breaking ranks from this position are the leading lending institutions, the World Bank/IFAD, the European Development Fund and the African Development Bank. The World Bank's ill-fated SOFRAIP has been mentioned above. Its replacement, the Participatory Agricultural Development and Empowerment Project (PADEP), is under preparation, and claims to be an improvement on SOFRAIP.[18] The International Fund for Agricultural Development (IFAD), a World Bank affiliate, has started implementing a $40 million Rural Financial Services Programme (Daily News 2002).

Finally, some recent observers cast doubt on whether the PRSP process can address the complex institutional issues discussed in this chapter. Craig and Porter note the 'striking sameness of PRSP documents addressing poverty in markedly different national contexts'. Drawing on the Uganda PRSP, they conclude that international donor agencies promoting PRSPs fall prey to 'structural predilections which favour the technical and juridical over the political, economic, [and] obscure power relations and restrict practical and political options' (Craig and Porter (2003: 1). Ellis and Freeman (2004) summarise the findings from the four-country LADDER research programme highlighting the negative impact of local government decentralisation, particularly fiscal decentralisation, on rural livelihoods, arguing that PRSPs need:

> to address those factors in the institutional and fiscal environment at local levels that are hostile and discouraging to trade, investment, risk-taking and enterprise in rural areas. And this means giving PRSPs some sort of coordinating or integrating influence over change processes put in motion by quite different branches of government. In the absence of this integrating role, it is likely that PRSP impacts will be limited to highly visible outcomes such as improved schooling and road provision, with little real impact on opportunities for the rural poor to devise their own routes out of poverty.

Partial evidence of stagnant rural incomes, growing inequalities and popular perceptions that few Tanzanians have gained much from nearly two decades of reform, are perfectly consistent with the picture of poor rural governance and counterproductive donor aid portrayed above. The 2001/2002 Poverty and Human Development Report finds no evidence of a significant reduction in rural food and basic needs poverty between 1991/1992 and 2000/2001 (Tanzania 2002b: 10). The Gini coefficient increased by 9 per cent between the same dates in rural areas,[19] and by 20 per cent in Dar es Salaam. Successful macro-economic reforms, rising foreign investment and export earnings from minerals, and a respectable level of growth have not translated into improvements at the 'micro' level. Survey and participatory rural appraisal data confirm this picture.

It is also evident that, if functioning regulatory institutions are a precondition for agricultural markets to work, and for the incidence of poverty to begin to decline, both government and donors still have a long way to go, even to conceptualise the key issues in a useful manner. A step in the right direction would be to try to understand existing institutions governing agriculture using the tools of institutional economics and political economy (Ponte 2002a).

Conclusions

The theory behind PRSP is neo-liberal with regard to both national and international economic options. The World Development Report 2002 *Building Institutions for Markets* makes the case for explaining most market failure in agriculture in developing countries in terms of 'lack of effective supporting institutions' (World Bank 2002a: 33). Explaining one absence (no properly functioning markets) in terms of another (no effective institutions) is hardly a promising starting point for understanding existing markets and support institutions. Similarly, the explanations for the failure of market liberalisation in agriculture frequently fail to incorporate a view of the counter-strategy pursued by incumbent elites to ward off the threat posed by the 'private sector'.

The Tanzanian example shares a number of similarities with other countries in the east–central–southern African region (Jayne *et al.* 2001: 2–4). They have all to varying degrees turned away from market-based policies, and are steadily 'bringing the state back in':

> politicians openly contend that agricultural market liberalisation has been a false promise, that private sector response has been too slow and too weak to spur rural development, and it is necessary to bring the state back into direct distribution of strategic inputs and/or commodities ... the policy environment in many Eastern and Southern African countries is not unambiguously more hospitable or conducive to private investment in key marketing functions than it was before the liberalisation process began ... most of these countries are generally less far along in the reform process at the time of this writing in early 2001 than they were five years earlier.

There are successes and failures to report from the experience of market liberalisation in Tanzania. The major success is that, in an average year, Tanzanian farmers have produced enough to feed themselves and the urban population with an increasing variety of grains, vegetables and fruits, and meat products. Urban horticulture, poultry and livestock raising have also flourished in the 'informal sector'. The fall in the consumption of fertiliser after 1995 seems not to have had a major impact on the overall supply of grains. Middlemen – from large, mostly Asian, trading companies, to smaller, largely African businesses – have expanded their roles in input and output markets, and agro-processing, often in spite of, rather than because of, official policies. Finally, not all marketing arrangements for traditional exports are equally distorted by interference from boards or local administrator–politicians.[20]

One of the key assumptions of government and donor agencies is that the government has in place policies that are gradually bringing about the liberalisation of agricultural marketing. This chapter challenges that assumption. Another assumption is that liberalisation of international trade, finance and capital movements – globalisation – is a precondition for the success of anti-poverty strategies, policies and programmes. A challenge for institutional research is to make the connection between international and national markets and market regulation, and to ask whose interests policies at both national and international levels are serving. Somehow, the impact of aid has to be factored into the equation. The gap between the declared pro-poor policies of the Tanzanian government and the quotidian abuses and indignities suffered by the poor at the hands of officialdom, both petty and grand, local and national, does not augur well for efforts at poverty reduction or the chances of social stability over the longer-term. Arguably, aid has contributed to this unsatisfactory state of affairs.[21]

In summary, this chapter has argued that the liberalisation of Tanzanian export agriculture from the early 1990s to date has not taken place to the extent claimed by the Tanzanian government and donor agencies. While internal food markets have been largely liberalised, donor-inspired attempts to liberalise export crop markets have been seriously undermined by the political–bureaucratic class. As in other countries undergoing adjustment under World Bank/International Monetary Fund programmes, a combination of local vested interests and concerns with the 'rigged rules and double standards'(Oxfam International 2002) of global commodity markets have led to a systematic but under-reported backlash against liberalisation. Tanzania's current status as a star HIPC/PRSP performer is belied by a growing rejection, whether principled or opportunistic, of the liberalisation project.

Notes

* The chapter draws on the results of two years of fieldwork by TASA, which is financed by DFID, Rockefeller Foundation, SIDA and Concern Worldwide. TASA members are Seithy Chachage, Suleman Chambo, Brian Cooksey (coordinator), Adolfo Mascarenhas, Marjorie Mbilinyi, John Shao and Andrew Temu. The chapter is an abridged, edited, and updated version of a paper that first appeared in *Development Policy Review* (Cooksey 2003). Material is reproduced here with permission of Blackwell Publishing. The chapter expresses the views solely of the author.

1 There is a substantial literature on the failure of conditionality to 'buy' reform. Gunning (2001: 132) cites Oyejide *et al.* (1999) who document that trade liberalisations have been reversed in seven of ten African countries.

2 In particular loans from the WB, IFAD and the AfDB.

3 An annual 2.4 per cent increase for 1985–1998 (Delgado and Minot 2000: 53).

4 Delgado and Minot (2000: 39) cite a figure of 14 per cent in 1986–1987. In the Southern Highlands, between a quarter and a half of farmers were said to use fertiliser.

5 Havenevik and Harsmar (1999) following Ponte (1998b). Farmers were successfully avoiding repayment of input loans with unions just as they were to do later with private companies.

6 The World Bank's Soil Fertility Recapitalisation and Agricultural Intensification Project (SOFRAIP) foresaw the massive importation of fertiliser as a means of 'recapitalising' Tanzania's heavily mined soils. The government originally requested a $350 million project, which was scaled down to $95 million by the World Bank (TASA 2001). Criticisms of the 'statist' ethos behind the project eventually led to its replacement by an investment loan fund project known as the Participatory Agricultural Development and Empowerment Project (PADEP) for companies and 'farmers groups' managed through district councils.

7 Tanzania (n.d.), National Fertiliser Policy, Dar es Salaam, p. 1. Large areas of central Tanzania are too dry to benefit from inorganic fertiliser.

8 Summarising the KCU '*fracasso*' Banturaki (2000: 79) concludes: 'government support of the interests of the co-op leadership against the interests of the members ... frustrated co-op efforts towards better performance'. The current

Minister of Cooperatives and Marketing, who subsequently headed the commission to draft the new cooperative policy, cited below, was a key player in this struggle. See Ponte (2002b) for an extended analysis.

9 Mediated by the trade, good commodity prices (e.g. for cashew) help dampen the negative impact of the 'squeeze' on farmers. Poor prices (e.g. for coffee) work in the opposite direction.

10 Some also argue that aid, currently running at $1 billion a year (gross), provides a perverse incentive to the government as regards the imperative for 'self reliance' on export earnings.

11 Quarterly Economic Review (1999: 2). In May 1999, President Mkapa removed the majority of private sector representatives from the boards of the major export crops, replacing them with ruling party members of parliament, military officers and senior party functionaries.

12 Ponte (2002b) and Shao (2002) document similar dubious deals between private actors and regulators in coffee and cotton respectively.

13 See for example Chachage and Nyoni (2001) on cashew and Ellis and Mdoe (2003) on maize. James *et al.* (2002) provides a detailed description of local institutions affecting farmers in Morogoro Region.

14 Although regional and local government have traditionally fallen under the Prime Minister's Office, they are now under the President's Office. At the formal presentation of the RDS it was proposed that a coordination unit should be set up under the President's Office, Regional and Local Government (PORALG) to coordinate implementation.

15 The last two sectors are under another new ministry.

16 Cooperative policy is an exception, reflecting donor reluctance to be involved in this sector. (Empowering 'farmer groups' often appears in project documents however, for example, in providing agricultural credit through SACCOS.)

17 Described by one observer, quoting a donor, as the quest for the four Cs: cars, cash, computers and cellphones (Holtom 2002). The manner in which aid serves to fuel the other big C (corruption) is described by Cooksey (2002).

18 Doubts remain. Local governments, who will house the project, have a generally poor track record in management and accountability, and independent investment funds provide rich opportunities for bureaucrats and politicians to pursue the five Cs mentioned above. In addition, 2005 is an election year.

19 From 0.33 to 0.36, and 0.30 to 0.36 respectively. Tanzania, op. cit., p. 13, quoting Household Budget Survey data.

20 Tea and cotton boards do not attract as much adverse commentary as cashew and coffee, for example.

21 According to Chabal and Daloz (1999) the systematic (mis)use of aid to finance political patronage agendas helps to explain how and why 'Africa works'.

11 Competition and coordination in liberalized African cotton market systems*

Colin Poulton, Peter Gibbon, Benjamine Hanyani-Mlambo, Jonathan Kydd, Wilbald Maro, Marianne Nylandsted Larsen, Afonso Osorio, David Tschirley and Ballard Zulu

Introduction

Cotton constitutes an important cash crop in more than a third of all countries in sub-Saharan Africa and one upon which millions of rural households depend for their livelihoods. In most Francophone West African countries, the cotton sector continues to be organized around a state-dominated, single-channel marketing system, albeit one under increasing pressure to liberalize. Elsewhere, in conformity with the general trend in sub-Saharan Africa, the sector has been liberalized and private operators now dominate input supply, crop buying, ginning and selling. However, liberalization has not necessarily led to greater competition between these private operators. Moreover, it is not clear that greater competition is associated with better system performance.

This chapter attempts to explain these phenomena, drawing on the liberalization experience of Ghana, Mozambique, Tanzania, Uganda, Zambia and Zimbabwe. It argues that, whilst the capacity of the state to regulate and support the cotton sector remains weak, there may be trade-offs to be made between the level of competition and the degree of coordination achieved between players within the sector. Different cotton system structures are observed, with a different role for the state appropriate for each.

These arguments have relevance beyond cotton. The chapter develops a framework that can be applied to the analysis of any market system where state capacity is weak. The framework also provides helpful insights into the appropriate role of the state in supporting and regulating private economic activity under different market conditions.

African cotton sector liberalization: successes and challenges

In their review of the liberalization of African cash crop sectors, Shepherd and Farolfi (1999) note that liberalization has been a broadly positive experience, but that there are a number of challenges yet to be resolved. These general findings are relevant to the particular case of cotton. Here, too, liberalization has had a number of positive impacts (Baffes 2001). The influx of private capital, management expertise and entrepreneurship associated with liberalization has, in most countries, contributed to a resurgence in production, albeit one that has recently been threatened by the depressed world prices for cotton lint. Almost everywhere, producers have benefited from prompter payment and now receive a higher share of the final price for lint than they did before. Nevertheless, liberalized African cotton sectors continue to confront a number of common challenges, including: how to maintain high quality standards for cotton lint; how to achieve efficient delivery of inputs to smallholder producers, in turn requiring an effective mechanism for disbursement and recovery of seasonal credit; and how to support research into improved seed varieties, pest control and cultural practices, complemented by effective extension to producers.

These challenges can be linked to the techno-economic attributes of cotton production. For example, cotton is widely acknowledged to be particularly input-demanding, partly because it is vulnerable to a large number of pests. In addition, cottonseed degenerates quickly, making good management of the seed resource critical. The recent excess supply in the world market for lint makes it particularly important that these challenges are met. Even when the market is saturated, producers of high and uniform quality lint will normally find ready buyers, whereas suppliers of a low and variable quality product may be forced to accept steep discounts. Furthermore, high productivity is essential to survival when prices are low. Though yields are only one component of productivity, we note that in most cases the resurgences in production post-liberalization are attributable primarily to an increase in the number of producers and/or an expansion of area, rather than to increased yields.

Having observed that the common challenges facing liberalized cotton sectors can be linked to the techno-economic attributes of cotton production, we also note that conditions are similar in many other cash crop systems (Shepherd and Farolfi 1999). Thus the case advanced here may have more general relevance. Our basic argument is that meeting these challenges requires a significant degree of coordination between players in the market system. In practice this coordination is most readily achieved where the number of cotton companies or ginners in the sector is low. Hence, insofar as coordination is achieved (good for both companies and producers), its achievement may come at the cost of reduced price competition within the system (bad for producers). Thus, there may be a trade-off in system performance between competition and coordination, with the most successful systems being those that strike the best balance between these two objectives.

In the sections that follow, we explain what we mean by coordination and why its achievement might require a trade-off with competition; briefly describe the six selected cotton systems and identify three distinct types of system structure and organization found among them; show how the six cotton systems have responded to the challenges outlined above and use this to illustrate the trade-off between competition and coordination; identify the competition and coordination challenges associated with each of the sectoral structures and observe the different role for the state (in terms of market development and regulation) that is consistent with each.

Framework: coordination and competition

We may think of coordination as effort or measures designed to make players within a market system act in a common or complementary way or towards a common goal. Coordination may be undertaken by private agents acting collectively or may be orchestrated by state agents defining the boundaries within which private agents can act. Two reasons why coordination may be required in a market systems are to protect investment in specific assets and to ensure the provision of public goods.

For example, in the cotton sector, when ginners provide pre-harvest loans to producers, they become exposed to free-riding actions by cotton-buying competitors. To tackle the side-selling[1] of cotton by producers, ginners are likely both to provide incentives directly to the producers (through the terms of the vertical relationship) and to seek ways of restraining the actions of competitors (horizontal coordination). This involves some restraints on competition for seed cotton supply from farmers.

A variety of public goods (e.g. effective quality control regulations and procedures, and high quality research) are critical to the long-run success of a cash crop system. Provision of public goods is often held to be the responsibility of the state. However, the state may not perform this function for various reasons. It may wish to fulfil its responsibility, but not have the capacity to do so. It may neglect the market system, leaving private actors to coordinate by themselves. Third, it may decide that the market system in question is a private arena and so delegate responsibility to its private participants. This could be a rational course of action for a state that was over-stretched, especially if it was decided that decisions within the market system did not compromise key national or political interests (e.g. food security). Public withdrawal from a sector might then be a way of communicating to private investors that the state would not interfere with their investments if they committed themselves to that sector.

Where this is the case, there are two coordination challenges involved if private players within a market system decide to provide these goods collectively: agreeing what should be done (what research to fund, which quality standards to opt for) and how it should be done (who has responsibility for which aspects, how it should be funded); and implementing and enforcing these agreements, including overcoming the problems of free-riding and other opportunistic actions. Private players thus have the following coordination options. They may fail to coordinate and suffer the consequences (lack of public goods, insecurity of investments). Alternatively, they may establish a collective organization that can set and enforce formal rules in an impartial manner and provide public goods[2] in place of the state. In practice, such an organization is unlikely to be independent of the more powerful interests that contributed to its establishment. However, it may give smaller players a stronger voice than the third alternative, which is to rely on relational or inter-personal, rather than impersonal, coordination mechanisms. This is most likely to occur when the number of players is small, as the time and associated costs of coordination depend on the number (and quality) of relationships involved.

In this chapter, we recognize that competition can occur along several dimensions. Cotton companies may compete on geographical coverage, the range of services they provide to producers, the timeliness with which these services are provided, and the prices they pay for seed cotton. In the short-term, producers may respond positively to better services even when they substitute for more competitive seed cotton prices. However, if prices remain depressed beyond a couple of seasons, farmers' commitment and output are likely to fall. We also recognize that conduct can be as important as structure in determining the competitiveness of a market or sector. Having few players within a market may make collusion on pricing feasible, but whether it occurs depends on the incentives facing those players. Large players within a concentrated market might still act in a highly competitive (or rivalrous) fashion. In all six cotton sectors examined here, total ginning capacity comfortably exceeds a typical annual harvest. The desire for high capacity utilization at ginnery level thus provides an important incentive to competition, even when the number of companies purchasing seed cotton is few.

From the foregoing discussion, we posit the following links between coordination and competition. First, impersonal coordination, through formal rule setting and enforcement, may be the only viable option when the number of companies in a sector is high. If effective, such coordination can also enhance competition. However, the institutional requirements for this are high. In practice, as is shown below, such coordination is often ineffective. Hence, where the number of companies in a sector is high, competition may be strong, but coordination weak.

Second, where private coordination is relied upon, competition could be lowered for a number of reasons. Obtaining agreements and monitoring their implementation is easier when few players are involved. Hence, more concentrated market systems are likely to be better coordinated. Whether or not they suffer from lower competition will depend on the nature of the incentives facing firms. Regular meetings between firms (essential to coordination) may lead to information sharing and may also foster the trust necessary to engage in price collusion. Furthermore, preventing free-riding or other opportunistic behaviour requires that players committed to the upholding of an agreement be able to sanction those that are tempted to break it. Such sanctions may be necessary if coordination is to be achieved. However, the power to sanction can also be used to discourage competitive behaviour by the same competitors.

At the start of this chapter, we noted three key challenges facing liberalized African cotton sectors. All of these require some form of coordinated response by the players within a sector. Our judgement is that those sectors that achieve effective coordination will perform better than those that do not. The experience of the six sectors to date suggests that this will be true, even if – in the absence of state capacity for effective impersonal coordination – coordination is achieved at the expense of some loss in competition. It is to this experience that we now turn.

The six country cotton sectors

Figure 11.1 shows cotton production trends in the six countries over the past 15 years.

Ghana

Ghana, the smallest of the six sectors, was the first to liberalize. In 1985 the assets of the parastatal Ghana Cotton Development Board were sold to key sector stakeholders to form the Ghana Cotton Company Ltd (GCCL). In the same year, the first private firm began competing in one of the country's three production regions (Upper West). The firms pursued a common path of input-intensive production, providing all producers with a standard

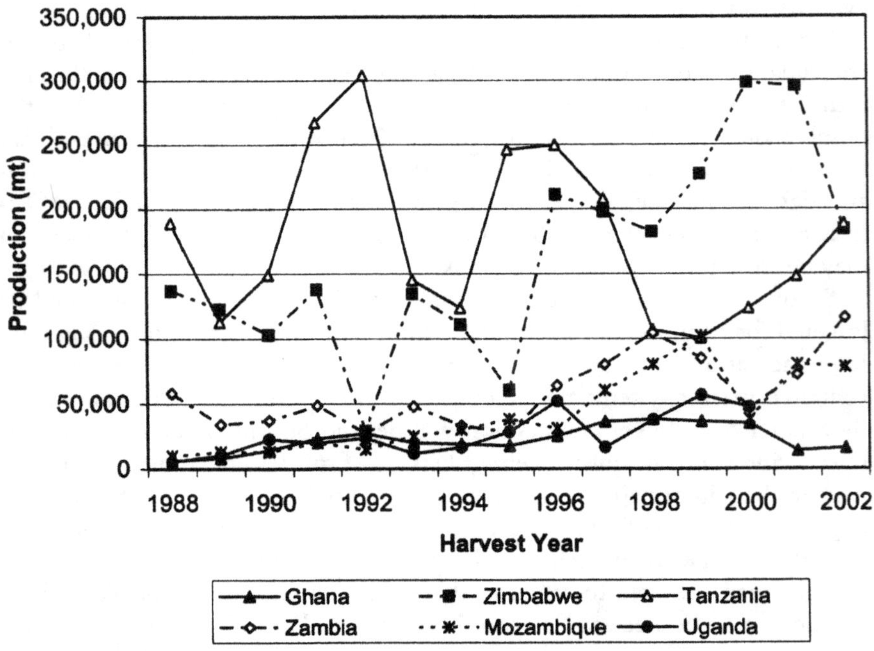

Figure 11.1 Seed cotton production 1988–2002 (source: Poulton *et al.* (2004).)

package (on credit) that included tractor ploughing, seed, fertilizer, pesticide spraying and extension advice. They also pursued a common pricing policy. Subsequent entrants have been expected to follow the same approach.[3]

The twin challenges of maintaining producer commitment to cotton production and ensuring seasonal credit recovery have dominated companies' thinking since liberalization. By 2000 the main players in the sector concluded that credit recovery could not be achieved where multiple companies were competing for business in a given village. They, therefore, persuaded the Ministry of Agriculture, to institute a local monopoly system, whereby each company was given exclusive rights to supply production services to, and buy seed cotton from, a given geographical area. The implementation of zoning did not start until 2001 and opposition to the plan by some players led to late planting in some areas, contributing to a large drop in production.

Mozambique

The recovery of the Mozambican cotton sector from the ravages of civil war began in the late 1980s with the formation of three joint venture companies,[4] which were given exclusive rights to organize cotton production in extensive 'concession' areas. Given that investment costs included road rehabilitation and private security, as well as investment in input supply and extension services, it was felt that only a monopoly system could provide the incentives needed to attract private capital. This monopoly system has remained intact since then, although it has also been subject to periodic challenges from new entrants wanting to establish themselves in the heart of existing concession areas. These challenges have typically been dealt with by creating new concession areas for major new entrants. In the mid-1990s new entry was encouraged by attractive world prices for cotton lint and by the perception that existing concession companies were providing poor services to producers. Cotton production increased rapidly in the mid–late 1990s, plummeted in 1999 due to the combined effects of problems with credit recovery and the collapse in world prices, and is now recovering again.

Tanzania

Tanzania's cotton production reached record levels just before liberalization. This, however, was achieved at some cost in terms of cooperative union debt. Large numbers of private firms entered the sector following liberalization in 1995 and soon reduced the remaining cooperatives to a minor role. However, strong competition during seed cotton purchase had negative impacts on both seed cotton and lint quality and on the possibility of delivering inputs to producers on credit (Gibbon 1999). The few firms that have tried to invest in extension provision have also found that most of the benefits are captured at harvest time by 'free-riding' competitors. Thus, after an initial increase coinciding with the high world lint prices of the mid-1990s, seed cotton production plummeted during 1997–1999. In response, the Tanzania Cotton Board (TCB) convened the first annual stakeholders' conference in 1999 to chart a way forward for the sector. This was followed by TCB-led interventions in seed and pesticide provision and quality control. Production levels have now begun to recover, despite recent adverse world prices.

Uganda

In 1994 the Ugandan government opened the cotton sector to private investment. Until then it had been based on cooperative ginnery operations with regional monopolies (Lundbaek 2002). Many local and international companies responded and activity within the sector rose quickly from its pre-liberalization trough. However, as in Tanzania, fierce competition in seed cotton buying has made it hard for these companies to recover investment in either input supply or extension provision. The Cotton Development Organization (CDO), the state body established at liberalization to regulate and promote the industry, and the Uganda Ginners and Exporters Association (UGEA) have tried to create the necessary investment incentives, but the challenge remains considerable. A UGEA-led scheme for providing pesticides on credit to producers had to be discontinued, but a system of private-sector regional investment plans was trialled in 2002–2003 to encourage investment in extension support.

Zambia

Liberalization of the Zambian cotton sector began with the privatization of the parastatal Lint Company of Zambia, sold in two parts to international buyers in 1995. The two resulting cotton operations (one of which was bought by Dunavant, the world's largest cotton trader, in 1999) have dominated the sector since then, although several small companies have also entered the sector as ginners and/or buyers. As in Mozambique, production grew rapidly in the mid-1990s, but growth was interrupted by problems with credit recovery, as new entry into the sector encouraged increased side-selling by producers. Dunavant's response to this, now being adopted by other players in the sector, is the so-called 'distributor' system, whereby extension agents are transformed into self-employed contractors, who on-lend and provide extension support to producers. The 'distributors' are paid by the cotton companies on the basis of seed cotton volume delivered and the level of loan recovery achieved. Whilst the system is still in its infancy, yields within the Zambian sector have been gradually increasing in recent years, production has surpassed its mid-1990s peak, and credit recovery has improved substantially.

Zimbabwe

In Zimbabwe, the Cotton Marketing Board (CMB) was first 'commercialized' (with many of CMB's debts being assumed by the government), then privatized, with shares offered publicly in 1997. The final government stake was sold in 2001. The main factor hampering CMB's financial performance in the 1980s and early 1990s was a requirement that it satisfy the demands of the domestic spinning sector at a heavily subsidized price before exporting lint. With this restriction removed, the new private company Cottco began life as a strong and highly viable business that has continued to dominate the market, despite entry by two competitors in 1994–1995 and several more since 2000. Its input credit scheme has been unrivalled within liberalized cash crop systems in Africa in terms of coverage and repayment record. One of the two early entrants, Cargill, maintained a market share of around 20 per cent until 2001, when it came under significant competitive pressure from a new, locally-based rival. Cargill's presence served primarily to spur Cottco to higher levels of service delivery and performance, until the subsequent general economic crisis in the country created adverse conditions affecting all enterprises, the eventual outcomes of which remain unknown to date.

Cotton market structures in the six countries

Three different market structures may be distinguished across the six countries. These are described in ensuing discussion as:

1 concentrated, market-based;
2 local monopoly, and;
3 numerous small players.

In Zambia and Zimbabwe, the concentrated market-based structure can be traced to the orderly privatization of the pre-liberalization cotton parastatals described above. In Zambia, the two businesses that were created out of Lint Company of Zambia continue to dominate the sector, competing only in one province (Eastern). In Zimbabwe, Cottco has preserved a 70 per cent market share even since the arrival of new competitors in 2001–2002. However, reasons for the relatively low entry in Zimbabwe (prior to 2001) and Zambia are still speculative.[5]

Until 2000 the Ghana cotton sector would have been classified in the 'concentrated, market-based' group, albeit with a fringe of small companies competing with the main three. As with Cottco in Zimbabwe, GCCL benefited from the physical assets and accumulated expertise of the pre-liberalization parastatal and from relationships with large numbers of experienced cotton farmers. Fifteen years after liberalization, GCCL maintained a 70 per cent share of the market. However, as already mentioned, in the 2001 production season Ghana adopted a local monopoly system.

A distinguishing feature of the local monopoly system in the Ghana and Mozambique sectors is that cotton companies are expected to provide production inputs on credit to all producers. In Mozambique this is a stipulation within the concession contracts; in Ghana it has been a condition required by the Agricultural Development Bank. There are benefits from such a requirement in terms of equity and possible 'collective good' benefits to the companies if credit access leads to the more rapid expansion of the sector. However, a universal access policy accentuates the adverse selection and moral hazard problems associated with smallholder seasonal credit, and the monopoly system provides a response to such problems.

Uganda and Tanzania have long histories of large numbers of cotton ginners, and interestingly today their cotton sectors correspond to the 'numerous small players' type. Asian businessmen led the development of the cotton sector in both countries as early as the 1920s, during which time a large number of small–medium sized enterprises were established. After independence, the Asian businessmen were forced out in both countries. In Uganda the sector went into precipitous decline; while in Tanzania private companies were encouraged to sell to cooperatives which preserved the de-concentrated character of the sector (Baffes 2002). Since liberalization, in Uganda 23 ginneries have been rehabilitated or upgraded by new private owners, and one new gin has been installed (Lundbaek 2002); while in Tanzania over twenty new private gins were built in the period up to 2002 (Gibbon 1999).

Cotton sector performance

Quality control

Maintaining high quality standards for cotton lint requires effective quality control procedures throughout the supply chain. Post-liberalization performance in this area has been mixed. While, at least until the last season or two, the liberalized Zimbabwean cotton sector succeeded in maintaining its international reputation as a producer of high quality lint, the International Textile Manufacturers Federation (2001) found that Tanzania, Uganda and Mozambique cotton lint were amongst the worst contaminated 'national origins' in the world.

Quality control in Zimbabwe begins with the grading of seed cotton into four grades at the time of purchase from the farmer. Approximately 35 per cent is classified as grade A and 40 per cent as grade B (Larsen 2002). A more thorough classification is undertaken prior to ginning to ensure that lint consignments are of uniform quality. However, there have been signs of deterioration in lint quality from Zimbabwe according to international lint traders interviewed in 2003. In Zambia, Dunavant has in recent seasons controlled polypropylene contamination by refusing to buy seed cotton that did not arrive at their buying posts in plastic bags and by introducing cleaning stations at their ginneries to remove polypropylene fibres before ginning.

Gibbon (1999) notes a number of reasons for a decline in the quality of Tanzanian lint since liberalization. These included the mixing of previously zoned seed varieties, the collapse of grading procedures at the time of primary purchase and a decline in insecticide use. A similar pattern, including mixing of seed varieties and the disappearance of grading at first purchase, has prevailed in Uganda.

Quality control in Mozambique represents a problem at all levels. There is little varietal zoning, and existing varieties have badly degenerated. Nearly all seed is distributed untreated. At the primary buying stage two grades are formally recognized, based on trash content, and prices are announced for each. However, in practice buyers do not always distinguish between the qualities, especially in recent years when the competition for seed cotton increased. With some exceptions, ginning equipment is dated and contributes to poor lint quality.

The Ghanian cotton sector has remained more dependent on sales to local textile firms than the other countries covered by this paper. One result is that incentives for raising product quality have been muted, although the International Textile Manufacturers Federation (2001) suggested that contamination of exported lint had been kept low.

Input credit

Each country's cotton sector response post-liberalization to the challenge of providing input credit to producers has been a determinant of, and has been influenced by, sector structure. As with quality control, success has varied from country to country.

Early players in the liberalized Ghana sector agreed to provide a common input package to all producers. Until 1995 no explicit charge was made for this package, except for ploughing cost. Instead, the per kilo price paid for seed cotton was adjusted downwards to recoup the costs of inputs supplied, based on a notional average yield of 600 kg seed cotton per half-hectare unit. The main strength of this so-called 'free input' system was that, when combined with common pricing by all cotton companies for inputs and seed cotton, it removed incentives for producers to side-sell. The two main disadvantages were that more productive farmers subsidized less productive ones and, more seriously, that common price setting removed competition from price formation (Poulton 1998).

In response, the sector moved during the mid-1990s to a more conventional system in which an explicit deduction was made for the inputs received by each producer. Side-selling escalated dramatically in the second half of the decade, as producers now had an incentive to sell to a company other than the one that provided them with inputs. This experience led to pressure for the introduction of the local monopoly system. Discussions with company representatives indicate that repayment rates of 85–90 per cent were achieved by some companies in 2002, despite the otherwise problematic start to this system.

Zimbabwe is the only other country of the six where many producers use inorganic fertilizer on their seed cotton crop. This, together with pesticide use, has been promoted particularly through Cottco's widely admired credit scheme. Established in 1992 (prior to liberalization), the scheme achieved exceptional repayment rates – a claimed 95–98 per cent in non-drought years – based on strong joint liability borrower groups, supported by extension and training support from Cottco staff, and backed up by the threat of asset seizure as a last resort (Gordon and Goodland 2000). Until recently an unanswered question was the extent to which Cottco's success was also due to the small number of buyers competing for seed cotton. However, as competition for seed cotton has intensified since 2000, side-selling has also become much more widespread and Cottco recently announced that they may have to suspend provision of credit to producers.

Similarly, in Zambia, side-selling has dogged attempts to provide pesticides to producers on credit since the entry into the market of several smaller buyers in 1997. Dunavant's response to this – their 'distributor' system – was described above. During the 2001/2002 marketing season, Dunavant had nearly 1,400 distributors, each working with an average of forty farmers. Since the start of the scheme in 1999, the company's credit repayment rate has risen from around 65 per cent to 85 per cent – a considerable improvement, but not yet sufficient for it to conclude that it has solved its input credit problem.

In Mozambique exemplary credit recovery rates (for pesticide loans) are claimed in circumstances where an effective local monopoly is preserved. The rapid growth of farmer organizations in recent years may also have contributed to this strong performance, although these have been formed for a number of different motives and so function with varying degrees of effectiveness. Meanwhile, during the two periods of intense 'pirate' buying within concession areas, credit repayment rates in Nampula fell as low as 60 per cent.

The biggest challenges for input credit are encountered in the two countries characterized by numerous small buyers. In Uganda and Tanzania, early post-liberalization experiments by individual ginners with input credit resulted in large losses (Gordon and Goodland 2000; Gibbon 1999). The Uganda Ginners and Exporters Association (UGEA) experimented unsuccessfully to deliver pesticides on credit to the majority of the country's 300,000 plus producers in 1998–1999. In Tanzania since 1999, levies paid on ginned seed cotton have been used by the Cotton Development Fund to procure insecticides for subsidized distribution to farmers through district and village governments. While this approach could potentially increase the volume of insecticide available at farm level, it also discourages private sector supply and depresses the seed cotton price. Moreover, there have been difficulties in implementation. A huge consignment of insecticides ordered by CDF for the 2002/2003 season was not of the type that producers are familiar with. Only 15 per cent of these insecticides were taken up by farmers and there are doubts as to whether the remainder of the stock will be moved before it goes out of code. The episode raises important questions about decision-making processes within the CDF.

More generally, the Ugandan and Tanzanian experiences highlight the issues of governance and accountability where either state organizations or private sector representatives take action on behalf of an entire sector. One of the major objectives of liberalization was to reduce the role of state agents in taking action of this nature. However, where liberalization comes closest to the ideal of multiple small players, this sort of action is still needed and the challenges remain.

Research and extension

There are currently no sector-wide success stories in supporting cotton research within the six countries. Small advances have occurred because large companies (within concentrated sectors) have taken individual initiatives, confident of capturing a reasonable share of resulting benefits. However, much remains to be done in all cases.

Perhaps the least discouraging story here is that of Zimbabwe, where Quton, a seed multiplication and distribution company wholly owned by Cottco, has a five-year contract with the state-owned Cotton Research Institute (CRI). The contract gives Quton exclusive rights to use the varieties developed by CRI, in return for which it undertakes to provide seed to the whole sector and pays CRI a royalty based on the volume of seed that it sells. This generates more funding for CRI than the state can afford to give it. At the same time, Quton is developing its own research programme, which could soon become larger than that of CRI.

Extension activity is more conducive to individual company effort than research, as the economies of scale are lower. However, company incentives to invest in extension are undermined by the now familiar problem of side-selling by producers to the competitors of those that provide the service. This occurs particularly in the numerous small players situation typified by Tanzania and Uganda.

Seed cotton pricing

Table 11.1 shows the range of seed cotton prices (in US$ terms) paid to producers in the six countries over the past five years. Not surprisingly, given trends in world prices, the highest price was paid in 1998 in four of the countries. Zimbabwe maintained high producer prices through 2000, but has since let its price slump in real terms. In Ghana producer prices have risen in the past two years. In comparing across countries, it should be noted that these prices are the product not just of competitive dynamics within the six sectors, but also other factors such as relative transport costs (highest in Uganda and Mozambique) and taxes (highest in Tanzania).

Table 11.1 Returns to producers across the six sectors, 1998–2002

	1998	*1999*	*2000*	*2001*	*2002*	*Mean*
Seed cotton price (US$/kg)						
Uganda	0.27	0.20	0.20	0.20	n/a	0.22
Tanzania	0.27	0.22	0.22	0.20	0.19	0.22
Mozambique	0.25	0.17	0.15	0.12	0.13	0.16
Ghana	n/a	0.18	0.10	0.20	0.19	0.17
Zambia	0.29	0.18	0.21	0.24	0.19	0.22
Zimbabwe	0.24	0.39	0.33	0.16	0.11	0.25
Returns to land (US$/ha)						
Tanzania	56	95	98	67	94	82
Zimbabwe	157	272	261	113	40	166
Mozambique	93	68	31	29	32	51
Zambia	105	53	73	98	75	81
Returns to labour (US$/family labour day)						
Tanzania	0.56	0.95	0.98	0.67	0.94	0.82
Zimbabwe	1.31	2.27	2.17	0.94	0.40	1.39
Mozambique	0.93	0.68	0.31	0.29	0.32	0.51
Zambia	1.05	0.53	0.73	0.98	0.75	0.81

Source: Poulton *et al.* (2004).

Nevertheless, it seems clear that seed cotton prices have been least attractive in the two cotton sectors now under local monopoly systems (Ghana and Mozambique). This flows directly from the fact that there have been no competitive pressures on seed cotton pricing in either country. In the countries with 'multiple small players', price competition is intense. In Tanzania, the Cotton Board sets a floor price for seed cotton, which generally acts as the opening price at the start of the official buying season. However, prices commonly rise 50 per cent above this level within a month or two. There is debate within the sector as to whether the floor price protects the most cash-strapped farmers, who are desperate to sell as soon as buying starts, or whether it actually depresses the price at the start of the season.

According to Table 11.1, the 'concentrated, market-based' countries have performed well on price. This is perhaps surprising, as there has been little direct price competition in either sector. The practice in both countries has been that the largest firm announces its price and competitors announce prices fractionally above this.[6] There are several possible reasons for the relatively good price performance. First, despite high transport costs in Zimbabwe (Pedersen 2002), it is possible that the costs of operation in these countries have been amongst the lowest of the six. Second, both countries are dominated by dynamic companies with ambitions of expansion that realize that you have to reward producers if they are to supply you in increasing quantities. Third, as in all six countries, ginning overcapacity encourages companies to keep their buying prices up, to maximize supplies.

Returns to producers

Best estimates of mean yields across the six sectors are presented in Table 11.2. This suggests a positive correlation between market concentration (as given by the CR3 ratio) and yield.[7] This is consistent with the argument in this chapter that, in the absence of a strong state, it is very difficult for sectors comprising numerous, small players to deliver the services that would assist smallholders to raise yields and productivity.

In Table 11.1 we present our estimates of returns to producers for the four countries for which we have sufficient data. Returns to land and labour are presented, as reliable estimates of family labour input into cotton systems are rarely available. Following Haggblade and Tembo (2003) for Zambia, we have estimated total labour input at 100 person-days per hectare for Mozambique, Tanzania and Zambia, and 120 person-days per hectare for Zimbabwe. Not surprisingly, returns in Mozambique are much lower than in the other three countries, reflecting both low yields and low price. Overall, returns in Zimbabwe are comfortably the highest, even though the combination of depressed prices and drought in 2002 dramatically reduced returns. The 2001 figures show that, even with weak prices, the Zimbabwe sector can generate higher returns to producers than those obtained in the other countries, because of the higher yields achieved.

Perhaps the most interesting comparison is between Tanzania and Zambia, which have offered similar prices to their producers over time. Whilst Zambian producers use more inputs and achieve higher yields, the difference in yields has not so far been sufficient to increase returns above Tanzanian levels. Finally, if we multiply the value added per kilogramme of seed cotton produced by the total production in each country, we get a crude estimate of the relative contribution to rural livelihoods in terms of direct income to land and labour that can then be spent on other rural goods and services across the six countries. Again using mean figures for 1998–2002, we find that the contribution in Zimbabwe (US$48.6m p.a.) is roughly twice that in Tanzania (US$26.4m p.a.) and four to five times that in Zambia and Mozambique.

Competition, coordination and the role of the state in the different sectors

In the previous sections, we have argued that, of the three distinct sectoral types observed within liberalized African cotton systems, the 'concentrated, market-based' sectors have been the most successful in meeting common coordination challenges. Moreover, they have done this whilst still maintaining reasonable prices to producers. Whilst local monopoly systems do offer a viable solution to several coordination problems, in Ghana and Mozambique the benefits are undermined by the absence of any competitive dynamic within these systems. Finally, the sectors with multiple small players have been fiercely competitive, but at the expense of effective coordination. We

Table 11.2 Comparison of the six surveyed cotton sectors, 2001–2002

Country	*First year of liberalization*	*Estimated number of seed cotton producers*	*Number of buying companies in first year of liberalization*	*Number of buying companies in 2001–2002 marketing season*	*% share of market of top 3 buyers (CR3) 2001–2002*	*% increase in seed cotton production since liberalization*	*Estimated average seed cotton yield 1998–2002 (kg/ha)*	*Mean seed cotton price 1998–2002 (US$ per kg)*
Ghana	1985	50,000	2	12	88	3,831	600	0.17
Mozambique	1989	230,000	3	15	50+	671	390	0.16
Tanzania	1994	300,000+	28	30	25	−32	421	0.22
Uganda	1994	300,000+	<15	27	50–60 (CR5)	167	310	0.22
Zambia	1995	80,000	2	6	90	119	568	0.22
Zimbabwe (smallholder)	1995	250,000+	2	5	95	130	752	0.25

Source: Poulton *et al.* (2004).

therefore conclude by suggesting that the appropriate role for the state in supporting and regulating private market activity depends on the character of the cotton sector under review.

In the 'concentrated, market-based' sectors, the main impetus for coordination tends to come from the dominant private companies. State agents may be required to oversee the enforcement of agreements reached between stakeholders (if capacity exists) and the state may need to arbitrate disputes between private parties. However, a large part of the burden for enforcing agreements rests with the firms themselves, both by their commitment and by the pressure that they can bring to bear on other (usually smaller) firms to comply. For example, larger firms may threaten to exclude smaller firms from ginning facilities if they poach seed cotton where the larger firm has provided inputs to producers on credit.

In the 'concentrated, local monopoly' sectors, the state has a critical role to play in the allocation of zones or concessions. This needs to be done impartially, as has apparently mainly been the case in both Mozambique and Ghana. However, to retain contestability, the state needs to establish procedures for evaluating the performance of concessionaires and periodically re-tendering concessions. No such procedures yet exist in either country.

Finally, in the sectors with 'multiple small players', the problem lies with inability to achieve coordination. In the absence of large private players, the onus is on the state to take the lead in public goods provision or on the multiple small players to organize themselves to tackle common problems. Tanzania illustrates the former approach and also illustrates its difficulties in a context of low state capacity. The failed Ugandan input credit experiment illustrates the difficulties of putting in place an effective formal private association approach.

All cotton system types, therefore, face their own particular challenges in striking the competition-coordination balance. So far, the 'concentrated, market-based' sectors have the slight performance edge.

Notes

* This chapter is an abridged and edited version of a paper published in *World Development* (Poulton *et al.* 2004). Material is reproduced here with permission of Elsevier. It is an output of a research project funded by the Social Science Research Unit of the UK Department for International Development (DFID), however the views and opinions expressed are those of the authors alone, and are not attributable to DFID.

1 Side-selling is the sale of seed cotton to a buyer other than the company that provided the producer with inputs on credit during the production season.

2 In a concentrated sector with limited new entry, such goods provided collectively by private players may more accurately be described as club goods than public goods. However, we use the term public goods throughout, as our emphasis is on the common challenge facing all sectors as to how to provide such goods.

3 Perhaps because of its small size, but perhaps also because of its commitment to the common input and pricing package, Ghana's cotton sector has remained the exclusive preserve of locally-based firms.

4 These were joint ventures between the Mozambican government and international (either Portuguese or multinational) firms. Strictly speaking, it is more accurate to talk of the privatization of the Mozambique cotton sector in 1989 than of its liberalization.

5 In Zambia, an unknown, but substantial, number of independent traders operated from 1997 until 1999 (or later). These contributed to the credit repayment problems experienced by the sector during this period.

6 In Zimbabwe Cottco also then pays an end-of-year bonus to all their producers after selling their lint. Under the so-called 'pool price' system, also now operated by Cargill, mid-season price rises (necessitated in 2002 by spiralling inflation) are also paid to all producers, irrespective of when they sold.

7 The Pearson correlation coefficient, calculated using CR3s for Uganda and Mozambique of 0.45 and 0.55 respectively, is 0.831, significant at the 0.05 level (2-tailed). If rankings are used instead of absolute values, the Pearson correlation coefficient is 0.771, significant at the 0.1 level (2-tailed). However, we accept that a correlation based on just six data points is only suggestive.

12 Comparative land tenure issues arising in four countries*

Sholto Cross

Introduction

Village reports arising from the LADDER project reveal a diverse picture of the pursuit of livelihoods by small rural producers in east and south-central Africa in the years 2001–2003.[1] At the micro level it is apparent that many new avenues, especially for off-farm income, are being explored. Different ecological systems pose new challenges and opportunities: there are declining coffee and cotton markets, but new opportunities in horticulture, improved smallstock breeds, processing and trading. Despite these diversities, there are significant commonalities, a number of which are discussed from a comparative point of view in Chapter 3 of this volume. What stands out plainly overall is that rural immiseration is deepening, and that the causes of this are intimately bound to the manner in which households gain and maintain access to land, the basis for most of their prospects for survival. It is the purpose of this chapter to review the themes and issues which arise from what may be termed a 'narrow aspect' of land reform – that is, the changing nature of customary tenure, and its interaction with policy initiatives which have impacted on it. These are then placed within the context of an overview of the developments in land reform at a more general level in these countries.

The aim is to situate the immediate and the concrete life experiences revealed by the village reports not only against this broader background of a political and historical narrative, but also in the context of the contemporary debate on land reform. If in doing so some light is thrown on what priorities there may be for policy interventions, and what lessons may be learned from the comparative contexts, then this chapter will have succeeded in its basic aims. But it is a large canvas, with a complex and confusing landscape, where dense thickets of legislation and bureaucratic procedures more often obscure than expose the interactions between land-users, administrators and policy-makers.

The structure of the chapter is as follows. Following a brief outline of the background to land reform (broadly, up to 1990) some of the key issues arising from the village reports are summarised and presented. There is here a necessary process of selection, but this takes the form of limiting the detail on specific variations rather than neglecting any major issue: it is remarkable how over the four countries the same motifs emerge. There are broadly three groupings of these. The first is that of the (in)security of tenure, which goes to the heart of the experience of land loss which has formed the consciousness of small producers over the past century. Allied to this are a range of issues and co-factors concerning the optimisation of the efficiency of land usage via the design of the tenurial relationship. Second is the question of inequality of access to land and associated economic opportunities, of which gender is the largest but by no means the only dimension. The third issue to be addressed arises directly from these: the nature of the obstacles to the implementation of the current land reform proposals which have rather agonisingly passed through political and legislative processes.

Background to land tenure reform

This chapter starts from the premise that land, as the key resource in Africa, is at the centre of its political struggles just as much as it is the fount of its economic wealth. The determinants of socio-economic status flow from the outcomes of these struggles. There are many dimensions. At the broadest level is the issue of dominance, by individuals and groups, their retainers and client base, over the system whereby land is made available to actual and potential supporters. Contemporary elites have found in the institution of freehold tenure, and the notion that the state has vested title to land, powerful weapons for consolidation. But contestation has extended downwards to the inter- and intra-household levels, where customary modes of access to land predominate.

While the latest wave of land reform has been characterised by attempts to remove the radical title to land from the state (and the official class which it subtends) and vest this in the people, and to 'rehabilitate' the customary sector in various ways (in particular through aligning it with freehold systems), many questions arise over whether the outcomes have in practice favoured small land-based households, or reduced inequitable stratification within them. An understanding of these struggles around land utilisation is of particular relevance for the analysis of sustainable livelihoods by the poor, as their life chances are predominantly determined by the terms on which they have access to land.

There are many common threads for this perspective in the four countries under consideration. In Uganda, Kenya and Malawi, English land law (as it existed prior to its reform in 1925) was imposed in such a manner as to facilitate the alienation of land to the state, for purposes of encouraging settlement and commercialisation. The existing, or customary mode of land-holding was accorded the fragile and subordinate status of occupancy (Okoth-Ogendo 2000). The German period in Tanganyika was no different, and although this process of alienation was frozen in terms of the C mandate granted to Britain, the customary sector was similarly made subordinate to the received law (McAuslan 2000).

This phase of reception of land law was followed during the 1920s to 1950s by what many proponents of a balanced approach to settler and indigenous rights refer to as the period of reconstruction (the maintenance of a dual system, whereby new systems such as trust lands were deployed, aimed at maximising political stability). Piecemeal attempts were thereafter made to evolve customary tenure in the direction of freehold, but at independence customary land-holders generally had the lowest degree of enforceable rights to land (Toulmin and Quan 2000).

While the political developments during the first three decades of independence in these countries took apparently different routes, there were fundamental similarities and continuities. In Malawi, the 1967 Land Act re-asserted the control of the state over land, and subsequently Banda proceeded both to subordinate the customary sector to the interests of a new rentier class of supporters and officials, and to transfer large areas of prime land out of the customary into the private leasehold sector (Cross 2002a). In Uganda much the same processes took place under Obote I (Amin) and Obote II, with Amin's 1975 Land Reform Decree (purporting to declare all land as public land, thus ostensibly destroying freehold tenure in Buganda and the other kingdoms – the 'lost counties') doing little more than open the door for large amounts of land to be transferred as leasehold to the benefit of senior politicians and officials, operating through district land boards and the Uganda Land Commission (Bosworth 2001). The development conditions attached to the land were rarely enforced, and much land remains under-utilised.

Kenya led the way in land policy in East Africa, but is now arguably the laggard. The background is complex, but central to current problems. The Swynnerton Plan (Swynnerton 1954) envisaged the intensification of agriculture as the road ahead for the customary sector, and also scouted the idea of converting customary tenure to individual freehold. This path was taken further by the recommendations of the East African Royal Commission in 1955. Presented in terms of economic rationalism, political considerations of a hoped for stabilisation of land matters were also a driving impulse for reform, which culminated in the Registered Land Act. This took into the independence era the system whereby land might be registered, consolidated and adjudicated as privately owned land, while the Trust Land Act (TLA) vested control over customary lands not so transferred to absolute proprietorship in county councils. Both were ill-suited instruments. They perpetuated the notion of state trusteeship for the customary sector, and the move towards titling and registration of agricultural land, but failed to install any effective means of policing the fiduciary duties of the state (Okoth-Ogendo 2000).

The Registered Land Act did not deal with issues of succession, where customary law continued to operate, while the registration approach often required adjudication on title, tilting access in favour of the powerful and wealthy, particularly where urban expansion brought rising land values (KLA 2002). The TLA was wide open to abuse by county councils whose fiduciary duties were neither supervised nor challenged, despite the wholesale transfer of land under customary use for registration by big men. The courts did attempt to establish some protection where customary systems continued to operate in purportedly privatised land, but upon sale or lease this involved the destruction of lesser rights and 'condemned customary land tenure to the ghetto of neglect' (Migai Akech 2001). In particular there was a large reduction in the welfarist role of the land, through the loss or further degradation of the weak rights of outsiders and women.

This was aggravated by the fate of much public land. At independence a considerable amount of land consisting of gazetted forests, national parks and reserves, bodies of water, wetlands (and unalienated range or agricultural lands in such areas as Lamu and Tana River Districts) passed to the state. In practice, this has been treated as if it were private property to be disposed of at will, without conditionalities or public scrutiny. All categories of government land (including land reserved for public purposes or in urban areas where leases expired) became vulnerable. The 'principle of first registration' in the law of Kenya originating from the colonial era has also meant that irregular allocations cannot easily be reversed.

In the pastoral areas covering two-thirds of Kenya (where Swynnerton did not envisage privatisation) group ranches were established in the early decades of independence, over a third of which were subsequently sub-divided, individualised and mainly sold to outsiders, leading to a resurgence of customary patterns of ownership (Scoones 1995). The redistribution of private land owned by white settlers after independence has also led to an extremely complex and inequitable situation. Farm areas are now of mixed size ranging from 10,000 hectares to less than one hectare. Smallholders rarely have registered titles and operate in accordance with customary law and land use systems. Apart from changes in the technical description of land title, land relations in registered areas of trust land have barely changed. Attempts to assert private title are often fiercely resisted by kinsmen and are a frequent cause of violent confrontations.

The replacement model, which characterised early post-colonial Kenya, thus failed. The extent to which private tenure regimes were installed has reflected a political market rather than an economic one, and the vast majority of farmers continue to access land via indigenous systems. This has led to arguments in favour of an adaptive model for customary tenure, driven by Boserupian forces and induced innovation (Bruce and Migot-Adholla 1994). But the overlapping and incoherent administrative measures surrounding access to land make a radical overhaul now imperative.

Tanzania has a somewhat different history, but with curiously similar outcomes (Sundet 1997). The German period of occupancy recognised formal title where it existed, and as with most other colonial powers, acquired land to the state by right of conquest, and subsequently made this available for commercial settlement. The mandatory terms established by the Treaty of Versailles prevented such transfers, however, and the Land Ordinance of 1923 vested radical title to land in the people, represented in the person of the governor, subsequently the president. This did not prevent signification alienation of land in the southern and northern highlands to settlers, but the mandate ensured that Tanganyika fell under the doctrine of the paramountcy of native interests. The adoption of a socialist *ujamaa* ideology following independence permitted land policies to flow smoothly on from the colonial dispensation, allowing the political leadership to dispose of land without challenge, a primary enablement for the villagisation programme. In 1963 the role of traditional chiefs was abolished, clearing the way for the rural revolution *vijiji*, which saw two-thirds of the rural population resettled via administrative fiat into nucleated villages (Coulson 1979; Hyden 1980). The collapse of the rural economy led to the formulation of the New Agricultural Policy in the 1980s, and the Economic Recovery Programme, heralding a process of liberalisation. This opened the way for widespread disputation over land rights. Apart from the direct dispossessions of customary land for resettlement, the state had also granted vast swathes of land to parastatals and individuals. The confusion in land affairs also saw a continuing process of land-grabbing.

The first post-colonial phase 1960–1990 thus saw, as Okoth-Ogendo (2000) has concisely summarised it, some deep commonalities in land policies across the four countries. These are the pre-eminent role of the state, which retained radical title to the land (or behaved as if it had), without any means of control or supervision of its trusteeship duties; a general attitude that customary tenure was an inferior system and should be allowed to wither away, if not actively suppressed; and an over-arching system whereby land matters were dealt with essentially through political and administrative means, rather than by any attempt to establish a coherent body of law.

Despite the very different apparent circumstances therefore of avowed socialist and capitalist systems, countries suffering civil war and anarchy or enjoying extended decades of peace, the political processes vis-à-vis land policy have shown some profound structural similarities. These are the continuance of the early colonial agenda by the new nationalist elites of providing a land-owning basis for the powerful and wealthy and those who would join their ranks; rent-seeking behaviour towards the customary sector, whose own production interests were largely neglected or utilised as a base for the extraction of profits; and their general downgrading to the status of tenants at will, with inferior rights of dubious enforceability, constantly subject to the threat of eviction.

A wave of land reform in the region took place broadly in the last decade of the twentieth century, provoked by rising popular dissatisfaction – given greater scope by the dawning of the multi-party era – together with the urgings of the donor community, and the broad shift in public policy perspectives towards poverty alleviation via liberalisation. These developments are not reviewed for each country in detail here, and the reader is referred to Cross (2002b) for the relevant details.

Land tenure and the village reports

The LADDER fieldwork locations were not intended as representative samples, but rather as illustrative of particular ways in which livelihoods are pursued in different and typical ecosystems. The Tanzania fieldwork was undertaken in two of the five districts within Morogoro region: Kilosa (intensive irrigated rice, semi-arid maize, livestock) and Morogoro Rural (south-west face of the Uluguru mountains, high value fruit and vegetable production; and remote and relatively inaccessible maize and sesame villages on the northern border of the Selous Game Reserve) (Ellis and Mdoe 2003). The Malawi surveys (Dedza, Zomba districts) covered villages with access to fish and paddy, and those confined to rainfed arable, significantly off-road. The Kenyan studies concentrated on the west (Suba district, lakeshore and hinterland districts) where rural land competition is as intense as anywhere in Africa. In Uganda (Mbale, Kamuli, Mubende districts) both highland coffee–banana *shambas* and lakeshore fishing villages were covered.

Land access: inheritance

Customary tenure predominates as the means for gaining access to land in these areas, affected as they are but not yet overly disturbed by peri-urbanisation. There have however been many modifications and adaptations from the archetypal mode of matrilineal or patrilineal inheritance, reflected both in mobility (incoming outsiders, clan movement to new land) and endogenous change. Generally it appears that the greater the pressure for land, the more adverse are the chances of women achieving access or security other than via marriage; women in better-off households have greater access to land and room to manoeuvre than do those in poorer households; and the risk to a household of early adult male death impinge hardest on women and the young. There is thus an apparent gradient of negative consequences of traditional inheritance systems running parallel to socio-economic status. There are exceptions to this, notably where *mailo* tenure is in operation in Uganda, and also where women's associations have been established. There is also a growing stratification between elders, those already established on the land, and 'outsiders' and 'insiders' with political access on the one hand, and the younger generation who may have no other choice than migration, landless labour, or inadequate survival on a fragment of inherited land on the other. Generally customary inheritance has retained its validity, even where registration and titling of land has purportedly occurred, or land has been removed from clan control by allocation. Yet its capacities do not appear to be able to contain fragmentation and deepening inequities.

Some examples illustrate this. Pinde village (irrigated vegetables, Uluguru, Tanzania) typifies a settlement with a major land constraint where the matrilineal system is still intact. Almost all available land is cultivated, some under perennial crops. The better off own up to four acres in three to four scattered plots, and rent in land. The poor own less land, much of which is fragmented and rented out. The old who cannot work are food insecure most of the year, and a large proportion of the youth migrates. Drastic declines in soil fertility have accompanied a shift away from coffee (falling prices) to intensive horticulture (cabbage, tomato, improved varieties of Irish potato). The position of women is noted as being quite balanced under a still strong matrilineal system, with considerable involvement in decision-making, and significant areas of independence, such as the freedom to raise credit (although constrained by a lack of collateral sources to raise capital).

Buwopuwa village (Mbale, Uganda) is populated almost exclusively by Bagishu clans, and patrilineal inheritance by sons predominates. The few outsiders in the village have purchased their land. More recently, however, some women have been free to inherit land and transact in this resource independent of men and clan influence. But only women whose parents recognise that both boys and girls have equal rights have been so favoured. Most fathers bequeath land to their male children only. Parents who allocate land to girls are those parents who are well off or only have daughters. Nonetheless, inheritance by women is frowned on by the community, as this status is associated with women who have separated from their husbands or are spinsters living on their own.

This may be contrasted with nearby Bunabuso village, where access to land occurs equally through outright purchase or inheritance (hiring and borrowing are not uncommon). Once one buys land it becomes private property. The most common source of this kind of land is from neighbours. Clan elders may stop the sale if they do not think there is a genuine reason for its sale or the interests of other members of the household are being neglected. Typical reasons for selling land accepted by the clan as valid include school fees, court fees, money for dowry, health problems, burial arrangements and purchase of land in other areas. The key distinguishing characteristic of the latter village is the prevalence of development institutions, some external, some homegrown, which suggests that these may help account for its more 'modern' attitudes towards the land market.

In Dedza and Zomba districts, Malawi, the predominant matrilineal system is starting to break down under the pressure of land scarcity, as is the case in Tanzania (see Gudugudu below). For example, at Lumwira village in Dedza, more sons than daughters are being given land by their mothers, and the traditional *chikwamwini* (matrilocal) system is declining in places (Mpango village) to be replaced by *chitengwa* (patrilocality). This has led to a structural change in village relationships, with household members preferring to devote time and resources to non-farm income generation rather than supporting family ties (Cross 2002a: 19). Malawi perhaps is nearing the endpoint where customary systems of land access via inheritance and marriage fulfil some social welfare function, and as the most extreme example of poverty and scarcity, may be the most obvious case for providing assistance to the adaptive capacity of indigenous systems through careful legislative reform.

Land access: purchase and rental

Land sales are generally most uncommon in the case study villages, except the *mailo* areas of Uganda, and even here it is infrequent. The rental market however is a rapidly growing one. In Kisanga sub-village (Morogoro Rural, Tanzania) land sales were noted as very uncommon but did occur, with renting or inheritance as the main means of access. The better-off rent in land, and a higher proportion of land is rented out as the poverty indicators increase. The very poor, with on average 0.5 acre, have little option but to rent out both their land and labour. There is an interesting positive relationship noted here between village authorities who are helpful (solve disputes, not corrupt) and rising income levels and micro-mobility.

In Kinamwanga village, (Kamuli district, Uganda), most villagers have only small pieces of land, some none, and gain access through renting at about Ush 30,000 per acre (on average up to one km distant). This trend has sharpened over the last five years. In the past, people used to lend out land free of charge for cultivation purposes; this is now rare. Land fragmentation is on the increase through inheritance, distress sales of small portions of land arising from sickness, marriage payments, burial arrangements, debt repayment and to finance outmigration. It is the latter category that is usually available for outsider cultivators to buy.

Gudugudu and Mlali villages (Morogoro Rural) are unusual villages, in that land (village and clan) is relatively freely available. Village land is accessible both to residents (and outsiders) through application to the village administration and the payment of Tsh 10,000 – Tsh 18,000 to cover stationary costs and allowances for the Village Land Committee. Clan land is acquired through matrilineal inheritance. But for the four major Luguru clans with land in Mlali (Kimri, Nkombe, Ndoto and Kikomi) this system has been in steady decline since the villagisation programme. Men now commonly inherit directly, and sales of clan land (Tsh 50–70,000 per acre) are reported. Other ways of gaining access to land for agricultural activities is through renting. Similarly the renting of both clan and village land is on the increase, specifically for cash cropping tomatoes (Tsh 5,000 per acre for two seasons).

Land access: *mailo* land

In the coffee–banana system of eastern Uganda, Bukhasusa village is an interesting case where patrilineal inheritance predominates, but customary and freehold (*mailo)* tenure mingle easily, and the not infrequent land sales suggest an evolutionary path from the former to the latter. This is accompanied by the privatisation of hill lands, which were previously under common property or open access regimes. Rich households may set aside land for a daughter, after provision had been made for sons. The delineation of a small piece of land for widows is frequent, but the purpose is primarily to meet funeral costs and continuing access is subject to clan approval. It was observed that women who are members of the savings and credit associations live a better life. They are able to pay for school fees, corrugated iron roofs, can purchase their own land and at least can pay hired labour for their separate fields. Some have acquired livestock, which gives them milk for domestic consumption and sale.

Similarly in Kabbo village, Mubende district, a father may allocate some land to his married sons. However, if the father dies before all the sons are married, then the wife inherits the land and she has the right over the land and the decision to allocate it to the remaining sons as they acquire their own homes. Land in the village is owned by private individuals with some having acquired leaseholds while others are at varying stages of formalising the title deeds. Many are sitting tenants (*Bibanja* holders) who pay no rent to the title holder, and are free to develop or sell the *Kibanja* without permission. Normally, wives have their own plots that they cultivate for home consumption. Produce from men's plots is usually sold. Women work both in their own and their husband's plots, but husbands rarely help in the women's plots. Single women may access land via rent and purchase, if they can.

Land scarcity

Not a single village study encountered a community where land availability was not a major constraint, regardless of scale factors. At one end of the spectrum are typical Kenyan villages such as Gingo village in Suba district where within living memories land holdings by the better off exceeded twenty acres, but have now more than halved, to the Malawian case where average holdings (across the three income categories) are in the 4–6:1 : less than 0.3 acre range. 'Those who did not get rich in the past will never get rich now' was the telling phrase.

Table 12.1 summarises trends in farm size as they have occurred in the case study villages. The data listed under 'current situation' represents typical farm sizes for the three wealth groups identified in wealth ranking exercises (Ellis and Freeman 2004).

Land distribution in Roo village (see Table 12.1), where communal land was originally freely available, is now essentially bimodal between the older generation of Basuba settlers with eight to twelve acres and the youth with between one and five acres. Similarly in Kilimani sub-village (Chakwale, Kilosa, Tanzania: maize, pigeon peas, sweet potato, beans) elders own most of the land, which can be between twenty and forty acres, while the poor average one acre. The youth have no option but to migrate or sell their labour. With declining soil fertility, little infrastructure, no or fake inputs,

Table 12.1 Suba District, Kenya: trends in holding size (acres) (current situation divided between three wealth categories)

Village	*10 years ago*	*5 years ago*	*Current situation*		
			I	*II*	*III*
Gingo	20	15	10	8	5
Roo	communal	n/a	12	6	2.5
Nyapuodi	120	n/a	10	12	1.5
Makende	20	15	10	7	2
Average	53	15	10	8	3

Source: research carried out in four villages in Suba District during 2001.

returns of less than four bags maize/acre indicate the non-viability of fragmented holdings. A similar picture emerges from Bunabuso village (Mbale district, Uganda). With increasing population, land fragmentation has increased and most young people have had to migrate out of the village in search of off-farm employment in North Mbale, Kenya and Buganda. Indeed, some of them have eventually settled where they migrated after securing land. Nonetheless they rarely relinquish the land they own in the village.

Land titling, registration, land use planning allocation

In Tanzania (Kilosa District) the growing demands for land as a result of increased population pressure has led to violent clashes between pastoralists and crop farmers resulting in forty-two deaths between 1998 and 2000. Whilst such outcomes are the exception, in all communities land demands are fuelling intensified grievances. Similar inequities in land demarcation and registration are noted for Chanzuru village in Kilosa district and Gingo village (Suba district, Kenya).

The clear conclusion from the LADDER village reports is that registration has not worked as an empowerment tool, rather the reverse. The bureaucratic procedures necessary to register and entitle land, and accord with land use planning by-laws, have reduced rather than enhanced the security of the customary sector, and it is to the informal rental market that producers mainly look in order to access additional land.

Gender balance

Both matrilineal and patrilineal systems reflect culturally embedded norms, which give men land entitlements not generally open to women. This is seen not only in inheritance, but in the division of labour, decision-making, control of income, livestock and access to credit. The examples are ubiquitous throughout the LADDER village reports. Women within marriage secure their land via their husband, with access to specific fields from which they are expected to provide for the reproductive needs of the household, providing most of the physical labour as well. Upon the husband's death, land is usually allocated to male relatives within the clan. Where land is made available for widows and daughters (rich families, coffee–banana area), it is land 'on the other side', land close to the homestead being reserved for sons. The increasing fragmentation and declining fertility of land means that women of remnant households often end up with non-economic holdings. Separation, divorce and early widowhood (through AIDS) are now common.

But there is some evidence to suggest that the declining opportunities within cultivation are episodically improving women's livelihood chances. Basic field labour is giving way perforce to trading, processing and catering, which are proving to be both more financially rewarding and capable of opening up some independent social space, whether individually or through women's groups. In many fishing villages, for example, where women are forbidden to go on the lake (although instances of women owning boats and nets occur) the drying and marketing of fish provides significant income. Brewing beer and *waragi* are similarly increasingly profitable undertakings open to women.

Village settlement and mobility

A striking feature of the village studies is the high level of physical mobility revealed, whether relatively large cross-border movements of both clans and individuals, or oscillating migration between a home village and local employment or trading node. Even Malawi is no exception, although movements here tend to be individual rather than clan-based, mainly consisting of *obwera* (outsiders) moving into new cash opportunities (fish, rice), men in a matrilocal system who retain land in their clan village, and a certain amount of rural–urban oscillation. The search for land is the predominant motive. Lundi sub-village (Morogoro Rural, Uluguru mountains) where land availability is the major constraint on livelihoods is typical. Almost all is clan land, with steep slopes prone to soil erosion, subject to fragmentation and declining plot size and soil fertility, except for areas reserved to tree planting. Something of a land market has developed, with a few sales but more commonly rentals (Tsh 60–120,000 per acre). This village shows a picture of increasing diversification within the agriculture sector, away from coffee and food staples towards new cash crops and improved livestock (Swiss goats). The problems are the limits to agricultural intensification of these production systems, with consequent outmigration, largely by young men, who in any event constitute the better-off. Women are relatively adversely affected by these changes as they have fewer opportunities for engaging in the new activities, are constrained into the less profitable forms of petty hawking and entrepreneurship, and have markedly less capacity to raise credit and accumulate capital.

Sogea Mbele sub-village (Bakwira, Morogoro Rural) is a settlement recently formed by such Luguru outmigration. It is isolated, with little infrastructure or services, but offers scope for young men. Non-clan access via rent (T2–5,000/- per acre of paddy) and sale (T50–80,000/- per acre) is common, mainly to men. Matrilineal inheritance is now breaking down into the patrilineal form. The upper stratum is composed mainly of hardworking young men with some education who cultivate up to ten acres (usually in non-adjacent plots), often hiring in (male) labour. Informal networking, revolving credit and support organisations (*kiwili, lugota*) contribute to their success. The local MP and village committee are resented for not having prevented land suitable for paddy being removed to a wildlife area, and generally failing to respond to requests.

Iyingo village (Lake Kyoga, Kamuli) reveals another dimension to population mobility. During the bush war fought by the NRM in the 1980s there was a large-scale outmigration (of all tribes) from Iyingo, followed by an influx of Iteso fleeing the insurgency in Teso (a district on the other side of the lake). These then returned home, retaining some stake, while the families who fled the area in the early 1980s have been filtering back. However, the returnees, faced with the decline in fishing prospects, have built homes in Iyingo, but practice oscillating migration (to Buganda and Kenya) to pursue livelihood activities. Wives are usually left in Iyingo, which is visited only at Christmas and Easter.

The elders of the fertile Roo fishing village (western Kenya) date the first settlements to around 1920. These were Basuba people from the northern parts of Tanzania, (later driven out by another clan of the same tribe). They then settled in other parts of Gembe division, and were joined by other Basuba clans from Uganda, now currently settled in Gwassi, Mfangano and Rusinga. The majority of the original Roo community are descendants of the Kakrinda and Kakyone clans founded by two brothers. Villagers therefore cannot intermarry. Marriages are strictly with immigrants from other areas, or uxorilocal with neighbouring clans. Apart from the predominant Luo and Basuba there are also Kisii who migrated from Migori in the early 1970s in search of farmland, relatively new Luhya settlers, Baganda and Tanzanians from the border towns of Mara, Tarime and Msoma, most of whom engage in fishing. The Tanzanians, some of whom have second identities as Kenyans, have not fully settled, instead opting to keep moving from Kenya to Tanzania and back. Wives may not accompany their husbands. In the early days land was communally owned and only one person, the clan elder, advised by counsellors whose appointments were entirely based on age and knowledge of the community, had the prerogative to allocate land. Quarrels over land were minimal or non-existent. Most of these powers and positions have now been pre-empted by the Provincial Administration and government appointees. Disputes occur every day. Population growth, exploitation of forest resources and water catchment areas for commercial farming by outsiders, some with political support, and the enactment and enforcement of forest legislation restricting further access to the forest have meant that they are faced with a shrinking, overexploited resource base. This has resulted in increased land pressure, and hence a reduction in the fallow periods, resulting in declining soil fertility and lower yields.

Overall assessment

The picture at grassroots is then of a world clinging to culturally embedded modes of access to land, which are however giving increasingly diminishing returns to both equity and efficiency. The resource base – soil fertility, tree cover, fishing stocks, livestock – tends to be subject to ever greater human pressure, resulting in land fragmentation and outmigration, where new opportunities are mainly seized by young men. The welfare function of the common property regime has largely given way in the face of shrinking per capita land availability, and has given a new dimension to patriarchy following the commoditisation of land and agricultural production. A considerable capacity for adaptation is however revealed in terms of moving to new forms of economic activity, both non-farm and off-farm, but this has been seriously undermined by a wholly inadequate supply of inputs and marketing support, and ubiquitous rent-seeking behaviour by local authorities. If there is one feature common to all the studies, it is the revelation of the absence of any effective or fair local land administration.

Emerging themes and issues

The LADDER village reports showed generally that customary tenure systems are dynamic rather than static, capable of evolution, yet also inadequate in a number of respects. Given the context of poor agricultural service delivery and adverse politico–administrative regimes, the direction of adaptation has been towards survival, and a shift of advantage for the upper stratum of small rural producers with some shift from matrilineal towards effectively patrilineal inheritance, rather than towards promoting efficiency, innovation and equitable access. Common property rights have been widely abused through privatisation and over-exploitation, and in particular the weaker rights of outsiders and migrants have been eroded. The evidence of the village reports confirms the conclusion that formalisation of tenure is unlikely to secure that which has not been attained through the operation of social networks (Meinzen-Dick *et al.* 2002: 7).

Thus neither the arguments for creating a fully fledged open property market, nor the conception that customary land rights evolve on their own in an optimal manner appear to be supported. The Kenyan case (Haugerud 1983; Migot-Adholla *et al.* 1991) classically illustrates the former, and Malawi (Cross 2002a) the latter. There is some evidence from the surveys that more secure tenure is positively correlated with better practices such as fallowing and tree-planting (as also noted by Place *et al.* 2002) but this is possibly as specific to farming systems as it is to tenure as such.

Do the proposals on the table in the land reform legislation passed or proposed in Malawi, Uganda and Tanzania offer a way ahead? Certainly there are some significant advances. Optional avenues for formal transition towards registration, while retaining safeguards against abuse, and the opening up of a potential land market are desirable, and there is little evidence that this per se leads towards overly large agricultural land accumulation. The latter occurs primarily in the peri-urban fringe driven by speculation, and does not address the issue of tenurial design as such. The key problem has been land grabbing by elites at the point of first registration rather than through the market (Bruce 1988; Sundet 1997: 118).

The main reason why rural land markets are likely to be thin, as Platteau points out (2000: 62), are attitudes towards the land, which is seen as a bank, a refuge of last resort, and a stake in the organic community rather than primarily as a commodity. The thrust of activity observed in the villages was towards the emergence of a rental rather than sales market, and the constraints on and imperfections in these are hardly addressed in current legislation. Land rental by individuals and collectives to more efficient producers (including outsiders and migrants) holds greater promise for optimisation and the maintenance of political stability than does the promotion of a land sale market. This ties in with the widely observed failure of the collateralisation effect (Platteau 2000: 71). Failure to access credit is less a function of land entitlement than it is of failures in the market for rural credit supply.

Of more importance perhaps for the drive towards efficient utilisation are means to promote production on those lands acquired by elites for reasons of prestige or speculation. Absentee landlordism in Uganda, leaseholding of erstwhile customary land in Malawi, elite transfers via registration and disposal in Kenya and Tanzania are cases in point. This has effectively created a dual agrarian structure (Otsuka and Place 2001: 28) in these countries, and is a large contributory factor to land scarcity. This is not an issue effectively addressed in recent legislations.

The land reform measures so far legislated in these countries (Cross 2002b) offer a vision for a degree of rehabilitation of customary rights of access. Uganda has gone furthest in recognising that land belongs to the people, not the state, with an elaborate decentralised mechanism on the drawing board. Malawi too has set up a process whereby customary ownership can be certified, and even extended to cover leased out land, which may then, theoretically at least, be recovered by original clan owners. The Tanzania legislation has exhaustive procedures which seek to control abuses in land administration, and a number of sensible provisions for village land security, but is gravely weakened by centralisation and the continuity with the past tradition of control by the state without judicial oversight.

However the central question that hangs over these measures is over what timescale they might be implemented. The case of Uganda, which led the way both in decentralisation and land reform, is instructive. Land reform properly carried out requires a large corps of people skilled in land survey, registration and jurisdiction matters (an estimated 32,000 in Uganda), this has considerable costs, as too in Uganda does the Land Fund which is supposedly the fulcrum of the land reform's political mechanism. Considering how remote these requirements are in 2003, it becomes clear that the operationalisation of the 1998 Land Act lies far in the future. Similar caveats apply to an even greater extent in Tanzania, Malawi and Kenya.

Notes

* This is a substantially shortened and edited version of a paper presented at the Nairobi Conference and is also available as LADDER Working Paper No. 31 (Cross 2002b).

1 There are thirty-seven village reports, all available in PDF format from the website: www.odg.uea.ac.uk/ladder.

13 Implications of livelihood strategies for agricultural research

A Kenya case study*

H. Ade Freeman and Frank Ellis

Introduction

Rural households in low income countries are pursuing diverse livelihood strategies deriving income from a wide range of farm, off-farm and non-farm sources (Reardon 1997; Ellis 1998; Bryceson 2000; Ellis 2000; Barrett *et al.* 2001c). There is also evidence that the share of non-farm income is increasing in the income portfolio of rural households (Bryceson 2000). However, despite increasing income diversification, agriculture remains an important income source for a large proportion of rural households (Ellis 1998; Bryceson 2000; IFAD 2001; Orr and Orr 2002). Moreover, a proportion of off-farm diversification in Africa is linked to agriculture through forward and backward production linkages (Reardon *et al.* 1998).[1]

Improved technology and better access to markets have been identified as crucial in fostering broad-based growth, enhancing sustainable management of natural resources, and poverty reduction in rural areas (de Janvry and Sadoulet 2000; IFAD 2001; Csaki 2001; Tripp 2001). Yet, there is scarce empirical evidence on the implications of household livelihood strategies for the design and development of agricultural technologies and rural institutions that benefit the poor. Agricultural researchers need to develop a critical understanding of the role that research can play in improving diverse livelihoods in order to enhance the effects of agricultural research investments on poverty reduction.

This chapter provides a holistic understanding of the factors that distinguish the rural poor from the better off and the multi-sectoral patterns of activities they pursue in constructing diverse livelihood strategies. This micro-level understanding of livelihood strategies is then used to draw implications for the design and development of agricultural technologies and institutions that enhance the poverty impacts from agricultural research investments. The conceptual framework for the research was based on the sustainable livelihoods framework that emphasizes a broad and systematic view of livelihoods and the factors that assist or block households' efforts to construct routes out of poverty (Carney 1998; Scoones 1998; Ellis 2000).

The chapter is organized as follows. The next section presents a brief discussion of the policy environment in Kenya. This is followed by a discussion of the survey research methods, results from descriptive statistics and probit regressions that examine factors associated with identified livelihood strategies. The chapter concludes with implications for agricultural research if it is to make effective contributions to rural poverty reduction.

The case study

Economic patterns and trends in Kenya set the context for any meaningful discussion of poverty reduction. Kenya has an estimated total population of 31 million in 2001, growing at 2.4 per cent per annum. Per capita gross national income was US$ 340 in 2001; lower than what it was in 1987. The Kenyan economy has experienced long-term decline in economic performance with growth in real income falling from 3.2 per cent per annum in the first decade of independence (1963–1972) to about 1 per cent per annum in the 1980s. National policy frameworks in Kenya, such as the Poverty Reduction Strategy Paper (PRSP) and the recent Strategy for Economic Recovery documents view agricultural research as a key instrument to raise agricultural productivity and enhance competitiveness in the agricultural sector.[2]

Public service delivery has deteriorated in rural Kenya over the past two decades. This is manifested by poor maintenance of rural feeder roads, high cost and poor delivery of education and health services, uneven provision of agricultural technology and advice, and poor market outreach for farm inputs and outputs. The findings of rural livelihoods research reported in this chapter must be interpreted in the light of these general considerations.

The fieldwork combined qualitative research methods and a quantitative household survey to examine the livelihood patterns and strategies of rural individuals and households (see Chapter 3). The qualitative component of the research addressed the institutional context of livelihoods and changing livelihood circumstances at the community level, while a quantitative component addressed assets, activities, incomes and vulnerability factors at household level. The qualitative research involved a wealth ranking exercise and focus group discussions formed around particular activities or issues. In other instances, specific understanding of strategies and constraints were obtained through discussions with individuals and households. The sample survey took place at the same time that qualitative, village research was conducted. Households were stratified into three wealth groups based on participatory wealth ranking procedures (Grandin 1988). A random sample was drawn from household lists in each wealth group. This resulted in a final sample of thirty-five households in each village, ten households each from the well-off and middle categories, and fifteen households from the poor category. The five villages studied thus provided a total sample of 175 households.

The fieldwork for this research was conducted in Suba District in Nyanza Province. The district was carved out of Homa Bay District in 1995, and is located in the south western part of Nyanza along Lake Victoria. It borders

Kisumu and Siaya districts to the north, Homa Bay District to the southeast, Migori District to the south, the Republic of Tanzania to the southwest and the Republic of Uganda to the west. Average annual rainfall ranges from 700 to 1,200 mm with 60 per cent reliability. There are two rainy seasons: the long rains occur from March to May while the short rains occur between August and December. Average temperatures range from 17.10°C to 34.8°C.

The villages selected for the study in Suba District are listed in Table 13.1. These villages were purposively selected bearing in mind poverty–relative wealth considerations given the overall research focus on poverty and food insecurity. Villages differed in the degree of reliance on different natural resources, market access, infrastructure and service support.

Survey results

Income and asset endowments of the sample households by income quartile are shown in Table 13.2.[3] Even though livelihoods and income are not synonymous, income data provides a direct and measurable outcome of livelihood circumstances and strategies (Ellis 2000). There are substantial differences in household incomes with average per capita income in the richest households being twenty times higher than that for the poorest households.[4] Poorer households also had smaller endowments of productive assets. The heads of poorer households had the least education and household members had the least average years of education. Poor households had larger families, owned smaller farms, had fewer livestock and productive tools and were least likely to own a bicycle.

Household activities and incomes

Sample households were involved in a range of activities that generated income. The portfolio of household income shares by source is shown in Table 13.3.

Even though 63 per cent of resident household members reported farming as their main occupation, crop and livestock income only accounted for 16 per cent of total household income. Poorer households obtained a greater share of household income from cropping and livestock activities. These households also derived substantial amounts of income from off-farm activities involving exploitation of common property resources such as collecting firewood, making ropes and charcoal. Low entry barriers and corresponding low returns to household assets characterize these activities. In contrast, the richest households derived over half of their income from non-farm sources. Remittance income and transfers were less important in overall income portfolios across all income groups. The data on household income portfolios show that the share of non-farm income in total income monotonically increased with wealth. This corroborates evidence on the positive correlation between the share of non-farm income and total incomes that has

Table 13.1 Characteristics of sample villages

Division	*Location*	*Sub-location*	*Village*	*Soils*	*Production systems*	*Market access*
Lambwe	Lambwe West	God-Jope	Nyapuodi	Poor soils due to erosion (due to occasional heavy downpours, overstocking and strong winds during dry season) and prevalence of weeds especially *kayongo*	Major crops are maize, sorghum, beans, vegetables (kale, onions and tomatoes), cassava, green grams, groundnuts, cotton and fruits (paw paw, pineapples and bananas introduced in 2001 and 2000) Livestock production (cattle, goats, sheep, poultry and donkeys) Typical farm size is 4 ha.	Good year-round vehicle access
Central	Kaksingri East	Sumba West	Makende	Low soil fertility Heavy erosion due to cutting down of trees, overgrazing and overstocking	Major crops are maize, sorghum, cassava, beans, groundnuts, sunflower and millet Livestock (zebu type cattle, goats, sheep and poultry) Typical farm size is 1.2 ha.	Poor year-round vehicle access
Mbita	Gembe West	Mbita Township	Gingo	Increased wind erosion and reduced soil fertility; Striga weed is on the increase	Fishing Major crops are sorghum, millet, maize intercrop with beans and marginal horticulture (onions, tomatoes and kale) Livestock (cattle, goats and poultry) Average land holding is 4 ha.	Dry season vehicle access only
Mbita	Gembe West	Mbita Township	Nyachebe	Soils are poor with increasing infestation of weeds especially Striga.	Fishing Major crops are sorghum, maize, beans, sweet potatoes and vegetables Livestock (cattle, goats and poultry) Average land holding is 8 ha.	Good year-round vehicle access
Central	Kaksingri West	Rangwe West	Roo	Soils are relatively fertile	Fishing Major crops are sorghum, maize, cassava, sweet potatoes, beans and groundnuts Livestock (cattle, goats, donkeys and poultry) Average land holding for older heads of households is 3–5 ha. while that of the younger head of households is about 1 ha.	Beach in poor year-round vehicle access

Source: research carried out in five villages in Suba District during 2001.

Table 13.2 Household characteristics by per capita quartiles

	I	*II*	*III*	*IV*
Income per capita (Ksh)	3,966	11,187	21,269	74,373
Age of household head	51.1	48.1	46.8	43.8
Years of education of household head	6.0	6.5	6.6	7.8
Average years of education of all resident	12.7	14.7	15.8	16.5
Household size	4.1	4.1	3.9	3.6
Ratio of workers to family size	0.4	0.4	0.4	0.5
Total land owned (ha.)	1.9	2.2	2.3	2.5
Land owed per capita (ha.)	0.6	0.7	0.6	0.8
Livestock (CEU)[a]	4.2	4.3	6.3	6.9
Tools[b]	7.8	7.1	14.1	9.0
Households with:				
Concrete or brick house (%)	2	10	11	16
Piped water (%)	0	2	0	0
Bicycle (%)	36	46	44	55

Source: research carried out in five villages in Suba District during 2001.

Notes
a CEU: Goats = 0.12; Sheep = 0.10; Chickens = 0.02.
b Tools is a value-based index based on productive assets owned by households.

Table 13.3 Per capita shares of different sources and income quartiles

	I	*II*	*III*	*IV*	*Total n = 175*
Crops	42.0	20.0	9.0	4.0	8.0
Livestock	19.0	22.0	13.0	4.0	8.0
Fishing	6.0	16.0	15.0	30.0	25.0
Rent	0.0	2.0	0.0	0.0	0.0
Other natural resources	13.0	18.0	14.0	7.0	10.0
Non-farm	11.0	20.0	42.0	53.0	46.0
Remittances	4.0	1.0	2.0	1.0	1.0
In-kind	5.0	1.0	5.0	1.0	2.0
Total	100.0	100.0	100.0	100.0	100.0

Source: research carried out in five villages in Suba District during 2001.

been reported in other African countries (Reardon 1997; Barrett *et al.* 2001d).

Survey data on output shares suggest a relatively low monetization of the agricultural economy in the survey area. Table 13.4 provides data on the output share of major crops grown and livestock that is consumed by households in the survey area.

The results show a striking reliance on subsistence consumption for crops with cereals predominantly retained for home consumption. The mean subsistence share show that maize, sorghum and millet are predominantly consumed within the household, while over 70 per cent of beans are on average

Table 13.4 Output share of selected crops and livestock products consumed by households (%)

Crops	*Total n = 175*
Maize	93
Sorghum	98
Millet	95
Beans	71
Livestock	
Milk	73
Cattle	37
Goats	41
Chickens	82

Source: research carried out in five villages in Suba District during 2001.

retained for home consumption. Amongst livestock products, milk and chicken are kept mainly for home consumption while goats and cattle are kept predominantly for other livelihood functions including cash sales. In general, the relatively high dependence on subsistence production in the sample suggests that food is a major wage good for all households in this area irrespective of their wealth.

The central role of subsistence in rural livelihoods is further explored by data on the share of own consumption in total income (Table 13.5).

The general pattern that emerges is the declining share of own consumption in total income as household income increases. Reliance on subsistence falls steeply from 51 per cent of household income among the poorest households to about 6 per cent of income among the richest households. These data suggest that rural poor are trapped in a subsistence economy that allows very limited scope to move out of poverty because their ability to generate cash income severely reduces their range of livelihood options.

Households build their livelihoods from decision-making processes involving the use of assets that individuals (or the household) own or have access to. This process characterizes a household livelihood strategy (Soussan *et al.* 2001). Following Ellis (2000) we developed typologies of household livelihood strategies using observable choice of activity and income data. A household is characterized as primarily pursuing a livelihood strategy if it obtains

Table 13.5 Share of own consumption in total income by income quartiles (%)

	Income quartiles				*Total n = 175*
	I	*II*	*III*	*IV*	
Whole sample	51.4	25	13.1	6.4	11.4

Source: research carried out in five villages in Suba District during 2001.

two-thirds or more of its income from an activity or combination of activities. As Ellis (2000) notes the income threshold selected can make a big difference to the pattern of household livelihood strategies.

The characterization of livelihood strategies resulted in four distinct household livelihood strategies. First, agricultural based livelihoods comprised households that earned their income primarily from cropping, livestock and fishing activities; a second livelihood strategy comprised households that earned their income from engaging primarily in non-farm activities. The data suggested two mixed livelihood strategies in which households combined agricultural activities and non-farm activities. Given that the returns to different non-farm activities varied substantially we distinguished low return non-farm activities from high return non-farm activities based on information obtained from the focus group discussions. Communities perceived activities such as collecting firewood, rope making and basket weaving as low return activities that poorer members of the community engaged in. In contrast, high return non-farm activities, such as obtaining salaried employment within the public or private sector, involved specialized skill or education. We therefore distinguished two mixed livelihood strategies; one defined as mixed livelihoods including diversification into low return non-farm activities and the other mixed livelihoods including diversification into high return non-farm activities.

The distribution of sample households according to the typologies described above is reported in Table 13.6. The table shows that households pursued distinct wealth-differentiated livelihood strategies. These result from differences in the level of entry barriers involved in pursuing each strategy (Barrett *et al.* 2001c).

The poorest households pursued agricultural livelihood strategies and low return mixed strategies that required limited specialized skills and involved little capital assets. Households with few *ex ante* asset endowments are compelled to diversify into these strategies because they have relatively low entry barriers. In contrast, wealthier households diversified into non-farm strategies that provided higher returns. Entry into these activities, however, required higher levels of skill, capital assets or both. Table 13.7 shows the relationship between household livelihood strategies and *ex ante* asset endowments, and

Table 13.6 Livelihood strategies by income quartiles (%)

Strategies	*I*	*II*	*III*	*IV*	*Total*
Principally agriculture	52.0	34.0	14.0	36.0	34.0
Principally non-farm	5.0	16.0	40.0	43.0	26.0
Mixed strategy with low return non-farm	23.0	41.0	28.0	14.0	26.0
Mixed strategy with high return non-farm	21.0	9.0	19.0	7.0	14.0
All strategies	100.0	100.0	100.0	100.0	100.0

Source: research carried out in five villages in Suba District during 2001.

Table 13.7 Distribution of assets by livelihood strategies

	Principally agriculture	*Principally non-farm*	*Mixed strategy 1*[a]	*Mixed strategy 2*[b]	*Total*
Age of household head	49.7	46.8	44.3	49.2	47.5
Total adult equivalent unit	3.6	4.1	3.9	4.4	3.9
Education of hh head	6.1	8.2	5.9	7.0	6.7
Education of resident members[c]	12.9	17.4	15.3	14.6	14.9
Total land owned (ha.)	2.1	2.1	2.3	2.5	2.2
Total cattle equivalent units	4.2	6.8	4.5	8.1	5.5
Tools	7.1	12.9	7.9	12.1	9.5
Households with:					
Concrete or brick house (%)	6.0	11.0	7.0	21.0	10.0
Stand pipe (%)	0.0	2.0	0.0	0.0	1.0
Bicycle (%)	32.0	51.0	50.0	58.0	45.0

Source: research carried out in five villages in Suba District during 2001.

Note

a Mixed strategy with low return non-farm activities.

b Mixed strategy with high return non-farm activities.

c Average number of years of education of resident household members.

provides additional insights into the importance of asset endowments in the choice of a household pursuing a particular livelihood strategy.

Our findings provide additional evidence that diversification into non-farm activities is related to greater upward income mobility. Given the importance of non-farm incomes and its importance in offering rural households a route out of poverty we further investigated non-farm income sources. The relationship between agriculture and the non-farm economy at the household level is shown in Table 13.8.

About 75 per cent of non-farm activities are directly linked to agriculture either as backward or forward production linkages. Forward production linkages involve diversification into agro-processing, trading and transportation services are particularly important while backward linkages in the form of supply of farm inputs and services are less important. This latter finding reflected, in part, the weak derived demand for farm inputs and services in an agricultural system that predominantly used traditional production technologies.

We further examined the determinants of household livelihood strategies

Table 13.8 Farm/non-farm linkages by per capita income quartiles

Linkages	*I*	*II*	*III*	*IV*	*Total n = 175*
Backward linkage	33	30	8	26	23
Forward linkage	50	40	58	53	51
No linkage	17	30	33	21	26

Source: research carried out in five villages in Suba District during 2001.

with probit regressions. The regression equations estimate the probability of a household pursuing a livelihood strategy as a function of its asset endowments and a community variable measuring market access. This provided additional insights into how household asset endowments influenced their choice of livelihood strategy. Given that several of the independent variables are choice variables the regression results only provide evidence about the correlation between livelihood strategies and household assets without implying causality. Even so, the probit regression results were instructive.

The results from the probit regressions link the probability of households pursuing three distinct livelihood strategies – agricultural strategy, mixed strategy including diversification into low return off-farm activities and non-farm strategy – as a function of household asset endowments and market access. The dependent variable takes a value of one for a household pursuing the ith livelihood strategy and zero otherwise.

The results are reported in Tables 13.9, 13.10, 13.11 and 13.12 for agricultural, mixed and non-farm livelihood strategies, respectively. Households with a higher proportion of workers were more likely to pursue an agricultural livelihood strategy. These households were also less likely to be members of credit or savings groups, or they received remittance income that could be used for financing farm investments. Households pursuing agricultural livelihood strategies were also less likely to own a bicycle, an important transportation asset in this area. The level of education of the household head did not have a significant influence on the choice of pursuing an agricultural livelihood strategy. A likely explanation is that farming activities in this area

Table 13.9 Description of regression equation variables

Variable	*Type*	*Description*
AGE	Continuous	Age of household head
AGE^2	Continuous	The square of the age of the household
GENDER	Binary	Gender of household head: 1 = male headed, 0 = otherwise
EDUCATION	Continuous	Number of years household head has spent in school
LANDOWN	Continuous	Total area owned (acres)
HOUSEHOLDSIZE	Continuous	Total number of resident household members in adult equivalent units
DEPENDENCY	Continuous	Ratio of workers to family size
LIVESTOCK	Continuous	Size of livestock herd in cattle equivalent units
CREDIT	Binary	1 = member belong to a credit scheme, 0 = otherwise
REMITTANCE	Binary	1 = receive income from remittances, 0 = otherwise
TOOLINDEX	Continuous	Tools index
BICYCLE	Continuous	Number of bicycles
MARKETACCESS	Binary	1 = good market access, 0 = otherwise

Table 13.10 Probit result for agricultural livelihood strategy

Variable	*Coefficient*	*Probability*
Constant	0.385	0.739
AGE	−0.049	0.293
AGE^2	0.001	0.169
GENDER	0.405	0.165
EDUCATION	−0.005	0.895
LANDOWN	0.012	0.614
HOUSEHOLDSIZE	−0.047	0.515
DEPENDENCY	0.696[b]	0.094
LIVESTOCK	0.001	0.943
CREDIT	−0.680[b]	0.080
REMITTANCE	−0.931[a]	0.020
TOOLSINDEX	−0.012	0.354
BICYCLE	−0.396[b]	0.066
MARKETACCESS	−0.075	0.733
Chi-squared	28.924	
Significance	0.007	

Notes
a Significant at 5% level.
b Significant at 10% level.

Table 13.11 Probit result for mixed livelihood strategy including low return off-farm

Variable	*Coefficient*	*Probability*
Constant	−0.884	0.507
AGE	0.056	0.339
AGE^2	−0.001	0.148
GENDER	0.199	0.524
EDUCATION	−0.114[a]	0.006
LANDOWN	0.015	0.526
HOUSEHOLDSIZE	0.074	0.342
DEPENDENCY	0.080	0.858
LIVESTOCK	−0.010	0.654
CREDIT	−0.806[a]	0.049
REMITTANCE	0.048	0.905
TOOLSINDEX	−0.016	0.271
BICYCLE	0.305	0.178
MARKETACCESS	0.020	0.932
Chi-squared	23.588	
Significance	0.035	

Notes
a Significant at 5% level.
b Significant at 10% level.

Table 13.12 Probit result for non-farm livelihood strategy

Variable	*Coefficient*	*Probability*
Constant	−1.208	0.319
AGE	0.009	0.856
AGE^2	0.000	0.981
GENDER	−0.343	0.293
EDUCATION	0.098[a]	0.010
LANDOWN	−0.034	0.218
HOUSEHOLDSIZE	−0.052	0.490
DEPENDENCY	−0.759	0.118
LIVESTOCK	−0.002	0.892
CREDIT	0.875[a]	0.006
REMITTANCE	0.574	0.104
TOOLSINDEX	0.020[b]	0.063
BICYCLE	0.005	0.983
MARKETACCESS	−0.021	0.930
Chi-squared	31.606	
Significance	0.003	

Notes

a Significant at 5% level.

b Significant at 10% level.

are based on traditional technologies that require limited skills. A surprising finding is that the coefficient on the land variable, though positive, did not significantly influence the choice of pursuing an agricultural livelihood strategy. A probable explanation is that in this area where farm sizes tended to be higher than average, it may be access to good quality land rather than large farm sizes that determine the successful pursuit of an agricultural strategy. This finding is consistent with the perception of the communities that low soil fertility and high rates of soil erosion reduced the quality of land resources, severely limiting the potential for agricultural production. Households pursuing livelihoods that primarily comprised agricultural and low return off-farm activities were more likely to be those with younger heads and without family members that belonged to credit or savings groups. Non-farm livelihood strategies were more likely in households where the head had a relatively high level of education, family members belonged to credit and savings groups, and the household received remittance income that could finance non-farm activities. These households had a higher level of initial wealth as proxied by the tools index. Together these results imply that human capital variables, and other capital assets, imposed important barriers to entry into non-farm activities that provided higher returns to household resources. This is consistent with findings in other parts of Africa that show barriers to entry into high return non-farm activities (Dercon and Krishnan 1996; Barrett *et al.* 2001c). Poorer households lacking in education, specialized skills or capital assets are compelled to diversify into low return livelihood strategies in agriculture and low return activities off-farm.

HIV/AIDS and the health situation of rural households

HIV/AIDS is a major development and social problem that severely affects the livelihoods and food security of a large number of households in the sample villages. We did not obtain data on the incidence of the disease at the household level but the communities overwhelmingly agreed that the incidence and extent of the disease has increased over the past ten years. HIV/AIDS had reduced the availability of labour for farm work and fishing; diverted household expenditure from food, clothing, school fees and productive investments into medical care; forced the sale of household assets including land and livestock, and reduced income generating activities. The disease has created large numbers of orphans who are either being supported by grandparents, who are poor themselves, and often too old to work, or left to fend for themselves. The quality of human capital assets have also declined as teachers succumb to the disease and children are withdrawn from school to care for the sick or because parents are unable to pay school fees. These communities expressed the view that these factors have increased poverty and vulnerability in many households.

Local taxation regimes and their impact on livelihood strategies

We also examined local taxation regimes in the focus group interviews, given that taxes influence relative prices and the incentives to pursue commercial activities. Households in Suba District pay a wide range of legal and illegal taxes on all commodities involving monetary transactions. Fisherfolk require a number of licenses from the fisheries and health departments and pay levies to the county council on fish sales. Farmers pay taxes on crop sales, and on movement of commodities outside the district, while a livestock trader needs a license to start trading and taxes are imposed on livestock sales and movement. Chiefs and local administration authorities also compel households to contribute to *harambees* (local fund-raising activities). Moreover, tax collection systems are not transparent, opening them up to all sorts of abuse. Indeed, the perception of the communities is that they are over-burdened by local taxes and other ill-defined payments to the authorities. The communities were unanimous that these payments discouraged commercial farming, fishing or livestock activities and limited their ability to undertake productive investments. Ellis and Bahiigwa (2003) reported similar findings on local taxation in rural Uganda (see also Chapter 9 above).

Conclusions and implications for agricultural research

The analysis of rural household livelihood strategies presented in this chapter is consistent with empirical evidence from other parts of Africa that most rural households obtain their livelihoods from a diverse portfolio of income sources (Reardon 1997; Ellis 1998; Bryceson 2000; Ellis 2000; Barrett *et al.* 2001c). The projection is that rural households will continue pursuing multi-locational and multi-occupational livelihood strategies (Ashley and Maxwell 2001). The main implication following from this is that the implicit assumption often made by policy makers that all rural households are primarily farming households is not valid and can lead to the wrong specification of technology needs. Technological change is critical in the transition from subsistence production to monetized farm and non-farm sectors. The challenge for agricultural research is to identify and develop the types of technologies that will help poor rural households work their way out of poverty. Such technologies need to recognize the linkages between agriculture and the rural non-farm sector, be compatible with household investment strategies, raise labour productivity in food production, improve the productivity of household assets and stimulate growth of the non-farm economy. Institutional innovation and enabling rural institutions are equally important in expanding growth opportunities for rural households.

The rising share of non-farm income in household income portfolios reported in this chapter does not diminish the role agriculture can play in rural poverty reduction or the importance of agricultural policy and research (Reardon *et al.* 1998; Kydd 2002). As Kydd (2002) argues, the challenge is to find ways to make agricultural research more successful. The study reported here shows that non-farm activities are closely linked to agriculture particularly through marketing, crop processing and distribution. Reardon *et al.* (1998) argue that this corresponds to a first stage of the rural non-farm sector transformation. In this stage a dynamic agriculture is necessary for development of the non-farm sector and vice versa. Gordon and Craig (2001) argue that many countries in sub-Saharan Africa are in the first stages of rural non-farm sector transformation.

The observed patterns of income diversification imply that rural households allocate their scarce resources in farming as well as between farm and non-farm enterprises according to relative returns to resource use and subjective assessment of the riskiness of alternative investments. Many rural households are part-time farmers, part-time workers and micro-entrepreneurs (de Janvry and Sadoulet 2000). Rural households will continue evaluating relative returns and risk of alternative enterprises when making investment decisions. Agricultural research strategies need to consider this in priority setting and technology design. Many rural households may seek to free farm labour to pursue more productive activities off-farm. HIV/AIDS also reduces labour availability for farm work. These households are likely to prioritize labour-saving technologies even in perceived labour-surplus areas. Other households with cash resources and access to information and markets may want to pursue intensified commercial agriculture with high labour demands. Such households may generate employment in agriculture and prioritize labour-using technologies. The simultaneous demand for labour-saving and labour-using technologies in rural areas underscores the need for agricultural research to emphasize the development of a wider range of technology options for households with differing technology needs.

The high share of the value of subsistence consumption in household income portfolios highlights the importance of food as a wage good in the study area. This finding is consistent with empirical evidence from other parts of Africa (Delgado *et al.* 1993; IFAD 2001; Lipton 2001). Improved technologies that increase food production in these semi-open economies would reduce food prices. Given that food is a major wage good, this is equivalent to an increase in per capita incomes of rural households (Schuh 2000). Most of these benefits would accrue to poorer rural households who tend to spend a larger share of income on food compared to better-off households. Increased labour productivity in food production would also free household labour to pursue higher return off-farm activities.

The finding that land and labour resources were not important factors conditioning the choice of agricultural livelihood strategies justifies the view that improvements in the quality of land and labour, key household assets, are necessary for lifting rural households out of poverty. Improving land productivity typically involves increased investment in natural resource management such as soil fertility and water management technologies. But rural households may not adopt improved natural resource management technologies if the returns to these investments accrue at a later date or are lower than returns to investments in alternative non-farm activities. Farmers producing a commercial crop are more likely to adopt improved soil and water management technologies. Thus, agricultural natural resource management research strategies need a paradigm shift away from a narrow agricultural production bias to a broad intersectoral perspective that emphasizes relative returns to household resources in alternative activities.

Tripp (2001) argues that future agricultural technologies will be knowledge intensive and inputs will increasingly be delivered by the private sector. It is therefore crucial to build the human capital of rural households if they are to benefit from new technologies and emerging opportunities for commercialization. Investment in human capital also facilitates the transition to non-farm employment. The projected increased role of the private sector in input supply calls for improving the technical knowledge of input suppliers so that they can effectively advise farmers on input use. All of this implies a changed role for extension systems, most of which are facing severe budgetary limitations and barely function in many rural areas. Rather than focus on information dissemination to farmers, extension systems might use their limited resources to improve the technical capacity of private traders so that they can provide effective advisory services for farmers.

Even though the data did not allow us to test the strength of farm and non-farm linkages, the importance of backward and forward production linkages in non-farm activities suggest that future research should put greater emphasis on strengthening farm–non-farm linkages. The farm sector will eventually decline with economic development (Schuh 2000). Agricultural research should help rural households make that transition. Diversification into non-farm activities is associated with improved living standards. But the probit regressions suggested that there are significant entry barriers to non-farm activities. Agricultural research and policy interventions should aim at reducing entry barriers into remunerative non-farm activities. Emerging local government business licensing and taxation policies require careful monitoring in this regard.

Within the farm sector, technology change can facilitate diversification of cropping patterns through choice of variety, choice of crops, improved product quality. On-farm crop diversification can benefit both semi-commercial and commercial farmers. The challenge is to identify market niches that exploit these opportunities (Orr and Orr 2002). Future crop improvement programmes may need to put more effort into incorporating preferred farmer and market traits into new varieties. Correspondingly, there has to be greater emphasis on improving farmer linkages into markets in ways that include market participation of smallholder farmers. This includes development of information and communication systems to improve the flow of information on products, markets and cropping options. Policy interventions should also facilitate the design and development of agro-processing suitable for small- and medium-scale rural entrepreneurs.

Institutional innovations that reduce transaction costs in marketing and distribution are equally important. Marketing arrangements that provide incentives for implementation of grades and standards in rural areas are necessary to facilitate access to high value urban, regional and international markets. Kydd (2002) observes that agricultural research needs to reflect the fact that technology and institutional development are co-evolutionary. An important implication of this is that institutional change that distorts or inhibits the participation by farmers in markets is likely at the same time to inhibit the uptake of technologies that can make strong contributions to future productivity and incomes in agriculture.

Notes

* This chapter was written especially for this volume, and draws on the LADDER data set as well as several of the LADDER Working Papers.

1 The importance of these linkages as comprising strictly rural growth opportunities, has, however, been exaggerated in much of the linkage literature. Many such linkages occur to towns and represent part of the transition from rural to urban lifestyles. Moreover, reduction of co-variant risk means that households often seek non-linked, non-farm activities in order to achieve better livelihood security overall.

2 Agricultural research organizations in Kenya include national agricultural research institutes, policy research institutes, public and private universities, international and regional research centres, and private sector research.

3 I is the first income quartile comprising households with the lowest income while IV is the fourth income quartile comprising households with the highest income.

4 This is partly of course an artifact of the stratification procedure adopted, and does not represent the degree of inequality in the underlying village populations.

Part IV

Natural resource management and rural poverty reduction

14 Crop-based farming systems and diverse livelihoods in Uganda

John McDonagh

Introduction

This chapter describes an analysis of crop farming-based livelihoods in Uganda undertaken as part of the LADDER research.[1] In particular it is concerned with the perspective of rural Ugandans on factors or processes that appear to be facilitating or blocking their attempts to accumulate assets and escape poverty. A number of these factors are linked to important policies in the agriculture sector currently being implemented under Uganda's broad poverty reduction strategy.

Uganda is one of the low income-economies of sub-Saharan Africa (SSA) and is among the poorest countries in the world. Poverty is most pronounced in rural areas, particularly in the north and east and this contributes to food shortages, child malnutrition, frequent illness, high rates of HIV/AIDS and widespread illiteracy (Uganda 2000b). Although there has been an overall decline in numbers of poor in recent years, the results from the 1999/2000 Uganda National Household Survey (UNHS) indicate that 35 per cent of the population, or 7.7 million Ugandans, were then living below the absolute poverty line and 80 per cent of these were from farming households (Appleton 2001b). The downward trend in poverty figures up to 2000 appear to have undergone a reverse according to the most recent survey conducted in 2002/2003 that puts the aggregate national incidence of poverty at 38 per cent (Uganda 2003c).

As part of its poverty reduction strategy the Government of Uganda (GoU) has embraced decentralization and is pursuing a cross sectoral approach to rural development with a strong poverty focus, articulated in the Plan for Eradication of Poverty (PEAP) (Uganda 2001d). Although a number of countries in SSA have voiced commitment to a poverty reduction strategy there are large differences in apparent levels of commitment, local ownership of the policy and the pace of implementation (Jayne *et al.* 2002; Ellis and Bahiigwa 2003). Uganda, however, is something of a showcase in Africa and would be somewhere near the top of any list compiled on the basis of these criteria.

The effects of the Economic Reform Programme (ERP) implemented in the late 1980s and early 1990s can be seen today in the agricultural sector. In common with many countries in the region the private sector was encouraged to take over as the main suppliers of agricultural inputs, credit and marketing services once the parastatals withdrew (Wiggins 2000). There have been some positive impacts from this, particularly in the marketing of the major cash crops coffee, cotton and tobacco (Djikstra and Van Donge 2001). However, this strategy has only been partially successful (James *et al.* 2001). In the LADDER research sites, small-scale coffee and cotton producers have suffered as farmers' access to reliable markets for these cash crops has worsened. In addition the complex and largely privatized system of local taxation appears to be having a particularly deleterious effect on the ability of farmers to market their agricultural produce on fair terms (Ellis and Bahiigwa 2003). It is clear that local taxation regimes can stifle attempts by poor farmers to move from subsistence into market-oriented farming and so they conflict directly with key Ugandan policy objectives.

Decentralization was initiated in Uganda in 1992. The 1997 Local Government Act began the process of devolving political, financial and planning responsibilities to District (LC5) and sub-county (LC3) level. Non-sectoral conditional grants became available for LC3 administrations to use on whatever they believe will best enhance poverty eradication. This approach should promote a more sensitive allocation of resources that is responsive to the local priorities. It is likely, however, that sectors that are somehow out of favour or poorly represented will receive few resources under this system and suffer as a consequence. This appears to be the case with agriculture generally and the state agricultural extension service in particular. The impact of this is discussed in the section on the NAADS below.

The Poverty Eradication Action Plan (PEAP) was launched in 1997, and revised in 2000. It aims to reduce mass poverty in Uganda to 10 per cent by 2017. It has four main goals:

1 creating a framework for economic growth and structural transformation;
2 ensuring good governance and security;
3 directly increasing the ability of the poor to raise incomes;
4 directly increasing the quality of life of the poor.

Implemented under the PEAP, and of profound importance for the future of the agricultural sector in Uganda, is the Plan for Modernization of Agriculture (the PMA). The PMA was developed in the late 1990s (Uganda 2000a) and is consistent with the cross-sectoral and decentralized approaches advocated in the PEAP. It is expected to contribute to the achievement of the third goal of the PEAP listed above. It promotes a move from largely subsistence to technology based export-oriented agriculture through a broad range of cross-sectoral initiatives. The PMA mission is to 'eradicate poverty by transforming subsistence agriculture to commercial agriculture'. It is an holistic, strategic framework for eradicating poverty through multi-sectoral interventions enabling the poor to improve their livelihoods in a sustainable manner.

The PMA vision is a future agricultural sector with the following qualities:

1 competitive, with lower unit production costs of production and marketing;
2 technology-based, by adoption of improved farming practices;
3 diversified, with higher value and higher demand for all agricultural products;
4 export-oriented, but at the same time ensuring food security in all households;
5 capable of increasing productivity of land and labour.

The PMA claims to have a strong poverty focus formulated with help from data drawn from the Uganda Participatory Poverty Assessment Project (UPPAP) carried out in sixty-seven communities in nine Ugandan districts. The PMA is being implemented through decentralized planning processes which are expected to identify the key constraints at the local government level and help to remove these constraints through 'joined-up' public sector interventions.

Uganda's National Agricultural Advisory Service (NAADS) programme is one of the five core programmes under the PMA. The vision for the NAADS is 'a decentralized, farmer-owned and private sector serviced extension system contributing to the realization of the agricultural sector objectives' (Uganda 2000d). The primary objective in restructuring NAADS is to facilitate the implementation and success of the PMA, though it is also unambiguously stated that the advisory services provided by the new body should be demand-driven.

Even without the negative impact of decentralization on the state extension service mentioned above conventional wisdom states that government extension services tend to be inefficient and ineffective (Carney 1998b; Anderson and Van Crowder 2000). Part of the recognized problem is that state services are generally over-staffed with inadequate operating funds and are rather over-bearing and top-down in their approach. With the current macro-policy trends to decentralize, devolve and liberalize, some alternative to the state-run service in Uganda was inevitable and probably desirable. Interestingly the current de facto situation is almost completely the reverse of what NAADS proposes with the government service being mobilized in an uneven fashion by private funds from donors and NGOs. This can be locally effective but does not produce a coordinated service with consistent coverage and approach across the country.

The NAADS vision for the long-term is a service based on private delivery and private finance though it is acknowledged that public finance will be required in the short-term, particularly if it is to be accessible to the poor. The role of the government becomes one of quality control, providing the supply side (i.e. the extension agents) with the support they require and improving the capacity of the demand side (i.e. the farmers) to identify needs and contract services accordingly. With regard to financing, it is important not to have over-optimistic expectations for the contribution that the private sector will make to the service (Schwartz 1994; Davidson *et al.* 2001). For NAADS it is still very early days and local government and farmers are initially expected to contribute relatively modestly to the costs of NAADS (12–19 per cent in the first five years) though this will rise to 50 per cent by the end of the twenty-year programme.

Anderson and Van Crowder (2000) argue that, for most situations, a model somewhere between a fully private or public service may be more practical and more effective than either extreme as fully private systems are less able to internalize broad long-term public concerns such as soil and water erosion and longer-term issues such as HIV/AIDS. This discussion will be returned to in the light of the fieldwork results below.

The above is the policy context of crop farming in Uganda. The fieldwork is presented next and the ensuing discussion will attempt to identify the linkages between this policy environment and the constraints and opportunities influencing the farmers' livelihoods.

Agriculture and diverse livelihoods in the LADDER study locations

The rich natural resource endowment of Uganda, in particular its humid tropical climate and large areas of fertile volcanic soils, distinguishes it from most other East African countries (Wortmann and Eledu 1999). These resources give much of Uganda the potential for high agricultural productivity and form part of the justification for the current policy emphasis on technology driven intensification and commercialization in rural small-holder agriculture (Uganda 2000a).

There is great agro-ecological diversity within the country with fourteen distinct zones (AEZs) recognized in the latest classification (Wortmann and Eledu 1999). Altitude has the strongest influence on climate and ranges from 610m a.s.l. in the Rift Valley to 4,324m a.s.l. on Mount Elgon. Though the LADDER research was carried out in only three districts, five of the fourteen zones are represented and together these account for approximately 30 per cent of the country's land area and many of the most densely populated and intensively utilized areas (Table 14.1). In addition many of the features of the hillside farming systems and livelihoods found in the study sites are similar to other parts of Uganda. For example, the southwest highlands within the densely populated Kabale district. For logistical and security reasons, some large and important districts and AEZs, particularly in the north, were not represented in the sampling. In spite of this, the sampling was successful in capturing study villages contrasting in a number of key livelihood-determining characteristics. These were population density, land use intensity, AEZ,

Table 14.1 Some characteristics of the agro-ecological zones represented by the research sites

District	*Sub-county/village*	*Agro-ecological zone*	*Soils*	*Rainfall (mm/yr)*	*Population density (persons/km²)*	*Major crops (and livestock)*	*Ugandan land area under same AEZ in km² (%)*
Mbale	Butiru/Bukhasusa Bududa/Bunabuso	Mount Elgon High farmlands	Very productive	Unimodal: >1200 mm/yr	High: 345	Banana, beans, maize, groundnuts, coffee	969 (0.5)
	Butiru/Buwopuwa	Jinja and Mbale farmlands	Very productive	Bimodal: >1200 mm/yr	High: 456*	Bananas, sweet potato, beans, maize, coffee	16,302 (9.1)
Kamuli	Kinamwanga/ Kidera Buyende/ Kiribairya Kagulu/Iyingo	Southern and Eastern Lake Kyoga Basin	Variable	Bimodal: >1200 mm/yr	Moderate: 129	Finger millet, banana, maize, rice, cassava, cotton	10,154 (5.7)
Mubende	Kasambya/Kabbo	South-western grass farmlands	Generally good	Bimodal: <1000 mm/yr	Quite low: 64	Bananas, beans, sweet potatoes, maize, cassava	11,659 (6.6)
	Bulera/Kalangaalo Madudu/ Kansambya	Western mid-altitude farmlands	Very variable	Bimodal 1000–1200 mm/yr	Quite low: 78	Bananas, maize, beans, sweet potatoes, cassava, groundnuts. Cattle very important in parts.	15,307 (8.6)

Source: LADDER fieldwork; Wortmann and Eledu (1999).

Note
*Most densely populated rural AEZ in Uganda.

farming system, quality of infrastructure, strength and competence of local administrations and access to markets.

In all villages in Mbale and Mubende districts, crop cultivation is the most important livelihood activity (Table 14.2). This is followed by various non-farm activities which include trading and off-farm activities such as brewing, brick making, cutting timber, etc. Livestock is the third most important source of income. Crop farming is also clearly important for many in the coastal villages in Kamuli district with one village, Kinamwanga, ranking farming above fishing in importance in group discussions. Significant farming system characteristics including production constraints, elicited from farmers in focus group discussions, have been summarized for each village in Table 14.3.

The communities in Kamuli District were purposively selected to capture rural people with livelihoods based around fishing. Despite the reported importance of crop farming in Kinamwanga, the income data indicate that agriculture is of minor importance in terms of its contribution to household income in the Kamuli villages. Non-farm activities contribute most (40 per cent) followed by fishing (36 per cent). Given the lack of a strong farming base to the livelihoods in this district the discussion will focus on Mbale and Mubende districts.

The size of land-holding was a major criterion used by villagers to distinguish wealth categories and its link with wealth shows up clearly in the data from both Mbale and Mubende districts (Tables 14.4 and 14.5). This observation is consistent with the national land-holding picture: it is reported that over 90 per cent of crop production in Uganda is occurring on farms averaging less than two hectares (4.9 acres: EIU 1997). In Mubende the lowest mean acreage owned by the 'poor' households in a village was 2.2 acres. However, in two of the three Mbale study villages, mean area owned was less than one acre.[2]

The average land-holding of 'poor' farmers was 0.6 acres in Mbale's Bukhasusa village and it was 0.9 acres in Buwopuwa village; in both cases unlikely to be enough to provide for household needs. These are mean figures and there are a large number of 'poor' households with less than 0.5

Table 14.2 Income portfolios of the three districts (%)

Income source	*Mbale*	*Kamuli*	*Mubende*
Crops	53.5	7.1	56.9
Livestock	5.9	5.3	7.2
Fisheries	0.0	36.1	0.0
Other NR	5.7	11.2	6.2
Non-farm	33.1	38.9	29.1
Remittances	1.8	1.4	0.6

Source: sample surveys carried out in nine villages, 2001.

Table 14.3 Farming systems and livelihoods of sample villages

Village	*Major crops grown*	*Major livestock farmed and fish types caught*	*Main production constraints*	*Main off-farm livelihoods*
Bukhasusa	Banana, maize, beans, sweet potatoes, finger millet, groundnut and coffee	Pigs, poultry, goats and cattle	Yield decline caused by drought, crop and livestock disease, poor access to and high cost of inputs, lack of Extension advice, soil erosion and fertility decline, land fragmentation	Sale of labour, banana vending, bicycle transport (produce)
Buwopuwa	Maize, beans, bananas, cotton, millet, cassava, sweet potatoes, sorghum and millet	Pigs, chickens, goats, and a few cattle (disease has greatly reduced numbers)	Yield decline caused by land over-use, drought, pests and diseases, inferior seed. Cattle lost through disease. Lack of access to manure and chemical inputs. No help from Extension Service	Sale of labour, brick making, bicycle transport (people and produce), brewing, produce vending
Bunabuso	Coffee, bananas, maize, beans, horticulture (tomatoes, cabbage, onions), sweet potatoes	Dairy cows, pigs, goats chickens	Yield decline due to soil exhaustion; fragmentation; poor access to and high cost of inputs; pests and diseases; unreliable weather, collapse of marketing co-ops	Sale of labour, shops, brick making, bicycle transport (people and produce), brewing
Lyingo	Maize, sweet potatoes, cassava, finger millet, groundnut, beans, and cotton	Livestock: Cattle (meat), goats, chickens and ducks Fish: Nile Perch, *Rastrineobola argentea*, Tilapia	Drought, crop disease, poor access to inputs, labour, markets	Sale of labour (fishing and agricultural), fish trading, transport (bicycles and boats) shop keeping, petty trading

continued

Table 14.3 continued

Village	*Major crops grown*	*Major livestock farmed and fish types caught*	*Main production constraints*	*Main off-farm livelihoods*
Kiribairya	Maize, sweet potatoes, cassava, finger millet, cotton, sorghum, groundnut, beans	Livestock: Cattle (meat), goats, chickens and ducks Fish: Nile Perch, *Rastrineobola argentea*, Tilapia, Lung fish	Drought, crop and cattle disease, poor access to inputs, labour, markets; no help from Extension Service	Sale of labour – to fish and to work on other farms, fish trading, transport (bicycles and boats), petty trading, brick making, firewood harvest, brewing
Kinamwanga	Maize, cassava, sweet potatoes, finger millet, cotton, sorghum, groundnut, beans	Livestock: Cattle (meat), goats, chickens and ducks Fish: Nile Perch, Tilapia	Drought, crop and cattle disease, poor access to inputs, labour, markets; no help from Extension Service	Sale of labour – to fish and to work on other farms, fish trading, transport (bicycles and boats), petty trading, brick making, firewood
Kabbo	Bananas, maize, beans, Irish potatoes, sweet potatoes, groundnut, cassava, coffee, vegetables	Cattle (milk and meat), chickens and goats	Yield decline due to decreasing soil fertility and intensive cultivation, drought, pests and diseases, high cost of inputs	Agricultural labour, produce trading, shop keeping, brewing, selling of clothes, petty trade, hunting
Kansambya	Maize, beans, sweet potatoes, Irish potatoes, cassava bananas, finger millet, sorghum, coffee	Cattle (milk and meat), chickens and goats	Yield decline due to drought, pests and diseases. Poor access to improved seed and other inputs	Agricultural labour, produce trading, shop keeping, brewing, brick making, transport activities, hunting
Kalangaalo	Maize, sweet potatoes, beans, Irish potatoes, bananas, groundnut, cassava, coffee, vegetables	Cattle (milk and meat), chickens and goats	Declining soil fertility, drought, land fragmentation, pests and disease, poor access to inputs and mechanization	Agricultural labour, government workers, produce trading, shop keeping, brewing, brick making, transport activities, builders

Source: sample surveys carried out in nine villages, 2001.

Table 14.4 Land-holdings in Mbale and Mubende Districts

Wealth group	*Mbale*	*Mubende*
	Area owned (acres)	
Rich	8.5	9.2
Middle	3.0	4.2
Poor	1.5	3.2
Total	3.9	5.5
Difference (p) between wealth groups*	<0.000	<0.000

Source: sample surveys carried out in nine villages, 2001.

Note
*An analysis of variance was carried out to look for significant differences between group mean incomes. p = probability value.

Table 14.5 Area owned by district

Area owned	*District (%)*			*Total*
	Mbale	*Kamuli*	*Mubende*	
Less than 0.5 ha.	37.1	67.6	21.9	42.2
0.5–1 ha.	24.8	11.4	14.3	16.8
1–2 ha.	15.2	11.4	26.7	17.8
2–3 ha.	6.7	2.9	14.3	7.9
3–4 ha.	4.8	1.0	9.5	5.1
More than 4 ha.	11.4	5.7	13.3	10.2
Total	100.0	100.0	100.0	100.0

Source: sample surveys carried out in nine villages, 2001.

acres or even no land at all. Buwopuwa is located on the drier plains where the Teso (cotton and maize) farming system dominates. Productivity is constrained by moisture availability here and cropping is less intensive than in the hills. Hence land holdings are on the large side for the district: 5.4 acres on average. Bukhasusa is located higher up in the Mount Elgon foothills where moisture and soils are conducive to intensive productive agriculture. Very intensive systems have developed, population densities are high and land fragmentation has led to an average land-holding of 1.3 acres. The third LADDER village in Mbale, Bunabuso, is similar in agro-ecological zone to Bukhasusa with similar intensive systems and high population densities though farm sizes are somewhat larger than in Bukhasusa. Generally, farmers farm most of the area they own with a general tendency for the medium and poor farmers to rent additional land.

On average the Mbale sample households had 30 per cent more crop-derived income and 60 per cent more total income than the Mubende sample (Table 14.6). Of the Mbale villages Bunabuso appears to be the richest with

Table 14.6 Crop and total income in Mbale and Mubende

Wealth group	*Mbale*		*Mubende*	
	Annual crop income	*Total annual income*	*Annual crop income*	*Total annual income*
Rich	1,770	5,100	1,057	2,130
Middle	1,130	1,990	875	1,405
Poor	470	760	478	798
Total	1,060	2,370	803	1,444
Difference (p) between income groups*	<0.001	0.020	0.001	<0.000

Source: sample surveys carried out in nine villages, 2001.

Note
*An analysis of variance was carried out to look for significant differences between group mean incomes. p = probability value.

mean incomes of Ush 4.31 million compared with Ush 1.50 million and Ush 1.15 million for Buwopuwa and Bukhasusa, respectively. For Mubende villages, the richest appear to be Kalangaalo with a mean income of Ush 1.69 million, compared with Ush 1.41 million and Ush 0.92 million for Kabbo and Kansambya, respectively. The latter result gives credibility to a widely held view by district officials that Madudu sub-county, in which Kansambya village is located, is the poorest sub-county in Mubende district.

Crop and livestock based income accounted for, on average, 59 per cent of total income in Mbale and 64 per cent in Mubende, suggesting that non-farm income generating activities are relatively more important in Mbale. Table 14.7 summarizes villagers' perceptions of their first and second most important activity for the three Mbale villages. In Bunabuso the pattern of activity is somewhat different from the other Mbale villages with only 61 per cent of respondents giving farming as their main current activity compared with 81 per cent and 80 per cent in Bukhasusa and Buwopuwa respectively. *Boda boda*, general trading and other forms of off-farm income generation are common in Bunabuso, perhaps linked to the particularly high land pressure in this area. It is interesting to note that this village does appear to be better-off than its more farming dependent neighbours, perhaps as a result of this diversification.

Most respondents mentioned major livelihood changes that had happened to them over the preceding five years. Whereas the environmental and socio-economic landscape may not appear to be changing very fast, the lives of individuals and households clearly are. There are a number of more or less predictable changes in their asset status as well as the effects of less predictable outcomes such as sickness and other livelihood shocks. The most common reason given for a change in livelihood activity over the last five years was one related to age or the major life events: either acquiring land on leaving

Table 14.7 Livelihood diversification in Mbale District

Activity	*1st and 2nd most significant household activities (% farmers)*					
	Bukhasusa		*Buwopuwa*		*Bunabuso*	
	1st	*2nd*	*1st*	*2nd*	*1st*	*2nd*
Farming (crop, crop + livestock)	81	17	80	14	61	33
Brewing	3	6	3	14		6
Boda boda* or other trading	3	3	6	9	12	6
Remittances	6		6	14		21
Selling labour	6	17	3	14	3	9
Teaching or other professional	3	6		11	9	6
Livestock farming			3	3	15	
None		43		11		
Artisanal activities		9		9		15
Renting						3

Source: sample surveys carried out in nine villages, 2001.

Note
*Boda boda = petty trading.

home or marriage, losing assets when obliged to pay bride prices for married daughters and loss of land with old age as it is passed on to children or sold because the owner no longer has the strength to work it.

Just as age and sickness are given as major agents of decline in livelihood activities, disease in livestock and crops were cited many times as contributing to the decline in agriculture. Soil fertility and lack of planting material were also mentioned by some farmers. It is likely that the effect of the large 'social' changes in people's lives partly obscure, in the minds of villagers at least, many of the external shocks and changes caused and influences of policy that we are eager to illuminate. The fact that many still mention pests and diseases and productivity (soil fertility) decline as major constraints suggests they are particularly significant.

Beer brewing and *boda boda* (bicycle taxis) are two popular activities households seem to have expanded into over the last five years. A number have also begun to receive remittances from household members working outside the area in that period.

Agricultural production constraints

The picture of rural Uganda painted by the field research is of a nation of small farmers largely dependent on subsistence agriculture but keen to move into more intensive market-oriented farming if the opportunity arises. Despite the inherent productivity of their land, most are suffering a combination of production-related problems that policy will need to address if agriculture is to be the foundation for economic growth. Farmers most frequently report problems of declining yield and offer the following explanations, most of which were also identified in the UPPAP:

Throughout the three districts (Kamuli included):

- Increased incidence of pests and diseases affecting both crops and livestock.
- More intensive farming, land fragmentation and reduced fallow causing a decline in soil fertility and productivity of the land.
- Lack of access to and/or high cost of agricultural inputs (notably improved seed and planting material, fertilizers and pesticides) and mechanization.
- No, or very little, help from or contact with the Agricultural Extension Service. This service seems largely to have ceased functioning in recent years.
- Unreliable weather, mostly periods of drought in the growing season but also very destructive intense rainfall events in some areas.
- Loss of marketing co-operatives and poor access to markets.

Area specific concerns:

- Land fragmentation, particularly in Mbale where population densities are several times those in the other districts studied.
- Soil erosion, again particularly in the Mbale hillsides communities.

Many of these concerns, in fact all but co-operatives and market access, are in some way linked to the poor and worsening agricultural support service. Combined with the trends of increases in population and land-use intensity and decreases in farm size these represent major challenges for many farmers, particularly the poor and vulnerable most of whom are suffering multiple production constraints.

Agricultural productivity in terms of production per unit area, is declining in much of Uganda and if current and future policy is to turn this around it has to address the production constraints listed above. Agricultural service provision could, if effective and well-resourced, address the majority of the listed constraints. The successful implementation of NAADS will be crucial in fulfilling this role and elements of the proposals are discussed below. Land fragmentation is, however, particularly important in Mbale and other intensively farmed Ugandan hillside areas and is so extreme that the viability of intensifying production in these areas needs special consideration. The next section examines the land fragmentation phenomenon and considers whether existing and proposed policy provides the support poor farmers with very small land-holdings need.

Land fragmentation is a particular concern in Mbale in this study and in much of the fertile hillside areas of southwest Uganda, notably in Kabale and surrounding districts, where land is typically divided between male children on inheritance. The productive potential of these areas is very high due to favourable soils and rainfall regimes and this has allowed high population densities and intensive production systems to develop. When the soils are producing at their best it is possible to meet household food requirements from very small parcels of land, often less than one acre. However, when land-holdings drop below about 0.5 acres or when substantial productivity decline occurs (it is clear, from focus group discussions, that this is the case in many areas) it becomes difficult to meet household food needs, despite the high inherent productivity of the land. Many farmers are clearly struggling with their farming in this way.

Counter-intuitively it is possible that farmers are struggling most in areas with inherently very high productive potential. Figure 14.1 explains this by representing the theoretical declines in productivity in two areas of land differing in initial productive potential. Area one is not particularly high potential, soil may be shallow and/or organic matter and nutrient reserves poor. Productivity declines steeply from the first season of cultivation, year X, when a population begins to settle the area. Then there is a period of more gradual productivity decline, eventually stabilizing at a low level but one that can more or less be sustained indefinitely by soil processes. The same line could also be taken to crudely represent the carrying capacity of the

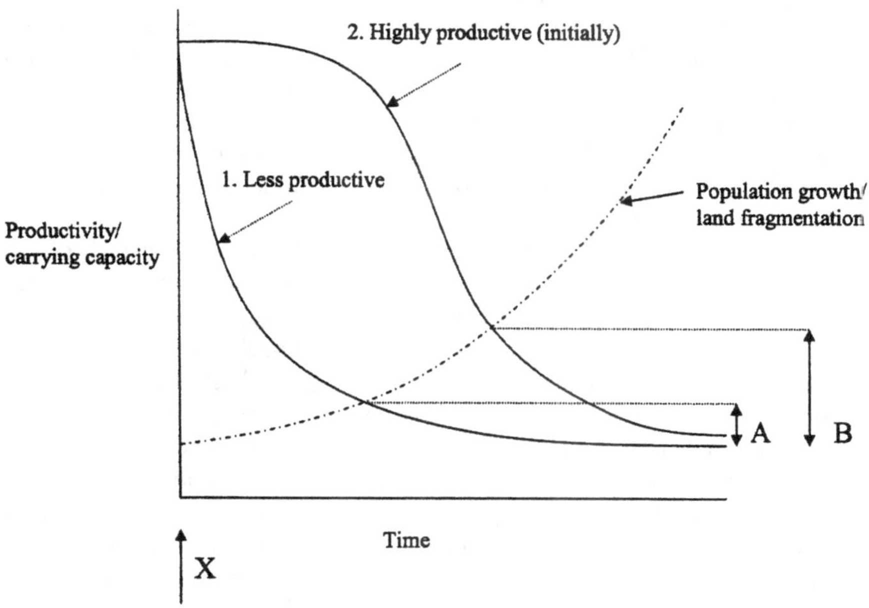

Figure 14.1 A stylized representation of the relationship between population growth and land productivity with time of cultivation.

environment in terms of the number of people it can support – this declines with decreasing system productivity.

The dotted line represents the population increase that develops exponentially from the time of settlement. By the time population reaches the carrying capacity of the land (i.e. land becomes a major constraint), households only have sufficient for household needs and there is strong resistance to further land fragmentation, the steepest productivity decline has already occurred. From this point forward, further increases in population cannot be supported by the NR base so strategies of non-farm income generation or out-migration develop. Although farmers are constrained by their environment, high densities of people dependent on farming have not developed and further declines in productivity are relatively modest and gradual (A). This scenario can be applied to large parts of SSA with poor soils and dry climates and perhaps also to some of the villages in this research e.g. Buwopuwa and its drier 'Teso' type farming system.

The second scenario applies to the inherently more productive areas in Uganda e.g. Bunabuso and Bukhasusa in Mbale. Productivity (and carrying capacity) of the land remains high for many years after the first settlement and this allows population densities to increase and farm size to reduce to a far greater extent than in scenario one. Eventually, however, mining of soil reserves, the increasing land use intensity and associated degradation lead to productivity decline. At some point the carrying capacity of the land is reached, as with scenario one, and the population begins to struggle with farming. There are two important differences, however, between the two scenarios that suggest that the numbers of people and the magnitude of the production constraints are likely to be much greater under scenario two. First, farm sizes are much smaller and there are many more people on the land. Second, carrying capacity has been reached at a point where the productivity is still steeply declining and has a long way to go (represented by B in Figure 14.1). Thus we can see, somewhat paradoxically, a potentially more difficult situation developing in the more productive areas where large numbers of poor farmers are trying to scrape a living on small parcels of land still rapidly declining in productivity. The research suggests that this somewhat pessimistic analysis is not far from reality in many of the high potential areas in Mbale District. An analysis of income portfolios across the districts suggests that already in Mbale farmers are having to rely strongly on off-farm income sources: 40 per cent of household income compared with 20 per cent in Mubende where pressure on land resources is much lower.

Whilst there is no way of increasing the amount of available land there are technical options for maintaining and/or improving agricultural productivity. The PMA recognizes that land scarcity is a major constraint in the areas of highest potential productivity and its central theme is the promotion of technologies for increasing agricultural productivity. Clearly the successful delivery of appropriate technologies and associated inputs and training are essential if the land constraint is to be overcome. The results of this research indicate that even farmers with less than 0.5 hectares of land sell, on average, 23 per cent of their crops but this is not the same as growing a cash crop – most crops are primarily grown for home consumption (though a portion might be sold) and so should still be classed as subsistence crops. The returns from the sale of a cash crop may make the adoption of resource-demanding technologies and/or external inputs feasible but it is quite rare for farmers to invest resources, particularly cash, in subsistence (or predominantly subsistence) production.

There is a danger, therefore, that the high input path to improved production will not be open to those farmers engaged in this type of production. Their assets are currently insufficient to resource a move into market-oriented agriculture. Indications are that many of the middling and poorest households in this study, the vast majority of the rural population, are in this situation. An example of an intensification initiative promoted by an NGO idea that suffered precisely this problem is given in Box 14.1. Dijkistra and Van Donge (2001) report something similar and suggest that the lack of an asset platform for investing in new agricultural activities is a considerable obstacle for many Ugandan small-holders.

Currently there is little if any access to agricultural support and advice for most rural Ugandans, and yet the current intensive land use, the aspirations of the farmers and the policy environment all point to an urgent need for an effective agricultural support service. The PMA and NAADS proposals recognize this but they may also need to acknowledge that many farmers will need assistance with their subsistence production, in non resource-demanding ways, before they can venture into input driven, market-oriented agriculture.

Box 14.1 IDEA in Mbale

This is an NGO promoting reduced tillage and pesticide use in maize production. Herbicides are used to clear the land of weeds rather than digging or ploughing, both of which can expose hillside land to severe erosion. High yielding maize seed is sown after herbicide application with basal and top dressings of fertilizers. Selective herbicides are applied once more to control weeds before the maize canopy closes and further weeding is not required. Small-holders in the Mbale hillsides were initially targeted with this technology as they were suffering severely from soil erosion. However there was no uptake as farmers were not able to devote large plots of land to cash crops – they needed all they had for subsistence crops. Neither could they afford to purchase the herbicides and improved seed required to practice the reduced tillage system. After several years of frustration the NGO began promoting the technologies among the wealthier commercial farmers growing maize in the lowland plans around Mbale. Several farmers have found the technology particularly cost effective and are achieving maize yields of over ten tonnes per hectare.

Source: LADDER Key Informant Interview.

Most respondents in Mbale and Mubende claimed they would rather consolidate their farming activities than diversify away from farming. This suggests that in many cases farmers have had to diversify in order to survive and not because they particularly wanted to. This conclusion is backed up by the data on land fragmentation. It is technically very difficult to consistently grow sufficient food for a typical Ugandan household on 0.25 hectares of land. Thus, for a quite large and increasing number of households, diversification off-farm is a route they must take. It is likely that, for most households, it is far easier to diversify away from farming than intensify and re-orient to cash-cropping. Whether resources generated off-farm are likely to be invested in agriculture ultimately seems to depend on the likely risk and return from farming versus returns from investment elsewhere (Evans and Ngau 1991).

In many parts of Uganda the potential returns from investment on-farm could be high so there is no reason why agriculture should not benefit from diversification. For the 50 per cent plus of the population in Mbale District currently tied to subsistence cropping it might be that facilitation of their involvement in off-farm activities will provide many with the resources they need for a move to the more intensive market oriented cropping envisaged by the PMA. Critically, however, these opportunities outside of agriculture have to exist before farmers are able to 'modernize' and this is rather different from the conventional notion that small-holder agriculture can first transform itself and then drive the development of marketing and processing opportunities and the development of a rural service sector.

In summary it seems that anything that can be done to facilitate livelihood diversification is likely to benefit agriculture and may provide resources and impetus for a degree of agricultural intensification.

Agricultural service provision

The participatory institutional analysis carried out as part of the LADDER research (though not reported in detail here) revealed that the research and extension services are currently considered by villagers to be among the least helpful institutions. In some cases they are even classed as unhelpful. Part of the explanation for this poor perception must be due to the fact that throughout the country the extension service has all but ceased to function (in one village sample nobody had encountered an extension officer since 1985).

This steep downturn in service delivery coincides rather ominously with the initial phases of decentralization. District agricultural officials in Mbale report that extension activities are given a low priority by district administrations and funds to the service cover salaries but allow for nothing else. Officials on the district councils accept this as a problem but complain themselves that the funds they have control of are barely sufficient to cover their sitting allowances. The extension service is generally staffed by competent officers, the older ones very experienced but lacking recent training, the younger members finding it difficult to establish themselves in their posts under conditions of low payment and poor resources. Though many NGOs do 'employ' extension officers in the field, coverage is, in general, poor and the co-ordination between NGOs with different funding sources and objectives inadequate. With the continuing trend of declining donor support for local level 'projects' and NGOs it would seem unwise to dismiss or dismantle the extension service too quickly unless there is an alternative with the potential to provide relevant coordinated support countrywide. It is in this light that the elements of the PMA and NAADS restructuring proposals need to be critically assessed.

Broad dissatisfaction with the AES, its outdated mode of operation and the high cost of running an effective service have all driven the development of a radical new framework for agricultural service delivery in Uganda embodied in NAADS. The above analysis has demonstrated how strong the demand for an effective service is and the importance of recognizing that much of this demand is likely to be for help with subsistence crops as this is what most, particularly the poor, are growing.

The commercially-oriented minority in any farming community will doubtless find it easier to articulate demand and pay for services. Evidence from outside Uganda suggests that providers of information for contract farmers, commodity crops, veterinary advice or advice linked to input supply, generally develop quite rapidly (Schwartz 1994; Davidson *et al.* 2001), largely in response to the willingness and ability of the customer to pay. However, there is a danger that, as it is in this commercial direction that policy is trying to drive agriculture, the needs of subsistence farmers (the poor majority) might be less well met. The NAADS proposal does recognize this, at least in part, and there is a commitment to finance services to subsistence farmers entirely from public resources. However, the public resourcing of the service will have to increase greatly if this commitment to support poor subsistence farmers is to be fulfilled. Though the mechanism for this has been carefully mapped out it will require hitherto hard to achieve levels of efficient, transparent, well-funded and organized administration, particularly at the district and sub-county levels.

The 'supply-driven' element to service provision may also become important. Much of the job of an agricultural service provider is to transmit information that already exists in some form to the farmer, rather than generate new information through research. The information may need to be simplified, screened or otherwise repackaged to make it more accessible but new research is not required to provide this part service. Indeed the PMA does recognize that a number of technologies have been developed at research institutions, but have largely remained on the shelf. What is needed is a mechanism that makes them available to farmers.

There remains, however, a need for basic and applied research in agriculture in Uganda, particularly for subsistence crops grown on small farms under low input conditions. It is technically very difficult to sustain intensive subsistence production with few or no inputs. Many of the past failures in extension and poor uptake of promoted management options can be blamed on advice that was based on assumptions concerning the production environment (biophysical and socio-economic) that were invalid or simply wrong. Real solutions may be complex, only partial or they may need time and research investment to develop. The uncertainty, costs and time involved in generating effective advice for low input farming are all likely to lead to the privatized service being reluctant to enter into contractual obligations with subsistence farmers and to a tendency to concentrate on commercial farmers and farming. This tendency would be reinforced if the funding for services to subsistence farmers is less secure. Again the example described in Box 14.1 demonstrated this point.

The mechanisms for commissioning and funding this research, some of which should be long-term, and the forming of research outputs into locally specific advice are not convincingly mapped out in the current policy documents. Whilst there does need to be a mechanism for adapting and refining research outputs and advice to fit with the local and even field-specific environment a lot can be said for co-ordinating and centralizing some aspects of these services. For example, in this research one of the strongest demands expressed by farmers was for help in dealing with some major crop pests and diseases, e.g. cassava mosaic virus and Sigatoka disease in bananas. Clearly it would be impractical for numerous privatized bodies all to tackle such issues independently. Probably few of the new service providers will have this type of long-term technical research capacity. This implies that the research institutions and in particular the National Agricultural Research Organization (NARO) will retain this role nationally and that two-way information flows between this institution and the many private service providers, NGOs, etc. must function well, particularly if subsistence farmers are to be better served. The difficulties in successfully maintaining and co-ordinating these flows and linkages between NARO and other research organizations and large numbers of different service providers appear, on paper, to be greater than the existing, albeit poorly functioning, research/extension system.

NAADS recognizes the requirement for a major improvement in the representation and empowerment of poor subsistence farmers. It describes farmer groups as 'the core institutions of the NAADS Programme' and proposes that farmers with common interests and/or similar socio-economic characteristics should form into groups that prioritize and articulate their demands to sub-county and district 'farmer fora'. These fora will further prioritize demands and then commission service providers. The fora also manage all aspects relating to costing, monitoring and evaluation of the advisory services. This proposal is radical and the system envisaged appears rather complex. There are several stages in this process where the original farmers' demands are summarized, prioritized and passed on by others. At each stage there is a danger that the commercialization imperative of the PMA and different agendas of those wielding power in the groups will disadvantage the poorer, less empowered farmer. In addition, although it would be unfair to assume these new groups and administrations will be hijacked by individuals intent on corruption and personal gain it would be naive to assume the potential for such problems will be any less than under current systems. It does seem that there are many points of entry for under-representing poor farmers and malpractice with the NAADS and this must be cause for concern.

Conclusions

In summary, the underlying assumption of both the PMA and NAADS is that, although most rural people are currently engaged in subsistence farming, with support, the majority can move into more intensive market-oriented agriculture. The picture emerging from this research is that most farmers want to do this. However, they are currently experiencing so much difficulty with their subsistence farming that the majority are a very long way from even beginning to contemplate the investments necessary to begin intensification. Both the PMA and the NAADS proposal appear to underestimate the size of the 'ready to intensify' market sector and there is a danger that resources allocated to the poorer, more vulnerable majority may be woefully inadequate. There remains a need for well-formulated research in the agriculture sector based on a recognition of the resource constraints under which small-holder subsistence farmers operate. Yet there is a danger that research will be under-emphasized in the new NAADS as easy access to research capability, long-term funding and efficient linkages with existing research institutions are somewhat in conflict with the fully privatized extension model.

The agricultural intensification focus of PMA is well placed in Uganda but this research suggests its vision of how this will develop and how long it will take needs to be more flexible. Rural livelihoods are diversifying away from agriculture in areas where land pressure is intensifying and the effects of this seem to be overwhelmingly positive. Although most people would prefer to remain in farming they benefit from diversifying and resources generated off-farm are just as likely to be reinvested in farming activities as elsewhere, particularly as most people's aspirations appear to revolve around farming. Paradoxically perhaps, policies associated with the PMA need to facilitate the diversification of the majority of households, particularly in intensively farmed areas, away from agriculture to generate some resources that could then allow them to take the intensification route.

Although some elements of the private sector will probably develop to serve specific niche demands relatively quickly under NAADS, this is not likely to happen across the board and it is important that the merits of a more pluralistic service are considered with public elements responsible for less commercially attractive areas of service provision. NAADS is relying heavily on the supply-side capacity of existing NGOs rather than trying to fully utilize the extension officers in the state system, yet this is where the majority of expertise in field level agriculture lies though more support is required to unite this field expertise with business skills that will allow them to operate from within the private sector. It would certainly be a missed opportunity if NAADS does not assimilate the strengths of the existing state service, i.e. good coverage, largely competent personnel and co-coordinated links with research institutions.

At the time of writing NAADS is in its second year of operation in the initial six pilot districts (started July 2001) and, due to strong demand, it is being rolled out more rapidly than originally intended to additional districts (a further nine in 2002). The most recent review (Adipala *et al.* 2003) identified emerging problems in many of the areas of concern highlighted in this research, i.e. the inability of poorer farmers to access cash cropping options focussed on by NAADS; the lack of support available for subsistence crops; a lack of capacity to address environmental issues; poor linkages with research institutions, a general lack of supply side capacity in NAADS and the difficulty experienced by most of the existing (government) extension personnel in equipping and positioning themselves such that they can market their services and compete for contracts.

Notes

1 The LADDER research programme is described in the Preface and Chapter 1 of this volume, and the field methods used in Uganda are described in Ellis and Bahiigwa (2003)

2 The area-farmed to area-owned ratio for Mbale district is 1.44, implying that, on average, Mbale households borrow or rent 44 per cent more land than they own. For Mubende, the ratio is 0.82, implying that land is not as constraining as it is in Mbale.

15 More than income

Pro-poor livestock development policy in Uganda

*Steve Ashley and William Nanyeenya**

Introduction

Approaches to livestock development throughout sub-Saharan Africa have conventionally aimed at increasing production in order to create a marketed surplus for consumption, trade and especially export or reduction of imports. In most countries this is still the case and is reflected in livestock sub-sectoral policies which tend to focus on production-related objectives and production-enhancing support. The Millennium Development Goals with its specific focus on reducing poverty by half by 2015 and the spread of national poverty reduction frameworks, often as PRSPs, has led to an enhanced profile for poverty reduction in the agendas of many countries. Uganda has taken a similar route, since its resolution in 1996 to prioritise poverty eradication as the major focus of its overall sustained growth and development strategy (Uganda 1999).

These changes are causing some to reflect on whether the focus on production is an appropriate model for livestock development in poor countries when poverty reduction is the prime objective. For example Livestock In Development (1999) propose a rethinking of approaches to the sector, and suggest that a new paradigm for poverty reduction through livestock may be required.

The Ugandan context

In the Ugandan case, the framework determining agricultural development strategy can be found in the Plan for the Modernisation of Agriculture (PMA); a holistic, strategic framework for eradicating poverty through multi-sectoral interventions, aimed at enabling the people to improve their livelihoods in a sustainable manner (Uganda 2000a). A broad objective of the PMA is to transform poor farmers from producing predominantly for subsistence to producing for the market with a view to reorienting them towards commercial agriculture in order to have a significant impact on poverty eradication in the country (Uganda 2000a).

The PMA does not go into specific detail on sub-sectoral strategy, but it contains a few clues as to what might be expected in terms of livestock development. In addition to addressing major problems felt by livestock-keepers such as disease and theft, it is implied that a general objective of livestock development strategy would be to increase yield per animal, and to enhance productivity. This would require the raising of improved animal breeds, and adoption of 'proper' feeding practices (Uganda 2000a). A clear implication is that agricultural (and other) sub-sectors are expected to incorporate the principles of the PMA framework into their plans, by providing a sub-sectoral interpretation of the overall PMA guidelines. This suggests a need across the agricultural sector for sub-sectors such as livestock to re-examine their approaches, and to reflect on their compatibility with the PMA and the likelihood of them contributing to the new goal of poverty reduction.

Given the changes to the wider national development agenda in Uganda, this chapter asks how livestock and the livestock sub-sector can best contribute to the overall goal of poverty reduction in Uganda, and in particular how best government can support that contribution.

Drawing on fieldwork conducted in the three districts of Mubende, Mbale and Kamuli (described in Ellis and Bahiigwa 2003), it describes the current livestock situation in Uganda in terms of the numbers, types and distributions of livestock, and then elaborates on who keeps livestock in Uganda, why they do so, and what problems they face. Based on this understanding, the chapter questions the assumption that livestock sub-sector contributions to poverty reduction are necessarily mediated through increasing livestock production and livestock income. It argues that in focusing on production and livestock income, current livestock policy approaches pay insufficient attention to the wider roles of livestock in contributing to rural livelihoods, and thereby miss opportunities to enhance the contribution of livestock, and livestock development, to poverty reduction.

The chapter then considers what this means for approaches to livestock development in Uganda, and wonders whether it is time for a national livestock sub-sector policy which states clearly the rationale for livestock development and the ways in which the government expect it to contribute to its wider poverty reduction goals. It further suggests that the PMA itself, as currently framed, sends the wrong messages to the livestock sub-sector because it focuses on a production-, commercialisation-, and intensification-led approach. This means that, if interpreted literally, application of the PMA principles to the livestock sub-sector would lead to policies and measures which are not pro-poor and would be unlikely to contribute significantly to the goal of poverty reduction.

The current livestock situation in Uganda

This section brings together data from a number of sources to describe current livestock numbers and distributions in Uganda, with a focus on mixed farming systems. This focus has been adopted because pastoralism and pastoralists have received considerable attention in post-independence

Uganda, but livestock kept in mixed farming systems have received much less attention, even though they are very widespread in these areas.

Data on overall holdings of livestock in Uganda are scarce, but a combination of incomplete sources combined with original fieldwork conducted during this study provides sufficient information to gain an overview of the national picture. Census data from 1995 are presented in Table 15.1. However, other than the relative magnitude of livestock species populations, this data does not provide much information on the poverty aspects of livestock-keeping or the distribution of livestock between households.

Data from the village surveys in three districts show that, overall, 78 per cent of households had some livestock at the time of the survey. This average figure obscures differences in the prevalence in livestock-keeping between districts, and differences between species held in different districts and villages, as illustrated in Tables 15.2 and 15.3.

This data is not statistically representative, but the sample is biased towards the poor (Ellis and Bahiigwa 2003), fewer of whom keep livestock (Table 15.8) so, if anything, is likely to be an underestimate. The most commonly held livestock by some distance are chickens, followed by goats, and then some way behind cattle and pigs (Table 15.3).

By far the majority of livestock in these areas are kept as part of small herds and flocks, with, for example, only 3 per cent of cattle herd sizes, and 2 per cent of goat flock sizes exceeding ten animals, as shown in Tables 15.4 and 15.5 below.

Table 15.1 Livestock census (1995)

Species	*Number*
Poultry	22,200,000
Goats	5,900,000
Cattle	5,600,000
Pigs	1,400,000
Sheep	1,100,000
Rabbits	500,000
Donkeys	23,000

Source: Uganda (2000e).

Table 15.2 Proportion of households keeping some livestock, by district

	Mbale %	*Kamuli* %	*Mubende* %	*All districts* %
No livestock	10.5	28.6	25.7	21.6
Some livestock	89.5	71.4	74.3	78.4
Total	100.0	100.0	100.0	100.0

Source: sample surveys carried out in nine villages, 2001.

Table 15.3 Livestock-keeping by species in three districts (household %)

Livestock type	*Mbale* %	*Kamuli* %	*Mubende* %	*Whole sample* %
Chickens	83.8	51.4	59.0	64.8
Goats	43.8	47.6	41.9	44.4
Cattle	37.1	23.8	25.7	28.9
Pigs	28.6	11.4	29.5	23.2
Other	1.9	24.8	1.0	9.2
Sheep	1.9	1.0	9.5	4.1
Turkeys	7.6	0.0	3.8	3.8

Source: sample surveys carried out in nine villages, 2001.

Table 15.4 Distribution of livestock herd sizes for different species

	Mbale %	*Kamuli* %	*Mubende* %	*Whole sample* %
Cattle				
None	62.9	76.2	74.3	71.1
1–5	35.2	15.2	18.1	22.9
6–10	1.9	2.9	4.8	3.2
More than 10	0.0	5.7	2.9	2.9
Total	100.0	100.0	100.0	100.0
Goats				
None	56.2	52.4	58.1	55.6
1–5	41.0	36.2	34.3	37.1
6–10	1.9	7.6	5.7	5.1
More than 10	1.0	3.8	1.9	2.2
Total	100.0	100.0	100.0	100.0
Chickens				
None	16.2	48.6	41.0	35.2
1–5	41.0	28.6	33.3	34.3
6–10	17.1	12.4	14.3	14.6
More than 10	25.7	10.5	11.4	15.9
Total	100.0	100.0	100.0	100.0
Pigs				
None	71.4	88.6	70.5	76.8
1–5	24.8	10.5	28.6	21.3
6–10	3.8	1.0	1.0	1.9
Total	100.0	100.0	100.0	100.0

Source: sample surveys carried out in nine villages, 2001.

Furthermore, livestock are kept across the spectrum of household wealth status, even by a large proportion of the relatively poor (Table 15.6).

However, there are differences in types of livestock held by different wealth ranks. Poor households were more likely to keep chickens, goats and pigs, and wealthier households more likely to keep all species, but notably with a greater likelihood of keeping cattle (Table 15.7).

Table 15.5 Distribution of livestock in Cattle Equivalent Units*, by district

Livestock herd/flock size	*Mbale* %	*Kamuli* %	*Mubende* %	*Whole sample* %
None	10.5	33.3	25.7	23.2
Less than 1	50.5	41.0	45.7	45.7
1–5	34.3	15.2	17.1	22.2
5–10	3.8	3.8	6.7	4.8
More than 10	1.0	6.7	4.8	4.1
Total	100.0	100.0	100.0	100.0

Source: sample surveys carried out in nine villages, 2001.

Notes
*CEUs: goats = 0.12; pigs = 0.14; sheep = 0.10; turkeys = 0.04; chickens = 0.02; other = (given price/5% trimmed mean price for cattle).

Table 15.6 Livestock-keeping by wealth group (household %)

Wealth rank	*Mbale* %	*Kamuli* %	*Mubende* %	*Whole sample* %
Poorer	79.5	59.5	57.4	65.4
Middle	96.7	78.8	75.0	83.5
Wealthier	96.7	80.0	100.0	92.2

Source: sample surveys carried out in nine villages, 2001.

Table 15.7 Different species held, by wealth rank (household %)

	Poorer %	*Middle* %	*Wealthier* %	*Whole sample* %
Chickens	56.4	67.0	74.4	64.6
Goats	28.6	47.3	64.4	44.3
Cattle	9.0	30.8	56.7	29.0
Pigs	20.3	24.2	26.7	23.2
Other	6.0	12.1	11.1	9.2
Sheep	1.5	4.4	7.8	4.1
Turkeys	3.8	4.4	3.3	3.8

Source: sample surveys carried out in nine villages, 2001.

It is apparent that livestock holdings are highly skewed, with wealthier households not only more likely to keep livestock, but also keeping proportionately more livestock than poorer households (Table 15.8). Indeed, livestock ownership was stated as one of the most important criteria defining household wealth status.

Going beyond survey data, recent estimates by Thornton *et al.* (2002) suggest that Uganda has 4.7 million poor livestock-keeping households, where poverty is defined by World Bank rural poverty criteria. The same

Table 15.8 Skewed livestock holdings by wealth

Wealth rank	*Mean livestock holding in CEUs – means of all HHs*			
	Mbale	*Kamuli*	*Mubende*	*Whole sample*
Poorer	0.68	0.25	0.38	0.44
Middle	1.39	1.45	0.52	1.15
Wealthier	2.16	6.40	6.51	5.02

Source: sample surveys carried out in nine villages, 2001.

study identifies the sort of environments in which these poor livestock-keepers may be found (Table 15.9), and shows that the vast majority of poor livestock-keepers in Uganda are to be found in mixed farming systems of the kinds described here. This suggests that the findings presented in this chapter may be broadly applicable to the majority of poor livestock-keepers in Uganda.

Together, these figures show very clearly that livestock are very widespread in Uganda beyond the areas normally considered to be where livestock are important, such as the 'cattle corridor'.

Contributions of livestock to livelihoods

The following data show how livestock incomes represent a relatively small proportion of the wider livelihood income portfolio, across the three districts.

Across the whole sample, livestock income was the sixth most important source of income. The finding is similar when the analysis is applied to livestock-keeping households only. In none of the cases shown in Table 15.10 does livestock income rank greater than fifth in order of magnitude.

The substance of these findings is strongly supported by major national household surveys conducted in 1992–1993 and 1999–2000, which calculate livestock incomes as representing 0.6 per cent and 0.8 per cent of household

Table 15.9 Numbers and percentages of poor livestock-keepers in Uganda, by livestock-keeping system

System	*Number of poor livestock-keeping households*	*% of poor livestock-keeping households*
Mixed rainfed humid/sub-humid	3,809,336	81.0
Mixed rainfed highland/temperate	718,710	15.0
Livestock only rangeland humid/sub-humid	147,462	3.0
Livestock only rangeland highland/temperate	2,753	<1.0
Total	4,678,261	100.0

Source: Thornton *et al.* (2002).

Table 15.10 Income portfolios by district and by village

	% shares of total aggregated income								
	Bananas	*Food crops*	*Cash crops*	*Wages*	*Self-employment*	*Transfers*	*Livestock*	*Fish*	*Total*
Whole sample	20.5	11.4	0.6	10.5	28.6	1.9	5.0	21.4	100.0
Rank	3rd	4th	8th	5th	1st	7th	6th	2nd	
District									
Mbale District	34.1	9.2	0.9	13.1	37.3	2.5	2.9	0.0	100.0
Kamuli District	0.0	6.4	0.0	6.4	24.5	1.2	3.2	58.4	100.0
Mubende District	29.5	23.4	0.9	12.5	19.8	2.1	11.6	0.0	100.0

Source: sample surveys carried out in nine villages, 2001.

income share, respectively (Uganda 1992; World Bank 1999). The percentage contributions of livestock to overall household income, at around 5 per cent, are therefore relatively high in comparison.[1]

These findings suggest that, according to income criteria, livestock are relatively unimportant in the livelihoods of rural Ugandans in the areas studied. However, if livestock provide such trivial contributions to household income, how can we reconcile this with the very wide ownership of livestock described in the previous section? Also, how can we reconcile this with the clear popularity of livestock: the fact that the majority of those who do not currently keep livestock aspire to do so? The answer lies in the fact that, despite the low contribution of livestock to household income, people commonly ranked livestock as the second or third most important means of livelihood (Table 15.11).

The analysis presented here shows that livestock contributed a relatively low share of income to households in a variety of rural contexts, and yet they remain very highly valued by these same households. The clear implication of this analysis is that the majority of livestock-keepers in mixed farming areas of Uganda do not keep livestock in order to provide direct income; they keep them for other reasons.

The real importance of livestock

The previous section has argued that income generation is not the primary objective of keeping livestock for the majority of poor livestock-keepers in Uganda. This section shows how livestock are valued for the multiple contributions they make to wider livelihoods, most of which are not captured by income data, and that this is the real reason why people, especially the poor, in mixed farming areas keep livestock.

Table 15.11 Comparison of importance of livestock to livelihoods and livestock contribution to household income

District	*Village*	*Livestock importance ranking*
Kamuli	Iyingo	F3, M2
	Kiribairya	4
	Kinamwanga	3
Mubende	Kalangalo	3
	Kansambya	2
	Kabbo	2

Source: sample surveys carried out in nine villages, 2001.

Note
No results for Mbale villages.

Why people keep livestock

The three district surveys show clearly that the main source of livelihood for the majority of rural households is farming (with fishing playing an important role in Kamuli), but that for most this is complemented by a variety of other diversified activities.

However it is equally clear that farming is defined as 'crops and livestock' rather than crops alone, illustrating that these are not considered to be separate activities but are parts of the same thing. Crops and livestock in the three districts studied are integrated in terms of farming systems, as is widely recognised (see, for example, Uganda's livestock breeding policy and animal health policy), but perhaps more importantly they are integrated in terms of wider livelihood systems.

In most cases crops (or fishing for some households in Kamuli) are the main outputs of the livelihood systems that people orient their strategies to deliver. But livestock have an essential input into this system, both directly and indirectly; to farming and also beyond farming. This is the key to understanding why people keep livestock: to 'oil the wheels' of their wider livelihoods.

Livestock-keeping roles and strategies

So in general terms, rather than keeping livestock for the relatively narrow contribution of income alone, most livestock-keepers in Uganda keep their livestock for the multiple contributions they make to their livelihoods. The following discussion, based on observations from this study, describes the most common roles and strategies that livestock-keepers adopt to achieve their objectives:

Enabling saving

Livestock are commonly purchased with money that does not need to be spent immediately, and therefore serve as a place in which savings may be kept until they are needed in similar ways to which others use banks. Livestock-keepers often argued that investing in livestock was better than putting money in a bank. First, this is because banks are perceived to be bureaucratic and livestock can be turned into cash more easily than it is to withdraw money from a bank. Second, livestock continue to grow and breed, so that all being well their value appreciates quicker than does money in a bank. Third, due to their multiple functions livestock provide many useful products while they are being accumulated, whereas money in a bank does not. On the down side, livestock-keeping is subject to major problems in the three districts, a point to which we will return in the next section.

Livestock are also felt to be a better form of savings than land. Land is neither so readily available nor so liquid, which is important because a key role of livestock is to be turned into cash in an emergency. Land ownership has many advantages, but providing access to accessible savings is not one of them.

Providing security

The converse of the savings role of livestock is that they may be sold when something goes wrong and when money is required urgently, for example to pay for a visit to hospital. Where people do not otherwise have access to cash savings, the essential role played by livestock in contributing to the sustainability of people's livelihoods, by making available lump sums of money is essential.

Accumulating assets

One of the routes out of poverty pursued by the poor is to progressively accumulate assets such that they can become productive and contribute to enhancing livelihood status. Livestock accumulation is a key objective for most rural households, and for many this begins with a process of acquiring small animals, increasing their numbers and sequentially trading up to larger species. In this way, people start with chickens, which they then rear and trade for a goat or pig, which they again multiply until they have sufficient resources for a cow or bull.

Financing planned expenditures

Livestock are a key source of funds for expenditures in the areas covered by this study. Regular or small expenditures such as for medicines, food, seed, or fertiliser can be financed by selling a chicken or a goat. Larger expenditures such as purchasing land, a boat, some new fishing gear, a house, starting a small business, paying school fees or making a dowry payment can be made through sale of larger numbers of smaller animals or fewer large animals such as cattle.

Maintaining social capital

It was observed that livestock are frequently shared, lent, borrowed, given as gifts, and slaughtered for a range of ceremonies and occasions. Activities such as these are often seen as 'unproductive' but in practice are highly valued for their ability to secure social capital which can play an important role in future livelihood security, especially for the vulnerable. They also contribute to households' overall sense of wellbeing and ability to be seen as a respected part of society.

Providing livestock products

In addition to the roles described above, livestock are also valued by some for the products they provide directly, including draught power from cattle, manure, meat, milk and eggs.

Livestock-keeping in Uganda: understanding reality

The following discussion helps to explain why the roles and strategies described above are important to the wider livelihoods of livestock-keepers, and why livestock-keepers in Uganda therefore value the multiple roles of livestock above production for income alone. It also begins to provide pointers to the need to re-evaluate Uganda's approach to livestock development, and starts to suggest possible directions of change.

The absence of alternatives

A key element in understanding the livestock-keeping strategies discussed above is that in most rural contexts there is no realistic alternative to the functions they play. Since these functions are themselves crucial elements of wider livelihood strategies, livestock continue to be seen as very important to rural Ugandans.

Livestock as rural finance

The availability of rural finance is considered to be a key constraint to livelihoods in Uganda (Uganda 2000a). From the discussion in this chapter, it is clear that livestock are currently fulfilling this role for the majority of rural households, although not without problems. Taking this point a step further: livestock disease, or other sources of livestock loss have the same effect as economic uncertainty does for credit use: it is destabilising, it reduces risk taking, and it reduces investment. Livestock mortality is the same as losing savings. Supporting livestock so that such problems are minimised might be expected to have a similar effect to providing rural finance.

The importance of all livestock species

The accumulation strategies for livestock mentioned above illustrate that for many poor households in particular, the route to increased livestock holdings begins with poultry, which are then multiplied and exchanged for goats, which in turn provide opportunities for acquiring pigs, steers and ultimately cows. However the process does not end there; cattle are then the springboard for investment in land, business, fishing gear, or other productive activities and assets.

This brings the importance of the much-neglected small animal species into clear focus, and is a lesson for livestock policy and strategy in Uganda. Supporting these species, including people with a few free-ranging village poultry, in such a way that enhances their livestock accumulation strategies may be a very effective way of supporting both livestock development in general and the wider livelihood strategies found in rural Uganda.

The logic of saving not selling

Livestock strategies are oriented largely to accumulate livestock numbers as savings so that they can either be invested productively (for example in other livestock, in crop farming, or in other business), or can be sold when needed to provide cash for specific needs (such as during sickness, for school fees, or for food when it has run out). In these situations, different types of livestock will be sold to meet different sized financial needs, with the objective of reducing livestock holdings as little as possible.

For many livestock-keeping households, especially the relatively poor, livestock sales – and therefore income from livestock – are frequently seen as undesirable since they compromise the accumulation strategy, and in many ways are indicative of a failure of other elements of the wider livelihood system. Consequently, increasing sales or income from livestock may be the very opposite of what livestock-keepers themselves are trying to achieve. On the other hand, everyone values income and one of the main functions of livestock in livelihood strategies is to be sold when needed. The point is that the majority of smallholder livestock systems, due to their multiple roles, are not aiming at profit maximisation, and therefore do not make decisions about investment and returns in the same way as someone who has this objective.

Livestock as a springboard to livelihood diversification

When the livestock accumulation strategy is successful people get into a position to make choices about disposal of livestock, and pursue productive investments such as small business or fishing gear as described above. In this case livestock play the role of a springboard to livelihood diversification, by providing investment funds which are frequently not available from any other source. However, even in this case, this does not mean that livestock are regarded as an enterprise in which enterprise efficiency is an important consideration, since this strategy requires accumulation until sufficient stock are kept to be able to sell them to invest in something else. Selling at an optimal time for production would not be compatible with this strategy. This sort of commercially-oriented selling behaviour therefore only occurs when productive investments are made in livestock specifically as a means to provide income.

It might therefore be expected that livestock numbers would increase as livelihood diversification beyond agriculture increases, since livestock are a home of savings and as people diversify they increase income and increase savings. This will create new demands for services, but not for services aimed at providing livestock income and increasing the efficiency of livestock production; it is more likely that the demand will be for services that will help protect people's savings.

The analysis above demonstrated that currently livestock are making a very important contribution to livelihoods in the three districts studied. This chapter has so far argued that the importance of livestock is not well captured by income data, and that this is primarily because livestock are not kept only for income: they are valued for the multiple roles they play in support of people's wider livelihoods.

This is a surprising conclusion to some, who assume that the key objective of keeping livestock is to produce in order to provide income or other tangible products. Others might even see these multiple functions as undesirable, and consider that livestock should be kept just for the purposes of production and income. However, when seen in terms of the wider livelihoods of the poor, the strategies described here represent an appropriate response to the challenging environment in which rural Ugandans make a living because they provide many valued roles which are not otherwise available.

Poor rural households do not live in sectors but have integrated holistic livelihoods. They are interested in livelihood goals, not sectoral goals. To poor rural people, their livelihoods are not a collection of individual sectoral businesses, as technical professionals tend to see them; they are in fact a system that needs to work as a whole. Livestock play a central and irreplaceable role within that system, but this is not always mediated through production and income. Since the livestock element of people's livelihoods is not seen as an enterprise, then it is unrealistic to expect 'enterprise-style' decision-making. This is why poor livestock-keeping systems tend to be based on low investment, and avoid unnecessary risk taking.

A practical implication of this view is that, because of the importance of all the wider contributions of livestock to livelihoods beyond production and income, livestock-keeping systems, objectives and strategies are unlikely to change unless there are suitable alternatives to those roles. Currently, as argued above this is not the case for most rural livestock-keepers in the three districts studied, especially the poor. The people who do modernise and invest in production are those who are able to fulfil those roles in ways other than through livestock. This analysis has far-reaching conclusions for livestock policy in Uganda, and beyond. Policies aiming to increase livestock income through increased production are not appropriate for the majority of livestock-keepers, and especially the poor, because this is not the objective of the livestock-keepers themselves.

Current constraints to livestock-keeping

Despite the importance of livestock to rural livelihoods in Uganda, livestock-keepers currently face many problems which inhibit the effectiveness of this contribution. Furthermore, fieldwork suggests that many of these problems are getting worse rather than improving. The two main problems identified during the study relate to poor animal health and animal theft. Interestingly marketing was felt not to be a problem. In all three districts livestock are easily sold, due to the itinerant traders who come to villages in search of animals.

Animal health and disease

One of the key problems felt by livestock-keepers is the presence of disease and corresponding poor animal health. Specifically mentioned are the problems of Newcastle Disease in poultry, African Swine Fever in pigs, and Foot and Mouth Disease in cattle. Part of the cause of this problem is the difficulty many livestock-keepers in all three districts in accessing animal health services. These are felt to be too distant, difficult to access, and if they are available they are prohibitively expensive for many due to the need to pay not only for drug costs but also often transport and fees. These findings are supported by several authoritative sources, including the Ministry's new Policy for Veterinary Services, by the PMA itself, and by UPPAP. It appears as though for most livestock-keepers, animal health services are inadequate for most of the time, and that the benefits of the changes made in the new animal health policy had yet to be translated into real progress for livestock-keepers at the time of this study's fieldwork.

The effect of animal health problems can be enormous and multi-faceted. For example, in Mbale, given the context of existing livestock-keeping strategies and the multiple roles livestock play, the weakness of animal health services, the high risk of disease and the consequent livestock mortality represents a substantial loss of savings as well as other wider effects. An outbreak of cattle disease in 1995 reduced the availability of draught power for cattle owners, but also increased the price for households who relied on hired draught for cultivation, affecting the poor disproportionately and putting it out of the reach of most. This led to a renewed reliance on hand hoes for cultivation, from which the area has still not recovered. It also reduced the amount of available manure, affecting crop yields for those who could not afford inorganic fertilisers. Furthermore, Newcastle Disease in poultry has reduced the numbers of chickens, and has consequently affected the role they play in livestock and wider asset accumulation strategies. These problems have together discouraged many from investing in livestock and influenced the social institutions around livestock, which are themselves very important for the poor.

Livestock theft

Theft of livestock was reported as the major constraint to livestock-keeping, and has discouraged some people from keeping livestock at all at several study sites. This was particularly the case in Mubende, which is not affected by the historical livestock raiding in eastern Uganda. Where theft is such a constraint, livestock development is fundamentally hampered, implying that it is an issue which the government cannot ignore when planning results-focused sub-sector strategies. The new animal health policy under the umbrella of the PMA acknowledges this and takes security consideration as a necessary condition for successful implementation of livestock development programmes.

The findings presented in this chapter show that though livestock currently play a central role in the livelihoods of the poor and other livestock-keepers, the current system has much room for improvement and this contribution could be significantly increased through appropriate support. The remaining sections considers what these findings mean for livestock development policy and practice.

The appropriateness of current approaches to livestock development in Uganda

Current livestock policy

Uganda does not have an over-arching national livestock policy. Instead it has a number of specific policies, strategies and masterplans focused on commodities or cross-cutting elements such as breeding, or animal health.

As such it is difficult to generalise about approaches to livestock development in Uganda, since there is no over-arching framework to provide guidance. Nevertheless, looking at the available policy documents, it is reasonable to conclude that the objective of current approaches to livestock development is 'to increase livestock production and productivity'. This is explicitly stated in the new Policy for Animal Health, which post-dates the PMA, and is implied by other documents.

Many of these policy documents recognise the multiple roles that livestock are expected to play in livestock-keepers' livelihoods, but they do not reflect them in the approaches they propose. Furthermore, with the possible exception of the animal health policy, existing policy documents do not address service provision or explicitly address poverty reduction objectives.

The prevailing approach to livestock development signified by these documents places emphasis on livestock and their products, and a focus on livestock as commodities. In order for such an approach to contribute to poverty reduction, it relies on an assumed causal link between increasing production and productivity, and reducing poverty. All analysis conducted for the PEAP, UPPAP and PMA, and the findings of this chapter, suggest that this is an over-simplification and that such a link cannot be assumed. This, in turn, indicates the need to revisit livestock policy if it is to contribute to the overall poverty reduction goal.

Livestock development at district level

Following the decentralisation provided for by the Local Government Act 1997 (Uganda 2001c), the role of national policies is to provide a framework which guide decisions taken at district and lower administrative levels. In terms of livestock development, national government is responsible for the provision of certain national public goods, but many functions and expenditures have been delegated to districts. The interpretation of national livestock policy and the PMA at district level is therefore of great importance in determining approaches to livestock development in practice. At district level, multi-disciplinary Production Committees are part of the team that produce district level development plans which outline how the district aims to achieve its objectives and its contribution to national development goals.

Unfortunately, when it comes to livestock development the three districts studied show little evidence of understanding the contributions of livestock to poverty reduction. This applies to their analysis of livestock-related issues, and also their response in terms of planned investments.

A synthesis of the three district case studies suggest that:

1 PMA principles have yet to be incorporated or are alternatively being applied literally in terms of commercialisation, intensification and modernisation.
2 There is a focus in all three districts on production, and intensification of existing livestock systems.
3 There is no evidence of recognition of the wider contribution of livestock to livelihoods.
4 Animal health problems are important in each district, but planned responses do not necessarily conform to the principles outlined in the new animal health policy, and do not necessarily meet poor livestock-keepers' needs.
5 A major share of attention and expenditure appears to be allocated to intensifying production through use of intensive production systems and the introduction of new breeds.

The analysis in this chapter suggests that both the analyses and the plans made in each of these three districts could be questioned. Given the importance of livestock and the problems people face in maintaining them, are the planned expenditures really the best pro-poor investments possible?

Lessons from this study

As the evidence from this study shows, the current approach to livestock development in Uganda as reflected in national policy documents does not reflect the objectives and strategies of the majority of livestock-keepers in practice. The study shows that livestock-keepers, especially the poor, want to keep their animals alive and expand their numbers so that they can contribute most effectively to wider livelihood strategies. However, the prevailing approach to livestock development revolves around improving management, breeds, and animal health services in order to enhance production and trade of livestock commodities. The outcome of this dichotomy is that many of the services being offered to livestock-keepers or being planned in their name are in fact inappropriate, as can be seen from the district plans.

Whilst improvements to current livestock-keeping practice are, of course, possible current efforts centre upon intensification. However, this analysis shows that this is precisely what most livestock-keepers do not want, or more accurately are not able to support at the current time due to the strategies they pursue as a result of their wider livelihood situation. Despite this, the study shows that livestock are very important, in fact central, to the livelihoods of the majority of rural households, and that these households suffer from many livestock-related problems. Overall, this means that due to the mismatch between the priorities of livestock-keepers and the support offered by government, Uganda is currently missing a major opportunity to maximise the contribution of livestock to the livelihoods of the poor, and consequently hampering its pursuit of the national goal of poverty reduction.

Implications for livestock development strategy under the PMA

The basic argument of this chapter is that farming, defined as 'crops and livestock', is the basis of relatively diversified rural livelihoods in the three districts studied. The role of livestock in this system is not as a profit-making enterprise where efficiency of production is the aim, but one of supporting the livelihood system as a whole in multiple ways. National livestock policy, however, emphasises livestock production in order to provide income. To many there may appear to be nothing new in these findings: most livestock professionals know that livestock are a part of farming systems, that they contribute in multiple ways to livelihoods, and that meat, milk and eggs are not their only products. However, it is the interpretation and depth of this understanding that is important in policy terms: current policy and its interpretation does not reflect this widely-held understanding.

The key argument here is that recognising this wider objective of livestock-keeping is essential to the definition of appropriate policies for the poor. An understanding of the roles livestock play in the livelihoods of the poor, the options they have and the constraints they face will result in different approaches compared to when production is the objective. It would also allow more specificity in targeting policy interventions to achieve the result that are being sought. Fundamentally, if livestock is used for savings and insurance, then it should be approached in a different way than if it is used to produce income. Good policy needs to reflect this fact. The conventional analysis, reflected in most current livestock policy, holds that increasing livestock production and productivity is the main objective of livestock development, and that the effect on the poor is achieved through the impact of increased income that this is expected to have.

The analysis presented here suggests that increasing livestock production and income is not necessarily compatible with the strategies being pursued by livestock-keepers. This implies that greater impact from livestock development could be achieved by a reorientation in which the multiple contributions of livestock to livelihoods are supported rather than just those related to production and income. Where a poverty agenda is the paramount concern, it is the overall income and security (or any other livelihood goals people may have) produced by people's wider livelihood strategies that is important, not livestock production and income per se. Ultimately, increased production, increased income and reduced poverty are important objectives. However, the big question is how to achieve that. This chapter argues that a production-focused approach will not achieve that objective. The reason for this is that the constraints to commercialisation and intensification of livestock lie in the constraints to wider livelihoods, not livestock alone. Commercialisation and intensification requires: risk-taking that poor households cannot bear; finance that is not available; means of asset management beyond livestock that do not exist in rural areas; and availability of cash for investment that poor households just do not have.

All of these issues will not be solved by commercialisation and intensification of livestock-keeping; they are prerequisites for it. In order to reduce poverty through livestock development, a different approach is required.

Pro-poor livestock development: the future

The implication of this chapter is that the reasoning underlying livestock development itself needs to be revisited, when poverty reduction is an important consideration. This means a rethink of the contribution of the livestock sub-sector to poverty reduction: at national level this implies a need to be supporting the contribution of livestock to national development goals (in this case poverty reduction), rather than marketed surplus; at a local level it implies a need to support the wider contributions of livestock to the livelihoods of the poor, rather than focusing on a limited selection of these potential contributions (namely production and income).

Though there are several livestock sub-sector policy documents currently to be found in Uganda, there is not one which provides an agenda for the whole sub-sector: which states the objective of livestock development, what it should aim to do, and how its success should be measured. In previous times this was less problematic because it was assumed that maximising livestock production was the obvious objective of livestock development. However, poverty reduction is now explicitly the main objective of government: people and not products are now what counts.

The findings of this study suggest that it is appropriate to redefine the objectives of livestock development in Uganda, to take account of the poverty agenda which is emphasised in the PEAP and the PMA, and the multiple contributions livestock make to livelihoods. Perhaps it is time for an over-arching policy and strategy for the sub-sector as a whole, which interprets the wider rules provided by the PMA, to ensure that efforts at livestock development do indeed contribute to national development goals.

A pro-poor approach to livestock development would differ in the following ways from current practice:

Get policy right

Policy needs to reflect the realities and aspirations of the poor if poverty reduction is to be an important objective. This means refocusing policy on the people who keep livestock themselves, rather than the animals, and their products. It also means that indicators which measure the success of livestock development should be based on its impact on people and their livelihoods, rather than on production and trade. The need to get policy right and ensuring it is well known and understood is an important part of eliciting the appropriate response for pro-poor approach within and outside the livestock profession. This is particularly important in the context of decentralisation where many of the real decisions and plans which affect livestock-keepers are being made at district level. It is also important for a wider group of stakeholders so that they can know what to expect from the livestock sub-sector.

Understand clients

A key element of being client-focused and demand driven is understanding people's objectives and strategies, and responding appropriately to these. This study shows that livestock-keepers in Uganda are not well understood by those who are meant to serve them. A client-oriented approach to service delivery and provision of an enabling environment, as envisaged by the PMA, requires a greater understanding of who are the clients and what are their priorities, on which to base policy, programmes and plans. It is important to recognise that differences exist between the objectives, strategies, constraints and priorities of different livestock-keepers. To assume a single objective (increasing production) therefore neglects the needs of all those – the majority – for whom other priorities are more important. This chapter argues that unless such differences are recognised and factored into livestock development planning, then the livestock sub-sector contribution to poverty reduction will be fundamentally hampered.

Address multiple roles

The reality of livestock-keeping, as outlined in this chapter, is that people do not see livestock as businesses or enterprises, but as the sources of multiple outputs and contributions to wider livelihoods. This is perfectly valid, but in focusing on production, the government continues to service only one of these many contributions. A pro-poor approach to livestock development will involve recognising the validity of these wider concerns and what really motivates livestock-keepers, and addressing these wider roles as well as addressing the production-related roles.

Support versus change

This chapter argues that livestock currently make a huge, irreplaceable and under-valued contribution to the livelihoods of the poor and others in the areas covered by this study. However, the fundamental approach of government policy and programmes is to change the systems which make this contribution into something else: something in which production features more highly, and which is based on commercialisation and intensification. This is still the case post-PMA.

A pro-poor approach to livestock development would seek to understand and appreciate the obvious value contributed by currently practiced livestock-keeping systems and strategies, most of which are subject to major problems, and seek to support those systems – rather than change them – so that they can contribute more effectively to people's routes out of poverty. To do otherwise is incompatible with a client-focused approach.

Implications for the PMA

This study has major implications for livestock development policy in Uganda, but does it also have potential implications for the PMA itself? The UPPAP studies (cited in Uganda 2000a) have shown us that poverty in Uganda is about more than just income; this study shows that the same applies to livestock development.

However, the PMA focuses on transformation towards market-oriented commercial production as the means to achieving poverty reduction. If the PMA is interpreted literally, as it clearly has been at district level, this study suggests that the PMA messages of increased commercialisation and a focus on income are not appropriate, or at least are not sufficient, as a basis for pro-poor livestock development. The PMA therefore currently sends the wrong message when it comes to sub-sectoral strategy for livestock development.

If it is not the intention of the PMA to send such a message, and a wider reading of the document suggests that it is not, then perhaps it is time for a deepening of its analysis at a sub-sectoral level, and an iteration of the document to reflect the emerging understanding of rural livelihoods emanating from studies such as the one described here.

Notes

* William Nanyeenya is a member of the Livestock Research Institute (LIRI)/ NARO, PO Box 96, Tororo, Uganda.

1 This can probably be explained by the influence of one village in Mubende (Kabbo village) where the livestock contribution was 21 per cent. This village was more pastoralist in nature, and in pastoralist systems the arguments made in this chapter about the importance of livestock income are less applicable.

16 The fisheries sector, livelihoods and poverty reduction in eastern and southern Africa*

Edward H. Allison

Introduction

The small-scale fisheries of developing countries are typically conceived of as an 'occupation of last resort' for the 'poorest of the poor'. Recent studies in Asia and Africa have, however, questioned this view both empirically and theoretically (Teitze *et al.* 2000; Pollnac *et al.* 2001; Béné 2003). The relative poverty status of fisherfolk and the role of the fisheries sector in the rural economy remains little understood in many countries. The primary aim of this chapter is therefore to review the role of the fisheries sector in four African countries (Kenya, Malawi, Tanzania and Uganda) and to assess whether that role is adequately recognised in policy processes such as decentralisation and poverty reduction strategies, as well as in the goals of fisheries policies.

Although the management of common property forests and wildlife and their contributions to rural livelihoods have constituted an important arena for debate in the study of development in Africa (e.g. Hulme and Murphree 2001), the fisheries sector, arguably of more importance to Africans than all other animal 'wildlife' taken together, makes only fleeting appearances in the literature. Being a rather specialised discipline dominated by biological scientists, fisheries science has engaged relatively little with the broad area of rural development. Radical changes are, however, taking place in governance regimes and institutional development in the sector (Allison 2001; Allison and McBride 2003). There is an evolving global policy focus on sustaining the contribution that fisheries make to food and livelihood security in developing countries, initiated by the FAO Code of Conduct for Responsible Fisheries (FAO 1995b), and given impetus by the adoption of livelihoods frameworks in recent fisheries development initiatives (Allison and Ellis 2001).

Contribution of fisheries to national economies

All four countries studied in this chapter have access to the Great Lakes of the East African Rift Valley. It is Lakes Victoria, Tanganyika and Malawi that provide the major contribution to fish supply and employment opportunity in the region, rather than the marine fisheries of Kenya and Tanzania which only account for a small fraction of total production (Table 16.1). As well as the other major rift valley lakes (Turkana, Albert, Edward), the region also abounds with shallow lakes and their associated wetlands (e.g. Lake Chilwa in Malawi, the Lake Kyoga complex in Uganda, Lakes Naivasha and Baringo in Kenya and Lake Rukwa in Tanzania). These wetlands can be immensely productive in some years and much less so in others, with fluctuations being largely driven by climate-induced variability in lake-levels (Sarch and Allison 2000; Jul-Larsen *et al.* 2003).

The fisheries sector makes important contributions to the national economies of all four countries, but it is difficult to assess exactly how important as the statistical data are rather unreliable. Using the estimated value of fisheries at the point of first sale, the sub-sector currently accounts for 2–4 per cent of GDP and 5–9 per cent of agricultural GDP at national level. Given that significant fisheries only occur in limited areas within the region, this implies considerable economic significance at sub-national level, notably in lakeshore and coastal districts.

Fish exports are currently among Uganda's top three foreign exchange earners (alongside coffee and tourism) and rank fourth among Kenya's agricultural exports; after tea, coffee and horticulture products. Of the four countries, only Malawi lacks a significant fish export trade. This export trade is relatively recent and has been driven not so much by policy intervention as by biological introductions. In the 1950s, Nile Perch were introduced into Lake Victoria and over the next thirty years this large, voracious predator gradually came to dominate the ecosystem so that the lake's fisheries switched from being based on a huge diversity of mostly small fish, to being based on three species – the introduced Nile Perch (*Lates niloticus*), the introduced Nile Tilapia (*Oreochromis niloticus*) and the native *omena/mukene/dagaa* (*Rastrineobola argentea*). These three species now support fisheries supplying three distinct markets – Nile Perch for high-value exports, Tilapia for medium value urban domestic markets and the tiny *dagaa* for widespread trade and consumption by lower-income groups (and, increasingly, for animal feed) throughout eastern, central and southern Africa.

The volume of export trade is now substantial. Of total fish production by weight in Tanzania, 63 per cent is used for domestic human consumption, 30 per cent is exported and 8 per cent is for animal feed or non-food uses. Fish comprised 12.3 per cent of the total export value in 1998 and the government also earned substantial tax revenue from fish exports (US$ 4.6 million in 2001: SSC Inc & OAFCC Ltd 2002). Trade figures may not include regional trade of lower-value but very abundant species. Small sardine-like fish (known as *dagaa*, *kapenta*, *mukene*, *omena* or *usipa*, depending on species and country) are widely traded, in sun-dried form, across national boundaries in the region but this trade is often unrecorded.

Although fish production increased steadily in the post-colonial era, total

Table 16.1 Contribution of fisheries to national economies

	Malawi	*Kenya*	*Tanzania*	*Uganda*
Total fish catch (tonnes)[a]	41,817	165,160	336,200	223,086
Inland fisheries catch (t)[a]	41,817	157,772	283,300	223,086
Marine fisheries catch (t)[a]		7,388	52,900	
First-sale value of landings (US$ million)[b]	49.5 (1995)	264.5 (1997)	580.0 (1997)	361.0 (1997)
Fisheries share of GDP (%)[c]	4.0 (1997)	2.0 (2000)	2.9 (1999)	2.2 (1999)
Agriculture share of GDP (%)[d]	41.6	19.9	45.1	42.5
Fisheries share of agricultural GDP (%)	9.0	8.7	6.4	5.2
Value of exports (US$ million)	0.3 (1999)[a]	50.0 (2001)[e]	75.5 (2000)[f]	87.5 (2002)[g]
Value of imports (US$ million, 1999)[a]	0.2	5.3	2.0	0.1
Per capita consumption (kg/year 2001)[h]	4.0	6.1	8.0	13.4
Fish as a share of protein in the diet (%, 1997)[h]	3.1	2.9	7.0	6.5
Fish as a share of animal protein (%, 1997)[h]	37.7	9.7	33.6	30.0
Employment in the catching sector	48,000 (2000)[i]	40,869 (1998)[e]	102,527 (1999)[f]	136,000 (1997)[j]
Total fishery-related employment (catching, trading, processing, etc.)	200,000 (1999)[i]	500,000 (2000)[e]	1,000,000 (1997)[b]	700,000 (1997)[j]

Sources:

a FAOSTAT Fisheries Data (last updated August 2003) Online. Available HTTP: http://apps.fao.org/page/collections?subset=fisheries (accessed 24 January 2004).

b FAO Fishery Country Profiles. Online. Available HTTP: http://www.fao.org/fi/fcp/fcp.asp (accessed 24 January 2004).

c Fisheries Department statistical bulletins and sector planning documents (see text for sources).

d World Bank (2002a) (Figures are for 2000).

e Kenya Fisheries Sector Study (JITAP 2002).

f Tanzania Fisheries Sector Master Plan (SSC Inc & OAFCC Ltd 2002).

g Uganda Investment Authority (2003) Online. Available HTTP: http://www.ugandainvest.com/4htm (accessed 17 January 2004).

h FAOSTAT Nutrition Data (last updated June 2003). Online. Available HTTP: http://apps.fao.org/page/collections?subset=nutrition (accessed 24 January 2004).

i Malawi (1999b) Ministry of Natural Resources and Environmental Affairs (MNREA), *The National Fisheries and Aquaculture Policy*, Department of Fisheries, Lilongwe: Government Printer.

j Uganda (2002b) Ministry of Agriculture, Animal Industry and Fisheries, *The National Fisheries Policy (final draft, June 2002)*, Kampala: Government Printer.

production in the region tended to plateau in the early 1990s, with production in Malawi declining since the 1980s. For three of the countries, per capita supply is on a long-term declining trend (Figure 16.1). Before a supply crisis is suggested, the figures need to be disaggregated. Data are scarce, but it can be assumed that dependence on fisheries in diets will be highly variable among different populations. For people in coastal villages in Tanzania, for example, fish makes up over 60 per cent of animal protein in the diet – double the national average (Shao *et al.* 2003: 35). *Dagaa* from Lake Victoria is the most cost-effective food in terms of energy and protein purchased per Tshs 100 (SSc Inc & OAFCC Ltd 2002). Fish accounts for between 6 and 7 per cent of cash expenditure on food by the poor in rural Malawi (rising to around 11 per cent in the urban poor). This is the third largest expense, after cereals and vegetables, of the fourteen food-group items identified in national household economic surveys (Allison and Mvula 2002).

Fisheries provide a source of income to large numbers of people, mostly young men, in the catching sector. For every job on the water there are up to five full or part-time jobs for both women and men in associated sectors such as processing, transport, trade, boat and net building and repair, and provision of other services to fishing communities (Table 16.1). If the figures are accurate, then one in ten members of Uganda's labour force are involved in the fisheries sector in some capacity. The number of people involved in fisheries is uncertain as some fisherfolk do not register with government, others are part-time or occasional fishers or internal migrants recorded as farmers in their place of origin in census data. There are also unregistered migrants from

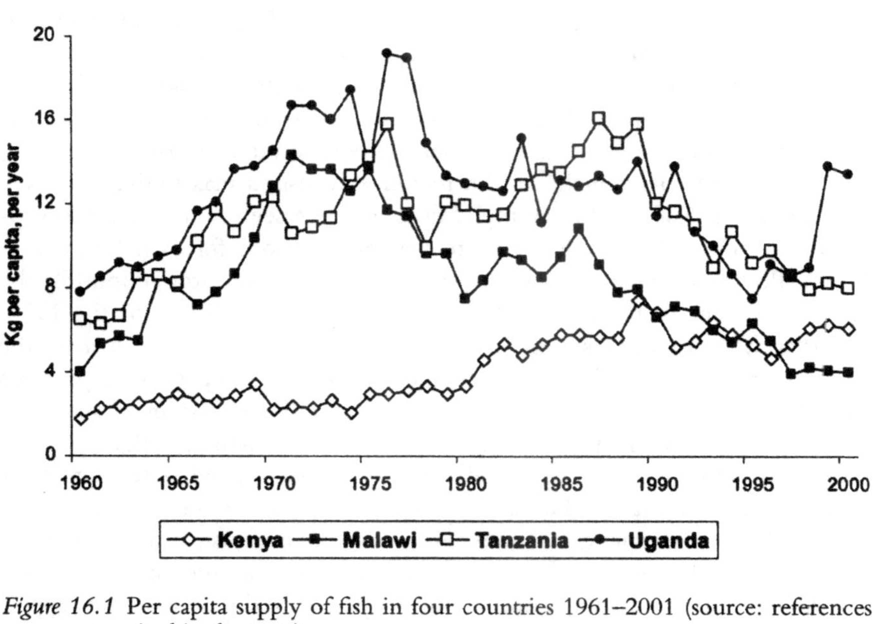

Figure 16.1 Per capita supply of fish in four countries 1961–2001 (source: references cited in the text.)

neighbouring countries (e.g. Congolese fisherfolk on the Tanzanian shores of Lake Tanganyika, Tanzanian fisherfolk on the Kenya Coast).

Small-scale or 'artisanal' fisheries dominate the catching sector in all four countries, with over 90 per cent of production originating from small boats – typically with crews of between one and five people and unmotorised or having only an outboard engine. In Coastal Tanzania, 20,000 fishermen work from over 5,000 small boats, only 10 per cent of which are motorised (Shao *et al.* 2003). Lake Victoria dominates Kenya's inland fisheries, with over 38,000 fishermen operating from over 10,000 vessels.

In summary, the four countries produce over 0.75 million tonnes of fish, worth in excess of a billion US dollars per year. The export trade, worth over US$ 200 million a year, is among the region's most significant foreign exchange earners. Fisheries also make an important contribution to the quality of people's diets. Between one and three million people are thought to be involved in fishing-related employment, supporting the livelihoods of four or five times that number of dependents. Recent censuses suggest there are almost 1,000 fish landing sites in Tanzania alone, signifying that a fishing village is located, on average, about every four km along the coastline of the countries' major water bodies (Indian Ocean, Great Lakes, etc.). Thus, fishing and its associated trades make a substantive contribution to rural societies throughout the region.

Policy directions and processes in fisheries

The potentially conflicting roles that fisheries play in the rural economy makes it important for governments to establish clear policy directions at national level. A fishery cannot be managed simultaneously to maximise the supply of cheap fish for domestic consumption, export earnings of high-value fish, and employment and income-generation to fisherfolk. Neither can the sector grow indefinitely; fisheries resources are renewable but finite.

Colonial fisheries policies in the region emphasised maximising domestic fish supply. In Malawi, for example, fisheries were seen as important in supplying nutritious food at low cost to plantation labour forces (Allison *et al.* 2002). Post-independence policies retained this focus on production 'for the masses'. The conventional development wisdom of the 1950s to the 1970s was that the cause of persistent poverty among small-scale fisherfolk lay in the limited productivity of small boats and 'artisanal' fishing gear, a problem curable though provision of more effective technologies (Bailey *et al.* 1986). Fisheries development projects of this era are not generally judged to have been successful (Cycon 1986) and a legacy of abandoned state-owned ice plants, disused central markets and rusting trawlers can be seen in most major fish landing centres in the region. Since structural adjustment programmes were instigated, state involvement in the production side of fisheries has gradually been withdrawn. Throughout the period of donor and state support for industrialisation of fisheries, artisanal or small-scale fisheries continued to expand with limited development assistance, with state-imposed regulations to protect fish stocks often being ineffective due to limited capacity of state institutions.

Fisheries are normally administered by departments within ministries of agriculture, environment or natural resources (Table 16.2). Despite recent changes in emphasis and governance arrangements, fisheries policies remain production-orientated. In all four countries, widespread concern about over-fishing co-exists with highly optimistic prognoses of maximum sustainable yields, based on the area of water available. For example, Tanzania's marine waters are estimated to support an output potential of around 100,000 tonnes per year, only half of which is currently caught (Shao *et al.* 2003) and Uganda's fishery policy estimates sustainable yields in excess of 300,000 tonnes although actual yields have never reached this level.

The region's fisheries policies also invariably contain highly optimistic statements of growth potential of aquaculture (fish farming) and its projected contribution to both national nutrition and rural livelihoods. Yet, at the moment, aquaculture makes a makes only a small contribution to food security and economic development in the four countries. Constraints to aquaculture for rural development may include lack of cash, shortage of labour and relevant labour skills, social levelling mechanisms and cultural constraints, quality of government extension, lack of land tenure and ownership arrangements and biophysical limitations such as limited or highly seasonal water supply and water quality and nutrient levels (Brummett and Williams 2000: 196).

The principles underlying national estimates of maximum sustainable production from capture fisheries are derived from the Gordon–Shaefer bioeconomic model (Charles 2001) that has been used for the last fifty years to provide target reference points for management policy in the world's fisheries. These reference points have, in the past, been set by government, with 'command and control' style regulation through limited licensing and a host of other input, output and technical control measures. With the current interest in community-based management, some of these responsibilities are now being devolved to fisherfolk themselves through community-based fisheries management initiatives. These are discussed in a later section of this chapter.

While livelihood issues are becoming more prominent, concern for resource sustainability continues to be the biggest influence on fisheries policy. Over the last decade, as the world's fisheries have reached crisis point, a broad consensus has emerged that the key task in fisheries management is to end the open-access nature of fishing and introduce 'rights-based' approaches to avert a 'tragedy of the commons' (or, more accurately, a tragedy of open-access). Responding to these global trends a wave of policy reforms have swept through the fisheries sector in Africa, under the influence of the 1995 FAO Code of Conduct for Responsible Fisheries (CCRF). The CCRF encompasses many of the provisions for fisheries in other international

Table 16.2 Key elements of national fisheries policy and legislation

	Malawi	*Kenya*	*Tanzania*	*Uganda*
Lead government ministry	Department of Fisheries, Ministry of Natural Resources and Environmental Affairs	Fisheries Department, Ministry of Agriculture and Rural Development	Fisheries Department, Ministry of Natural Resources and Tourism	Department of Fisheries Resources, Ministry of Agriculture, Animal Husbandry and Fisheries
Policy framework	National Fisheries and Aquaculture Policy, October 1999	Evolving rapidly – the old fisheries policy is no longer relevant (e.g. no legal mandate for community involvement in fisheries management)	National Fisheries Sector Policy and Strategy Statement, 1997 and Master Plan on Fisheries Development, 2002; the latter is informed by the PRSP	The National Fisheries Policy, 2002. Informed by the Plan for the Modernisation of Agriculture and the PRSP process
Legislative framework	Fisheries Conservation and Management Act, 1997	Fisheries Act, Chapter 378, Laws of Kenya (revised 1991)	Fisheries Act, 1970, supplemented by eight technical amendments between 1975 and 1997; Territorial Sea and Exclusive Economic Zone Act; Marine Park and Reserves Act, 1994	The Fish and Crocodile Act (1964 and 1967). A new Fisheries Act is under consideration by parliament at the time of writing.
Policy goals	'To improve the efficiency of all aspects of the national fisheries industry, production and supply of existing fisheries products, as well as the development of new products to satisfy local demand and potential export markets'	'No stated goals, a series of policy objectives: maximise production, increase per capita fish consumption, increase quality and value of fish products; conserve biodiversity; increase employment; enhance living conditions of fisherfolk; encourage exports'	'Exploiting fisheries resources in a sustainable manner to enhance food security by increasing availability of animal protein in local markets and to create employment for local populations'	'Ensure increased and sustainable fish production and utilisation by properly managing capture fisheries, promoting aquaculture and reducing post harvest losses'

Source: synthesised from Government Acts, Policies and Plans cited in the text.

environmental agreements (e.g. UN Convention on Law of the Sea, Agenda 21, Convention on Biological Diversity) and is in broad conformity with contemporary neo-liberal development policy in its emphasis on withdrawal of the state, removal of subsidies, participation by resource users in management and, latterly, emphasis on poverty eradication (Table 16.3).

The CCRF is applied on a voluntary basis. It aims to provide policy direction for legal regimes and may become binding, at global, regional and national levels when its provisions are adopted in state legislation or by regional and global conventions. In eastern and southern Africa, policy reforms funded by donors and influenced by the CCRF have initiated a process that then leads to formulation of new fisheries legislation and creation of a Master Plan for policy implementation (Table 16.2 above). Latterly, fisheries sector Master Plans have been competing for funds in Medium Term Expenditure Frameworks (MTEFs), necessitating some re-working to fit with PRSP objectives. The process is analogous to the evolution of sector-wide approaches (SWAPs) and agricultural sector investment plans (ASIPs) and is likewise challenged by the cross-sectoral nature of rural livelihoods (Gillings *et al.* 2001).

Table 16.3 Key elements of the FAO Code of Conduct for Responsible Fisheries

Policy objectives (to be implemented at national level)
Provide institutions and incentive structures for fishers and investors to assume increased responsibility for management of resources, through the provision of exclusive use rights such as ITQs,[a] limited licences and TURFs.[b]
Maintain/restore fisheries benefits – food, revenues, jobs, recreation, biodiversity.
Increase supplies to meet future demand through, e.g. waste reduction, productivity enhancement, use intensification and aquaculture.
Increase economic efficiency by reducing overcapacity, eliminating subsidies, promoting free trade and ensuring local values and equity are considered.
Protect the resource base and its environment, including through a precautionary approach.
Improve the priority given to small-scale fisheries to boost incomes and food security.
Develop the capacity to monitor and assess fish stocks at national and regional (transboundary) levels.
Institutional support from FAO
Advise developing countries in implementing the Code of Conduct
Assist regional cooperation, decision making and consultation
Provide technical support for implementation of the code at national/regional level
Monitor and Report on the Code's implementation
Finance for implementation
Development banks, Global Environment Facility, national governments, bilateral and multilateral donors, private banks, co-operation with NGOs

Source: Allison (2001).

Notes

a Individual Transferable Quotas.

b Territorial Use Rights in Fisheries.

Although now broadly supportive of a range of livelihood issues, fisheries policy objectives seldom explicitly address poverty objectives, probably because the available data on relative poverty of fisherfolk have not been available. To enable broad policy statements to guide sectoral investment and regulation at relevant scales, a better understanding of the local-level contribution of fisheries to rural livelihoods is required.

Characteristics of fishing-based livelihoods

There has existed in the fisheries literature a dominant narrative describing 'artisanal' fisherfolk as landless, unskilled, uneducated poor people, locked into fishing through lack of alternative opportunities. It has been assumed that fisheries are easy to get into, but difficult to get out of, leading to overcapitalisation and dissipation of resource rents as the growing population of poor fisherfolk scramble to catch the last fish (Pauly 1997). This narrative has been difficult to challenge, particularly in the face of undeniable resource declines, because there has been little information on the relationship between fisheries and poverty (Béné 2003). In Tanzania's recent national Household Budget Survey, for example, agriculture, livestock and fisheries are not disaggregated (Shao *et al.* 2003) and in surveys of poverty in Malawi, such as the Integrated Household Survey of 1997 and 1998 (Malawi 2000) households involved in fishing and related activities were not sampled, so that national-level generalisations about poverty and livelihoods are not necessarily applicable to understanding the particular circumstances of fisherfolk.

The LADDER research programme (see Preface and Chapter 1 of this volume) and some other recent projects in the region have begun to apply the livelihoods framework to bring a better understanding of the dynamics of poverty in small-scale fisheries into the fisheries policy arena. The research aimed to identify the role played by fishing in livelihood strategies in places where this is a livelihood option, the relative poverty status of fishing and non-fishing households in the same localities, and the effects on livelihoods of reforms in fisheries governance, principally the shift towards community-based or co-management. The research was then used to identify policy reforms, institutional changes or management or development interventions that might help to strengthen livelihoods.

LADDER field research, conducted during 2001 and 2002, included eight lakeshore villages in Kenya (Lake Victoria), Malawi (Lake Chilwa) and Uganda (Lake Kyoga). The research was conducted in partnership with national policy research institutions. It combined analysis of macro-level policies with studies of local-level institutions, household-level analysis of activities, assets and incomes, group and key informant interviews and individual life-history studies (Allison and Mvula 2002; Allison 2003; Freeman *et al.* 2004).

Livelihoods incorporating fishing tend to be structured in one of two main ways. One group are specialist fisherfolk who tend to be migratory and can be found living temporarily in lakeshore and coastal villages, or in makeshift fishing camps, sometimes with their families, but often with other fishermen in all-male groups. The second group of fisherfolk are residents of lakeshore villages, who tend to fish part-time, or may not fish at all but may own some fishing-related assets and depend on hired labour to do the actual fishing. They usually have household members engaged in farming or other activities and own land and livestock. Lakeshore fishing villages also include farmers who have minimal or no involvement in the fishing sector, so it cannot be assumed that lakeshore dwellers always have strong direct vested interests in fishing. It may be misleading to characterise these villages as 'fishing communities' and we prefer the term lakeshore or coastal village. Fishing activities are highly gender-specific. In most cases, only men are involved in fish-catching activities, although women are involved in beach or reef-based fishing, and in processing and trading fish.

On Lake Chilwa, in Malawi, for example, the range of combinations of migratory and resident fisherman include: residents who mostly farm but have some involvement in part-time fishing or fish-trading, residents specialising in fishing and/or fish-trading, migrants living with their families who also farm, migrant fishermen and itinerant male and female fish traders without their families. The breakdown in main income sources of these groups is indicated in Figure 16.2

Fisherfolk not only exhibit occupational diversity at any given moment; entry into and out of the fisheries sector is also highly dynamic. From analysis

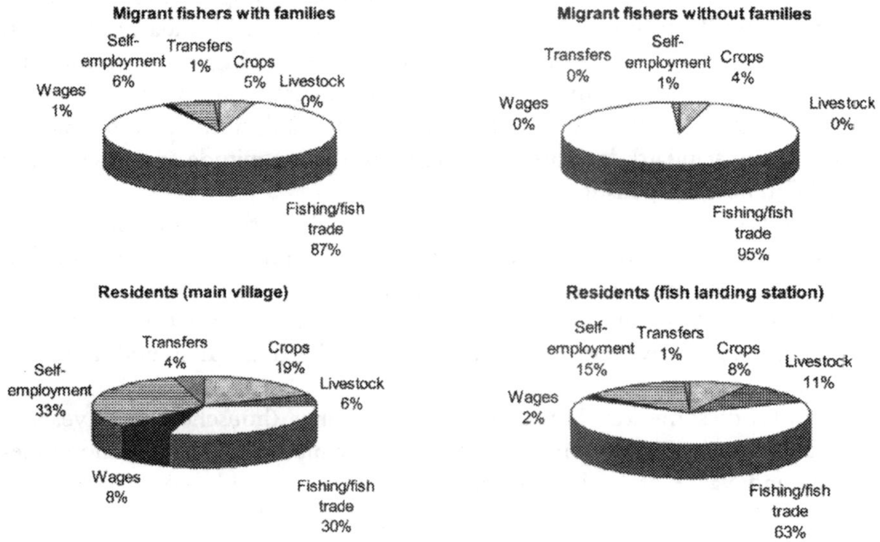

Figure 16.2 Household income sources for resident and migrant households in the lakeshore villages of Zomba District, Malawi (source: sample surveys carried out in two Zomba villages, 2001.)

of the individual life histories of over 100 fishermen and male and female fish traders, a picture emerges of initial engagement in the fishing industry through a diversity of means. For example, older fishing boat owners in Malawi accumulated capital towards fishing equipment by working outside Malawi as cooks, waiters, mineworkers and traders; others borrowed money from relations or friends; a good number started by working as fishing labour. The latter slowly accumulate money that enable them to buy fishing equipment in phases, often starting with the ownership of a lamp for night-fishing, or part-ownership of a gillnet.

In the case of settled farmer-fishers, decreasing availability of land and the decline of livestock-keeping due to theft and lack of veterinary support services threatens to reduce the diversity of the economic base for lakeshore dwellers. This may push more people into full-time fishing, thereby increasing the number of fisherfolk with a high level of dependence on fishing. Increased dependency on fishing is not desirable in the long-run, even if it may be profitable in the short-run. The livestock–farming–fishing 'tri-economy' is a common livelihood strategy in lakeshore areas throughout Africa and has proved resilient to extensive biophysical and economic changes (e.g. Geheb and Binns 1997; Neiland *et al.* 2000; Sarch and Birkett 2000), and could remain viable if flaws in the current institutional context are addressed by improved local-level governance. The removal of barriers to mobility and active support for livelihood diversification are relevant overall policy directions in this context.

Comparison of average incomes of households in lakeshore district villages that had some involvement in fishing with non-fishing households in the eight LADDER fishing villages in Kenya, Malawi and Uganda (Table 16.4) suggest that mean and median per capita incomes are higher for households involved in fishing than for those in the same district with no involvement in fishing activities. Because the data are synthesised from wealth-stratified samples, the standard deviations are large, but the magnitude and direction of the differences are consistent.

Fisherfolk are not rich. Only in the top quartile of the sample of Ugandan fishing households do per capita incomes average more than US$1 per day. Their incomes are, however, higher than those of non-fishing households in the same village, and higher or similar to income distributions of farmers and other rural dwellers in other regions in Uganda (Ellis and Bahiigwa 2003).

Profiles of some key household asset categories (household size, years in education, area of land owned, livestock ownership, value of tools and implements and value of fishing-related assets) are not readily comparable with non-fishing households, as migrant fishing households, for example, often live in poor housing and own no land or livestock and few non-fishing related tools and assets. This cautions against the uncritical use of asset profiles as proxy poverty indicators. There are, moreover, no indications that household size and educational levels differ significantly between fishing and

Table 16.4 Per capita income[a] comparisons between fishing and non-fishing households

	Fishing HH	*Non-fishing HH*
Kenya (Suba)		
N[b]	105	70
Mean	440.09	212.33
st.dev.	784.22	230.06
Median	213.33	147.99
Malawi (Zomba)		
N	50	60
Mean	86.98	79.81
st.dev.	77.72	49.00
Median	70.04	51.75
Uganda (Kamuli)		
N	53	52
Mean	532.11	184.61
st.dev.	1131.71	282.99
Median	238.91	95.58

Source: LADDER project database, unpublished data.

Notes

a Average per capita incomes (US$) of fishing and non-fishing households in LADDER project sites in lakeshore areas of Kenya (Lake Victoria), Malawi (Lake Chilwa) and Uganda (Lake Kyoga). Per capita income for each household is calculated from total household income divided by the number of people (adult male equivalent units). US$ values are calculated using exchange rates at the time of sampling

b N = number of households sampled.

non-fishing households. The main asset group differentiating wealth groups *within* fishing household samples are the value of fishing-related assets owned.

Although fisherfolk are not always among the 'poorest of the poor' in terms of income, other dimensions of poverty and vulnerability must be considered. Like other rural people, fisherfolk tend to be poorly served by access to basic needs such as education and health service provision, financial services and practical and technical support provided by extension or small business advisory services. Several features of fisheries also make fishing households vulnerable: fishing is one of the riskiest of occupations (ILO 2000); it is hard manual labour and requires good physical health; increasing levels of theft are widely reported, requiring monitoring of nets at night; as temporary residents or recent migrants fisherfolk are often marginalised from local decision-making structures, and they are prey to rent-seeking officials – often, the first person a fisherman sees on returning from a night's fishing is the local tax revenue collector.

Despite these risks, fishing remains an occupation of choice for many in Africa, as it does in South-East Asia (Pollnac *et al.* 2001). The lifestyle attractions of fishing are often overlooked. To young men, the chance to earn cash income outside the social strictures of their home village and enjoy the masculine camaraderie of a migrant fishing fleet may be a significant 'pull' factor, for which it is worth putting up with danger and drudgery.

To summarise thus far, the four most striking features of lakeshore livelihoods in east and southern Africa are the degree of monetisation in the fisheries sector, the relative wealth of those with access to fishing-related assets and to the resources themselves, the importance of mobility to specialist fisherfolk, and the degree to which fishing is an integral part of livelihoods for settled farmer-fishers. Mobility and diversity present important challenges to efforts to introduce community-based management as a means of regulating fisheries.

Community-based or co-management in the region's fisheries

In 'developed' countries with industrialised fisheries, the transition to rights-based fishing has centred on the introduction of various instruments granting private rights to go fishing. In the south, it is the community – rather than the individual or firm – that is widely seen as the unit in which to invest access rights to fish resources. Often, such communities are externally defined and a critical analysis of the notion of 'community' has been lacking (Allison and Ellis 2001). The devolution of responsibility for management to communities or user-groups has typically been partial, with government and community-based organisations working in some form of partnership, known as co-management (Wilson *et al.* 2003). Recent fisheries legislation such as that in Malawi and Uganda (Table 16.3) explicitly recognises community rights to resource management, but retains a strong element of government power over communities' roles and responsibilities (Allison *et al.* 2002; Allison 2003).

A number of major donor-funded projects to pilot the introduction of community-based management have been underway in the four countries of the region, notably the GTZ-funded National Aquatic Resource Management Programme (NARMAP) which has been working with government and fishing communities in southern Malawi since 1993, and the more recent Lake Victoria EU fisheries (LVFP) and GEF environmental management programme (LVEMP), and the DFID-funded Integrated Lake Management Project (ILM) in Uganda's Lakes George and Kyoga.

These programmes have made considerable progress in achieving their aims. Beach Management Units (BMUs) or Beach Village Committees (BVCs) have been created, stakeholder dialogue initiated, policies reformed, legislation to grant communities rights over the resources they use passed, and both fisheries officers and community leaders have been trained in carrying out their designated duties. A number of problems have arisen, however, principally around the way that CBFM has been conceived and implemented. Prominent among these is the fact that participatory, decentralised management is a donor-driven agenda. Fisheries department staff have not always been eager to participate in a programme that reduces their powers and forces them to collaborate with fisherfolk as partners rather than law enforcers and expert advisors. Similarly, communities have rather negative experiences of government fisheries staff and trust is lacking. The externally driven agenda also means that ownership of new 'community' based initiatives by fisherfolk is sometimes limited (e.g. Hara *et al.* 2002).

Co-management programmes have often seemed to ignore or deliberately bypass existing informal local institutions governing fisheries. On the Tanzanian shores of Lake Victoria, BMUs were created under the auspices of the Lake Victoria Environmental Management Programme (LVEMP). Conflict arose between BMUs, which had no legal mandate, and Village Environmental Committees, which have legal powers under government village establishment laws. BVCs in Malawi have been susceptible to elite capture and ordinary fisherfolk currently perceive little benefit from some of them (Allison and Mvula 2002). The legitimacy of some of the new devolved institutions is therefore sometimes limited and it may be necessary to look to the remnants of existing or past 'traditional' institutions regulating conflict and access to fisheries in order to build sustainable CBFM systems.

A great variety of informal organisations and institutions with a bearing on fishery issues exist independently of major donor programmes and central government policy. On the Kenyan coast, for example, these include co-operatives, unions, clubs, beach committees and youth groups (Malleret-King *et al.* 2003). Kenya's Fishery Department has recently focused on inclusion of coastal fisherfolk in beach management committees as a means of improving management. The structures of these committees are closely tied to previous traditional institutions that had become largely defunct following the introduction of state-based fisheries management (Malleret-King *et al.* 2003). Typically, these institutions comprised sets of beliefs, taboos and traditional practices that had resource conservation effects as a by product to their main function in regulating safety and social order. Similar institutions exist in Uganda's lakes, where traditional fishing leaders (the *Gabunga*) are a feature of fish landing sites (Allison 2003).

One of the difficulties encountered in community-based management in the region's fisheries is that lake-side villages, far from being the homogenous and clearly bounded entities considered ideal for the establishment of functional common property resource management regimes (Agrawal 2001), actually incorporate a range of occupational interests, ethnic groups and transient and long-term migrants, all having access to differential assets and pursuing different livelihood strategies. A common vision of the benefits of resource stewardship and expectation of future benefits of current restraint cannot be expected in such a group. Institutions capable of brokering compromises between conflicting interests and enforcing the results of negotiated outcomes are required, rather than mere 'community representatives'.

Migrant fisherfolk are usually regarded as problematic by fisheries managers promoting CBFM as the conception of such management centres around village fishing territories and exclusion of outsiders. In many cases in the LADDER research, migrants were found to play a positive role in the villages where they are based (for anything between two weeks and thirty years) as consumers of agricultural produce, patrons of various service industries (bars, restaurants, shops etc.) and employers of crew members from the resident farming households. They attract the fish traders into villages, which further stimulates economic activities. These relationships between migrants and settled farmer-fishers are generally mutually beneficial. Policies to exclude migrants undermine these beneficial effects.

In all cases, the vision for 'community-based management' continues to come from the top down. There may be donor and NGO projects that have a vision of co-management that is more genuinely participatory and empowering, but the message from central government policy is very much that communities will 'be participated' in management. Policy documents clearly state the expected role of communities and would appear to form a non-negotiable contract between state and subject rather than the embodiment of citizens' rights that the rhetoric suggests. Where communities have difficulty complying with government directives, then NGOs and CBOs are supposed to help them (e.g. Uganda's fisheries policy: Uganda 2002c: 17–18). Malawi's fisheries policy devolves management planning to communities but states that all such plans must be approved by the Director of Fisheries (Allison *et al.* 2002). On the coast of Kenya it is envisaged that under co-management, communities will implement government fisheries legislation through creating awareness of destructive fishing gear (i.e. an extension function), assisting in data collection and dealing with minor conflicts. The vision of CBFM or co-management at state level thus seems to see communities as instruments for cost-effective implementation of the state's management responsibilities.

The transition to CBFM is challenging and if it is to succeed then it requires careful attention to its underlying assumptions and to issues of how such programmes are introduced at all levels. Lind and Cappon (2001: 60) criticise the model of decentralised natural resource management in Uganda as being driven by assumptions that 'communities are willing and undivided wholes ready to assume a greater role in management of natural resources in accordance with policies and paradigms over which they have little influence or ownership'. This is clearly not the case and success in co-management beyond the life of current projects is the only real test of whether the problems inherent in this form of institutional development have been successfully overcome.

Fisheries policy in poverty reduction strategy papers

Fisheries policy has been carried along by the currents of three major governance and policy trends: decentralisation, market liberalisation and sustainable development (Allison 2001). PRSPs share these orientations, so that policies informed by FAO's CCRF appear to complement the main thrust of PRSPs in combining global market integration with effective governance to generate sustained growth (Craig and Porter 2003). Figure 16.3 identifies potential contributions of fishery sector objectives to poverty reduction strategies.

Although there are many synergies between poverty reduction strategies and fishery policy objectives, fisheries issues have a very limited profile in PRSP documents. In West Africa the sector was mentioned in only two out of twenty-three interim and full PRSPs, despite the economic and social importance of fisheries, particularly along the coast and around Lake Chad and the Niger Inland delta (SFLP 2002). Lack of coverage of the fisheries sector in national poverty data collection is an important reason for this absence. Poverty assessments are used to derive policy priorities, which are then allocated funds through either Medium Term Expenditure Frameworks (MTEFs) or Poverty Action Funds (PAFs).

In the four countries reviewed here, fisheries issues are present to some degree in two out of the four country PRSPs. Fisheries concerns feature prominently in Malawi's PRSP, as part of a natural resources sub-goal (Malawi 2002), and a specific budget allocation for the fisheries sector is identified in the MTEF. The Kenya interim PRSP (Kenya 2000a) briefly mentions fisheries in the context of the agriculture sub-sector. The PRSP process in Kenya has, however, been rather marginalised in favour of a coalition government 'strategy for economic recovery' (Mule *et al.* 2003). The latter document fails to identify fisheries products as one of the high value export crops important to meeting Kenya's drive towards economic recovery.

In Tanzania the 2002 Master Plan for fisheries specifically mentions the need to integrate fisheries development with the PRSP process. The Tanzanian PRSP highlights the dependence of the poor on environmental resources such as charcoal, firewood, honey and wild fruits (Tanzania 2000a: 27) but it makes no mention of fisheries. The Master Plan has been costed at just under

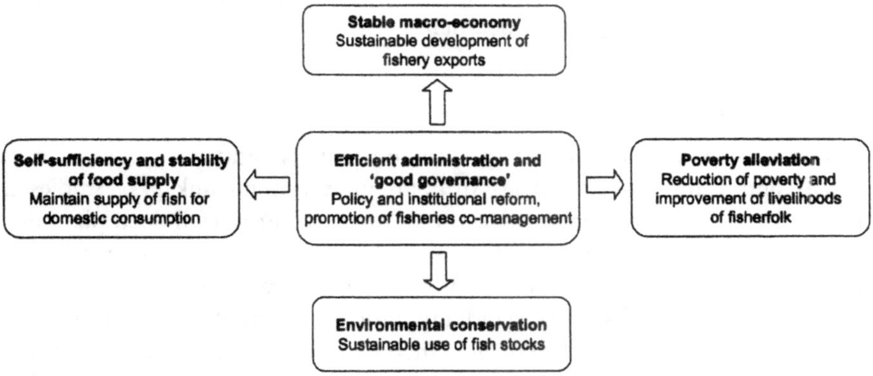

Figure 16.3 Policy agendas typical of PRSPs, with corresponding fisheries sector policy goals (source: author's own interpretation.)

US$ twenty-two million, of which US$ fifteen million is to be invested in facilities and equipment and the remaining US$ seven million will be used to cover the cost of training and personnel. There is a risk that the requested donor and government funds will not be allocated through the MTEF if fisheries are not mentioned in the PRSP.

The Ugandan PRSP of 31 March 2000 (Uganda 2000f) contained no specific mention of the fisheries sub-sector. Instead, fisheries are grouped with agriculture and livestock, and since agriculture is considered central to Uganda's development, the fisheries may benefit from appropriate investment as part of the Plan for the Modernisation of Agriculture (PMA). The PMA does not go into specific detail on sub-sectoral strategy, and the clear implication is that sub-sectors such as fisheries are expected to incorporate the principles of the PMA into their plans, by providing a sub-sectoral interpretation of the overall PMA guidelines (Ashley and Nanyeena 2002). With both fisheries policy and the PRSP process evolving rapidly in Uganda, and the ILM project's active involvement in influencing policy reform, this may now have changed.

The growing realisation of the importance of fisheries to Africa is reflected in the recent commitment of the World Fish Centre (of the CGIAR group) to a major new programme strategy focused on the continent (Dugan 2003), and in fisheries development programmes such as the DFID-funded, FAO-implemented Sustainable Fisheries Livelihoods Programme, involving twenty-five countries in West Africa (SFLP 2002). These programmes are helping put fisheries development on the national poverty reduction policy agenda, but fisheries policy needs to be coherent when it gets there. Fisheries development involves hard choices between incompatible objectives. At present, the national fisheries policies include the goals of increasing the supply of fish to domestic markets and promoting the export of fisheries products; increasing the level of fisherfolks' incomes and providing new employment opportunities in fisheries. These are all individually valid goals, but are mutually incompatible (Bailey and Jentoft 1990: 339). This analysis of trade-offs between conflicting policy options and priorities does not seem to have informed current policy documents.

Conclusions

In order to act as a stimulus to growth and poverty reduction, a sector must create significant spin-off effects through inter-sectoral linkages. Studies in four African countries suggest that the fisheries sector does indeed play these roles. Income from fishing enables investment in other rural enterprises or in building household assets and therefore security against poverty. This may include investing in livestock, land and agricultural inputs and education for children, or spending on healthcare. Income generated from fisheries is also spent on consumption of a range of goods and services that support markets for goods and services in some of the poorest areas of eastern and southern Africa.

However, in situations where fishing effort exceeds maximum economic yield, growth in the sector cannot be promoted without diminishing the benefits that are derived from the resources. Thus, policymakers have the difficult task of balancing the contribution to the rural economy from fisheries against concerns for the sustainability of the fish stocks that generate those benefits. State-enforced licensing and technical regulations have been the primary instrument of fisheries regulation in the past and, although the management targets remain similar, the approach has now shifted towards involving fisherfolk in the management of their own resources through community-based or government–community 'co-management' partnerships.

Most national fisheries policies avoid the 'hard choices'. Since all the different contributions of artisanal fishing are apparently compatible with poverty reduction strategies, PRSPs provide little guidance as to which fishery goal should be prioritised. For fisheries policy to provide useful direction the most straightforward way to make trade-offs between incompatible policy goals may be to set different policy priorities for different water-bodies or other non-overlapping sub-sectors of the fishery, as the Tanzanian Fisheries Master Plan has done.

The integration of fisheries development with broader poverty-focused development programmes would benefit from:

- maintaining sufficient profile in national poverty reduction strategies to ensure the sector receives funding commensurate with its potential contributions to pro-poor economic growth;
- adopting a more critical and politically engaged approach to promoting community-based fisheries management;
- ensuring that sub-sectoral studies that highlight the contribution of fisheries to national and local economies are disseminated widely amongst opinion formers in the policy domain;
- incorporation of fishing households explicitly in national poverty surveys.

There are welcome signs that all these processes are underway in Africa, so that the continent's fishing people can continue to provide economic, social and cultural benefits to their countries.

Note

* Thanks to Nancy Gitonga, Ade Freeman and Sunita Kapila (Kenya); Peter Mvula, Milton Kutengule and Alfred Nyasulu (Malawi); Ben Ngatunga (Tanzania); and Godfrey Bahiigwa and Jim Scullion (Uganda) for their help in supporting fieldwork conducted under the DFID-funded LADDER project. I am grateful to Laurence Mathieu, John Mims and Marie-Caroline Badjeck for research assistance, and to Frank Ellis for helping to extract this chapter from a longer manuscript.

17 Irrigation, livelihoods and river basins*

Bruce Lankford

Introduction

This chapter examines irrigation policy in Tanzania utilising a livelihoods and river basin perspective. It first analyses the current tone of thinking regarding irrigation and suggests that this is mainly predicated on the benefits of irrigation with little recognition of the costs and complexities of irrigation. The discussion explores access to irrigation within the livelihoods framework, including the subject of livelihoods diversification alongside irrigation. Finally, the chapter reveals how policy interventions for irrigation support are often flawed and goes on to propose several ways in which policy-makers might support irrigated agriculture in Tanzania and sub-Saharan Africa using a livelihoods and basin approach.

The context of irrigation development in Tanzania

The Tanzanian agricultural sector, in official statistics, forms the greatest share of GDP; 49.1 per cent in 1998, and 56 per cent in 2000. It absorbs 80 per cent of the employed population of the 32 million Tanzanians (Tanzania 2001d; JICA 2001). Although different strategies are being suggested to raise agricultural incomes, recently, the government has placed particular emphasis on the development of irrigation. Related to national interests, there has been a resurgence of donor interest in irrigation in sub-Saharan Africa as an engine of rural development and food security as, evidenced by the activity of regional institutions working in these fields; (e.g. SWIMNET, SACCAR and IWMI) and renewed donor support of irrigation, (e.g. from the Danish Agency for Development Assistance (DANIDA), the Japanese International Cooperation Agency (JICA), the African Development Bank (AfDB), and the Department for International Development (DFID).

In Tanzanian policy documents, irrigation is addressed in the Poverty Reduction Strategy Paper (PRSP), the Agricultural Strategy Paper (ASP) and the Rural Development Strategy Paper (RDSP). These documents give the perception that the government should take a leading and interventionist role in irrigation development.

Connected to these views is the related argument that considerable potential exists for new irrigation in Tanzania. Tanzania (2001e) states that only 15 per cent (6.3 million hectares) of all suitable land is used for agriculture and only a fraction of that is used for irrigation. Schultz (2001) echoes this view on realising potential in a recent paper on the scope for irrigation in southern and eastern Africa. The mechanisms by which this potential might be developed are outlined in the National Irrigation Development Plan (NIDP), which was prepared in 1994 with an overall objective of stabilising and increasing food production. NIDP can be summarised into three priorities:

1 Rehabilitation or upgrading of traditional irrigation schemes.
2 Upgrading water harvesting technology where irrigation is not possible.
3 Develop new smallholder schemes, where demand exists and conditions are appropriate.

Although these priorities remain, donor emphasis has mainly focussed on the initial two. In 2001, JICA formulated a National Irrigation Master Plan (NIMP) for Tanzania. The objectives of the NIMP are rather unclear and circular. However, they appear to be a review of existing policies with the intention of expressing lessons learnt to establish new methods of delivering irrigation development. The principles of the latter are also unclear but emphasise 'software' rather than 'hardware'. In other words, NIMP realises that farmers need to 'own' irrigation schemes – and that this will be achieved through government training of participants. This is an interesting 'top-down' viewpoint that argues that farmers have to be trained to own irrigation schemes. Furthermore, it is not clear how irrigation potential will be fulfilled if only the first two priorities remain.

Yet, the government understands the limits of its reach as demonstrated in ASP and NIDP, both of which attempt to define the scope of what governments can and cannot do at central and local levels versus the role of the private sector. Therefore, as indicated in the updated NIDP (Kalinga *et al.* 2001) the government view allows for private sector involvement in irrigation, either by privatising the existing irrigated state farms or in the construction of new irrigation. Although it may be viable and contribute to national food security targets, commercial private irrigation is not within the remit of this chapter, which tackles the risks, benefits and costs associated with smallholder irrigation.

Implicit in the narratives is a consensus that irrigation is automatically beneficial, that performance needs 'fixing', and but for the removal of a few constraints irrigation would grow to meet national objectives. However, irrigation is in reality contrary and complex, and an approach to irrigation requires a livelihoods and river basin perspective. Irrigation policy has to deal with a set of dilemmas. On the one hand irrigation requires government policy and support, and on other, irrigation is effected, controlled and improved by farmers. How can irrigation 'facilitation' be formulated in ways that is pro-poor rather than pro-commercial farming; that does not waste resources; that assists but does not undermine the farmers; that encourages 'ownership' but does not force it; that uses available water but does not promote overuse and exacerbate conflict? A balanced methodology is needed for irrigation support – something that ASPS (2000) also argues for.

Research methods

The discussion is supported by data collected in the Morogoro region of Tanzania. Three out of six sub-villages in the village of Chanzuru in Kilosa district were sampled; Kati, Darajani and Chekereni, although visits were paid to all sub-villages. Chanzuru is found on the road between Kilosa and the junction on the main Dar es Salaam to Iringa road. The village encompasses the Chanzuru Irrigation System, which is typical of Tanzanian smallholder systems in that it taps river water running off an escarpment before draining into pools and swamps or supplies to other rivers. Equally typical is that Chanzuru is one of a sequence of intakes on the river, called the Ilonga (Figure 17.1). More importantly, the Chanzuru irrigation system is downstream of an improved intake that supplies the Ilonga Irrigation System

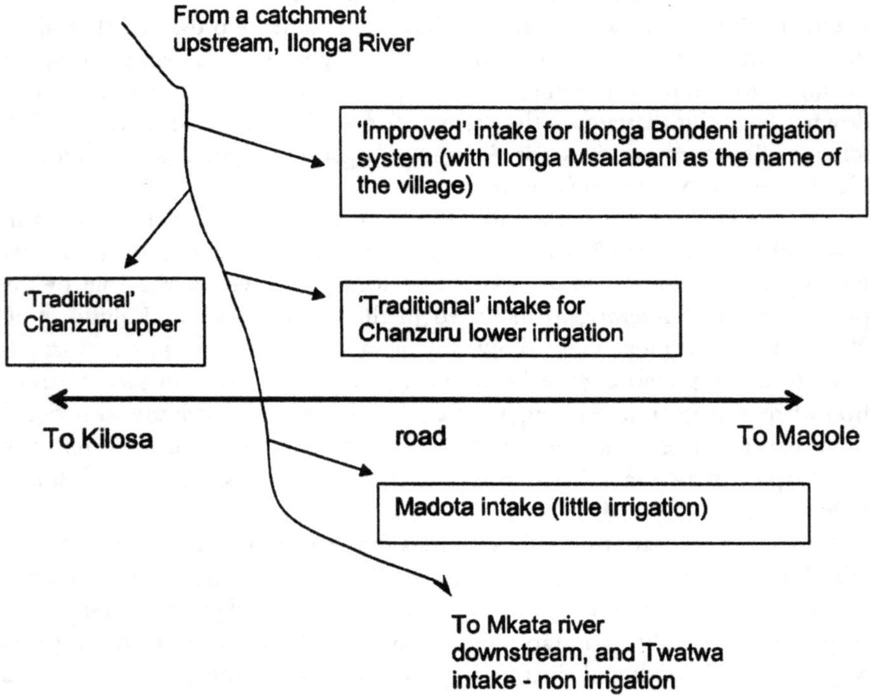

Figure 17.1 Schematic map of the four intakes of the River Ilonga (source: author's own interpretation.)

belonging to a neighbouring village. The area is representative of the debate on irrigation potential; 3 per cent of Morogoro rivers are used for irrigation (DANIDA/JICA 2001).

Sampling followed a similar format in each sub-village and is described in more detail in Chapter 1. PRA wealth-ranking identified three wealth groups that were then sub-sampled using a stratified random technique giving rise to ten households in the middle and richer household and fifteen households in the poorest group. Alongside qualitative and quantitative surveys, PRA exercises and more focussed irrigation interviews were conducted.

Understanding irrigation

The benefits of irrigation

On smaller-scale systems, and on some farmer plots within larger-scale systems, evidence can be found that farmers benefit greatly from irrigation. Irrigation was mentioned by many of the villagers at Chanzuru as a means of securing greater income. Benefits occur because:

- irrigation secures crop productivity against shortfalls or breaks in rainfall;
- irrigation allows rice and other crops that generate a cash margin to be grown;
- by adding more water, irrigation raises crop productivity to profitable levels;
- security of water improves the planning and timing of the start of the cropping season by farmers;
- water extends the season length, reducing labour calendar overlaps and assisting farmers in farm management;
- irrigation extends the area under cultivation and brings more farmers into production;
- irrigation raises the number of jobs conducted on the land (e.g. irrigating, weeding) and provides for secondary job creation (crop marketing, trading);
- irrigation raises the landesque capital of irrigated land, attracting commerce related to land such as renting of plots (clearly visible from increasing rents year on year, which now stand at 20–30,000 Tsh/acre).

A variety of knock-on effects of these benefits can be identified. In Chanzuru, farmers who had been irrigating at subsistence level then chose to irrigate 'for the market', growing and selling whole-stick sugarcane and tomatoes. Here, irrigation provided the platform and exposure to home-level entrepreneurship. Some farmers bought produce from others to sell.

In addition, as the size of irrigation increases, so do the number of people, and importantly the number of economic transactions between active irrigating farmers, labourers, landowners, service providers and surrounding householders. Many studies support this picture of success from irrigation. DFID (1997), Shah (2000) and van Koppen (1998) found that irrigation generated extra cash and jobs in the wider economy. Studies in Zimbabwe (Lovell 2000) found that groundwater use in dryland areas brought considerable livelihood benefits to those villages with access to the wells. Schulz (2001) argued that food security at the national and international level is dependent on the contribution of irrigation. Chambers wrote cogently in 1988 that benefits of irrigation-based livelihoods occur at household, regional and national levels.

Due to these advantages, irrigation has what might be described as 'honey-pot' attractions. Policy-makers are lured to a notionally attractive intervention which, when scaled up in size has trap-like qualities; becoming more glutinous, intractable and risk-prone. Thus, the main message of research of the last twenty to thirty years has also highlighted the transaction costs, institutional problems, low economic return and environmental impacts of irrigation (Bottrall 1985; Chambers 1988; Postel 1992; Mazungu 2000). The next section explores how irrigation systems at the larger scale become more complex.

The complexities and costs of irrigation

Medium- and large-scale systems acquire scalar-related characteristics that make large irrigation analysis and intervention markedly more complex – this relationship is captured in Table 17.1. Note too, small-scale systems increase in complexity when they agglomerate into a connected patchwork of systems fed by one river or one aquifer. Thus in Usangu in Tanzania, it is the total area of many small systems that has led to problems associated with water shortage (Tanzania 2001g).

The net effect of the complex nature of 'larger irrigation systems' is to generate inter-farmer, inter-system and inter-sector competition over a scarce resource. The downside of irrigation is increased conflict over water. It is a key thesis of this chapter that in water-scarce situations (which nowadays are more common) governments and donors should be aware of the need for land and water conflict mediation as much as irrigation development itself.

Donors and agencies are not unaware of the issues of low performance, social conflict and environmental impacts (e.g. over-abstraction from river basins) associated with irrigation. However, the solutions and interventions designed to improve water management are often problematic and based on an incomplete understanding of water. Part of this understanding, it is argued, can be obtained from a more complete livelihoods analysis of irrigation.

Analysis of irrigation livelihoods

This section (with Tables 17.2 and 17.3) explores the factors that affect exposure to and ensuing success of an irrigation-based livelihood, in other words

Table 17.1 Complexity typology for irrigated water management

Types	*Characteristic*	*Irrigation–livelihood implications*
Rainfed farming (no irrigation)	Non-interconnected farming	Farmers are not inter-dependent for their water. Success dependent on timing/amount of rain
Rainfall harvesting	Smaller, less connected systems	Farmers have high-risk attitude to RH cropping. Success dependent on timing/amount of rain
Supplementary irrigation	Rainfall contributes significantly to crop	Farmers not critically dependent on irrigation, but irrigation can extend area cultivated
Groundwater-sourced individual surface system	Energy required to source water Non-sequential access	Security of access and costs can promote marginal use of water, higher performance, timely planting and fewer top-to-tail differences
Piped irrigation systems (sprinkler and drip)	Energy required to source water. Non-sequential access because of pressurised piped delivery	Particular type of cropping system unlikely to be faced by majority of poor irrigators. Piped highly-structured systems ensure minimised problems of subtractability and sequential access
Small-scale surface irrigation (<25 ha.)	Smaller, lesser-connected systems	On small systems, farmers likely to have built their own canal system have higher social cohesion; have smaller canal distances and fewer bifurcation points
Medium-to-large surface scale irrigation	Social and canal complexity increasing. Water demand increases	Systemic properties and complexity non-linearly increases in size; sensitises system to water shortages, inequality, water shortages and social conflict
Irrigated river basins and catchments	A number of systems inter-connected by riverine/aquifer resources	Large distances involved; high complexity, little sense of community, difficult to redress water abstraction, considerable transaction costs in water management, control and re-allocation

Source: author's own classification and summary.

Table 17.2 Four resources and characteristics of irrigated livelihoods affecting access to irrigated plots of land

Access resource	*What is it?*	*Why does it arise?*	*What does it lead to?*	*What is the household livelihoods approach to the solution?*	*What is the group, village NGO, district and river basin solution?*
Access to irrigation land	Below a defined area, people are excluded from accessing direct benefits of cultivating their own crops. In Chanzuru, the area is about 0.5 to 1.0 hectare	There is often intense competition for small plots of land. Landlords tend not to rent out smaller plots, plus farmers feel that that 1 acre provides work and income for a small family unit and more money would be required for larger plots	The poorest of the poor are not able to get a foothold on the benefits of cultivating and selling their own crops	People cope by selling their labour to other growers, by cultivating small areas of rainfed land and by micro-diversification	Demarcate land for micro-plots of irrigation? Revolve plots on an annual basis? (Applicable to village owned land). IMT* and settlement
Access to water (conflict-area tradeoffs)	Access depends on water availability. Improved internal supply and distribution of water resolves conflicts but extends area irrigated leading to additional farmers and increased risk of new competition	Irrigation interconnectivity between users reflects a common-pool resource. In middle or tailend reaches, or in downstream irrigation systems, water supply is variable and insecure. Getting access to small amounts of water may have high marginal benefits to the poor. Resolving waste and inefficiency in upstream areas releases water to downstream farmers	Extending irrigation provides benefits but increases chances of conflict in normal and drier periods when water supply contracts, necessitating conflict resolution, a search for increased supply or a contraction in irrigated area	People respond. Farmers may move to better served plots. Labour transactions change. Individuals may attempt to hoard water	Group planning is required to limit and improve irrigation in zones beyond which risky water supply occurs. Improve upstream/downstream control via river basin management. Deliver small amounts of water for lifeline needs (e.g. compensation flows or piped domestic supply)

Access to capital	Farmers in Chanzuru need money to rent land	Irrigated farming has become increasingly commercialised. Obtaining financial capital to purchase land or water may be via borrowed money or selling labour. Very poor farmers may be excluded from this, but increasingly will consider credit	Borrowing of money against future cropping Savings from cropping or other incomes	Formal or informal credit systems were found to exist in Chanzuru either at household level or from an NGO in Ilonga	Formal or informal credit systems managed by an NGO, with a wider enabling environment influence by government
Access to labour/energy	To gain access to irrigated land at the bottom rung necessitates the provision of labour	Labour may provide initial means to derive benefits from irrigated land either through direct access, sharecropping or paid labour	Labour or energy is required either to prepare land, or to work on another land or to access water	People cope by working for water or land. Labour duties are shared out. Planting mosaics arise	Engage with impact of labour-selling on water management and efficiency

Source: author's own classification and summary.

Note
*IMT – Irrigation Management Transfer.

Table 17.3 Factors affecting deepening/widening access to irrigation-based livelihoods

Factors affecting movement up/down	*Brief explanation*	*Move up*	*Move down*
Land Land availability Land given and inherited Land bought and sold Land rented	The amount of total land available, and the degree to which portions of it are available to villagers affects irrigated livelihood options	Land becomes more available, small plots made available, prices stabilise, landlords provide good contracts	Land becomes less available or market for smaller plots becomes more competitive. Richer farmers rent more land marginalising poorer farmers. Prices increase raising risk element when borrowing money
Water and climate Water availability Improve intake Acquire new intake or pump Equitable predictable climate Control of upstream users	The amount, predictability, timeliness, location, distribution of water enables farmers to plan and manage water accordingly, enhancing irrigation livelihoods	Water becomes more secure, available, predictable, better distributed, less prone to disruption by upstream irrigators	Water becomes less secure, less available, more frequently taken by upstream irrigators, or affected by weeds, leaks etc.
Crop Yellow spot Rainfed maize yield	Potential yields are blighted by disease and lack of rainfall	Good maize and rice yields raise incomes, allowing farmers to invest in further assets	A poor rice yield due to yellow spot infestation or poor maize reduces income and can lead to debt. Poor maize can also knock farmers down
Labour/energy Availability of own/other labour Cost of labour/energy	Providing energy for farm work either prepares land or ensures water	Energy/labour cost benefit ratio is advantageous providing land and water	Land or water has an energy/labour cost exceeding benefits from energy/labour
Diversified livelihoods e.g. Micro-enterprise, urban-rural migration, rainfed agriculture/dry season irrigation, livestock, labouring	An ability to save money from other activities and not borrow money creates bi-directional investment between agriculture and other streams	Other income sources become developed. Capital used to access irrigation land or vice versa – irrigation income used to build other enterprises	Opportunities erode, individuals rely on few sources or permanently/temporarily migrate. Access to rainfed land decreases. Failure in one activity drains others

Economic and financial Capital, debt, borrowing Input and labour costs, demand Credit and financial planning management Market prices, stability and transaction costs	Access to capital, and costs of borrowing money as a household or individual affect ability to change one's livelihood. Access to functioning markets with acceptable prices and minimal transaction costs	Terms and cost of borrowing amenable to cover access and initial start-up costs with leeway to allow for delays in payment. Market is accessible, predictable, easy to enter into, prices profitable	Borrowing costs are high and terms are unfavourable, capturing or depleting other resources previously built up. Markets not accessible, prices crash, transaction costs high
Social Social cohesion and conflict resolution Social/customary access to land 'Competition'	The access to land and water can be affected by social factors such as desire and competition to add to assets, and by organisation and conflict resolution	Village and water user association communicate, incomers bring new ideas, farmers meet to resolve conflicts	Competition, bullying and intimidation present, poor WUA organisation, break-down in village communication, and gender or age marginalisation/exclusion to land
Water institutions Local village and WUA bye-laws Control of river basin abstraction Support by zonal irrigation office	Some social factors affecting access explicitly acknowledge in commonly agreed, written bye-laws and legislation. Supporting policy and project environment	Bye-laws understood, adopted, and used in assisting protection and or development of resources and in resolving conflicts	Organisation breaks down, legislation is no longer utilised or known about. Policy environment erodes activities/plans made at the household and village level

Source: author's own classification and summary.

how a rainfed farmer or non-farmer becomes an irrigator, and an irrigator becomes a more secure irrigator or irrigator with more land.

Research in Chanzuru revealed a ladder of irrigation-related wealth. At the bottom exist those with no exposure to irrigation; these often tend to be women, the poorest, poor rainfed farmers, incomers or youth (LADDER 2001). Above them lie a number of tiers that represent greater wealth in irrigation terms. At the top of the scale are found wealthier landlords who rent land out but do not cultivate themselves. A person can occupy more than one rung; he or she can be a cultivator waiting for water to arrive at their field, whilst labouring for a cultivator further up in the irrigation system. There are several dimensions that interplay here, described briefly in the following subsections.

Initial access to irrigation

Obtaining a foothold in irrigation is a precursor to an irrigation-based livelihood – and is therefore a critical step. The Chanzuru study showed that initial access does not need to go via labouring, it can leap directly to renting or owning irrigated land depending on circumstances. Initial access occurs in four interrelated ways, through land, water, capital and labour, as explained in Table 17.2.

Gaining a satisfactory irrigation-based livelihood is not unproblematic. Because water is often the limiting resource, irrigation is a privileged not a widespread solution (Moris 1987). This is evidenced in Usangu and Chanzuru where it secures benefits at the rate of about one farmer or two farmers per acre for those able to rent land. In Tanzania, most irrigation systems are found between 10 to 500 hectares, providing for households that number in tens and hundreds, not thousands. Furthermore, in areas with a history of irrigation it is a choice of cropping that accrues to farmers who already have sufficient assets, either as a result of irrigated cropping, from other jobs, or by borrowing to rent into irrigation. For example, when the Ilonga system was extended, incomers were reasonably well-off villagers and staff from the nearby research station.

Furthermore, irrigation space is limited on a per capita basis. Villagers in Chanzuru said that rainfed land was needed to make up the food requirements that irrigation alone could not provide for. In fact a total of 42 per cent of the three Chanzuru villagers owned no land at all, even though these were sub-villagers that had access to an irrigation system, and even though land was available to rent, only 41 per cent of the total village respondents cultivated rice, the key indicator of irrigation activity.

Moderating influences on access to irrigation

The play of the above factors affects initial access to irrigation. After that, the direction can be upwards, downwards or stationary. Table 17.3 demonstrates ways that undermine or benefit irrigated livelihoods, some of which are the same factors that govern initial access, while others mediate the benefit derived from irrigation. With regards to crop productivity, the Ilonga River irrigators tend to solve their own cultivation problems, including the judicious use of fertiliser on certain kinds of crops. According to the villagers, the extension officer, once reasonably visible, now hardly visits the village (LADDER 2001). However, there were certain yield problems that farmers could not fix, such as yellow spot on rice. Here, farmers felt yellow spot was a major problem halving yields, and the lack of extension advice damaging. In Usangu, farmers complained that top-end fields were declining in soil fertility (i.e. twelve bags/acre), while tail-end fields with water yielded eighteen bags/acre. Yet, farmers with secure water at the top of the Kimani system in Usangu are carting in farmyard manure, an interesting sign of perceived balance between security of water and the costs and benefits of additional inputs.

Villagers state that the increasing price of rice relative to costs of inputs was one important reason why rice cultivation had increased in area. Counter-balancing this was a decline in the rice price for 2001 from 25,000 Tsh/bag to 8–10,000 Tsh/bag because of good rains throughout Tanzania and a glut of rice on the market. The location of Chanzuru on the main road between Ilonga and Morogoro benefits market access – another aspect of irrigation that farmers implicitly factor in.

By mass-producing high yielding cash crops, irrigation systems become function-orientated, responding to a wider economic environment. Farmers both sense this and the nature of the incentive environment into which they fit. Thus a highly appropriate irrigation-livelihood intervention is not necessarily the upgrading of infrastructure or establishment of WUA's, but the provision of predictable, accessible markets. Lower transaction costs (e.g. reducing the number of rural taxes on the movement of goods) explored by Ellis and Mdoe (2003) help incentivise the desire of farmers to participate in irrigated agriculture.

Furthermore, market signals generate comparative incentives for farmers to improve water management manifested by investments in infrastructure. Thus farmers will decide to line or rebuild canals when the value of doing so outweighs the costs of not doing so. Examples of these decisions are found in Usangu; farmers do not upgrade the intake but will rebuild a canal wall that has collapsed. In the former, the water supply is not under threat, whereas in the latter it is. It is the argument of this chapter that farmers are better placed than governments to make these detailed system-level economic decisions.

With regards institutional and social factors, villagers did not readily identify strong influences (LADDER 2001). Yet a variety of cultural and social norms appear to be affecting access to land and water. For example, female farmers cannot own land, but were renting land and providing labour on other farms. Of the irrigator respondents, 67 per cent were male and 32 per cent were female. Regarding plans by village youth (16–24 years) to grow rice, interesting observations were made by villagers: 'Previously into beer drinking, they now expect great changes in the next two years from the land released by the Masai'.

Villagers also held the view that the 'vision to adopt new technologies' was constrained by low levels of education – though this contradicts the rapid adoption of basin irrigation by villagers copied from Sukuma incomers. In addition, although not expressed during the Chanzuru PRA exercises, the purposive irrigation interviews revealed that underlying the conflict between the village and WUA leaderships is the desire by irrigators to question the existing socially-determined incentives and penalties of the WUA in order to enhance water management.

The study of Chanzuru irrigation demonstrates that irrigation expands and is competed over because of livelihood benefits. At the moment irrigation is growing in interest amongst farmers, including some of the youth of the village. This favourable view, the area growth and increasing investments made by farmers are telling points for policy; irrigation is attractive despite a lack of visible intervention or provision of inputs by the government.

Diversification and irrigation

The causal direction of success in irrigation and success in diversifying into other activities cannot always be predicted but it is possible to say that success in irrigation provides a means to diversify, whereas in Chanzuru, diversifying without irrigation is more problematic.

Interviews with irrigation-involved villagers suggest that irrigation is a mainstay of income and that most interviewees wished, where possible, to have both irrigation and at least one other activity in order to maximise income. Two further facets can be identified. First, farmers with small-scale diversifications (such as selling beer or labour) saw irrigation as an important but seasonal activity providing much needed income ('One cannot forget irrigation'). During irrigating periods, other enterprises can become dormant. There were also examples where minor business people (such as sugarcane sellers and café-owners) point to irrigation being the source of capital to start their other activities. They used sums of 5,000 Tshs to obtain materials or rent land to try other crops. Although irrigation was less necessary in these cases, it was highly desirable and could be 100 per cent prioritised when necessary, with respondents claiming that another family member would cover non-agricultural duties.

Diversification into irrigation (out of rainfed agriculture) occurs because villagers see the benefit of good prices from rice and dry season crops and because they are aware of the security of production when compared to dry season maize; one frequently heard 'the rains are not certain'. One of the sub-villages, Chanzuru, provided a third reason for movement into irrigation, namely the closure of access to rainfed lands by a powerful landowner in the area. This is compensating rather than diversifying but it does influence farmers moving in and out of different types of agriculture. Thus, it is for a number of reasons that irrigation rental has increased in the last five years.

Movement into irrigation currently requires rental capital (whereas some years ago, land was given out for a nominal sum by the Chanzuru village government). This money, which had been increasing steeply in the preceding three years, is obtained mostly by borrowing, but augmented by some savings from, and labour within, agriculture.

At the river basin level, increasing livelihood needs for water inevitably means that water is abstracted into irrigation intakes without much regard to downstream users.[1] Constraining this is necessary because of other-sector needs. Theoretically, water rights and intake designs should balance upstream–downstream needs, but this is unlikely while river basin officers have minimal presence in places like Kilosa District and irrigation intakes are over-designed for peak flow periods. If and when water is throttled, one consequence will be irrigators having to make decisions about alternative sources of income; but there is no evidence that diversification helps reduce water demand. This is because irrigation is so much more profitable than other rural activities available in Chanzuru. Without further water supplies being added, it may be necessary to target abstraction throttling rather than to expect it to happen as a consequence of livelihood 'progress'.

As far as *in-system* management is concerned, there was conflicting evidence that diversification into other activities negatively affects land and water management. One neutral stance is that water management does not deteriorate because most diversification occurs during the off-crop season. A more negative outlook is that diversifying into temporary labouring when a farmer has received their water leads to a mosaic of uncultivated irrigated plots which evaporates water that is more urgently required by other farmers for crop evapotranspiration thereby reducing overall productivity. Farmers clearly experience the individual costs and benefits of this, so that final outcomes depend on collective decisions, as exemplified in Usangu.

There may be evidence that diversification, by further raising incomes, is an impetus to improved in-system management. The link is tenuous, but several people expressed plans to increase the area of irrigation to raise capital for various home and business needs. Without storage, meeting more people's needs and increasing the irrigated area can only be met by better distribution and management of water. While this has improved over the last ten years, villagers are aware of the need to make further changes, as seen in the disputes surrounding the Water User Association (WUA). The village government wants to replace the current WUA chairman to reorganise canal maintenance and draw up new rules and schedules.

Policy recommendations

Table 17.4 summarises two interpretations of policy on a variety of issues. Various players in Tanzania, including donor agencies, hold an existing view

Table 17.4 Existing and 'livelihoods-river basin' views of irrigation policy

Stage	*Current view informing policy*	*Irrigation river basin livelihoods view*
Irrigation understanding		
Whose irrigation performance? (Farmer–livelihood integration)	'Irrigation suffers from performance problems.' Solutions are then imposed by external players who often see narrow 'disciplinary' problems	Farmers with irrigation-based livelihoods are integrating across a wide range of social, economic and technical issues, responding and succeeding accordingly
'Normal' vs. cautionary irrigation approach	'Irrigation is the addition of water to crops.' Fad-type thinking influences refinements to this theory	Irrigation is complex and needs engaging with using long-term programmes. Approach and fund with care, using long-term interdisciplinary, facilitator-type teams
Irrigation potential vs. actual irrigation livelihoods (see main text)	'Irrigation potential exists.' This becomes a policy narrative, requiring engagement: find it with land suitability mapping and planning.	It exists, can be fulfilled, but observe and understand how farmers see potential, choose to locate and develop irrigation. Assist this by ensuring market signals and economy reduces farmer risk and transaction costs
A balanced irrigation–river basin livelihoods approach	'Irrigation potential should be fully realised.' Consideration of downstream multi-sectoral demands tends to be forgotten	Irrigation consumes water, which dries downstream sectors, this is especially important in a river basin with a seasonal hydrograph. River basin and conflict mediation approach vital.
Irrigation policy formulation and delivery		
New large-scale systems	No longer popular among donors, but when they are considered; whole system is designed by consulting engineers who do not operate it	Might be necessary, but only in certain locations and only construct headworks? Let farmers build or sub-contract inter-disciplinary teams to create remainder
Policy vs. cognitive approach (situational analysis)	Policy-hegemony. (e.g. 'Water must be paid for.' 'Rights must be introduced.' 'Community management is required.')	Adopt a problem-focus priority. 'What realistically can be done to improve water management and reduce water use in this particular irrigation or riverine system?'

Institutional review and strengthening	Create irrigation WUAs[a] (then these tend to be left to own devices)	Three tier institutions; 1) WUA at irrigation level (related to village govt); 2) RUA[b] at river level; 3) Higher at district/river basin level. Promote synergy between levels/other institutions
Water rights	Train farmers to own irrigation systems	Respond to farmer requests for help
Conflict mediation	Impose formal water rights	Determine ways of building on indigenous rights as means to manage water
(See main text)	Conflict resolution is unrecognised by agencies as evidenced by lack of formal support	Conflict given equal weighting along irrigation development. Capacity and awareness building needed. Responsive, problem-orientated, demand-led. Continue to assist in facilitation and mediation training of all institutional levels
Pro-poor land and water distribution	Generally unrecognised by agencies	Conditional with new or rehabilitated systems. Special focus within institutional mediation projects and programmes? (Koopman *et al.* 2001). Farmer management transfer on govt. farms. Domestic/lifeline water supplies are critical
Technical issues: intake bias (see main text)	Intake improvements over-emphasise abstraction	Either leave traditional intakes alone or consider proportional weirs to divide water
Within-irrigation technical options	Engineers like to line canals; create divisional networks and insist on water cycling or suggest drip/sprinkler	Observe/build on what farmers consider are ways of saving/extending water. Help them focus on where water is being mismanaged
Formulating water demand and design	The conventional method of demand planning = specific field demand × efficiency × area	Other methods: socially agreed division; design in drought; prior use; relate right accurately to actual design. Re-tune design if necessary

Source: author's own classification and summary.

Notes
a WUA – Water User Association
b RUA – River User Association.

which argues that irrigation has clear benefits, is inefficient and has undeveloped potential or room for improvement. The alternative view is a more conditional understanding. This says that irrigation potential exists in Tanzania, but comes with unforeseen complexities; that it should be balanced against competing demands for water; that it is only realised by farmers operating within a complex irrigation–rural livelihoods system; and that it should be accompanied by a river basin perspective and an appreciation of the role of conflict mediation. Table 17.4 is further divided into two main sections; the upper argues for a better understanding of the irrigation–livelihood–river basin approach; while the lower argues that certain policies and strategies should reflect this approach. The discussion in this section explores in more detail three issues from Table 17.4.

The potential and suitability of irrigation

There are dangers in believing that government can 'roll out' irrigation expansion without risks; a lack of contextual analysis could be blamed for the placement of large-scale systems in places where smaller systems were already competing over water (e.g. Lower Moshi in the Pangani Basin). In other ways too, particularly from a farmer's perspective, irrigation is not always appropriate, economically feasible, required, or likely to be successful in all situations. When left to farmers, a rather narrow window of opportunity exists because of the range of constraints and risks. Too dry, and there is insufficient rainfall to create large enough streams to provide secure flows for a season length of at least 120 days. Too wet and farmers utilise rainfall to grow crops. In addition, catchments need to be 'just so', having aquifers or being large enough to yield secure and sufficient water. The economic and demographic context also affects farmers' decisions regarding irrigation. Farmers may see no reason to invest in socially complex irrigation when rainfall meets their needs or when no effective market demand exists for their produce. This farmer-perspective contrasts with the formal institutional view that the government should deliver the considerable potential for irrigation. There is potential, but this needs to be divided into the following:

1. Large smallholder schemes located on the eastern floodplains of Tanzania where large rivers are found incising tracts of relatively under-utilised land;
2. New farmer-owned smallholder schemes that might be found in some inland regions of the country;
3. Extension of existing smallholder systems via upgrading and modernising intakes to increase water distribution where this can be done without impinging on downstream users.

Conflict resolution – institutional arrangements

Special consideration needs to be given to irrigation conflict management, in terms of pre-emptive institutional frameworks and then specific resolution support. Conflict mediation specifically applies to river basins that are closing or are closed where demand outstrips supply. A range of institutional arrangements (relating organisations, legislation and agreements) can assist communities in regulating and managing their water abstraction, providing important on-going mediating processes affecting access to natural resources. Three tiers seem appropriate; irrigation-level user agreements; sub-catchment level user agreements, and a higher-level overview. Of the first, water user associations (WUAs) are common examples of this – and such an organisation, albeit moribund, was found in Chanzuru. Of the second, both traditional and river user associations (RUAs) are found in various part of Tanzania. For example the SMUWC project (2001) set up a RUA termed a sub-catchment management resource programme on the Kimani river, which was seen as highly desirable by users. Farmers in the Mkoji sub-catchment in Usangu already meet, without outside involvement, to agree a share of water abstracted between different intakes. In Chanzuru, river conflicts were rarely mentioned, a reflection of the positive ratio of supply to demand, and the design of the improved Ilonga intake that allows water downstream. Clearly, water-sharing institutions are not always required.

At a tertiary level, farmers primarily turn to their district council to sort out disagreements, and in rare circumstances, where they exist, to a river basin authority. Even if the latter arrangement is available, its success depends on the relationship between the water rights, application and appeals procedure, cost, design and service delivered in terms of conflict resolution (van Koppen *et al.* 2004). In Usangu, formal water rights were imposed to share water but did not relate to infrastructure and did not recognise existing indigenous arrangements or provide for environmental water demands.

With the provision of a sub-water office in Usangu, some conflict resolution is now being provided to resource users but this is only when the situation has deteriorated to the extent that outside help is necessary. The current arrangement is partly satisfactory if a little ad hoc, and could be strengthened by a more carefully delivered and resourced conflict resolution service.

Infrastructural approach to improvements

Irrigation lends itself to, indeed requires, technological interventions. This fact means that it is subject to risks of under-design and inappropriate design. The predominant approach to irrigation interventions in the last twenty years in Tanzania is defined by an infrastructural emphasis, notably in the construction of concrete intakes to replace traditional intakes. Chanzuru farmers all mentioned that an improved intake would benefit them. Yet, Lankford and Gillingham (2001) reviewed the evidence from the Usangu Basin and saw that improved intakes caused the system to over-abstract, leaving the environment or lower irrigation systems dry (even if they, too, had new intakes). There is no evidence that Chanzuru irrigators are short of water because of a traditional intake; their desire for a concrete one stems from lower maintenance costs.

There are two policy insights here. First, a policy of non-intervention may be the best; irrigation does not necessarily require considerable investment in infrastructure, though this is what most farmers would wish. Second, if intakes are to be built, they should not be simply for meeting crop water requirements to the exclusion of other river basin or livelihood priorities (Lankford 2004). Intakes could be designed to explicitly share water between upstream and downstream demands as is the function of proportional or castellated weirs (Lankford 2001).

Conclusion

In summary, three issues stand out:

1 farmers choose to irrigate depending on livelihood, environmental and water circumstances;
2 in under-irrigating areas, it is advisable for the government to generate an enabling environment that encourages farmers to consider irrigating, and while this may still not provide the first type of capital-intensive scheme, it would attract farmers to invest in new and existing systems;
3 the 'potential irrigation' narrative of the Government of Tanzania's strategy papers misses a more pressing issue of conflict mediation in existing irrigated areas where the demand to expand irrigation is ever present.

The first two issues reflect conclusions made by Guijt and Thompson (1994) on the importance of context in determining the interest in and benefits of irrigation through a livelihoods perspective.

Furthermore, it is argued, a rural livelihoods approach to irrigation can be formulated as:

1 An approach that recognises the many dimensions and complexities of irrigation arising from its role as a sector, input, system and activity.
2 An understanding that farmers are integrating across a wide range of constraints, costs, benefits and risks when deciding whether to develop, expand or improve irrigation.
3 An argument that states farmers, rather than officials, are better placed to decide on how irrigation can be improved or potential be realised.
4 A river basin approach that recognises the subtractability of water resources due to irrigation, and therefore the balance between upstream irrigation livelihoods and downstream environmental and livelihood needs.

5 A recognition that conflict mediation at different irrigation-river basin scales may be as important as promoting irrigation.
6 An appreciation of the site, stage and context elements of irrigation so that 'problems' of irrigation are addressed using a cognitive, problem-solving approach, rather than the hurried application of theory informed by 'normal' viewpoints of agencies.
7 An acknowledgement of the strong technical nature of irrigation (often underplayed in rural livelihood frameworks) – yet recognising the social and depletive nature of irrigation so that irrigation design provides for river basin and livelihood needs (Lankford 2004).
8 A recognition that farmers are interested in irrigation because of a number of benefits: income generation; food; food security; and jobs. The links between these farmer-level benefits and national poverty, food security and unemployment strategies are not direct; suggesting the latter three are by-products of farmer interests.
9 A recognition that the surrounding economic and cultural environment stimulates irrigation activity and the desire to resolve water-based conflicts (land tenure, markets, crop pricing, etc.)
10 The provision, where necessary, of services and infrastructure to facilitate access to very small amounts of water and/or irrigated land for the poor.
11 The provision, where necessary, of the capital for major works beyond the reach of poor farmers.
12 That, within the debate over national food security; a distinction is made between strategies for private-sector involvement and those required to support pro-poor livelihoods.

Notes

* This chapter is an abridged and edited version of a paper published in *Physics and Chemistry of the Earth* (Lankford 2003).

1 This is certainly the case in the Ilonga river system where water is taken from the Ilonga and Chanzuru offtakes up to their respective design maximum flows, in wet and dry season, leaving little water for the downstream intake of Madota.

18 Community-based natural resource management in Malawi and Botswana*

Piers Blaikie

Setting up the argument

The idea of community-based natural resource management (CBNRM) is, in various forms, an established policy goal of rural development, especially in Africa. It is also a simple and attractive one: that communities, defined by their tight spatial boundaries of jurisdiction and responsibilities, by their distinct and integrated social structure and common interests, can manage their natural resources in an efficient, equitable and sustainable way. The natural resources in question are usually, though not exclusively, common pool resources. In southern Africa, these are typically forest, open woodland or grasslands for livestock grazing, wood supply, medicines and famine foods; farm land for gleaning, grazing after harvest and crop residues; wildlife for game meat and safari incomes; fish in fresh water lakes; and aquifers, tanks and irrigation channels for domestic and livestock water supply and irrigation (Adams *et al.* 2000: 12).

Case studies and in-country research are concentrated in two contrasting African nations. The first is Malawi, the rural people of which have endured decades of sustained dispossession by a neo-patrimonial despot and currently face serious food insecurities, extreme absolute poverty and currently (in early 2003) widespread famine. The government has pursued a programme of progressive legislation for forests removing restrictions on the access and use of woodland, and has specifically targeted women as key resource users (National Forest Policy 1997 and Forest Act 1997). It has had a decentralisation policy since 1998, approved a Strategic Plan for CBNRM as recently as November 2001, and has proceeded since with some CBNRM implementation especially in forestry and artisanal fisheries. However, policy reform has had to contend with decades of institutional destruction at the local level, and a rural population, which had grown weary and wary of any further interventions by government.

The second country is Botswana, a comparatively wealthy African country, resource-rich in minerals and with low population–land resource ratios, whose government has taken devolution of powers to manage natural resources seriously since the mid-1980s, and specifically CBNRM since 1998 following assistance from USAID. These countries have had very different histories of government, but have both witnessed at times in the past growing interference in local chiefly government, territorial incursions by the state and private capital to establish plantations, state forests, game and nature reserves and various parastatal adventures into business enterprises by their bureaucratic elites.

Although the term CBNRM was not generally in use until the 1980s, the notion that communities should, and could, satisfactorily manage their own resources according to their local custom, knowledge and technologies has a long history. However, the ideas of community and the local have constantly been shaped and reshaped by different outsiders through time (from colonial Governor-Generals, political advisors, European settlers, rural development consultants and academic writers). Thus, the idea of CBNRM has evolved through time and been specific to particular countries, but over the past fifteen years, there has been a convergence of various strands of meanings in the international development literature and practice by International Funding Institutions (IFIs). Today for example, social and community forestry in India and Nepal, and Natural Resource Management Committees in Malawi have some quite close similarities at a general level, which have resulted from a range of accepted policy design from IFIs.

Still, at the level of the detail of administrative, legal and financial structures and of daily practice, it continues to mean widely different things to different people. In the colonial period in Africa, the practice of indirect rule was developed in which 'native institutions' were adapted and shaped for that purpose by colonial rulers, dividing the rural from the urban and one ethnicity from another, and forming an institutional segregation. Africans were relegated to a sphere of customary law, while Europeans obeyed civil law (Ribot 1999: 23). These institutions, based upon 'traditional' (usually chiefly) leadership amounted to what Mamdani (1996) called decentralised despotism, and analogous to *apartheid*. They were essentially local and varied according to a great variety of cultures, ecologies and material needs but usually underpinned by communal tenure and chiefly authority. They were in many ways neglected except for purposes of political and strategic control, labour mobilisation, and latterly, just before independence, for soil and water conservation. Otherwise, they were treated with a degree of disdain or neglect by most colonial observers, who assumed that processes of 'natural evolution' would lead to individual tenure, a market in land and the commercialisation of agriculture (Lugard 1922). The presumptions behind this thinking had become standard development wisdom by the time of independence by African states, and remain powerful today (even in the minds of many government officials who implement CBNRM programmes, see Taylor (2001), with reference to Botswana). These presumptions were that individualisation of land tenure with registration of title would encourage long term investment in natural resource management, would inhibit (what was later styled as) the 'tragedy of the commons' (Hardin 1968), and would help to provide collateral for production loans, and create incentives to shift production from subsistence to the market – a late colonial narrative with a very contemporary ring.

Contemporary CBNRM can be seen as an attempt to re-unite the rural and urban, and the policy elites and civil society across the divide which had been created by colonial rule. It also runs counter to various post-colonial projects in newly independent states of modernisation, centralisation and, in many cases, patrimonial robbery of the small peasantries using coercive state powers. It remains a touchstone for much of rural development and sustainable natural resource management and has been promoted by most major international funding institutions (IFIs) since the early 1990s. Yet, as this chapter argues, it has largely failed to deliver the expected and theoretically predicted benefits to local communities. CBNRM became, and remain, popular to IFIs, but often so *un*popular with target communities themselves. Faced with such disappointing results and many critiques, it still flourishes as a central policy goal in all countries in central and southern Africa. In this sense, CBNRM *succeeds!* This chapter examines why.

All roads lead to CBNRM

CBNRM combines a number of powerful ideas, which contribute to its popularity or, more sceptically, '[its] warm emotional pull' (Taylor 2002: 125) in much of academic writing and funding agencies. The first is part of the phrase itself – 'community', the meaning of which may be understood in three ways (Agrawal and Gibson 2001: 1–31): community as a spatial unit, as a distinct social structure and as a set of shared norms. As this chapter will discuss, empirical evidence shows that the three are seldom co-terminous, and that community boundaries of jurisdiction may make little sense in the rational management of an identified natural resource with boundaries that may bear no resemblance to community boundaries (for example, a watershed or the habitat of an endangered species of fauna). There is also an extensive and powerful critique of the idea of the 'community', which will be alluded to later (Cleaver (1999, 2002) on the 'myths of community'), and, while the critique contributes to an explanation of the failure of many CBNRM projects, it has failed to tarnish their attraction to IFIs.

Another powerful discursive tool in the label 'CBNRM' is the elision of the notion of sustainable natural resource management (defined by rational and scientific criteria) with 'community', implying that this vehicle for management is well suited for the task, with its connotations of *gemeinschaft* ('intimate, private and exclusive living together' Bender (1978) in Agrawal and Gibson 2001: 8), local ownership and indigenous expertise. It is supposed to be able to deliver on scientifically specified NRM principles (which are by definition seldom, if ever, community-constructed and local). Herein lies the first contradiction in the label CBNRM: the first confrontation between formal science with its foundations in logical positivism and the independence between observer and observed on the one hand – and on the other, local knowledge, which is embedded in a particular environmental and social history and continuously negotiated on-site and face-to-face. However, the CBNRM policy narrative goes, this unequal relation of power to name the environment and its processes and trends, can be palliated or even negated by participatory and inclusionary techniques by which some form of hybrid knowledge can be negotiated and implemented. Here again, there are many instances where local knowledge has not been able to negotiate on an equal basis with official scientific knowledge, but has instead been shaped by what is offered by outsiders, who make strategic choices about which 'local knowledge' is heard and conforms to their scientifically given environmental goals (Mosse 2002).

CBNRM also derives its power from the promise of a diverse range of benefits predicted by social science theory and of a more sustainable management of natural resources. The latter focuses on environmental conservation and the current perceived failures identified through the coercive application of modern environmental knowledge, which is assumed to be scientific, reliable, authoritative and reproducible – the very antithesis of local knowledge. In this sense CBNRM often makes more of its promises over Natural Resource Management than Community, and thus the promise is not made for, and delivered to, the community at all, but rather to target-chasing, fund-raising members of the development industry worried about the environment. As Taylor, among many others notes: 'one of the expatriate NRMP team members in Botswana admitted informally that their real aim is conservation, and community development is included as a means to achieve this' (Taylor 2001).

A major argument here will be that it is the *practice* of CBNRM (its production, representation in policy documents and implementation), situated at the interface between the 'community' and outside institutions, which creates profound contradictions between theoretically derived promise and actual delivery. There are two key related but distinct ideas which represent the bridging between the outsider and the local. These are decentralisation and participation. Both imply a movement of decision-making and real political power from the central to more local levels (for example, district, county, parish or community-based organisation). Participation in decision-making about the management of natural resources requires a wide range of quite radical reforms, including transparency in transactions, accountability downwards, the granting of a considerable degree of local discretion over environmental decision-making (termed 'environmental subsidiarity') and a degree of competence, confidence and political savvy by local institutions (Agrawal and Ribot 1999; Ribot 2001, 2002).

Many of the theoretical benefits of CBNRM are 'small-scale' dependent, and weave through most of this disparate collection of pro-CBNRM theories and sentiments:

1 There is a pro-poor and safety net argument because of the privileging of small-scale insiders (labour intensive, surpluses retained locally, maximisation of internal trade transactions) to the exclusion of outside capital (which would lead to mechanisation, loss of artisanal jobs, enclosure, privatisation, export of profits and re-investment elsewhere). This argument has become particularly serviceable in the current round of Poverty Reduction Strategy Papers which most African countries are obliged to produce as a condition of debt relief, in which CBNRM are, in a sense, retro-fitted to poverty reduction strategies. Here a case of the opportunistic grabbing a set of propositions about the benefits of CBNRM off the shelf and putting them to discursive work in the day-to-day life of IFIs and senior government in Lilongwe or Gaberone. CBNRM is well endowed with promise.
2 CBNRMs promote efficient resource use and allocation, locally appropriate technologies and the successful application of indigenous technical knowledge (ITK), because local ecological specificities can be addressed by local experience and experimentation, adaptive agricultural practice, wildlife and hunting practices and forest use, local farmer networks etc. There are formidable problems of negotiating these knowledges at the development interface (a classic treatment being Long and Long's aptly named *Battlefields of Knowledge* (1992)). These too will be illustrated later in the chapter.
3 New institutional economics and public choice theory indicate that locally managed resource systems with clearly recognisable territorial boundaries will tend to internalise externalities (the decision-makers pay for the costs of their actions); will tend to deploy all information where local decision makers have most information about that resource, enabling service provision to match needs; and will create local institutions as problem solving solutions to issues of trust and malfeasance in economic life, and assist in issues of representation and transparency, which requires in rural environments face-to-face discussion and witnessing (thus, the small scale, small number, low transaction costs argument holds) (Cleaver 1999: 601; Ribot 2002)
4 CBNRM will solve or palliate open access problems resulting from coercive and insufficiently policed state property regimes. Policing will be undertaken by local people, who are on the spot and can see and directly apprehend wrong doers (another functional advantage of the 'local'). The community will have a stake in the protection of the resource and secure tenurial rights, either *de jure* or informally, de facto.
5 CBNRM can be styled as a 'local site of resistance', a bulwark against modernist and de-humanising invasions, and which can withstand the depredations of the colonial and post-colonial state, and globalising forces (Escobar 1995: 46–52).
6 CBNRM can initiate a benign cycle of effective participation, empowerment and the development of political confidence and expertise (drawing

on Mamdani's (1996) work 'from subject to citizen') financial independence, as the 'fulcrum for democratic change' (Ribot 2001).

7 CBNRM is described as an antidote to the acknowledged failure of state-run natural resources (Adams and Hulme 2001), where 'fences and fines' approaches to wildlife protection have too high economic costs for the state to meet), and disenchantment with fortress conservation, (Ghimire and Pimbert 1997; Inamdar *et al.* 1999; Songorwa *et al.* 2000).

Of course, there are counter arguments against CBNRM too. The CB institution can be seen as no more than a 'rascal's charter' as it protects archaic and regressive forms (e.g. chieftancy and patriarchy), and encourages cronyism. There are also some epistemological challenges from conservationists and arch-modernists with proven ecological imperatives who look on 'post-modern influences' and associated community-based approaches as an assault on rational ecology-based conservation, (Attwell and Cotterill 2000). These views however do not prevail in most international policy documents – the local is progressive and transformative, not laggard and traditional. Small is indeed beautiful. So the story goes...

Yet arrival is elusive...

For all the theoretical benefits promised, by and large, CBNRM policy has failed to deliver, in terms of its stated aims. Shackleton *et al.* (2002) concludes from thirteen case studies in Africa that 'most devolved natural resources management reflects rhetoric more than substance' and that 'the ways in which local people realise the benefits of devolution differ widely, and negative trade-offs, mostly felt by the poor, are common'. Shackleton and Campbell (2001), in an evaluation of fourteen case studies in eight countries of Africa assessed the outlook for CBNRM as poor overall, although they identify a number of CBNRM projects which show some signs of success. They take the well-trodden path towards the conclusion that the less the state and its line ministries impose and limit local NRM, the more local people can reshape social–environmental relationships in ways which suit them. There are success 'stories' too, although they are stories told by the initiating agencies themselves. The well-known CAMPFIRE project in Zimbabwe, boxed up in commentaries as a successful case study, has since been widely criticised (Sullivan 2001). A visit to the Compass Tamis website for documentation on CBNRM initiatives in Malawi has, as its column title for documents 'success story title', leaving little doubt over the quality of outcomes (Compass Tamis 2004). There are huge difficulties in establishing clear criteria of success and failure, requiring baseline studies and monitoring the before and after situation, establishing evidence of 'better' conservation, better production, improved incomes and institutional development (Ribot 2001: 45) But a generalised conclusion may be fairly confidently made that CBNRM programmes have substantially failed to deliver the promises to both communities and the environment. Why?

. . . And as many roads lead back again: 'our theories are inadequate'

There are a number of epistemologically distinct approaches to explain the failure of CBNRM programmes and policies. The first is to take theories seriously, and to try and rectify or improve them, on the assumption that, if there were better theories, there would be better CBNRM outcomes. However, this presupposes that there is a rational and instrumental model of policy-making and implementation. Here, better theory, which predicts more accurately the outcomes of CBNRM from initial characteristics of the community and the natural resource, appeals to rational policy-makers, who then change or adapt the policy in directions suggested by the theory. While a complete abandonment of this naïve version of the rationale of policy making leads the whole project of government and the possibility of progress into some fairly desolate destinations, it needs to be comprehensively critiqued and modified (see Keeley and Scoones (1999), on understanding environmental policy process, and Apthorpe and Gasper (1996) on arguing development policy).

There are a number of examples which illustrate well how a particular theory with powerful discursive leverage in policy-making discourses in Malawi and Botswana has been overturned but still has legitimacy. Two examples will suffice. The first is the eclipse of Hardin's Tragedy of the Commons as a general and inevitable condition following the establishment of a network of scholars (mostly economists on the USA) who theorised and championed common property management systems (see for example, the works of Bromley (1992), Oakerson (1985), Feeney *et al.* (1995), McKean (1992), and Ostrom (1990)). In Botswana, Hardin's theory was linked to a large volume of ecological studies of rangelands, which identified serious environmental degradation there due to what was assumed to be over-grazing on an open access resource. Science in this case provided a most important 'apolitical' and authoritative evidence, and it came from outside consultants, uncontaminated by political and economic interests from within Botswana. The Tribal Grazing Land Policy (TGLP) of 1975, followed by the implementation of a fencing component of the National Policy on Agricultural Development (NPAD) of 1991 both drew their legitimacy from a particular social theory (or 'parable' as its author has it) and supported by an impressive weight of evidence of degradation of the range. In short, local people could not look after their local resources – therefore, in the name of scientific and sustainable management, they must be privatised through fencing and exclusion of local cattle hitherto grazed on communal lands. The local, it was implied, was incompetent, therefore it would be invaded and used more responsibly by non-locals.

The considerable lapse of time between these two policy enactments attests to the resilience of Hardin's theory and the scientific evidence of the existence of serious environmental degradation in policy circles, even in the face of overwhelming empirical and theoretical attack, and asks searching questions about the (contingent) role of theory in policy-making. The scientific basis for defining rangeland degradation has been marked by the collapse of the stocking density controversy in the face of new models of natural variability and pastoral adaptation, thus largely exonerating local herders from over stocking and being the major perpetrators of degradation (although the debate of the significance of non-equilibrium theories in range ecology still continues (Abel and Blaikie 1989; Behnke *et al.* 1993; Illius and O'Connor 1999; Sullivan 2002). Needless to say, local voices that had been denying overgrazing were raised but never heard. Nonetheless, the political momentum for privatisation continues, with the result that rangeland is one sector which has been almost entirely neglected in the CBNRM project in Botswana (Shackleton *et al.* 2002: 19).

The next avenue for exploring the inadequacy of theory supporting CBNRM is to identify where the initial conditions for a satisfactory establishment of a local institution fail to be met. In this sense, it is an inductive failure of theory exposed by empirical trial. This has led to an ever-growing number of ever-growing lists. There is Ostrom's list of eight attributes (Ostrom 1990), and Roe *et al.* (2000: 114–120) have five tables of characteristics of communities plus internal and external factors of desirable attributes. Adams and Hulme (2001) have assembled a list of contra-indications, where CBNRM, in this case wildlife, simply is 'not the answer'. This includes, among other sets of conditions, for which CBNRM could never fulfil any of the major objectives (for example, the existing wildlife is not sustainable, or a range of wildlife which cannot yield a sustainable revenue flow, and when there is deep resentment at earlier dispossession of land). For example, in Lake Mburo National Park the inhabitants cleared all wildlife so the government would lose interest in the area (Hulme and Infield 2001). In the case of the Okavango Delta in Botswana, resentment and passive resistance regarding earlier and continuing coercive resettlement of the Basarwa (Koi-San) have been revived by the appearance of CBNRM policies. The Chobi National Park was formed in 1960 followed by The Moremi Game Reserve in 1964 and involved wholesale relocation of settlements. Special Game Licences (SGL) were established for each community which themselves imposed quite serious restrictions on the level of offtake of wildlife, but were rescinded at the time of the formation of CBNRM Trusts (where village 'communities' were strongly encouraged to form Trusts as the only legitimate vehicle for the CBNRM), and the quota of wildlife available for hunting was further radically reduced. Official visits to encourage the Baswara to form these Trusts were seen as yet another attempt to dispossess them of hunting rights and hunting territory. The list of contra-indications for the successful formation of CBNRM is unfortunately very long.

Agrawal (2001) questions the wisdom of pursuing this seemingly endless task of specifying 'facilitating conditions' for successful CBNRM (and implicitly accounting for failure when they do not apply), and lists a synthesis of about thirty, most of which describe the three main attributes of an idealised 'community' and the local outlined at the beginning of this chapter. More specifically, these include the small area extent of the natural resource, well-defined boundaries, small group size, shared norms, homogeneity of identities and interests and so on. Agrawal (2001) identifies the sets of causal links which are specified in research about common property institutions, with particular attention paid to external factors such as population growth (see also Lipton (1984), where the author draws attention to the growth of population and attendant growth of transaction costs involved in CBNRM management on account of the size of the group), the nature of enforcement, support or coercion by the state. These will be addressed in the Botswana and Malawi cases below. The conclusion the author draws is that careful research and statistical comparison may hold out the prospect of a 'coherent, empirically relevant theory of the commons' (Agrawal 2001: 1649). This effort may be helpful for the choice of likely communities for the successful establishment of CBNRMs (see the Malawi Country Report for the establishment of promising sites for CBNRM (Mwabumba *et al.* 2000)), but it leaves policymakers with the task of finding a needle in a haystack (an existing community with its natural resources which fulfil an impossibly large number of criteria), where the location of the haystack itself is far from clear.

Of course, there is an unknown, but probably very large, number of CBNRMs throughout most of Africa, which operate beyond the searching eye of decentralised government, or zealous NGOs. For example, there are many village committees in Malawi which organise the maintenance of contour *bunds* originally set up by colonial authorities, repair footpaths which can turn into serious gullies, and stabilise marker ridges with vetiver grass, and all this with minimal government support or interference (Evans *et al.* 1999). There are less exemplary examples. There are small fishing 'CBNRMs' (in inverted commas since the participants would call their institution by a variety of local names) throughout Malawi as well as Uganda and western Zambia. Along the shores of Lake Kyoga, there are attenuated and rather ineffective fishing regulatory bodies headed by a *gabunga,* who attempts to control illegal fishing practice (the use of seine nets close to Nile Perch breeding areas, mosquito nets used for catching *mukene*, and fish poisoning). The latter was satisfactorily controlled by the *gabunga*, but nets are confiscated only when a levy to the *gabunga* is not paid. It is rumoured that the confiscated nets are sold on to neighbouring villages. Such a description resonates with accounts of local government in many parts of the developed world as well (ramshackle, sometimes effective, sometimes not, liable to corruption from time to time, and liable to change). In more general terms, it is the variety and complexity of ways in which rural people manage their natural resources which tend to frustrate efforts to improve the predictive capacities of existing theories, to standardise the local as it were, so as to reproduce it in ways which conform to the theories about it.

CBNRM and the state – blowing on cold embers?

There are two sets of external forces, which pose serious, and in some cases, insurmountable challenges to the promotion of CBNRM in ways beneficial to local environments and people in the ways predicted by theory. The first concerns the political interface of the international and national at which CBNRM is produced and negotiated. The history of state formation at Independence in Malawi and Botswana sets the political environment for the interface between IFIs promoting CBNRM and government officials. Malawi for example has been characterised as a neo-patrimonial state (see Chapter 8 above). The notion suggested by CBNRM policy that the local may be able to reclaim control of resources, and taxation may be devolved to regional and district level threatens the conduit of patrimony from the local, via the Chief, to district officials and other 'Big Men' and upwards to the capital. This is not an attractive proposition for those at the top of the network. However, coercion on the part of IFIs, promises of training, equipment and opportunities of professional advancement also form part of the neo-patrimony in many states of developing nations. Official acceptance of (and more personally, acquiescence) to the policy, the waving through of some local NGO projects and some rhetorical gestures in the form of policy papers, may be enough to ensure the continuing flow of the neo-patrimony of aid without really compromising the flow from the capillaries which draw patrimony from the local to the national level. While there were several training and skills development workshops facilitated by the Malawi Department of Forests, foot-dragging over approving regulations and management plans has meant that many communities have lost interest.

CBNRM also creates widespread feelings of professional disempowerment from foresters, agricultural research and extension officers, wildlife rangers and so on. The local for them is a site for instruction, implementation and control with specific scientific objectives in mind. Not any longer. Partnership, social engineering and taking local politics and local technical knowledge seriously are emphatically not what professionals are currently trained for. Furthermore, IFIs are constantly changing their policies even within the CBNRM sector, there are different donor practices with low levels of donor coordination, all of which undermine purpose, initiative and a sense of routine for in-country officials. In the words of one forester in Malawi 'participatory forestry has become a talking shop – we are never left with any clear idea of what we should do' (personal communication, Lilongwe 2001). Here, it is the professional not the local farmer who feels disempowered and with not much to do for which they are trained (Mayers *et al.* (2001) for an excellent account of the forging of a forestry policy in Malawi, where these issues are discussed).

Botswana on the other hand, has taken much more serious political steps to decentralise powers of management to the local level (The Wildlife Conservation Policy (1986), National Conservation Policy (1990), Tourism

Policy (1990), and finally CBNRM since 1990, (Rozemeier and van der Jagt 2000)). In any case, there exists a long history of decentralised planning where democratically elected District Councils play an important role. There are also Land Boards at the district level, which have the power to make a number of decisions about natural resource use, although the Boards are only partly elected by the local population and are an arena of conflicting interests. Also, the Department of Wildlife and National Parks keeps quite close scrutiny of wildlife matters through its Technical Committee, which is largely detached from the District Council (which sends a few members to the meetings but receives very little of the income which may derive from commercial wildlife ventures). A much higher degree of accountability in government and a very much better resourced administration, have contributed to a more visible presence for CBNRM. In spite of this, the range of CBNRM issues and the extent of the powers of local CBNRM Trusts are quite circumscribed and mainly deal with wildlife only. A number of CBNRM Trusts to manage wildlife have been successfully set up. However, the management skills and capital necessary to run a safari enterprise usually cannot be found in a local Village Development Committee (VDC), with the result that it is foreigners who successfully bid for them, pay a licence fee to the VDC and make little attempt to employ local people, develop local skills in guide work, building construction, catering, driving, etc. This has meant that the 'local community' have often become little more than rentiers with no opportunity for widening livelihood options and associated skills.

Other sectors such as rangelands are largely excluded from CBNRM briefs. The management decisions concerning what is left of communal grazing areas after privatisation devolves onto the local chiefs, the traditional meeting (the *kgotla).* The VDC has more to do with community activities other than NRM anyway. Thus, in Botswana, official engagement with the local has had a long history, been much more intensive and is better financed and organised than in Malawi. However, the power of the *kgotla* to make management decisions over land has been undermined by the Land Boards, engagement is limited to wildlife which has largely been taken over by foreigners, and the Trusts have tended to take the form of wealthy enclaves the benefits from which do not flow to the local VDCs.

CBNRM As Trojan horse: theory and practice

The practice of implementing policies for re-invigorating the local and conserving the environment through CBNRM usually starts with detailed design of policy and projects, terms of reference, organigrams of devolved government, a new legal framework, financing, training of both government officers as well local leaders, new political structures and even, as in the case of Malawi, amendments to the national constitution. In contrast, the subject of the policy is the community which is socially and environmentally diverse, complex, which, even within one community, has a wide array of different social constructions of the same 'resource' (for example a wood may be a sacred grove, a supply of fuel wood, a biodiverse collection of medicinal plants, high quality carving wood for tourist curios, or act as protection of a watershed). These may be contested, but meanings will always be multiple and be different from one community to the next. Also, the technical specifications of the resource itself have different political implications. For example, multi-species indigenous forest and single species eucalyptus wood fuel lots have a completely different set of management demands and therefore different local politics. Faced with such complexity (as it appears to the eye of the outsider), manageability becomes a nightmare. To render the local manageable, standardisation and replicability become essential.

Re-imagining the local so as to render it manageable requires its black-boxing and containerisation. A black box simplifies by hiding troubling complexities within, and obscuring even smaller scales (the household, women, children, ethnic minorities), and a local politics of control and inequality. CBNRM projects in practice may become an opportunity for new political entrepreneurs, both internal and external, rather than an opportunity for target groups (the poor, women, minorities and disabled), as the egalitarian and pro-poor objectives of CBNRM may demand. Gender issues, particularly of the asset position of women-headed households, are seldom addressed, (because they are so difficult to do so within the formula of CBNRM) and reliance on chiefs (who are almost invariably male) may reinforce these inequalities, and exclude (most) women from the negotiations which local scale management is supposed to facilitate.

The containerisation of the local in CBNRM policy is another reductionism to render manageable what is diverse and complex, involving movement of people (and sometimes resources such as freshwater fish and wildlife) through space and time, which transgresses simple mapping of boundaries. Boundaries, which make sense for managing natural resources and local territorial boundaries often do not coincide. To whom do the wildlife of the Kalahari or the fish of Lake Malawi, which both migrate across territorial community boundaries, belong, and whose responsibility are they? These are not insuperable problems but they require a deep understanding of the political economy of local resource use. A failure to understand existing management arrangements often results in inept attempts to territorialise common property jurisdictions. Fishing in Lake Chiuta in Malawi for example, was regulated through complex arrangements between local and migrant fishermen, which were ignored by the setting up of territorially-based Beach Village Committees (BVCs). Local fishermen, who tended to land lower catches than the migrants, then used the new BVC to attempt to evict the migrants on the grounds that the latter were responsible for over-fishing. BVCs crosscut the jurisdiction of the local chiefs, inducements were brought to bear by some of the contestants with outcomes which varied from chaotic to partly successful (see a review of Africa's inland fisheries and CBNRM projects by Geheb and Sarch (2000)).

For all the rhetorical intentions of CBNRM policies, the contradictions of engagement between the local and centralised institutions still tend to reproduce the local in a bureaucratically manageable form. There are of course local strategies of resistance. Non-participation in CBNRM may become a rational strategy of resistance, or getting what one wants by other means (stealth, stealing, using through existing networks). The CBNRM project is also an opportunity where changes in authority, local by-laws and sites of decision making provide a disturbance, an opening for new political entrepreneurs, new rents and control of resources. There are winners and losers but the prospect of being the former may induce a form of provisional acceptance of a CBNRM, subject to fears of dispossession by the state and on conditions which will favour the likely winners. Outright resistance is not uncommon and evokes coercive responses from the local state. For example, the Basarwa (or Bushmen) in Botswana objected to further incursions into their hunting rights, and were met with cajoling by local officials along the lines that 'we are all Batswana now' and you should not try and preserve your identity as Basarwa, and 'if you do not agree to form a CBNRM Trust [as the vehicle for CBNRM] the government will set it up without you, and you will lose out' (Taylor 2001: 7).

Conclusion

The notion of local management of natural resources has taken many turns in southern Africa, even over short periods in the two countries discussed here. Under colonial or Protectorate rule, the chief became the conduit of indirect rule, and the local was relegated to a stagnant backwater, which might, at some point, be slowly drawn back into mainstream economic life. However, environmental conservation was and remains today, an important warrant for invasions, instructions and dispossessions. Scientific evidence such as land degradation and the extermination of wildlife (Anderson and Grove 1987) was brought to bear. Scientific expertise as the rational enforcement agency in the hands of the state was not long in forcing entry in the name of conservation.

Furthermore, and in contradiction to the premises of CBNRM, both the colonial and post-colonial state have long presided over the encroachment and undermining of common property and the control and management of local natural resources by local people. Plantations, estates, state forestry programs, private farms, game parks and national parks encroached on the territory of local people, and the state has also invaded it with conservation expertise. Instruct, fence out, dismantle and resettle, and turn the local inside out (with locals on the wrong side of the fence). External driving forces continue this process. Structural adjustment programs, global trade agreements (the south must liberalise its markets of course, but the north will continue to subsidise its farmers) and population growth with a lack of non-agricultural employment all combine to reduce people's well being and confidence to manage their own lives, and to make material conditions more onerous in which to do so. Here, it is the global impacting in all sorts of specific ways upon the local (Watts 2000).

Then at this point in the argument, CBNRM makes its stage entrance. It is an arena where individual agents feel they can have an impact. It is adorned with an impressive armoury of theory and populist sentiment and promises rescue of the local and many benefits to nature and society. There is a confusing variability in CBNRM and related administrative and legal reforms, such as decentralisation even across a single country. It is porous, can absorb all manner of different agendas, and is rich in variety, something in it for all, especially for the aid industry and its clients. However, the warrant for CBNRM still remains environmentally focused. If local people are managing their natural resources sustainably, why is there NRM in the title? Why not merely CB and the notion of community development which was in vogue (especially in south Asia) in the 1960s? An answer to this might point to the failure of 'fence and fine' coercive conservation, now no longer enforceable by weak states such as Malawi. Also, sometimes the state and its science are found to be mistaken (as in the case of the overstocking controversy in Botswana and other southern African countries). It would be better to negotiate with the local, the counter-argument goes, and allow the functional advantages of the small scale to operate as theory predicts; and advantageously, to pass on the costs of policing forests, wildlife and range lands which the state was finding impossible to meet.

The success or failure of CBNRM may be judged by the outcomes, in terms of degree to which it has delivered on sustainable environmental management, enhanced incomes especially for the poor and institutional learning at all levels. These criteria suggest difficult and costly monitoring and evaluations. Where clear evidence on these criteria is missing (or adverse), other measures may be substituted. If this is not done, a CBNRM programme or project is seen 'not to work'. In any case, results are always mixed and open to all sorts of interpretation. There are cases where it is clear that local people, including the politically marginalised, *have* benefited, especially when the state really has let go of professional and economic control. Also, there are so many others which have messy and not too encouraging outcomes in terms of CBNRM's stated goals. However, it is in the implementation of CBNRM that the 'community' and the social and environmental variability which comes with the local, have to be regularised, reduced, manualised, replicated and inserted into program targets – but lionised and idealised too, if CBNRM is to succeed discursively and the project is to survive at all.

Note

* This chapter is an abridged and edited version of a paper published in *World Development* (Blaikie 2004).

Part V

Macro–micro linkages in rural poverty reduction policies

19 Poverty reduction strategies for addressing multi-level poverty traps

Reflections from Kenya*

Brent Swallow

Introduction

At the Millennium Summit in September 2000, the United Nations General Assembly adopted the eight Millennium Development Goals and agreed upon the eighteen targets and forty-eight indicators that would be used to measure progress toward those goals. The first goal is to eradicate extreme hunger and poverty, with the targets of halving, between 1990 and 2015, the proportion of people whose income is less than $1/day and the proportion of people who suffer from hunger.[1] The UN World Summit on Sustainable Development in Johannesburg considered the progress toward those goals and the need for concerted action by all levels of government and development assistance in order to achieve better progress. Progress toward the poverty and hunger goals has been particularly poor in Africa.

In the past, most African governments have not had clearly-articulated approaches for reducing poverty or addressing the needs of the most impoverished members of the society. Since the late-1990s a number of United Nations agencies – especially the World Bank, International Monetary Fund, United Nations Development Programme – have been promoting the formulation of Poverty Reduction Strategy Papers by African governments. At the annual meetings of the World Bank Group and the IMF in September 1999, it was agreed that concessional lending and debt relief under the Highly Indebted Poor Countries initiative would be based on Poverty Reduction Strategy Papers (PRSPs) developed by national authorities. Extensive guidelines on how to develop PRSPs are provided by the World Bank and UNDP. PRSPs must be developed according to five general principles:

1 country-driven – involving broad-based participation by civil society and the private sector;
2 results-oriented – focusing on outcomes that would benefit the poor;
3 comprehensive in recognizing the multidimensional nature of poverty;
4 partnership-oriented – involving coordinated participation of development partners (bilateral, multilateral and non-governmental);

5 based on a long-term perspective for poverty reduction.[2] A great deal of resource material and data are provided to assist countries to prepare PRSPs.

The development of the PRSPs has generated a great deal of analysis, discussion and comment. Wilks and Lefrancois (2002) produced a report for the Bretton Woods Project and World Vision in which they criticize the World Bank for taking such an activist role in guiding the development of the PRSPs and for dominating the production of the empirical evidence on which the strategies are based. They note that 'Ministers from indebted countries and prominent academics have recently voiced concerns about the conflicts of interest underlying the Bank's role as analyst and lender' (HIPC Ministerial Declaration in Wilks and Lefrancois 2002: 10). The World Bank now conducts at least five types of core reports and eighteen sector or issue reports in every client country. These reports are all conducted using standard methodology, with limited room for debate or alternative perspectives.

National PRSPs, such as that developed for Kenya, have been criticized for:

1 reporting the incidence of poverty in a way that conceals important differences by region, population group, or gender;
2 reporting the incidence of expenditure poverty, but not clarifying the causes of that poverty;
3 not providing information on the quality and quantity of public services provided to different groups or regions;
4 concentrating on income and consumption measures of poverty;
5 restricting the final preparation of the papers to a few individuals in the Ministries responsible for finance and planning;
6 not providing adequate opportunities for the voices and opinions of poor people or Members of Parliament to be incorporated in the planning process;
7 downplaying important issues for the poor such as water;
8 proposing expenditure priorities that do not match the apparent needs of the poor;
9 poor planning of district-level consultations (Maji Na Ufanisi 2002; Wilks and Lefrancois 2002; Calaguas and McConnell 2002; Kiringai and Manda 2002).

In this chapter I reflect on poverty reduction strategies from the perspective of agriculture and rural development planning. I emphasize two related propositions. First, village or community-level perspectives need to be incorporated more systematically into poverty reduction planning and implementation processes. Second, priorities for poverty reduction programmes should be aggregated up from individual to community to region to nation, with the focus at each level being on the provision of public goods and services that impede progress at lower levels. Here I consider the case of Kenya, where good data on the village perspective is readily available through the participatory rural appraisal and community action plan approach adopted by the Ministry of Agriculture and Rural Development under the National Agriculture and Livestock Extension Programme. Most other African countries also have a wealth of community-level data that is not currently used for national-level poverty reduction planning.

Background to the case study

Poverty in Kenya

The Republic of Kenya experiences levels of poverty that place it at number 146 of the 175 countries that are ranked by the United Nations Development Programme in terms of Human Development Index (HDI), with an HDI of 0.489 and per capita Gross Domestic Product of US$ 371 in 2001. Kenya's economic and development performance has fallen continually since 1990, with a growth rate in per capita income of -0.6 per cent and a fall in Human Development Index from 0.535 to 0.489.[3] The deepening of poverty has been particularly severe in Nyanza District in Western Kenya, which is estimated to have had a poverty rate of 63 per cent in the year 2000 (Kenya 2000b). Nyanza also experiences the highest rate of HIV/AIDS infection in Kenya, 22 per cent in the year 2000 (Kenya 2001b).

Jayne *et al.* (2003) have assembled the best set of evidence regarding multi-level determinants of poverty in Kenya, as well as Ethiopia, Zambia, Rwanda and Mozambique. For Kenya, Jayne *et al.* (2003) had access to a panel of household survey data from almost 1,500 agricultural households in twenty-four districts collected by the Tegemeo Institute and Michigan State University. They assessed location and household-level factors contributing to differences in household income in each of the five countries. For Kenya, they conclude that:

1 Income per household is $827/household for the wealthiest 25 per cent of the households and $53/household for the poorest 25 per cent of the rural population (a difference of over fifteen times).
2 Average land size per household member is 1.1 hectares per person in the wealthiest 25 per cent of the households and 0.08 hectares per person in the poorest 25 per cent of the rural population (a difference of about fourteen times).
3 There is a significant positive, but non-linear relationship between land size and income. An increase in land size from 0.08 to 0.25 hectares per person is associated with a 30 per cent increase in income, while an increase in land size from 0.30 to 0.50 hectares is associated with a 3 per cent increase in income.

4 Other significant determinants of per capita income include: years of primary education, years of post-primary education, value of livestock assets, and sex of household head (single female-headed households have less income, while married female-headed households have more income).
5 Total variation in household per capita income is accounted for by between-province differences (6.4 per cent), between district differences (14.3 per cent), between village differences (23.5 per cent), and household and village attributes (50 per cent).
6 Total variation in household per capita land access is accounted for by between province differences (7.7 per cent), between district differences (15.9 per cent), between village differences (33.3 per cent), and household and village attributes (52.4 per cent).

Kenya's Poverty Reduction Strategy Paper

Kenya's final Poverty Reduction Strategy Paper for the period 2001–2004 was published by the Ministry of Finance and Planning of the Government of Kenya in September 2001 (Kenya 2001c). The PRSP was developed on the basis of an analysis of the poverty and macro-economic situation, consultations among thematic working groups and sector working groups, a National Stakeholders' Forum, and one-day consultations in each of Kenya's then seventy districts. The major results are:

1 an implementation matrix that lists objectives, activities, outputs, costs and implementing agencies;
2 a matrix of issues and priorities for each of seven sectors and forty subsectors;
3 a matrix of issues and priorities for each of the seventy districts. The main sources of data used in the development of the PRSP were macroeconomic and aggregate sectoral data and household-level welfare data generated through the Welfare Monitoring Surveys of 1994 and 1997.

Description of Nyando district

At the time of the 1999 population census, Nyando District had a human population of 299,930 persons living in an area of 1,164 square kilometres (258 persons per square kilometre). Population density ranged from about 50 persons per square kilometre to over 1,200 persons per square kilometre. Physically, Nyando district is defined by the lower and mid-altitude parts of the Nyando River drainage area, a river that is formed from tributaries originating in the Mau forest, the Tinderet forest, and the Nyabondo Plateau. The Nyando River carries high levels of sediment, nutrients and other pollutants into the Winam Gulf of Lake Victoria. The relief of Nyando district can be divided into the lakeshore areas, the Kano plains, and the hillsides and escarpment areas of the Nyanbondo Plateau. The major cropping patterns are as follows: lakeshore areas – irrigated rice, irrigated vegetables; Kano plains – maize, beans, sorghum, sugar cane and cotton; hillsides and escarpment areas – maize, beans, sugar cane, coffee and bananas. Nyando is one of Kenya's poorest districts, with 65 per cent of the population falling below the absolute poverty line, and has one of the highest HIV prevalence rates in Kenya (28 per cent). Research conducted by the World Agroforestry Centre over the last four years has shown the high prevalence of soil fertility decline, soil erosion and deforestation that characterizes the district. The long-term average rate of erosion in the most degraded parts of the district is about 90 tonnes per hectare per year (Swallow *et al.* 2002).

Community planning under the NALEP focal area approach

The National Agriculture and Livestock Extension Programme (NALEP) is implemented by the Kenya Ministry of Agriculture and Rural Development in forty-two districts. The Swedish International Development Agency (SIDA) and the Government of Kenya provide financing. The basis of the NALEP approach is the shifting focal area – extension staff concentrate their support in one or two focal areas of about 300 hectares and 400 households in each division each financial year, shifting to new areas at the beginning of each new financial year. The goal is to engage with about 100,000 new households every year across the country. The NALEP programme began in 2000–2001.

The NALEP approach begins with a five-day participatory rural appraisal involving subject-matter specialists, front-line extension workers and the rural communities. The PRA concludes with the preparation of a participatory appraisal of problems, a community action plan for addressing those problems, and the election of a focal area development committee. In the following weeks and months, the MOARD facilitates the implementation of the community action plan, the activities of common interest groups, and the specification of farm-specific action plans and farm business plans for every farm in the focal area. The MOARD staff provide specific information on technologies and enterprises, link community groups with other providers of material, technical and market support, provide training in technical and business skills, arrange cross-site exchange visits to other communities, and provide a few material inputs for community infrastructure.

Programming to alleviate multi-level poverty traps

There are many challenges inherent in the design and implementation of poverty reduction strategies. Here I want to draw attention to four related challenges affecting design: distribution, dynamics, synergies and levels. I use 'poverty distribution' here to refer to social–spatial variation in the incidence and severity of poverty. There is a growing body of evidence from around the developing world that poverty levels vary not only between countries and between individuals within countries, but also between regions within countries and between communities within regions (see the bibliography on chronic poverty by Hecky and Moore 2001). Poverty reduction planners must consider whether they will address only problems that are common to all communities and regions, or also more region or community specific problems. They must also consider the amounts of resources they will invest in regions or communities with more or less severe poverty problems. In other words, how much will poverty reduction strategies be geared to address redistribution or equity enhancement?

The challenge of 'poverty dynamics' concerns both the duration of poverty – roughly classified into chronic and transitory, and the cause and effect relationships that unfold over time. Poverty reduction planners must decide on the priority to give to alleviating short-term consequences of poverty versus the underlying forces that perpetuate poverty over long periods of time. Will poverty reduction strategies also be safety net programmes? Will they address the proximate causes of rural poverty, such as low use of fertilizer, or more distal causes such as the systematic under-education of women in certain ethnic groups?

The challenge of 'synergies' refers to the complementarities or tradeoffs between public investments and complementary investments by groups and private individuals. It is clear that the most efficient use of public resources is to create goods and services that 'crowd in' collective and private investments and to avoid investments that 'crowd out' such investment. Taken to an extreme, however, this focus on efficiency can become an argument in favour of making the relatively well-off – those who have access to private funds to invest – even richer.

The challenge of 'levels' refers to two inter-related questions. First, what level of public administration or collective action is most efficient and effective in implementing poverty reduction programmes? The emphasis put on decentralization of public administration by the World Bank, the United Nations Development Programme, and the United Nations Capital Fund is mostly a reflection of the view that more decentralized government is less susceptible to corruption, more accountable to target recipients and less susceptible to capture by elites (Bardhan and Mookherjee 2000). The principle of 'vertical subsidiarity' is that public services should be provided at the lowest administrative level that they can be efficiently produced.

The second 'level' issue that I would like to emphasize here is the existence of multi-level dynamic poverty traps (see Chapter 2 in this volume). In brief, dynamic poverty traps are self-re-enforcing processes that maintain multiple equilibria in which some units attain higher welfare from more productive strategies, with higher levels of productive assets, while other units are mired in greater poverty, less productive strategies, and under-investment in productive assets. Poverty traps are multi-level, affecting individuals, households, communities, regions and nations. At each of these levels, the causes of poverty traps are the same: credit and insurance market failures, asset accumulation thresholds, and transformation functions with increasing returns to scale at low levels of production. Poverty reduction strategies should seek to address common and idiosyncratic poverty traps at all levels.

Data, analysis and results

Data and analysis

In this section I evaluate how well the outputs from Kenya's PRSPs match with the priorities expressed by village groups in the Nyando district of Western Kenya. I consider information from three sources. First, I assembled and synthesized results from participatory rural appraisals and community action plans conducted by the Kenya Ministry of Agriculture and Rural Development in ten focal areas in Nyando district under the National Agriculture and Livestock Extension Programme. Two focal areas were covered in each of the five divisions of Nyando district, three in the 2000/2001 financial year, three in the 2001/2002 financial year, and two in the 2002/2003 financial year. One strong advantage of the focal area approach is that the communities undertake a rigorous ranking exercise in order to identify priority problems for their community. I summarized priorities across the ten focal areas by counting the number of areas in which an issue was mentioned and assigning weights ranging between one and twelve to the priorities elicited from each area, with a weight of twelve given to the highest priority and one given to the eleventh highest priority (if mentioned).

I then compiled information about the activities that the communities planned to undertake in response to each of the highest priority issues and compared those activities to the issues and possible actions listed in the national PRSP implementation framework and elicited in the Nyando district consultation.

Kenya's Interim Poverty Reduction Strategy Paper (IPRSP) was adopted by the Government of Kenya in June 2000 (Kenya 2000a) on the basis of household data from the 1994 and 1997 Welfare Monitoring Survey as summarized in the reports entitled *Poverty in Kenya*. The IPRSP was then updated and revised on the basis of national-level consultations held around key themes and sectors, district-level consultations held in all seventy districts, and participatory poverty assessments held in 10 districts. The finalized national PRSP was published in September 2001 (Kenya 2001c).

The Nyando district consultation was conducted on 2 March 2001 at the Ahero Multipurpose Institute, with leadership from the Widows and Orphans Society of Kenya. Participants at the consultation included representatives of widows and orphans, women's organizations, youth groups, people with disabilities, retrenchees, farmers, business people, teachers, small-scale artisans, hawkers, politicians, church leaders, the District Commissioner and government department heads (Kenya 2001d).

Issues and priorities

The PRSP implementation framework lists eight priority sectors, 106 objectives and 539 activities. The sectors, listed in order of priority, are:

1 Agriculture and rural development;
2 Human resource development;
3 Physical infrastructure;
4 Tourism, trade and industry;
5 Public safety, law and order;
6 Public administration;
7 Information technology.

No clear priorities are set within this list of objectives or actions. The sectors and objectives are listed in Table 19.1. At first glance, the list appears to contain most of the activities of the public sector in the country.

The one-day district level PRSP consultation in Nyando listed issues by sector and sub-sector and indicated interventions and solutions to each of those issues. The interventions/solutions are not stated in terms of objectives. See Table 19.2.

Tables 19.3a and 19.3b present information on the priority problems that were listed in the course of participatory rural appraisals in ten NALEP focal areas.

Table 19.4 presents information on the activities proposed by the villages for the eight priority areas and a comparison of those activities with activities proposed in the National PRSP and the Nyando district consultation for corresponding problems.

Evaluation of consistency

Process

The national-level process involved a large number of stakeholders over more than a year, it involved many of the government ministries that would be responsible for implementing the proposed actions at the central level, and it relied on household-level data on living conditions from across Kenya. The village-level process involved Ministry of Agriculture and Rural Development staff responsible for the NALEP programme and a significant portion of the community residents who were directly affected by the problems, would directly benefit from solutions to those problems and would contribute resources to the solution of those problems. The village-level process unfolded over five days of intensive analysis and discussion. In contrast, the district level process was conducted in a single day, involved only a sample of implementing and representative organizations, and did not give any consideration to the resource requirements of recommended actions. These

Table 19.1 Sectors and objectives of the Kenyan poverty reduction strategy

Sector	*Objectives*
Agriculture and rural development	improve crop development; enhance food security; improve market development; improve livestock development; research and development; enhance cooperative movement; enhance fisheries production; promote fish farming; institute a viable land policy; disseminate an appropriate land use policy; sustainable management and use of forests; conservation, sustainable utilization and management of environment and natural resources; promote inter-sectoral coordination and streamlining of policy, legal and institutional framework
Human resource development	promote early childhood education; enhance access, retention, completion rates and attainment at the primary school level; monitor and control exploitation of parents; expand provision of bursaries, subsidies and school feeding programmes; enhance educational opportunities for the poor at secondary and post-secondary levels; provision of science equipment and other materials; provision of loans and scholarships to needy students; encourage private sector partnership in school development; provision of educational opportunities to children not able to participate in the formal system; improve management and utilization of resources within the education sector; eradication of illiteracy among adults; improve services in water provision; provide effective and efficient forestry services; enhance entrepreneurial development and management; enhance equity, quality, accessibility and affordability of health care; implement health activities for women and children under five years; decentralize health services; combat the HIV/AIDS scourge; increase knowledge and awareness of transmission of HIV/AIDS; treat and support care for the infected and affected; mitigate socio-economic impact of HIV/AIDS; create employment opportunities; improve work environment; improve planning and resource mobilization for shelter and housing; facilitate provision of affordable housing; prolong economic lifespan of government buildings; complete ongoing building projects; terminate stalled and suspended building projects; suspend construction of new government projects except emergency projects

continued

Table 19.1 Continued

Sector	*Objectives*
Physical infrastructure	improve road transport especially in rural areas; foster transparency and accountability in the road sector; maintain main road network; reform operations of the Mechanical and Transport Department; implement urgent measures to minimize the effect of the power crisis on economy; ensure adequate supply of energy to sustain economic growth; boost power accessibility in rural areas; diversify energy sources; reduce dependency on imported petrol; improve quality of early children education centres; construct a National Centre for Early Childhood Education; maintain teacher training buildings; provide housing for police; increase access to improved water and sanitation; increase coverage of urban sewage and sanitation; rehabilitate and augment rural water supplies; provide water and sewage to public universities; protect land and encroachment from the sea; improve rail delivery services; increase efficiency of air transport; increase efficiency of meteorological services
Tourism, trade and industry	promote product and market development; industrial mineral development; promote internal and external trade; enhance tourism; enhance information network
Public safety, law and order	protect life and property; ensure maintenance of peace; protect national sovereignty; ensure safety of people, food and livestock; institutional rehabilitation of children and juvenile delinquents; rehabilitate offenders; provide legal protection to children; create conducive legal environment and efficient delivery of legal services; improve efficiency of justice system; provide children's services within the districts; provide probation services in the districts; preserve birth and death records; enhance accountability and integrity; prevent crime; gender mainstreaming
Public administration	improve efficiency and effectiveness of local authorities; provide uniform housing benefit to civil servants; continue reform of public sector; develop and maintain a respectable international image; facilitate constitutional reforms; improve budgeting and public finances; strengthen audit of public finances; promote accounting of government finances; prepare economic planning; enhance governance system; effective coordination of disaster operations; improve population statistics; update household income indicators; update poverty indicators; improve socio-economic indicators; update economic indicators
Information technology	strengthen IT capacity in ministries; establish GoK network to link ministries; computerize government records; support Kenya's participation in the global economy; reduce the digital divide

Source: Kenya (2000c).

Table 19.2 Nyando District issues per sector/sub-sector, in order of priority

Sector	*Sub-sector*	*Issues*
Agriculture and rural development	Crop development	outdated technology unreliable rainfall high costs of inputs inadequate marketing channels inadequate capital
	Livestock development	high prevalence of livestock diseases and use of local breeds
	Lands and settlement	lack of title deeds
	Environmental management	droughts and floods
	Cooperatives	mismanagement and untrained personnel
	Fisheries	lack of cold storage and processing facilities
Human resource development	Education	poor management of public schools inappropriate education system costly education due to cost sharing understaffing inadequate physical and learning facilities
	Health	inadequate physical facilities lack of health education cost sharing too expensive for the poor
	Labour, social security and capacity building	unemployment
Physical infrastructure	Roads	inadequate classified, feeder and minor road network
	Energy	inadequate coverage of the district by the national electricity grid
	Transport and communication	poor telephone and postal services, and absence of railway services
Trade, tourism and industry	Industries	mismanagement of local industries
	Tourism	neglected tourist attractions inadequate facilities and marketing of potential tourist sites
	Trade	high taxation delayed payments for delivered produce marketing corrupt tendering system
	Small-scale industries	absence of small-scale industries marketing
Public safety, law and order	Administration of justice	delays in bringing cases to court inadequate physical facilities for law and order staff inadequate number of personnel need for laws to protect orphans and children

Source: Kenya (2001d).

Table 19.3a Priority problems identified in the village participatory appraisals and community action plans

Issue	*Orego*[a]	*Kipsamwe*	*Olwalo-Nyabula*	*Holo-Angoro*	*Kango*	*Siany*
Food crop production and shortages						
Food shortage			1[b]		1	
Poor diets						
Low crop yield		6		4		1
Inadequate knowledge of agriculture						
Livestock diseases and production						
Livestock diseases	6	5	6	8		2
Low milk yield	8	7	8			2
Human diseases and health care						
HIV/AIDS/human diseases	2	1	5	3	3	9
Inadequate health facilities				6		
Inadequate knowledge of human health						5
Lack of clean water	5	2	3	1	7	
Lack of fuelwood and tree products	10	8	7	9	6	4
Soil degradation						
Soil infertility	4					
Soil erosion						3
Poor roads	7	9	4	11	2	
Marketing						
Problems with sugar cane marketing	1			12		
Poor market for farm produce		10				
Lack of market for cotton and sisal						
Insecurity						
Cattle theft	3	3				
Low income			2			
Flooding					5	
Inadequate vegetables and fruit				7		
Inadequate farm inputs				2		
High illiteracy					4	
Lack of credit facilities				5		
Lack of employment						
Inadequate farm labour					8	
Traditional and cultural practices						
Communal grazing		9				
Inadequate pasture/fodder						
Inadequate land preparation equipment	9					
Mismanagement of community groups			10			
Poor leadership				10		

Source: focal area reports compiled by the Nyando District and division offices of the Ministry of Agriculture and Rural Development.

Notes

a Obago and Kango focal areas are in Miwani Division, Orego and Kipsamwe are in Muhoroni Division, Holo-Angora and Kawandola are in Nyando Division.

b The numbers in the columns indicate the priority that was established by the community through matrix prioritization, with one being the highest priority.

Table 19.3b Priority problems from the village participatory appraisals and community action plans – four focal areas, total score and number of focal areas mentioning problem

Issue	*Kawandola*	*Obago*	*Nyamaroka*	*Asao*	*Total score*	*Mentioned*
Food crop production and shortages					109[b]	9[c]
Food shortage		1[a]		4	44	4
Poor diets	5				7	1
Low crop yield	1		3		47	5
Inadequate knowledge of agriculture			2		11	1
Livestock diseases and production					94	9
Livestock diseases		5	8	8	49	8
Low milk yield	2		10	2	47	7
Human diseases and health care					92	9
HIV/AIDS/human diseases		2	4	5	77	9
Inadequate health facilities					6	1
Inadequate knowledge of human health					7	1
Lack of clean water			1	6	62	7
Lack of fuelwood and tree products	7	7	11	7	47	10
Soil degradation					45	5
Soil infertility					8	1
Soil erosion	4	4		1	37	4
Poor roads		3	12		39	7
Marketing					25	5
Problems with sugar cane marketing					13	2
Poor market for farm produce						1
No market for cotton and sisal	6	6			12	2
Insecurity						
Cattle theft			6		24	2
Low income			5		18	2
Flooding		4			15	2
Inadequate vegetables	3				14	2
and fruit					11	1
					8	1
Inadequate farm inputs					7	1
High illiteracy			7		5	1
Lack of credit facilities					4	1
Lack of employment		8			4	1
Inadequate farm labour					3	1
Traditional and cultural practices			9		3	1
Inadequate land preparation equipment					3	1
Mismanagement of community groups					2	1
Poor leadership					2	1

Source: focal area reports compiled by the Nyando District and division offices of the Ministry of Agriculture and Rural Development.

Notes

a The numbers in the columns indicate the priority that was established by the community through matrix prioritization, with one being highest priority.

b Total score is a weighted sum of the priorities across the ten focal areas, with number one priorities given a weight of 12, number two priorities given a weight of 11 and so on.

c Mentioned is the number of focal areas in which the issue was considered to be a priority.

Table 19.4 Issues and activities from the Nyando focal areas and comparison with national and Nyando District PRSP

PRA issues in FAs	*FADC actions*	*National PRSP matching objective*	*National PRSP action*	*Nyando PRSP issue*	*Nyando PRSP action*
Food crop production and shortages					
Food shortage	use certified seed, improve soil management, striga control, grow drought and water resistant crops, improve water management	enhance food security	food reserves, strengthen drought management and mitigation system	food shortage	technology, canal irrigation, subsidize inputs, develop industries, give cheap credit, subsidize development of fallow land
Poor diets	training in improved cookery				
Low crop yield	test and demonstrate improved soil management practices	improve crop development, improve market development, research and development	strengthen extension through public/private collaboration, provide modalities for credit provision, develop referral databank of best practices, introduce appropriate technologies, maintenance plans for sub-sectors, develop pro-poor technologies, strengthen research – extension linkages		

Livestock diseases and production					
Livestock diseases	training on livestock husbandry and livestock diseases, demonstrate safe use of chemicals	improve livestock development	develop community based animal health services, promote private insemination services	livestock diseases	subsidize improved breeds, subsidize disease control
Low milk yield	establish napier/ fodder bulking plots, bull scheme, fence plots	improve livestock development	privatize KMC, complete dairy development policy, develop specialized extension		
Human diseases and health care					
HIV/AIDS/human diseases	stop wife inheritance, testing for AIDS, promote abstinence, launch awareness campaign, supply condoms	combating the HIV/ AIDS scourge	blood screening, condom promotion, information and awareness campaign		information and awareness campaign
Inadequate health facilities				inadequate health care, poor sanitation and water supply	provide health care facilities
Inadequate knowledge of human health				lack of preventive health education	
Lack of clean water for domestic and livestock	spring protection, water pans, extend pipes, repair boreholes, rainwater harvesting	improve availability and management of rural water supplies	private GOK water supplies, transfer schemes to communities, extend one pipeline		
Inadequate fuel-wood and tree products	plant trees in woodlots, terraces, hedges, commercial tree farms, establish group and individual nurseries, demonstrate energy saving devices	increased forest and tree cover	strengthen forest regulations, strengthen community participation in forest management, promote agroforestry		

continued

Table 19.4 Continued

PRA issues in FAs	*FADC actions*	*National PRSP matching objective*	*National PRSP action*	*Nyando PRSP issue*	*Nyando PRSP action*
Soil degradation					
Soil infertility					
Soil erosion	spring protection, gulley rehabilitation, tree planting, water pans, construct terraces, fence eroded areas				
Poor roads	rehabilitate existing roads and paths, improve drainage from roads	improve road transport	upgrading and maintenance of trunk roads and feeder roads	poor roads	improve roads
Marketing					
Problems with sugar cane marketing	diversify away from sugar cane	improve market development, regulation and stabilization	marketing reforms, market Kenya products abroad, establish commodities exchange		
	mismanagement of sugar cane industry	refinance and revive sugar factories, private ownership of factories			
Poor market for farm produce				poor marketing, lack of small-scale industries	establish new industries, form cooperatives, revive rice and cotton factories

Source: focal area reports compiled by the Nyando District and division offices of the Ministry of Agriculture and Rural Development.

differences in the level of input into the processes were reflected in the quality and useful of the outputs.

Priority issues

The list of 108 national-level objectives included, in some form, all but one of the priority issues raised in the Nyando district focal areas. Low soil fertility was specifically mentioned in one focal area and soil erosion was mentioned in four focal areas, but was not mentioned in the national PRSP.

There was a surprising lack of correspondence between the Nyando district PRSP and the priorities from the ten focal areas. Four of the most important issues in the focal areas – high HIV/AIDS prevalence, shortage of clean water for domestic use and livestock, inadequate fuelwood and tree products, and soil erosion – were given very little attention in the Nyando district consultation. Neither the high prevalence of HIV/AIDS, nor the socio-cultural or demographic factors contributing to its high prevalence, are mentioned in the report of the Nyando district consultation. Only one of the ten proposed health actions relates specifically to HIV/AIDS. In contrast, the high prevalence of HIV/AIDS and other human diseases was mentioned as one of the top five priorities in eight of the ten focal areas, despite the fact that no public health or medical officer was involved in the PRA exercises. Lack of clean water for domestic use and livestock was mentioned as a priority problem in seven of the ten focal areas, and was the highest priority problem in two focal areas. The district consultation mentions lack of clean water as one of several human health problems and lack of irrigation canals and dams as one of many problems affecting agriculture. Lack of fuelwood was mentioned in all ten focal areas and soil erosion was mentioned in four focal areas, yet neither problem was mentioned in the district consultation (see Table 19.4).

Clarity of priorities and plans

Priorities are clearest at the village level, somewhat opaque at the national level, and missing at the district level.

Allocation of effort and resources

There are massive differences in allocation of resources in the national PRSP implementation framework and the village-level community action plans. Agriculture and livestock receive the greatest attention in the community action plans, but receive only 10 per cent of the resources in the PRSP implementation framework. Although water infrastructure was mentioned more frequently than transport infrastructure, it is allocated less than 1 per cent as much financial resources as roads in the PRSP implementation framework.

Responsibility for proposed actions

The implementation framework in the national PRSP describes activities that will be undertaken by the national government, the community action plans describe activities that will be undertaken by village residents and the extension staff of the Ministry of Agriculture and Rural Development, the district-level PRSP describes activities that ought to be undertaken by the national government to serve the needs of the district. There appear to be mismatches at all levels. First, I would have expected the national-level PRSP to include much more reference to the activities that would be devolved to the other levels of government. Full completion of activities by the central ministries, on their own, may in fact have little impact on the behaviour or welfare of the poor. The district-level PRSP shows a distinct lack of district-level planning and responsibility. Nowhere in the Nyando district document is there any mention of who might implement any proposed intervention or strategy. Indeed the district-level document implies that the problems can only be addressed through massive infusions of capital and recurrent subsidies into the district. In contrast, the focal area plans are very clear on the responsibilities of community residents and the MOARD staff, are very modest in terms of capital and financial puts, but are unclear on how issues outside of agriculture (e.g. greater awareness of HIV/AIDS problems) can be addressed.

Conclusions

The conclusions section contains two sub-sections of reflections on the Kenya PRSP document and process in light of the results presented above. The first sub-section draws conclusions on poverty planning in Kenya, with particular emphasis on the issues of poverty distribution, poverty dynamics, synergies, and levels in light of the analysis that was presented from Kenya. The second sub-section returns back to two propositions that were raised in the introduction regarding the need for community and regional level inputs into PRSP processes.

Reflections on poverty planning in Kenya

Kenya's PRSP process has been generally endorsed by the World Bank and IMF, criticized by some international observers, and given somewhat mixed reviews by local experts. The analysis in this paper suggests that the national-level PRSP process did reveal sector issues and priorities of relevance to village residents in one poor district in Western Kenya, but that many of the activities indicated in the implementation matrix would have relatively little relevance to those village residents. For example, the top six sets of issues from the village-level PRAs (agriculture, livestock, human health, water supply, fuelwood and tree products, soil degradation) together are allocated less than 20 per cent of the funds in the implementation framework.

Poverty distribution

The presentation of the Kenya PRSP national document imply that a blanket approach to poverty reduction will be taken throughout the country, while the district-level documents imply that each district will make a case for consideration by the central government. Little explicit recognition is given to the large regional differences that do exist across the country in severity of poverty, in resources available to individuals or communities to improve their livelihoods, or in public services currently available to rural and urban residents. Fortunately, improved data on the regional distribution of poverty across Kenya is now being made available through a collaborative project of the Central Bureau of Statistics, the International Livestock Research Institute, the World Bank and the Rockefeller Foundation. Hopefully these data will allow explicit targeting of poverty reduction programmes to the most needy.

Poverty dynamics

The priorities in the national PRSP reflect some consideration of the causes and effects of income and consumption poverty, although this does not carry through to the implementation matrix. The implementation matrix focuses almost exclusively on transportation infrastructure, whereas education comes out of the poverty assessment studies as one of the most important determinants of individual differences in poverty, while agriculture, health and water are identified as key priorities for communities in Nyando district.

Synergies

The national poverty reduction strategy for Kenya does provide some discussion of the importance of public investments that synergize private sector investments. No quantitative analysis is presented, however, of the mechanisms by which different types of public investments are expected to catalyze private or collective investments.

Levels

One of the most striking aspects of the PRSPs is the lack of attention to investments and the provision of public services at different social–spatial levels. The overwhelming impression that is given is that all poverty reduction programmes will be undertaken by the central government; indeed, Kenya has not yet implemented the type of decentralization or devolution that many other developing countries have implemented in the last ten years. Elected officials in rural Kenya – councillors at the county and municipal levels – still command less real power and resources than the appointed

District Commissioners. Nonetheless, there is a capacity in Kenya to implement decentralized poverty reduction through the district and division offices of the various line ministries. However, at least for Nyando district, the district poverty reduction strategy does not provide a credible basis for district-level implementation.

Using community-level data to guide decentralized poverty reduction strategies

This final sub-section of the chapter expounds upon the two propositions that I presented in the introduction. The first proposition is that community-level perspectives need to be incorporated more systematically into poverty reduction planning. I defend this proposition by reference to the theory and evidence on multi-level poverty traps: poverty in Kenya and elsewhere in the developing world varies from community to community and that variation is in part related to differences in assets with thresholds in their transformation into goods and services. I also defend this proposition by reference to the results from the participatory rural appraisals from Nyando district. Community-level priorities vary from community to community within Nyando district, with some consistent priorities (such as soil fertility, fuelwood shortages, water quality) barely mentioned in the national-level Poverty Reduction Strategy Paper.

The second related proposition is that priorities for poverty reduction programmes should be aggregated up from individual to community to region to nation, with the focus at each level being on the provision of public goods and services that impede progress at lower levels. I defend this proposition in three ways. First, I re-iterate the finding that poverty varies among individuals within households (e.g. gender and age biases), among households within communities, among communities within regions, and among regions within countries. Second, I note that some of the causes of rural poverty – poor education, small land holdings, small numbers of livestock – might be best addressed through interventions aimed at thresholds at multiple levels. Third, from the results presented in this chapter, I note that there are both differences and similarities in community level priorities in Nyando district – issues that are important in all villages provide a good basis for planning activities at the district level. Priorities that span across districts will in turn provide a good basis for planning activities across districts.

Notes

* The author acknowledges the research assistance of David Nyantika and Wilson Nindo, the Kenya Ministry of Agriculture and Rural Development staff who worked in the ten communities, and the participants in the ICRISAT/LADDER Conference on Rural Livelihoods and Poverty Reduction Policies, 13–14 January 2003, who provided many helpful and stimulating comments on a previous version of this chapter.

1 The millennium development goals can be found at: http://www.un.org/millenniumgoals/

2 See website: www.worldbank.org/poverty/strategies/overview.htm

3 See website: http://www.undp.org/hdr2003/indicator/cty_f_KEN.html

20 Predicting rural household poverty

Methodological issues and the PRSP process in Kenya*

Germano Mwabu, Mwangi S. Kimenyi, Paul K. Kimalu, Nancy Nafula and Damiano K. Manda

Overview

Since independence, the Kenyan government has had a stated goal of fighting illiteracy, disease and poverty in order to achieve sustainable national development. However in the last decade, the educational attainment, health and poverty status of Kenyans have shown declining trends. Rural poverty has worsened from an estimated 46.8 per cent in 1994 to 52.9 per cent in 1997 and is estimated at 59.6 per cent in 2000. The increase in poverty in the country is observed from the rising number of people without adequate food and nutrition, and inadequate access to basic necessities such as education, safe water and sanitation, employment, health facilities and decent housing.

National level household surveys provide data that is used for identifying and measuring poverty status. However, carrying out such surveys is relatively expensive. Thus it is important to make maximum use of available survey data when it has been collected. This chapter develops a simple method for using poverty indices derived from survey data for a given year to predict poverty rates in subsequent periods without having to conduct a new household survey. We illustrate the workings of the method with data from the Kenya Welfare Monitoring Surveys for 1994 and 1997. The methodology is thought to provide reasonable predictions of poverty in Kenya over the period analysed. The predictions are useful in monitoring changes in poverty over time. The success of the PRSP depends on a sound system for monitoring implementation of the strategies identified via the PRSP process and for evaluating the outcome of those strategies.

Introduction

Poverty in Africa is a rural phenomenon, a situation that is also true of other world regions (Bigsten 1986; Ravallion 1994; World Bank 2001a; International Fund for Agricultural Development 2001). Rural poverty accounts for a significant proportion of overall poverty in many countries. In sub-Saharan Africa, the challenge of poverty reduction is particularly daunting in rural areas, where the bulk of the population earns its livelihood from agriculture. At the close of the twentieth century, nearly a half of the population in sub-Saharan Africa – 320 million people – lived in absolute poverty (Fields 2000).

Poverty in rural areas is largely due to the depletion of assets upon which men and women rely as sources of their livelihood. In addition to income poverty, the rural population is vulnerable to natural disasters such as drought or flooding. The rural population is isolated from schools, clinics, extension services and markets. These factors act as catalysts that promote gradual exclusion of the poor from society and the broader economy. In addition there are large numbers of individuals who are landless and rely on seasonal and casual labour as their primary source of livelihood.

In Kenya, the incidence of poverty in rural areas is higher than in urban areas. However, it does not follow that urban poverty in Kenya is not a matter of concern. Urban poverty in Kenya has risen rapidly in recent years not only because of growth in urban population but also as a result of a worsening employment situation.

Available poverty estimates since the 1970s clearly point to a rapidly deteriorating poverty situation in the country, especially in the last two decades (see Table 20.1). Collier and Lal (1980) showed that in 1974 about 29 per

Table 20.1 Summary poverty estimates of past studies in Kenya

Author	*Reference year*	*Data source*	*Poverty incidence*
Collier and Lal (1980)	1974/1975	IRS I Smallholder	34.2% of smallholder population 29% for all population
Vandemoortele (1982)	1976	IRS I 1974/1975; Nairobi Household Budget Survey (1974); Social Accounting Matrix	33.1% of smallholder household
Greer and Thorbecke (1986)	1974/1975	IRS (1977)	38.6% of smallholders
World Bank (1991)	1981/1982	1981/1982 penal survey and complementary statistics	22% of rural population
World Bank (1995) and Mukui (1993)	1981/1982 1992	1981/1982 rural survey and 1992 WMS I	Rural: 48% for 1981/1982 and 46% for 1992
Kenya (1998a)	1994	1994 WMS I	46.8% rural population 40% national estimates
Mwabu *et al.* (2000)	1994	1994 WMS II	39.7% rural population 38.8% national estimates
Kenya (2000c)	1997	1997 WMS III	52.9% rural population 52.3% national estimates

Source: adapted from Kenya (1998b) and updated.

cent (4.2 million) of the total Kenyan population were poor (they used a poverty line of Kshs 2,000 per year for rural households and Kshs 2,150 per annum for urban households). The majority of the poor (about 60 per cent) were the smallholder population followed by pastoralists, the landless, squatters in large farms and migrant workers. According to the Government of Kenya (Kenya 1998a), the number of people below the poverty line had sharply increased to about 47 per cent (nine million) of the rural population in 1994. The total number of poor Kenyans has also been increasing over time, for example from 11.5 million in 1994 to 12.6 million in 1997.

There exist large disparities in rural poverty incidence in the country. Regional disparities in the incidence of rural poverty are strongly associated with rainfall and dependence on rainfed agriculture (Webb *et al.* 1991). In Kenya, poverty varies by province with the poorest provinces being north-eastern, western and the Rift Valley. In addition, very large proportions of the population in arid and semi-arid areas of the country like Marsabit, Turkana, Isiolo, Samburu and Tana River districts experience higher incidences of poverty than other areas of the country (Kenya 1998a).

Rural poverty is marked by its common connection to agriculture and land. The rural poor are more dependent on agriculture than the non-poor. Also, the few non-farm activities in rural areas derive their prosperity on forward and backward production linkages with agriculture. Thus, poverty in rural areas tends to be explained largely by low access to natural assets (particularly land), non-farm employment opportunities and health care and schooling, than by labour market distortions as in the urban sector (Manda *et al.* 2000).

Associated with the increased poverty is the decline in primary school enrolment and the deteriorating health status of Kenyans. For instance, the gross primary school enrolment declined from 92.2 per cent in 1990 to stand at 86.9 per cent in 1999. Between 1992 and 1999, the health status of Kenyans worsened. Infant and under-five mortality rates increased from 51 for every 1,000 children and 74 for every 1,000 children in 1992 to 74 and 112 per 1,000 children in 1998 respectively. Life expectancy, from the early 1990s, experienced a declining trend from 60 years in 1993 to 51 years in 1998. Female and male average years of living declined from 58.4 and 55.3 in 1992 to 51.9 and 50.2 in 1998 respectively. The declining health status is only partly due to HIV/AIDS. According to the National Aids and Sexually Transmitted Disease Control Program (NASCOP 2001), urban HIV/AIDS adult prevalence was 18.1 per cent in 2000 whilst rural adult prevalence was 12.5 per cent. According to the Economic Survey (Kenya 2002) the national HIV prevalence rate declined from 13.5 per cent in 2000 to 13.0 in 2001. By the early 1990s, 13 million Kenyans (about 50 per cent) had no access to safe water while six million had no access to sanitation (UNDP 1994).

The above poverty estimates have been compiled using surveys carried at different time periods. Identifying and measuring poverty requires data on economic conditions of households and individuals. Such data are typically gathered through household surveys. Household surveys collect data on demographics, incomes, expenditure and other characteristics such as area of residence and participation in the labour force. Thus, data from household surveys are suitable not only for identifying and aggregating poverty, but also for constructing poverty profiles. A poverty profile shows how aggregate poverty indices differ according to various household characteristics (Foster *et al.* 1984).

Household surveys have two shortcomings, however: first, they require considerable expertise to conduct, and, second, they involve large expenditures in collecting and analysing data. For these reasons, household surveys are conducted only occasionally. Moreover, there is usually a long time interval between one survey and the next, except when the survey is designed to collect panel data. As a consequence, household surveys cannot be used to construct annual or high frequency poverty indices or profiles. Yet, such indices and profiles are key in evaluating the effectiveness of poverty reduction strategies. Indeed, the performance of these strategies cannot be monitored and evaluated without *periodic* information on changes in poverty indices and profiles.

Poverty Reduction Strategy Papers (PRSPs) have become a requirement for foreign assistance to low-income developing countries (Kenya 2000a), and many countries have invested substantial resources in preparing them. Moreover, substantial resources are required for investments in programmes to achieve the poverty reduction objectives of the strategy papers. There is need, therefore, to develop a workable method for predicting poverty rates for periods covered by PRSPs so that the effects of poverty reduction policies can be monitored and evaluated. Fortunately, it is possible to develop a simple statistical method for predicting poverty rates on the basis of rates computed from a reference household survey data.

It is necessary to start by indicating why there is a need to predict poverty. First, predicting poverty helps to monitor the performance of national poverty reduction strategies. Second, to assess the effectiveness of an antipoverty programme over a given period, the government must have information on poverty rates for the start and end of the programme. Third, for active programmes, the government needs information on the poverty status of the population over at least two time periods covered by the programme. Key to the evaluation exercise is information on the poverty status at a reference time period and at a later date. If such programmes or reforms are considered to be the main factors influencing poverty, the task of the evaluation is to determine the extent of poverty reduction following the implementation of the antipoverty programme.

The rest of this discussion outlines a methodology for determining poverty rates at a reference and subsequent periods and shows how the information obtained can be used to assess the effectiveness of antipoverty programmes.

The PRSP process

In 1963, the Kenyan government identified illiteracy, disease, ignorance and poverty as the main problems to be addressed in order to achieve sustainable national development. The government has tried to address the above problems through National Development Plans, Sessional Papers, Presidential Commissions and Task Forces among others. The first three post-independence decades saw modest improvement in some social and economic indicators such as health status and educational attainment. However, in the last decade, educational attainment, health and poverty status of Kenyans have shown a declining trend thus necessitating the preparation of the Poverty Reduction Strategy Paper (PRSP).

In December 1999, the Boards of the World Bank and the IMF approved the PRSP approach to reduction of poverty in low-income countries. Poverty Reduction Strategies are said to be country driven, participatory and results-oriented. The process of developing PRSPs places countries themselves in the lead in terms of devising and driving their own development strategies and agenda. A PRSP is a description of a country's macro, social and other policies and programmes designed to promote growth and reduce poverty. Thus a PRSP is an outcome of a broad-based consultative process between governments and stakeholders in society and serve as the main framework for donor assistance. Due to this, the preparation of the PRSP has been on the agenda of all low-income African countries including Kenya.

Kenya's PRSP document was prepared with multiple objectives directed towards reducing poverty and increasing economic growth. The PRSP process was expected to ensure country ownership of poverty reduction strategies and to develop comprehensive strategies to fight poverty. The specific objectives of the PRSP include linking policy, planning and budgeting; identifying national development objectives and priorities; improving the quality of expenditures and thus leading to efficiency gains; harmonisation of development financing frameworks; and monitoring and evaluation of poverty reduction programmes (Kiringai and Manda 2002).

The PRSP is linked to the long-term vision outlined in the National Poverty Eradication Plan (NPEP) which proposes a fifteen-year time horizon to fight poverty and has adopted the UN Millennium Development Goals, which aim at reducing global poverty by half by 2015. The National Poverty Eradication Plan (NPEP) describes the extent of poverty and sets poverty reduction targets. On the other hand, the PRSP is a short-term strategy, which seeks to implement the NPEP in a series of three-year plans. The Medium Term Expenditure Framework (MTEF) is linked to the PRSP by providing budgetary allocations to specific measures set out in the PRSP.

The strategy paper has detailed poverty analysis, containing the extent and magnitude of poverty, the nature and characteristics of the poor and determinants of poverty. There is also poverty analysis by region. The PRSP compares poverty levels over time especially for the 1990s and uses both the

1994 and 1997 Welfare Monitoring Surveys (WMS) data to analyse poverty levels and variations across regions.

The PRSP contains short-term and long-term targets for economic growth, poverty reduction and improvement in education and health outcomes. The PRSP targets have some appropriate links with the Millennium Development Goals (MDGs). Some of the targets include universal primary education, provision of two million textbooks annually, expansion of the bursary scheme with improved targeting and 2 per cent annual reduction of school dropouts. Further decentralisation of health services, reduction of HIV prevalence and reduction of infant and child mortality rates are some of the health targets in the PRSP. In the agricultural sector a long-term annual growth rate of up to 6 per cent is targeted to contribute to positive national growth and poverty reduction. Maintenance, and rehabilitation of the existing infrastructural facilities, and providing necessary infrastructure to areas that are disadvantaged are priorities in the paper.

The success of the PRSP will greatly depend on a sound and systematic monitoring and evaluation system that ensures that strategies and priorities identified are efficiently implemented so as to achieve the desired outcomes. The monitoring and evaluation system should provide a continuous tracking and feedback mechanisms to all stakeholders in the process especially the poor themselves. A poverty monitoring system is needed to track key indicators over time and space and assess changes as a result of the strategy. The tracking of public expenditures and outputs and quick monitoring of the household well-being need special attention. We develop a methodology of measuring rural poverty in the next sections of this chapter.

Problem and methodology

The problem is how to compute the poverty rates for years t and t + j, given that household survey data are available for only year t − j (note that for year t, the present period, j = 0). This is the problem that the policy makers in Kenya faced in preparing the Poverty Reduction Strategy Paper (PRSP) in the late 1990s. The PRSP process entails an assessment and discussion of the *baseline* poverty rates so that these rates can be compared with the poverty rates at some point in the future when effects of the poverty reduction programme are to be evaluated. However, the baseline poverty rates were not available. Furthermore, it was not clear to the government how the poverty rate for the end date (the evaluation date) would be obtained. To concretise the problem, suppose that the government wants to establish the poverty rates for 2000 (the implementation date of pro-poor reforms) and 2004 (the year when the performance of the reforms is evaluated). How should the government proceed? The magnitudes of the poverty rates for 2000 and 2004 are easy to establish, at least in theory. If the government has the required expertise and resources, it can conduct household surveys in 2000 and 2004 and compute the poverty rates for these years. However, if the government does not have the resources to mount the surveys, then this option is not available. The following demonstration will show how this problem can be resolved.

The method we develop is based on the idea that changes in poverty over time and space are determined mainly by changes in economic growth and distribution of income (see for example, Ravallion (1994), Ali and Thorbecke (2000), Oyugi *et al.* (2000)). As economic growth increases, poverty decreases, and as inequality worsens, poverty increases. Formally, this idea can be expressed as:

$$\text{Poverty rate for year } j = \alpha + \beta \text{ (GDP growth)} + \delta \text{ (Gini coefficient)} + \epsilon_j \quad \text{(1a)}$$

Where β and δ are the effects of growth and distribution, respectively, on poverty for year j; α is a constant term; and ϵ is the error term, which has a mathematical expectation of zero.

Note from equation (1a) that to compute the poverty rate for year j, information is needed on the GDP growth rate and the Gini coefficient for that year. Given the preceding information, and noting that α is a constant, the change in poverty rate from one year to the next can be stated as:

$$\Delta \text{ (Poverty rate)} = \beta\Delta \text{ (GDP growth)} + \delta\Delta \text{ (Gini coefficient)} \quad \text{(1b)}$$

Once the change (Δ) in poverty for adjacent periods has been computed, the poverty rate for the terminal period can be obtained by updating the base year figure (the poverty rate for the previous year) using a simple equation:

$$\text{Poverty rate for year } j = \text{poverty rate year } j - 1 + (\text{poverty year } j - \text{poverty year } j - 1) \quad \text{(2)}$$

From equations (1a), (1b) and (2) we have

$$\text{Poverty year } j - \text{poverty year } j - 1 = \beta\Delta \text{ (GDP growth)} + \delta\Delta \text{ (Gini coefficient)} \quad \text{(3)}$$

To apply equation (3), information is needed on the values for coefficients α, β and δ, GDP growth rates, and income distribution (see equation (1a)).

Obtaining data on the values for α, β and δ for a given country is not an easy matter, and there are two ways of doing this. The first method involves estimating regression coefficients for equation (1a) using time series data for the country. However, this approach is unfeasible, because data on annual poverty rates are not available. The second approach, which is used here, involves borrowing the values for α, β and δ from cross-country poverty regressions for sub-Saharan Africa. For Kenya, we borrowed these values from results of poverty regressions in Ali and Thorbecke (2000), who estimated equation (1a) for a sample of sub-Saharan African countries, including Kenya (Appendix Table 20.1). Equation (1a) shows that the average values for α, β and δ are the same for all the sample countries. That is, the effect of growth on poverty, for example, is the same for each country in the sample.

We make a strong assumption that the estimated coefficients apply outside the sample period. The sample data used by Ali and Thorbecke (2000) were collected during the early 1990s. We assume that the parameters for α, β and δ obtained with these data are relevant for the early years of the twenty-first century (that is, 2000–2005). Since the elasticities of poverty with respect to GDP growth and income distribution appear to be of the same order of magnitude across regions of the same country (Mwabu *et al.* 2000) and across different countries (Ravallion 1994), the constancy assumption we make with respect to α, β and δ is reasonable.

The data on GDP growth and income distribution were obtained from government documents and published literature (Kenya 1998c, 2000a). As already noted, we used the Gini coefficient as a measure of income distribution. Since income distribution change over time is very slow, it is reasonable, in the absence of annual data, to assume that a given Gini coefficient is valid for several years. Data on GDP growth rates are easily available from government documents. In Kenya, this information is available in the government's *Economic Survey* published by the Central Bureau of Statistics of the Ministry of Planning and National Development, and the *Statistical Abstract* and the *Development Plan*, also published by the same ministry. Another reliable source of such data on Kenya is the Central Bank of Kenya, which predicts short-term growth rates of the economy fairly accurately. We used the GDP growth rates provided by the Central Bank of Kenya in its quarterly *Statistical Bulletin*.

To provide a concrete illustration of the application of equation (2) in the Kenyan context, we use poverty rates obtained using the 1997 household survey (the most recent survey) to calculate the poverty rates for 2000. Poverty values for 1997 are updated to 2000 values using the formula:

$$\text{Poverty\_2000R}_i = \text{Poverty\_1997R}_i{}^*(1 + \tau_i) \tag{4a}$$

$$\text{Poverty\_2000R}_i = \text{Poverty\_1997R}_i + \Psi_I \tag{4b}$$

where Poverty_2000R_i is the head-count index for region i (province or district) in 2000; Poverty_1997R_i is the head-count index for region i (province or district) in 1997; τ_i is the percentage change in the poverty index for region i (nation, province or district) over the period 1997–2000; and Ψ is the level of change in the poverty index for region i (nation or rural area).

Equation (4a) was used to obtain head-count poverty indices for provinces and districts, while (4b) was used to obtain national and rural indices. Equations (4a) and (4b) differ in the following respects. In (4b), Ψ is the level change in the poverty index as indicated in equation (3). Ψ can be computed uniquely for each region (national or rural area), because, according to equation (1a), different values for α, β and δ are available for all these areas. In Ali and Thorbecke's (2000) regressions for sub-Saharan Africa (from which we borrowed the coefficients), equation (1a) was separately run for urban and rural areas. National-level values for α, β and δ were computed as simple averages of these same parameters for urban and rural areas. For example, if we let 'n = nation', 'r = rural' and 'u = urban', then $\beta_n = (\beta_r + \beta_u)/2$; and similarly for the other parameters.

Equation (4a) was used to obtain poverty indices for provinces and districts. The rural values for α, β and δ were used to compute poverty indices for provinces and districts, that is, all provinces and districts had the same values for α, β and δ. This was so because there were no coefficients to borrow for provinces and districts.

The term τ in equation (4a) is the percentage change in the rural poverty index over the 1997–2000 period. This change is assumed to apply to all rural provinces and districts. However, since the base poverty indices for provinces and districts differ, *the percentage changes* in *base* poverty indices over a specified time period (for example, 1997–2000) also will differ, except where the bases happen to be the same. The provincial and district base poverty rates were adjusted assuming that each rate changed by a percentage, τ, over the period 1997–2000.

From the above discussion, if rural poverty increased by 20 percentage points, for example from 50 per cent in 1997 to 70 per cent in 2000, it would be not be correct to adjust provincial and district poverty rates by adding 20 per cent to the 1997 poverty rates. The correct procedure involves setting τ to 40 per cent (20/50*100), and then using equation (4a) to adjust the base poverty rate. It is easily checked that the resultant level changes in provincial and district poverty rates *do* differ despite the uniform τ. This is because the poverty indices change from different bases.

Data and results

Poverty estimates for 2000 were obtained by adjusting 1997 estimates using the methodology described above. We used growth in GDP as a proxy of economic growth. The Kenyan economy has been declining since 1995. In 1997, the growth rate was 2.4 per cent, but it declined to -0.3 per cent in 2000 (Table 20.2). The Gini coefficient increased from 0.445 in 1994 to 0.57 in 1997 (UNDP 1999). The coefficients borrowed for the growth and distribution in equation (1a) are provided in Appendix Table 20.1.

The information presented in Table 20.2 and the regression coefficients in Appendix Table 20.1 were used along with equations (1–4) to obtain poverty estimates for 2000 (Kimalu *et al.* 2001).

Our estimates show that the national head-count index increased from 52.3 per cent in 1997 to 56.8 per cent in 2000. This can partly be attributed to the decline in economic growth and to a worsening in income distribution

Table 20.2 GDP growth rates and Gini coefficients for Kenya

Year	*GDP growth rate (%)*	*Gini coefficient estimates*
1997	2.4	0.570
1998	1.8	0.612*
1999	1.4	0.653*
2000	−0.3	0.695*

Source: Kenya (2000a), Kenya (1998b), World Bank (2000a).

Note

*Predicted values of Gini coefficient.

over the period analysed. During the same period, rural poverty increased by 6.63 percentage points, from 52.9 per cent to 59.6 per cent. Table 20.3 shows the changes in poverty measures over 1997–2000.

The results show great regional variation in poverty rates. North-eastern was the poorest province, with 73.1 per cent of its rural population living below the poverty line. At 35.3 per cent, central province's poverty rate was the lowest. The poverty rate for north-eastern province for 2000 was estimated from the predicted 1997 poverty rate, as the province was not covered in the 1997 survey.

To check whether the predicted poverty rates for 2000 (based on the 1997 survey) are reasonable, we use the same methodology to predict poverty rates for 1997 based on the 1994 survey. In this case, the poverty rates data for 1994 and 1997 are obtained from the Central Bureau of Statistics (Kenya 1998a, 2000a). Thus, it is possible to check whether the *predicted* values for 1997 (based on the 1994 survey) are close enough to the *actual* values. If they are close, it means that our methodology had a high degree of accuracy in predicting poverty rates for 1997 based on the poverty rates computed using the 1994 survey. A correspondence of the predicted and the actual poverty indices for 1997 would provide support for the reliability of the poverty rates predicted for 2000 using poverty rates for 1997 (Table 20.4). Table 20.4

Table 20.3 Rural head-count poverty indices, 1997–2000

Region	*1997 (actual poverty indices)*	*2000 (predicted poverty indices)*
Central	31.39	35.32
Coast	62.10	69.88
Eastern	58.56	65.90
North-eastern	65.48	73.06
Nyanza	63.05	70.95
Rift Valley	50.10	56.38
Western	58.75	66.11
Rural	52.93	59.56
National	52.32	56.78

Source: Kenya (2000c) and own predictions using data for 1997.

Table 20.4 Rural head-count poverty indices by province, 1994–1997

Province or region	*1994 (actual poverty indices)*	*1997 (actual poverty rates)*	*1997 (predicted poverty rates)*
Central	31.93	31.39	35.74
Coast	55.63	62.10	62.27
Eastern	57.75	58.56	64.64
North-eastern	58.00	Na	64.92
Nyanza	42.21	63.05	47.25
Rift Valley	42.87	50.10	47.99
Western	53.83	58.75	60.25
Rural	46.75	52.93	52.33
National	43.84	52.32	47.52

Source: Kenya (1998a, 2000c) and own predictions using data for 1994.

shows that in most cases the predicted and the actual values for 1997 are very close.

Column two and three of Table 20.4 shows that most of the predicted poverty rates mimic actual rates quite closely. For example, the predicted poverty rate for the coast province is 62.3 per cent, while the actual rate is 62.1 per cent. Similarly, the predicted rates for central, eastern, Rift Valley and western provinces are not far from the actual rates, and the 1997 estimate for rural poverty is 52.3 per cent, compared with the actual rate of 52.9 per cent.

An anomaly exists only with regard to the predicted and the actual rates for Nyanza province. The actual poverty rate for Nyanza in 1997 is 63.1 per cent, whereas the predicted rate is about 47.3 per cent, which compares favourably with 42.2 per cent, the actual poverty rate for 1994. If the 1994 poverty rate for Nyanza was actually 42.2 per cent, it is unlikely that it had increased to 63.1 per cent by 1997. It appears that the actual poverty rate for 1997 was not calculated correctly or that there were changes in data coverage. We can conclude that the methodology we have developed predicts poverty quite accurately; however, it works better when prediction is done within short time intervals (Kimalu *et al.* 2001), as the further away the evaluation date is from the reference household survey date, the less precise the poverty estimates for that date become.

Appendix Table 20.2 reports poverty predictions for provinces and districts. Kiambu district had the lowest poverty rate in 2000 with only 28.2 per cent of its population living below the poverty line. Homa Bay district had the highest poverty rate (87.2 per cent), followed by Mandera district (85.7 per cent).

Table 20.5 presents poverty profiles by social group. Estimates for 2000 were projected using 1997 poverty profiles (Kenya 2000c). As expected, all social groups experienced deterioration in well-being between 1997 and 2000.

Table 20.5 Rural poverty head-count indices by social characteristics, 1997–2000

Social characteristics	*1997 (actual poverty rates)*	*2000 (predicted poverty rates)*
Household head		
Male	52.50	59.08
Female	54.10	60.88
Marital status		
Male married	52.70	59.31
Male other	48.40	54.47
Female married	52.30	58.86
Female other	56.10	63.13
Education		
None	64.00	72.02
Primary	53.60	60.32
Secondary	33.40	37.59
Higher (form 5–university)	6.80	7.65
Higher (technical)	38.90	43.78
Household size		
1–3 persons	35.50	39.95
4–6 persons	49.60	55.82
7 persons plus	61.70	69.43
Age group of head		
15–29	37.90	42.65
30–44	49.10	55.25
45–55	58.10	65.38
56 plus	57.70	64.93

Source: Kenya (2000c) and own predictions using data for 1997.

Education emerges as the most important determinant in poverty. In 2000, poverty rates among household heads without education were 72 per cent in rural areas, which were the highest among all groups. This is a clear indication of the inverse relationship between poverty and education level. Moreover, the people with at least secondary-level of education were less affected by the increase in poverty between 1997 and 2000 than those with lower levels of schooling.

On average, women are the hardest hit by poverty, and female-headed households have the highest poverty rates in rural areas (Table 20.5). One of the explanations for this is that female household heads (single, separated, divorced or widowed), especially in rural areas, are largely responsible for the upkeep of families, without much support from absent husbands (Table 20.5). However, the rate of increase in poverty is the same for men and women.

Household-size data were grouped into three categories for ease of analysis. The results in Table 20.5 indicate that households with seven or more members were the poorest. These households had poverty rates of 69.4 per cent in 2000. Households with four to six members had average poverty rates of 55.8 per cent in rural areas.

The data for 2000 show that in rural areas, poverty levels increase with age with the age group 45–55 years having the highest level of poverty. The older groups had higher increases in poverty levels than the younger groups.

Conclusion

This chapter has developed a methodology for updating poverty rates based on the most recent household survey. In particular, we have demonstrated that poverty rates from the most recent household survey can be used to predict rural poverty rates for subsequent years using information external to the survey. Using the poverty rates from the 1997 Kenya household survey, we have predicted the poverty rates for 2000 and shown how these rates vary by region and by social characteristics of households.

The novelty of our approach is that no additional household data are required for the predictions, as the predictions can be made for any year after 1997, provided that information is available on growth rates and income distribution. Since growth rate data are easily available from routine predictions of government planning units, our methodology can be used to assess the effects of antipoverty programmes. For example, if antipoverty programmes are expected to improve growth and income distribution by certain magnitudes over the subsequent years, our methodology would assess the poverty reduction effects of such policies without the necessity for a household survey. That is why this methodology is a convenient and important tool for monitoring and evaluating the success of such programmes.

Appendix

Table A20.1 Sensitivity of rural poverty to growth and distribution, in sub-Saharan Africa, 1990s

Dependent variable	*Constant*	*Log income*	*Log Gini coefficient*	R^2
Log head-count ratio	5.2175 (14.33)	−0.5028 (−10.75)	0.4792 (7.61)	0.93
Log poverty-gap ratio	2.5105 (4.6)	−0.7648 (10.92)	1.3801 (14.63)	0.96
Log squared poverty gap ratio	0.2894 (0.35)	−0.9585 (−9.0)	2.1116 (14.72)	0.96

Source: Ali and Thorbecke (2000).

Table A20.2 Kenya: poverty rates by province and district, 1997–2000

Region	*1997 (actual poverty rates)*	*2000 (predicted poverty rates)*
Central (rural)	31.39	35.32
Kiambu	25.08	28.22
Kirinyaga	35.70	40.18
Muranga	38.62	43.46
Nyandarua	26.95	30.33
Nyeri	31.05	34.94
Coast (rural)	62.10	69.88
Kilifi	66.30	74.61
Kwale	60.55	68.14
Lamu	39.35	44.28
Taita-Taveta	65.82	74.07
Tana River	34.22	38.51
Eastern (rural)	58.56	65.90
Mbeere	51.36	57.80
Embu	55.76	62.75
Isiolo	–	–
Kitui	64.91	73.05
Machakos	62.96	70.85
Marsabit	–	–
Meru	40.96	46.09
Makueni	73.51	82.72
Tharaka Nithi	55.58	62.55
Nyambene	47.29	53.22
North-eastern (rural)	65.48*	73.06
Garissa	54.43*	60.73
Mandera	76.81*	85.69
Wajir	64.40*	71.85
Nyanza (rural)	63.05	70.95
Kisii	57.22	64.39
Kisumu	65.44	73.64
Siaya	58.02	65.29
Homa Bay	77.49	87.20
Migori	57.63	64.85
Nyamira	66.74	75.11
Rift Valley (rural)	50.10	56.38
Kajiado	27.87	31.36
Kericho	52.42	58.99
Laikipia	33.88	38.13
Nakuru	45.08	50.73
Nandi	64.15	72.19
Narok	52.17	58.71
Bomet	61.80	69.55
Transmara	56.59	63.68
Baringo	36.95	41.58
Elgeyo Marakwet	47.82	53.81
Samburu	–	–
Trans Nzoia	54.83	61.70
Turkana	–	–

continued

Table A20.2 Continued

Region	*1997 (actual poverty rates)*	*2000 (predicted poverty rates)*
Uasin Gishu	42.22	47.51
West Pokot	68.46	77.04
Western (rural)	58.75	66.11
Bungoma	55.21	62.13
Busia	65.99	74.26
Kakamega	56.69	63.80
Vihiga	61.97	69.74
Total rural	52.93	59.56
National	52.32	56.78

Source: Kenya (2000c) and own predictions using data for 1997.

Note
*Predicted values.

Note

* This chapter was first presented as a paper at the LADDER Conference on Rural Livelihoods and Poverty Reduction held in Nairobi 13–14 January 2003 and has benefited from comments by participants at that conference.

21 Economic reform and rural livelihood diversification

Case studies from Malawi, Tanzania and Uganda*

Kunal Sen

Introduction

This chapter examines the outcomes of economic reform processes in the three sub-Saharan African countries of Malawi, Tanzania and Uganda, in terms of their impacts on micro-level livelihoods in rural areas. Economic reform refers here to the structural adjustment programmes that were in place in all three countries from the early to mid-1980s until the late 1990s when they were replaced by Poverty Reduction Strategy Papers (PRSPs). More specifically, it refers to the economic disciplines imposed on countries by SAPs, exemplified by strict monetary policies, controls over government expenditures, market-determined exchange rates and liberalised markets.

Economic reforms are fundamentally macro in character, and relatively little work has been done on linking them to micro level outcomes. Yet these macro–micro links, even if kept solely in the economic sphere, should be of great interest to policy makers concerned with formulating and implementing poverty reduction policies. As discussed by Bryceson in Chapter 4 of this book, it is possible that rather than boost productivity, employment and incomes in agriculture, economic reform has instead produced micro-level conditions and signals that have led to increasing livelihood diversification in rural areas as families struggle to combine stagnant and declining agricultural prospects with growing reliance on non-farm activities in trading and services. If this is indeed the case, and a lot of evidence suggests that it is so, then one of the fundamental original goals of reform was never realised, and understanding the reasons for this is important for future approaches to poverty reduction.

Macro–micro linkages in the economic sphere can occur in three main ways. Firstly, inflation is a macroeconomic outcome (principally determined by excess money supply growth and cost-push factors such as the price of oil). Yet high rates of inflation tend to lead to high variability in relative prices, creating a more risky environment for farmers to engage in agricultural and non-agricultural activities. A second macro–micro linkage is via the real exchange rate. Changes in the real exchange rate influences the relative profitability of tradeable activities (agriculture, industry) relative to the non-tradeable sector (construction, retail trade). A depreciation of the real exchange rate can provide an incentive to farmers to engage in export agriculture, by far the most important exporting sector in the sub-Saharan African context. The final macro–micro linkage is the rural–urban terms of trade (the price of agricultural products relative to the price of manufacturing products) which influences the relative profitability of agricultural activities relative to non-agricultural activities. An increase in the terms of trade will increase the returns to farming and increase the incentive for farmers to invest in agricultural activities.

The rest of the chapter has four sections. The next section provides an overview of the key elements of economic reform as applied in the three countries. This is followed by a look at macro-level outcomes, in terms of GDP growth, the sectoral distribution of GDP and agricultural production. The fourth section traces macro–micro linkages with respect to inflation, the exchange rate and the rural–urban terms of trade. The final section synthesises what one has learned from the case studies with respect to the effects of economic reforms on rural livelihoods in the three countries.

An overview of the economic reform process in Malawi, Tanzania and Uganda

Malawi

Since independence in 1964 to the late 1970s, Malawi was one of the strongest economic performers in sub-Saharan Africa. During this period, economic growth was largely driven by an export-oriented agricultural sector, as Malawi exploited its comparative advantage in agriculture, particularly in cash crops such as tobacco and tea (Sahn and Arulpragasam 1994). At the same time, the economic development strategy was based on the promotion of large-scale commercial agriculture by the state in the estate sector. Much of the resources that were needed to finance the expansion of the estate sector were extracted from the smallholder agriculture sector via implicit taxation of food crops (Kydd and Christiansen 1982). Thus, peasant households, the bulk of the population, shared little in the economic gains experienced by the Malawian economy in the 1960s and 1970s.

The fragility of the development strategy was exposed when the economy was buffeted by external shocks in the late 1970s. Following the second oil shock, the external terms of trade deteriorated sharply, and by 1980 it was less than 0.56 per cent of its 1970 level (Sahn and Arulpragasam *op cit.*). Along with this came an influx of refugees from war-torn Mozambique and the cutting off of Malawi's transport corridor to the Indian ocean. Finally, the drought of 1980/1981 severely impacted on agricultural production.

In response to the deteriorating macroeconomic situation, the government of Malawi began an adjustment programme late in 1979, with support from the IMF. Structural adjustment programmes continued through the 1980s and 1990s, supported by successive IMF stand-by operations and World Bank structural and sector adjustment loans. More recent developments along these lines have been the adoption by the government of Malawi of the Poverty Reduction and Growth Facilities (PRGF), sponsored by the IMF.

The main focus of the economic reform programme in the 1990s was to redress the policy bias against the smallholder agriculture sector that was evident in the previous three decades. Thus, the agriculture sector adjustment loan approved in 1990 included agreements to legalise the production of burley tobacco on a limited scale by smallholder farmers and to discourage the transfer of the land from the latter to the estate sector. More such policy reforms were adopted later in the 1990s including the decontrol of the prices of many crops grown by smallholder agriculturists in 1992–1993, and the liberalisation of the import and domestic distribution of fertilisers and the production and marketing of hybrid maize seeds in 1993–1994 (fertiliser subsidies were phased out much earlier beginning in 1985–1986). A more detailed account of the policy reforms undertaken in Malawi during this period is provided in the Appendix to Sen and Chinkunda (2002).

Tanzania

Since the Arusha Declaration in 1967 till the beginning of the reform process in 1986, Tanzania followed a development strategy based on the principles of socialism and self-reliance involving state intervention in almost all areas of economic activity. In the rural economy, beginning in 1973, the Tanzanian government set up a system of crop-specific parastatal authorities who were responsible for the collection of crops from villages, transport, storage, further processing and final sale either to domestic consumers or export markets. Along with this centralised procurement system, the government implemented a single pan-territorial producer price for each crop, to be determined annually by the Economic Committee of the Cabinet. In the period from 1967, many large private businesses were nationalised, including bank, insurance companies, plantations, estates, importers/exporters and food processors. The major milling companies were nationalised and merged to form the National Milling Corporation. Finally, to facilitate cooperative agricultural production and the delivery of social services, the villagisation campaign was launched in 1973, and within four years, millions of farmers were relocated.

The parastatal agricultural marketing system was highly inefficient and the steeply rising cost of operation had to be supported by both a substantial transfer of resources from small-holder agriculture (by a continuous decline in the producer share of crop value from 66.4 per cent in 1970 to 41.6 per cent in 1980 (Ellis 1983) and by very substantial borrowing from the commercial banking system, leading to growing fiscal deficits and the emergence of inflation. In the 1970s, the persistent deterioration in the real returns to agricultural production (due to the declining producer share of sales value and a steady fall in terms of trade for the rural economy) led to stagnation in marketed output, and a long-term decline in export crops production in particular (Ellis 1988). The bias against export crops inherent in the parastatal marketing system and in the pan-territorial pricing policy was compounded by a real overvaluation of the Tanzanian shilling occurring since the late 1970s.

By the mid-1980s, it was apparent that the centralised marketing and pricing regime in the agricultural sector was unsustainable (see Bigsten *et al.* 2000 and Sarris and Van den Brink 1994 for further details on the economic crisis facing the Tanzania state in the 1980s), and the government initiated a series of deregulation measures, with the adoption of the three-year Economic Recovery Program in 1986, supported by the IMF and the World Bank, and other international donors. Domestic food markets were liberalised first, and between 1986–1989, private trade in food crops was initiated, starting with minor crops and eventually including maize and rice. Controls on the movement of food crops were also abolished in 1987. By 1989, the pan-territorial pricing policy was effectively abandoned, and the National Milling Corporation was re-organised to work along the lines of a Strategic Grains Reserve to cover emergency food needs. There was a major devaluation in 1984, followed by another major devaluation in 1986. Liberalisation of the marketing of agricultural inputs was initiated in 1992, and subsidies on fertilisers were gradually reduced over the first few years of the 1990s, reaching zero in 1994. With respect to export crops, export taxes were gradually lifted, beginning with coffee and cotton in 1981. In 1993, private traders were allowed to buy, process and export coffee, cotton, tobacco and cashewnut, and private traders were legally operating in the coffee and cotton sectors in 1994–1995, and in the tobacco sector the following year. Finally, crop authorities were restructured as crop boards, responsible for regulation, research and information services.

Uganda

The economic reform programme initiated in 1987 was one of the most ambitious programmes of economic liberalisation in the African continent (Collier and Reinikka 2001). The National Resistance Movement (NRM) government attempted a comprehensive program of trade liberalisation, the main elements of which were the granting of the retention of 100 per cent of foreign exchange export earnings to exporters, the liberalisation of exports and imports procedures by the establishment of export and import certificate systems, the abolition of an export tax on coffee, and the liberalisation of the Balance of Payments Current Account. In mid-1990s, these measures were followed by the reduction of import tariff, which declined from 34 per cent in 1994 to 15 per cent in 1999. There also was a reduction in the dispersion of tariffs as measured by the standard deviation from 47 per cent to 23 per cent during the same period (Short 2000). With respect to exchange rate reform, there was a devaluation of the shilling in 1997 by 77 per cent, followed by two more rounds of devaluation in 1988 (60 per cent) and 1989 (17.5 per cent), and the legalisation of the parallel foreign exchange market in July 1990 and liberalisation of the foreign exchange market in the same year.

Agricultural liberalisation has mainly consisted of the liberalisation of the marketing of cash and non-cash crops by breaking up the marketing boards, the deregulation of the prices paid to farmers for their produce including cash crops, and the liberalisation of agricultural input prices. With respect to the dismantling of the marketing boards, the most significant policy initiative in this area has been the conversion of the Coffee Marketing Board to a publicly owned corporation in 1991–1992, with regulatory and quality issues assigned to the newly created Uganda Coffee Development Authority (UCDA). This was followed by the dismantling of the Lint Marketing Board – the marketing board for cotton – in 1994, and the setting up of an independent cotton promoting agency – the Cotton Development Organisation (CDO) – in 1995. Other measures taken were the transfer of crop financing responsibilities from the Bank of Uganda to commercial banks and the deregulation of the mode of transportation of cash crops, which was previously monopolised by the state-owned railways. Within a relatively short period of about fifteen years, Uganda has implemented a wide-ranging and comprehensive set of reforms, and at the same time, maintained a high degree of 'ownership' over its reforms (Holmgren *et al.* 1999; Dijkstra and Van Donge 2001).

The evolution of the macro economy

In this section, we present macro-level evidence on the impact of economic reforms on the agricultural sectors of the three sample countries. The analysis here is subject to several caveats. First, macro-level data may not be representative of the livelihood strategies of many households, given the heterogeneity one observes at the micro-level. Second, much of the macro-level data is heavily biased towards agricultural production data, and there is little information available at the economy-wide level of off-farm and nonfarm income sources. Third, macro-level data is obtained from country statistical offices, and one is aware of the limitations of such data, especially those drawn from agricultural censuses. Notwithstanding these caveats, the macro-level data may highlight broad trends evident in the rural economy in the country in question, and offer insights on why we seem to see differing outcomes with respect to poverty reduction among the countries considered.

Growth of output

Figure 21.1 presents the growth rate of output for the three countries for the post-reform period. In the case of Malawi, growth in output of the economy has been dominated by rain-fed agriculture, especially the smallholder

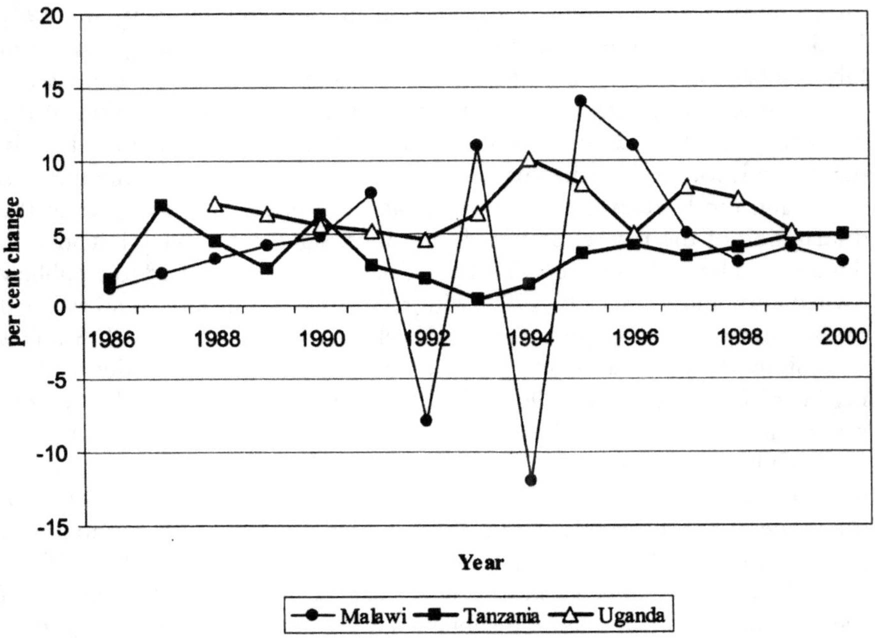

Figure 21.1 Growth of output (source: Malawi (1993, 2003), Tanzania (1993, 2003) and Uganda (1993, 2003c).)

agricultural sector. Between 1964 and 1979, the economy registered an average annual growth rate of about six per cent, well above the population growth rate of 2.9 per cent. The economy slowed down in the 1980s averaging only three per cent per annum, with most of the growth emanating from the estate agriculture, government services and manufacturing sector. In the 1990s, economic growth further slowed down because of weak output growth in the smallholder agricultural sector due to effects of weather. As a result, the average growth rate between 1990 and 1994 was only 0.6 per cent. Furthermore, relative to Tanzania and Uganda, output growth in Malawi has been significantly more volatile.

Tanzania's growth performance in the post-reform period has also been disappointing, with an average annual growth rate of Gross Domestic Product (GDP) of 3.5 per cent. With an average annual population growth rate of three per cent, Tanzania's per capita income growth for this period has been a dismal 0.5 per cent per year.

In contrast to Malawi and Tanzania, output growth in Uganda has been around six per cent per annum, with a clear acceleration in the growth rate since 1992. The sustained high growth rates of the 1990s has been driven primarily by the growth of the monetised sector of the economy, which grew at around 9 per cent per year since 1992.

Structure of production

Table 21.1 presents the composition of output in the three countries for the periods 1985–1989, 1990–1995 and 1996–2000. In the case of Malawi, it is interesting to observe that despite the aim of the economic reform process to rejuvenate the smallholder agricultural sector, its share in total output does not show a significant increase over the period 1985–2000. In the case of the Ugandan economy, perhaps its most remarkable feature relative to that of Tanzania is the rapid increase in the monetised proportion of the economy in the former economy compared to that of the latter. In fact, in the Tanzanian case, monetised GDP has been stagnant at 73 per cent of total monetised and non-monetised output over the mid-1980s to the late 1990s. Much of the increase in monetised GDP in Uganda has occurred in the non-agricultural sector, suggesting that non-agricultural activities have been the primary source of growth in the latter economy.

Agricultural production

In examining the behaviour of the agricultural sector in the three sample countries in the post-reform period, it is useful to distinguish between the export crop and food crop sectors. We first consider the effects of economic

Table 21.1 Composition of output

	Period		
	1985–1989[a]	*1990–1995*	*1996–2000[b]*
Malawi			
Agriculture	36.4	33.9	37.9
Small-scale	28.1	24.1	29.5
Large-scale	8.3	9.8	8.4
Non-agriculture	63.6	66.1	62.1
Tanzania			
Monetary GDP	72.6	72.9	72.6
Agriculture	27.4	27.2	27.7
Non-agriculture	72.6	72.8	72.3
Non-monetary GDP	27.4	27.1	27.4
Uganda			
Monetary GDP	65.5	70.3	76.6
Agriculture	23.7	24.4	23.0
Non-agriculture	41.8	45.9	53.6
Non-monetary GDP	34.5	29.7	23.4

Source: Malawi (1993, 2003), Tanzania (1993, 2003) and Uganda Bureau of Statistics (1993, 2003).

Notes

a Data for Uganda is for 1987–1989.

b Data for Tanzania and Uganda is for 1996–1999.

reforms on the food crops sector. In the case of Malawi, there was an increase of 262 per cent in the total production of food crops in 2000–2002 as compared to 1988–1990 (Table 21.2). However, the growth of food output mostly occurred in sweet potatoes and cassava, both crops which have lower nutrient value per unit output compared to the staple foodgrain – maize (so that the share of maize in total food output fell to 28 per cent in 2000–2002 from 76 per cent in 1988–1990). In the case of maize in particular, there was a 32 per cent increase in the same period; however, from 1999, the production of maize has steadily fallen. The decline in maize production in the recent period can be mostly attributed to the removal of fertiliser subsidies and the increasing cost of imported fertilisers with the depreciation of the Malawian Kwacha since 1995 (Harrigan (2003) for an elaboration of the argument relating to fertiliser subsidies). In the case of Tanzania, there was a meagre 4 per cent increase in food output in 1997–1999 as compared to 1988–1990. This was primarily due to stagnant production of the main food crop – maize – for the whole period. Unlike the case of Malawi, maize still accounts for the bulk of food crops grown by farmers in Tanzania, with a share of 67 per cent in total food crops production over the period 1997–1999. Finally, in the case of Uganda, we have seen robust growth in

Table 21.2 Food crops production, all three countries (thousand tonnes)

Country	*1988–1990*	*2000–2002*	*% change*
Malawi			
Maize	1,425.4	1,889.3	32.5
Rice	41.0	84.1	105.3
Other grains	30.2	57.9	92.0
Groundnut	43.4	143.1	229.7
Sweet potatoes and cassava	269.4	4,314.1	1,501.2
Pulses	60.0	278.4	364.0
Total	1,869.4	6,766.4	262.0
Tanzania			
Maize	2,329.1	2,421.7	4.0
Paddy	636.3	597.6	−6.1
Wheat	90.3	75.3	−16.6
Pulses	398.1	521.7	31.0
Total	3,453.7	3,616.3	4.7
Uganda			
Bananas	7,534.7	9,182.3	21.9
Maize	555.3	967.0	74.1
Other grains	983.0	1,110.3	13.0
Sweet potatoes and cassava	5,329.3	6,089.7	14.3
Pulses	215.7	296.0	37.2
Beans	374.3	336.3	−10.2
Total	21,304.7	25,194.3	18.3

Source: Malawi (1993, 2003), Tanzania (1993, 2003) and Uganda Bureau of Statistics (1993, 2003).

food crop output, with an 18 per cent increase in the level of output in 1997–1999 as compared to 1988–1990. Bananas, the staple food crop, grew at 22 per cent over this period, and its share in total food output has remained stable at around 35 per cent.

Turning to export crops next, we find that in the case of Malawi, there has been an impressive increase in tobacco production over the period 1988–2002 (Table 21.3). This has happened in spite of a fall in world tobacco prices in the late 1990s, and can be explained by the lifting of restrictions on smallholder farmers to grow burley tobacco. By 1998, smallholders accounted for 70 per cent of the country's total tobacco production compare to 12.8 per cent in 1990. The surge in smallholder incomes brought about by tobacco production led to multiplier linkages to the non-farm economy (Harrigan 2003). While this may have contributed to a fall in poverty among some smallholder farmers, burley tobacco cultivation has been mostly undertaken by households with a mean landholding size of 1.6 hectares (Orr 2000), when the average land-holding of poor households is 0.9 hectares (Malawi 2000). Furthermore, increases in the tobacco quota for smallholder farmers by the Malawian government may lead to a fall in tobacco prices, given Malawi's large market share in the world burley tobacco market. Thus, burley tobacco production by itself cannot be seen as a major driver of the process of poverty reduction in Malawi.

In the case of Tanzania, there is clear evidence of an increase in export crops production in the post-reform period, with total output from the export crops sector increasing by 45 per cent in the period 1997–1999 as compared to 1988–1990. The increase in export crops production seems to be driven primarily by an increase in the production of cashewnuts, from 22.1 thousand tonnes in 1988–1990 to 105.9 thousand tonnes in 2000–2002. There also was an increase in the production of tobacco from 11.5 thousand tonnes in 1988–1990 to 40.6 thousand tonnes in 1997–1999. On the other hand, sisal, which was an important export crop at the beginning of the 1980s, witnessed a fall in its share in total export crop output from 29 per cent in 1980 to 7 per cent in 1997–1999.

In the case of Uganda, prior studies (such as Djikstra and Van Donge (2001)) have found that the economic reforms initiated in the 1980s led to a significant supply response from the agricultural export sector. Table 21.3 confirms this finding. We observe a significant increase in the procurement of coffee (this is true of both Robusta and Arabica varieties), tea and tobacco from 1988–1990 to 1997–1999. The increase in coffee production over the 1990s has continued, in spite of a fall in coffee prices in the late 1990s. Coffee remains the dominant export crop in the case of Uganda, with a share of 86 per cent in 1997–1999.

What have been the effects of the trends in agricultural production on poverty? Unfortunately, we do not have longitudinal data on poverty for all three countries. The Ugandan data is the most reliable and it suggests a dramatic fall in the head count ratio for rural poverty from 69.4 per cent in 1992

Table 21.3 Export crops production, all three countries (thousand tonnes)

Country	*1988–1990*	*2000–2002*	*% change*
Malawi			
Tobacco	10.3	90.2	778.3
Cotton	32.5	37.5	15.5
Total	42.7	127.7	198.7
Tanzania			
Coffee	49.5	44.2	−10.7
Cotton	58.8	48.0	−18.5
Tea	20.8	24.3	16.6
Cashewnuts	22.1	105.9	379.5
Tobacco	11.5	40.6	252.9
Sisal	33.1	21.5	−34.9
Pyrethrum	1.5	2.7	72.8
Total	197.4	286.2	45.0
Uganda			
Coffee	149,648.7	220,308.3	47.2
Tea	4,958.0	23,902.0	382.1
Tobacco	3,139.0	9,852.7	213.9
Total	157,745.7	254,063.0	61.1

Source: Malawi (1993, 2003), Tanzania (1993, 2003) and Uganda Bureau of Statistics (1993, 2003).

to 39 per cent in 1999/2000 (Appleton 2001b). Data for Tanzania is more problematic but suggests a minimal decline in the head count ratio from 23.1 per cent in 1991/2 to 19.6 per cent in 2000/2001 (Tanzania 2002a). Poverty in Malawi is very high at 66.5 per cent in 1997/1998 (according the Integrated Household Survey, held that year) and is mostly concentrated amongst smallholder agriculturists (Malawi 2000).

Macro–micro economic linkages

As discussed earlier, three sets of variables can be said to link macro-policies to micro-outcomes in the economic sphere. These are the inflation rate, the real exchange rate and the terms of trade between agriculture and non-agriculture. Low inflation leads to a lower degree of variability in relative prices, and offers a more stable environment for households to engage in high return but more risky activities in the rural economy. Among the three countries, Uganda's success in reducing inflation to below 5 per cent is quite remarkable (Figure 21.2). In contrast, Malawi has witnessed high and variable rates of inflation for much of the 1990s. Here, the slippage in macroeconomic policy evident in Malawi and to some extent, in Tanzania, can be seen as a failure in implementing successful macroeconomic stabilisation that would have supported the longer term objectives of economic reform programmes.

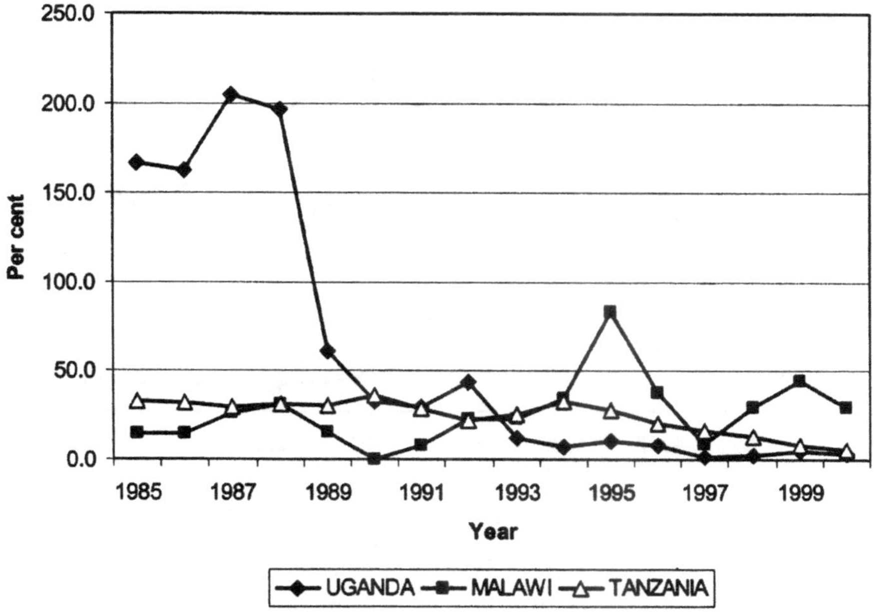

Figure 21.2 The inflation rate, Malawi, Tanzania and Uganda (source: Malawi (1993, 2003), Tanzania (1993, 2003) and Uganda (1993, 2003c).)

The real exchange rate is another key variable that links macro-policies to micro-outcomes. An overvalued real exchange rate can act as a serious constraint to the expansion of the tradable sector – which in the sub-Saharan African context, is mostly the export agriculture sector, and may nullify the otherwise positive effects of economic reforms on the rural economy. In the case of Malawi, the Malawi Kwacha (MK) was floated in February 1994 and subsequently, the real effective exchange rate depreciated by 41.7 per cent through to the first half of 1995. The MK depreciated again by 15 per cent in July 1997. The fiscal slippage in 1997/1998, a slowdown in donor inflows and a decline in tobacco export earnings owing to a drop in export prices, led to a further depreciation of the Malawi Kwacha of about 60 per cent in August 1998. The period between 1998 and 2000 has witnessed further depreciation of the Malawi Kwacha resulting directly from low foreign exchange earnings from the export sector reaching an average of 80 Malawi Kwacha per 1 US$ in January 2001. However, after January 2001, there has been a marked appreciation of the Malawi Kwacha against major trading partner currencies with the rate going as high as 63 Malawi Kwacha per 1 US$ in August 2001. Reflecting changes in the nominal exchange rate and the domestic price level, the real exchange rate shows a period of relative stability in the 1980s followed by a period of considerable volatility in the 1990s, especially after the move to market-determined exchange rates in 1994 (Figure 21.3).

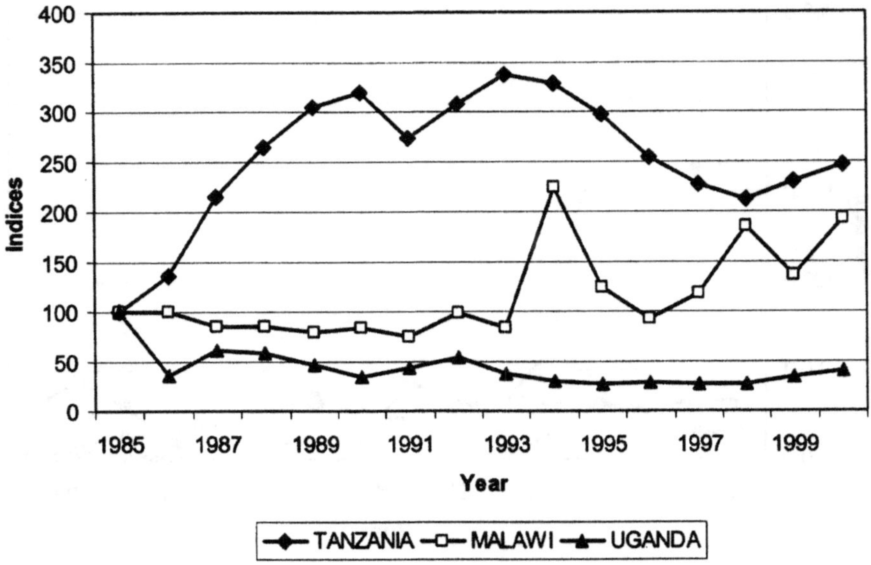

Figure 21.3 The real exchange rate, Malawi, Tanzania and Uganda (source: Malawi (1993, 2003), Tanzania (1993, 2003) and Uganda (1993, 2003c).)

In the case of Tanzania, the decline in the inflation rate is not, however, reflected in a real depreciation of the real exchange rate, at least in the period 1993–1998. On the contrary, during this period, the Tanzanian shilling appreciated significantly in real terms, nullifying to a great extent the positive effect on the tradable sector of the real depreciation of the exchange rate that occurred during the period 1985–1993. The Tanzanian shilling has been depreciating in nominal terms continuously since 1986. However, it is clear that the nominal depreciation that occurred in the mid-1990s was not sufficient to counteract the pressure on the real exchange rate to appreciate that originated from the inflation rate in Tanzania being higher than that observed in its trading partners.

In Uganda, the Bank of Uganda was able to hold the real exchange rate at a constant level for the period 1994–1997, with a steady depreciation since then. This may have been largely a result of the low inflationary environment and the maintenance of fiscal discipline (Henstridge and Kasekende 2001). The successful management of the real exchange rate by the central bank may have been an important contributing factor behind the large supply response observed from the agricultural tradable sector from the mid-1990s onwards (such a response is not evident until the mid-1990s as pointed out by Belshaw *et al.* 1999).

The third variable that connects macro-policies to micro-outcomes is the rural–urban terms of trade. An upward trend in the terms of trade provides an incentive to farmers to invest in agricultural activities. Perhaps the most important objective of the reform programmes initiated in sub-Saharan Africa was to redress the historical bias against the agricultural sector (particularly smallholder agriculture) by increasing the rural–urban terms of trade via marketing reforms and product price deregulation. In the case of Tanzania, the terms of trade has improved significantly for export crops in the 1990s, after a period of little or no change in the 1980s (Figure 21.4). The increase in terms of trade for export crops in the post-reform period contrasts sharply with a persistent decline in this variable in the pre-reform period. As Ellis (1982) has shown, the price terms of trade for export crops fell by 42.6 in the period 1970–1980. Thus, the evidence from the terms of trade analysis suggests that the deregulation of agricultural pricing and marketing reforms may have led to a reversal of the long-standing bias against export agriculture in the Tanzanian economy that was evident under a policy regime of pan-territorial pricing and highly centralised state procurement systems in the pre-reform period (Ellis 1983). However, there has been no similar increase in the terms of trade for food crops in the 1990s. Thus, economic reforms have not led to any significant reversal of the slow but steady long-term rate of decline that has been observed in the case of food crops for Tanzanian agriculture since the 1970s.

In Uganda, the terms of trade of food crops shows a slow but steady increase since the mid 1990s (Figure 21.5). However, the terms of trend for

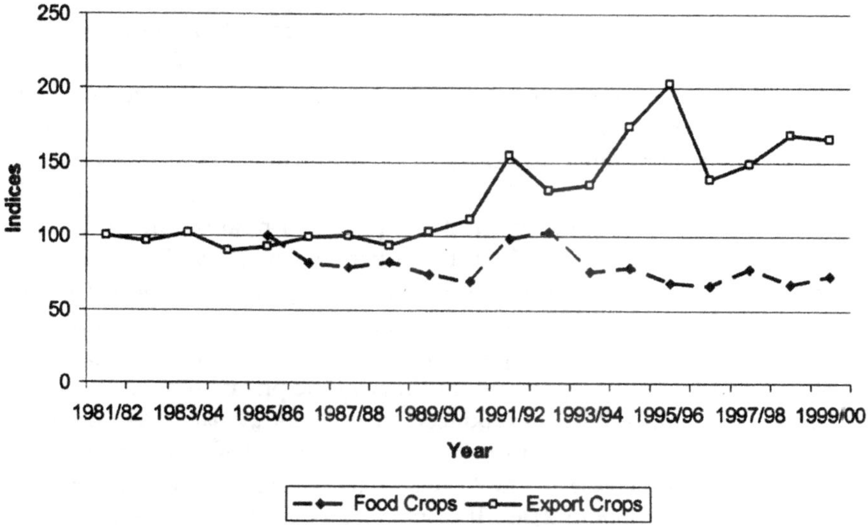

Figure 21.4 Terms of trade, Tanzania (source: author's calculations; from Tanzania (2000b).)

Note
Price terms of trade; Food crops: maize, rice and wheat; Export crops: cashewnut, coffee, cotton, tea and tobacco. Price deflator: Non-food National Consumer Price Index.

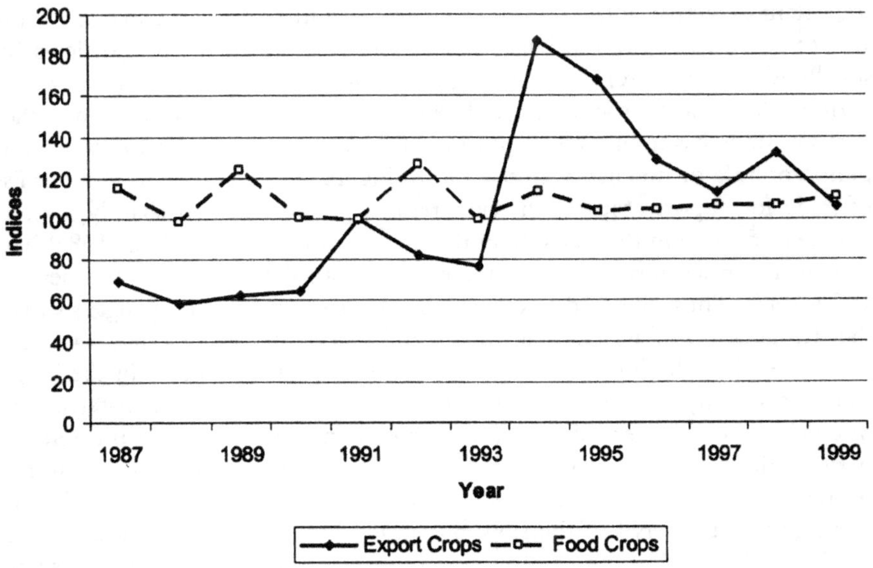

Figure 21.5 Terms of trade, Uganda (source: Uganda (1993, 2003c).)

Note
Price deflators for agriculture, cash crops and food crops deflated by the implicit price deflator for manufacturing.

cash crops shows a sharp fall from 1994 (driven by the fall in the world price of coffee), after showing a steady increase in previous years. With the entry of the private sector in coffee marketing and processing leading to increased competition, there have been significant efficiency gains in these areas (Uganda 1996). For coffee, the share of producer prices as a ratio of world prices has also steadily increased from 12 per cent in 1987 to 79 per cent in 1998. In the case of cotton, real producer price as a ratio of lint world price increased from 56 per cent in 1990 to 65 per cent in 1998. The increase in the returns to cash crop farming could also be explained by the fall in real input prices, following the decontrol of input prices and the greater competition in these markets following government withdrawal from direct procurement and distribution of inputs and the entry of the private sector.

For Malawi, similar data on producer prices is not available. We use retail price data to construct a pseudo-terms of trade for Malawi. While the graph shows a sustained increase in the 'terms of trade', one should interpret this figure with caution (Figure 21.6). It may well be that the increase is primarily driven by increased profit margins of traders in the period of deregulation. Moreover, such a terms of trade rise may not be beneficial to many smallholder farmers who are net buyers of food crops, mostly maize.

It is clear that economic reforms seem to have had a differential impact on returns to farming in the two countries where we have reliable data –

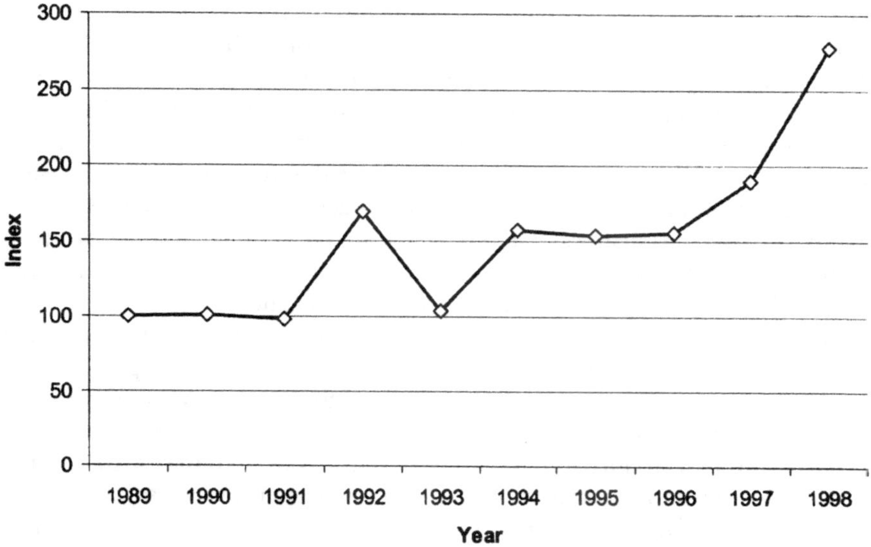

Figure 21.6 'Pseudo-terms of trade', Malawi (source: author's calculations from raw data provided by the Ministry of Agriculture, Government of Malawi.)

Tanzania and Uganda. For Uganda, the impact is, on the whole, positive, with the sustained increase in the terms of trade for food crops. In the case of export crops, while the terms of trade is more volatile, farmers are getting an increasingly higher proportion of the world price of the two major export crops – coffee and cotton. This is not the case in Tanzania, where the food crops terms of trade seem to have stagnated.

Perhaps the most important reason for the differences in impact is the more positive response of the private sector to the space left void by the parastatals in the marketing arena in Uganda as compared to Tanzania. This in turn could be linked to the ambivalence of the Tanzanian government, particularly at the local level, to private traders about their role in agricultural marketing, with the latter often subject to harassment by the local authorities (Amani *et al.* 1992). This has resulted in a high degree of uncertainty in the minds of traders about their future, and may have led to under-investment in storage capacities (30–40 per cent of maize produced in Tanzania is lost due to poor or non-existent storage every year (Kahkonen and Leathers 1997)).

Conclusions

In this chapter, we find that the effects of economic reforms on rural livelihood diversification, as evident from the macro-level data, have been complex. Economic reforms have had a positive impact on the livelihoods of smallholder farmers in Uganda, many of whom have moved out of poverty in the 1990s. The response of Ugandan smallholder farmers to the reforms thus far has been positive with increasing production evident in the cash crops and to a lesser extent, the food crops sectors. That this happened in spite of a precipitous fall in the world coffee price (Uganda's main export crop) could be in part due to the micro-level effects of reforms that has led to an increase in the share of producer prices for coffee and cotton farmers in world prices of these commodities, and in part due to an increasing engagement in non-farm activities by many smallholder farmers (Ellis and Bahiigwa 2003). In the Ugandan case, there seems to be a causal linkage between increasing livelihood diversification evident at the household level and the observed fall in rural poverty in the 1990s (Balihuta and Sen 2001).

In Malawi and Tanzania, economic reforms seem to have had a somewhat different impact, one that is not so positive in all respects. The export agriculture in both countries seem to have benefited from economic reforms, with strong growth in output, linked to the increase in the terms of trade for export crops in Tanzania and the lifting of restrictions on burley tobacco production for smallholder farmers in the case of Malawi. However, the impact of the growth of the export crops sector on rural poverty in these two countries does not seem noticeable yet, and it is arguable to what extent an export crop-driven growth strategy can be a vehicle for sustained poverty reduction on its own accord, in the absence of a rapid expansion in non-farm economic activities.

In contrast to the relatively positive response of the export crops sector to the reforms, one finds a different outcome in the food crops sector. The food crops sector in Malawi and Tanzania have not showed signs of growth in spite of over two decades of economic reforms. It could be argued that part of the blame for this stagnation could be attributed to economic reforms themselves, in particular the removal of fertiliser subsidies and the scaling back of public investment in agricultural extension services, which has led to an increase in the riskiness of the economic environment for poor smallholder farmers (World Bank 2000d and 2001b; Harrigan 2003). Certainly, such an argument is supported from the micro-level evidence that is available in many of the studies contained in this volume (see Chapters 3, 4, 7 and 14 above). Another possible reason for the dismal performance of the food crop sector is that staple food crop supplies may be roughly in balance with domestic demand (this would be true of bananas in Uganda and maize in Tanzania), so that an increase in supply would be met with falling prices, and consequently, lower returns to food crop farming.

Along with the negative or indeterminate effects of the reforms on the returns to food crop agriculture has been a significant 'market failure' in agricultural credit with the withdrawal of directed credit programmes to the rural areas in Malawi and Tanzania, and the limited entry of the private sector into rural credit markets (Sen 2002; Sen and Chikunda 2002). However, it is not obvious that economic reforms alone can be held responsible for the somewhat adverse outcomes witnessed in Malawi and Tanzania. Certainly, in

Tanzania, the weakness of the marketing system – one important reason for the lack of effectiveness of reforms in this country – can be attributed to 'government failure' in the lack of a supportive environment for private sector involvement in marketing. Incomplete macroeconomic stabilisation in Malawi may have also contributed to the weak impact of the economic reforms on the agricultural sector.

Note

* The author would like to thank Frank Ellis for detailed comments on an earlier version of this chapter.

Part VI

Towards improved rural poverty reduction strategies

22 Synthesis and policy implications

H. Ade Freeman and Frank Ellis

The chapters of this book provide a rich tapestry of conceptual and empirical information regarding rural livelihood patterns at the micro-level in a set of low income countries in eastern and southern Africa, and connections, or lack of them, to poverty reduction strategies at the macro-scale. The regional focus deriving from the research programme entitled LADDER is also supplemented by material from other places, particularly India (Chapter 5) as well as other sub-Saharan African countries. As stated at the outset, making micro–macro links is at the centre of the research endeavour that this collection represents. Of course not all chapters do this explicitly because they have other preoccupations of their own, nevertheless the overall direction of the book is to bring out into the open the critical mismatches that occur between the priorities and constraints confronted by ordinary rural people in their pursuit of diverse livelihoods, and the eventual sectoral and sub-sectoral priorities that emerge from PRSP or PRSP-type processes at macro policy levels.

The livelihoods approach (Chapter 1) informs much of the empirical work described in different chapters. As stated in the first chapter, this approach has demonstrated strengths, especially in recognising or discovering:

- the multiple and diverse character of people's livelihoods;
- the prevalence of institutionalised blockages to improving livelihoods;
- the social as well as economic character of livelihood strategies;
- the principle factors implicated in rising or diminishing vulnerability;
- the micro–macro (or macro–micro) links that connect livelihoods to policies.

The livelihoods approach comes together with the concepts of poverty traps (Chapters 2 and 19) and chronic poverty (Chapter 7) through the notions of cumulative processes and poverty thresholds. Exit routes from poverty involve a virtuous cumulative process in which asset levels are raised, asset substitutions occur, and the vulnerability factors of seasonality and risk are diminished by diversifying assets and activities across economic sectors and sub-sectors. Livestock can play a critical role in such a process (Chapter 15).

So can diversification away from subsistence crop production into non-farm activities that can generate cash, the latter being the most substitutable of all assets and difficult to secure through financial markets that work sporadically, if at all, in rural areas. Comparative livelihoods research (Chapter 3) suggests that the most vulnerable position for a rural family to be situated in is excessive reliance on subsistence food production coupled with low wage seasonal work on other farms.

The concepts of poverty traps and thresholds (Chapter 2) provide additional valuable insights into cumulative processes. They indicate that the transition from severe poverty and vulnerability towards secure and improving livelihoods cannot be characterised as a smoothly continuous process, rather it exhibits discontinuities or thresholds that represent barriers that people must overcome in order to move out of poverty. Some of these barriers are to do with particular asset deficits that are acutely difficult to overcome (no land; low or no education); some are to do with social exclusion factors (divorce, widowhood, disability, etc.); and some are to do with factors in the institutional context that are more difficult for the poor to navigate than the better-off (permits, licenses, taxes, fees, roadblocks, etc.). There are close complementarities between chronic poverty understandings of the reasons for persistent poverty (Chapter 7) and the poverty traps approach. Also relevant here are downward trajectories, whereby asset erosion, often to do with personal misfortune (e.g. HIV/AIDS in the family) result in previously livelihood secure families falling into chronic poverty (Chapter 7).

The diversity of rural livelihoods in low income countries constitutes a recurring and important theme throughout the book. No longer is it remotely accurate to characterise entire populations in the rural economy as smallholders or small poor farmers. The degree to which rural households nowadays depend on non-farm earnings, and evidence that this constitutes a trend of diminishing reliance on agriculture, leads to the description of this process as 'deagrarianisation' (Chapter 4). It seems that economic liberalisation in sub-Saharan Africa (SSA) may have inadvertently accelerated this process, instead of creating the resurgence of agriculture that it aimed to promote. The reasons for this are, first, that the expected higher real returns to agricultural production spectacularly failed to occur during the 1990s (partly due to declining real world price trends); and, second, that agricultural input and output markets became unreliable and unstable post-liberalisation to a degree that substantially added to production risks. Instead of growing and becoming more market-oriented, much of SSA agriculture slipped back towards subsistence (Chapter 3) wherein the achievement of food security from own production was reinforced as the fundamental objective of agricultural producers.

The case study from Andhra Pradesh, India (Chapter 5) suggests that diversity is facilitated by prior higher levels of assets excluding the household's own labour. This finding is consistent with the notion of poverty–wealth thresholds advanced in Chapter 2. The case study also suggests that remittances ('unearned income') can substitute for other forms of diversity ('earned income') in terms of reducing risk, and that the type of activities in which household members engage is a more important determinant of per capita household income than the mere number of such different activities. These relationships clearly merit further exploration since the concept of gains from specialisation that holds such a central place in the history of economic thought appears to be contravened by the findings of much livelihoods research in poor countries, yet this may be due to peculiarities of the way production opportunities and labour markets work in low income rural and urban settings that become less relevant as incomes rise in well-performing or fast-growing economies.

Livelihood diversity does not, of course, work in the same way for different individuals, nor necessarily in different economic and social contexts. In particular, it is often strongly gender differentiated, with options for men being substantially broader in scope than for women (Chapter 6). This may occur more strongly in SSA than in places where manufacturing growth has created new labour markets for women (as in southeast Asia, for example). In SSA increased diversity can represent some widening of opportunities for women, but, offsetting this, it can increase the burden of women 'left behind on the farm' to take care of the young and the old as well as to undertake heavy agricultural work.

The scope for rural households to construct their own pathways out of poverty is heavily dependent on the institutional environment, including public sector behaviours, the working of markets, and social and cultural norms and expectations. A generally facilitating environment may be counterposed to a blocking or hampering environment. In SSA, the facilitation of individuals and families to break out of the limiting circumstances in which they find themselves is a rare occurrence. The contrary is more widely the case, with those in positions of power or authority tending to interpret their roles as blockers and gatekeepers rather than facilitators. Very often there is a personal economic subtext to this. Public servants are so poorly remunerated that they have little choice but to seek alternative sources of income in order to provide themselves and their families with a sufficient livelihood.

Part III of the book provides ample examples of this difficult policy and institutional environment. A case study of Malawi (Chapter 8) conveys the message that democratic decentralisation may exacerbate rather than ameliorate predatory behaviour by local officials. This is because in the typical patrimonial state where authority, power and wealth originate from loyalty and patronage rather than effectiveness at achieving stated government goals, decentralisation merely serves to recreate patronage politics at local levels. Local taxation in Uganda supports this broad viewpoint (Chapter 9). Here, decentralisation creates an appetite for local revenue generation in order to provide councillors with sitting allowances; however, the ensuing local tax system is multiple and complex, and imposes unreasonable burdens on families and businesses.

Two chapters explore markets as part of the institutional environment surrounding rural livelihoods. In Tanzania, it is found that market liberalisation has failed to fulfil its promise, not due to too much liberalisation, but because the state never really 'let go' its involvement in markets, and policy reversals are in progress that seek to recapture markets that private traders were successful in taking out of the state umbrella (Chapter 10). Meanwhile a study of cotton markets in several sub-Saharan African countries (Chapter 11) suggests that while private markets work best, those where a degree of market power can be exercised by the leading private players (who can, for example, ensure that quality standards are maintained) work better than those characterised by excessive competition between numerous small players.

Next in this context is an exploration of recent or intended changes in land tenure legislation in the four LADDER countries (Chapter 12). It is found that new legislation is timid and inadequate, and potentially creates more difficulties for poverty reduction than it sets out to solve by biasing the ability to create freehold land registration towards the better-off and men. Women's land rights are consistently woefully inadequately addressed in new or proposed laws, so that previous customary rights, for example, at widowhood, are eroded rather than strengthened. By clinging to weakened forms of customary tenure under an umbrella of state land ownership, the power and patronage of traditional or state authorities is preserved, while at the same time enough of a gesture towards freehold is created to enable the well-off to secure private land rights wherever customary ownership can be successfully challenged.

The institutional context of livelihoods includes the delivery of agricultural services, especially research and extension support (Chapter 13). The past twenty years has seen the accelerated disintegration of public sector capabilities in this area, a theme also taken up in other chapters (for example, in different ways, Chapters 4 and 14). Previous crop or sub-sector based public research and extension systems are no longer underpinned by linkages to public sector marketing and input delivery organisations, and are poorly adapted to market induced diversification pressures, both farm and off-farm. Semi-moribund extension services comprising officers trained years ago in single crops or particular food crop systems are unable to provide useful advice relevant to rapidly changing domestic and export markets (advent of supermarket supply systems even in poor countries; urban demand for high value horticultural crops; export demand for new commodities); nor are they familiar with taking non-farm labour demands into account in considering on-farm alternatives; nor have they ever been that good at responding to the real gender division of labour on farms (Chapter 6). The policy challenges here relate to incipient privatisation planned or in process in several countries, and how to harness the knowledge intensity enabled by evolving information technology to useful effect in a low income setting.

Rural livelihoods, however diverse they are, depend, of course, on access to natural resources and on the management regimes that regulate such access. Some natural resources, principally farm land and livestock, tend to be under private control, while others represent varying types of common property. The distinction between private and common property is blurred in most African rural settings, and important overlaps and interdependencies occur. For example, livestock may be privately owned but communally grazed, and implicit rules exist on permissible versus unacceptable behaviour regarding the roaming of livestock in settled agricultural areas. The continued fuzziness of land tenure in the LADDER countries despite recent legislation has already been mentioned and a considerable body of evidence suggests that this works against the poor and women (Chapter 12 again). Major institutional changes occurred in common property regimes during the 1990s and into the first decade of the new century. This refers to the replacement of hierarchical state management of resources such as fisheries, forests, irrigation and wildlife by community based natural resource management (CBNRM) or co-management.

Part IV of the book begins with looking at livelihoods and policy contexts related to crop production (Chapter 14) and livestock (Chapter 15). Chapter 14 extends the discussion of the preceding chapter on the theme of support services to agriculture, utilising Uganda as a particular case study, and drawing on the evidence provided by the LADDER village studies and household data set. It is noted that Ugandan agricultural policy, as articulated in the Plan for the Modernisation of Agriculture, is strongly towards making crop production more market-oriented, and bringing a privatised agricultural advice service behind such an objective. However, the LADDER studies reveal how strongly subsistence-oriented are the poor, so that an advice service biased towards rapid commercialisation will be inherently prone to exclude poor food-crop farmers from its remit.

Chapter 15 emphasises the multiple roles of livestock in successful livelihood strategies, which means, in a poverty reduction context, that effective livestock policy has a considerably more important role to play than is indicated by considering it simply as a production sub-sector on its own. The LADDER studies confirmed these multiple roles, revealed at the most basic level by a high correlation between levels of livestock ownership and overall livelihood success, in respect of which, it is the stock of animals rather than the level of recurrent output from them (milk or meat) that is the pertinent variable.

The following three chapters examine livelihood and institutional context findings in relation to common property problems in the fisheries sector (Chapter 16), with respect to small-farm irrigation (Chapter 17), and in relation to the conceptual approach to community management of natural resources more generally (Chapter 18). The application of CBNRM in the fisheries sector has been rife with misunderstandings leading to the potential failure of initiatives and few demonstrable gains in terms of realising poverty reduction objectives. As described in Chapter 16, livelihoods research in fishing villages revealed the flexible role of fishing income in diverse livelihood strategies, the generally higher income of those who engage in fishing compared with those solely dependent on farming in the same locations, the importance of migrants in inland fisheries, and the ease of entrance and exit strategies in the artisanal fishing sub-sector. By contrast CBNRM has tended to be based on principles of specialisation, territoriality and exclusion, as well as lack of understanding of pre-existing institutions adapted to the mobile and flexible strategies of fisherfolk.

As shown in Chapter 17, some similar and some different findings are reported with respect to small-farm irrigation where the tendency even today is to assume that growth in the irrigated area depends almost exclusively on external support to irrigation infrastructure, with minimal attention being given to the existing and evolving capabilities of farmers themselves to instigate and manage their own irrigation systems. In particular, small-farm irrigation is deeply prone to conflict (for example, between head-end and tail-end users of a particular canal; between downstream and upstream abstracters of a particular river; between water use of a particular river and the ecological needs of a river basin; between competing users and uses in a river basin – crop producers, livestock herders, domestic water supply, urban water supply). These potential sources of conflict can only be 'managed' through social processes of coordination that involve all such users within the river basin.

Finally, in this context Chapter 18 offers an overall assessment of CBNRM experience, drawing on the conceptual literature as well as on case studies from Malawi and Botswana. Certain flaws in the practical implementation of CBNRM are inevitable given the preconceptions of its advocates (for example, the assumption of relative homogeneous communities with a close identity of interests between community members), and the mixed and ambivalent reasons for its advocacy by donors (for example, reducing central government regulatory costs), as well as the tendency to impose an organisational model from outside and to do so irrespective of pre-existing social mechanisms for handling conflicts of access to a communal resource. In addition politics and patronage play ever-present background roles never fully understood by outsiders. Outcomes will necessarily be variable and disappointing compared to intentions, and may just as likely exclude the intended beneficiaries of CBNRM policies (the poor, women) as to include them.

The penultimate part of the book (Chapters 19 to 21) pursues, in an admittedly fragmentary and incomplete way, the theme of macro–micro (or micro–macro) links between central level policies and processes and micro-level livelihood realities. A narrow interpretation of macro–micro links tends to place this wholly in the economic domain, and then poses the question as to what is new about the livelihoods approach that was not available to earlier economic analyses of these links. Economic macro–micro links are of course important and are examined for the LADDER case study countries in Chapter 21. However, they comprise only part of the overall picture, and, indeed, often not the most important part. People's livelihoods are facilitated or inhibited by a great deal more than just the economic signals (exchange rates, interest rates, fiscal policy) that pass in an uneven way from the central level to the remote corners of national economic space in the form of changing relative input and output prices, and borrowing costs.

Institutional, social and political contexts also tend to take shape at central levels, sometimes modified by pressures originating in outlying locations but more often responding in an adaptive way to donor priorities, and are transmitted or interpreted or utilised for gain by those in positions of authority on their way from the centre to the community and to the family and individual. These contexts comprise constraints on individual action as well as determining the opportunities available and how these may be accessed. They consist of rights, rules, regulations, laws, social customs, political allegiance, land tenure institutions and so on, and they collectively modify to a considerable degree, and may even entirely overwhelm, the opportunities and capabilities apparently represented by price signals in the economic sphere.

In general, PRSPs do not even attempt to address the livelihood blockages that tend to be represented by these social, political and institutional macro–micro links. To the extent that they do so, they rely on an essentially untested conviction that decentralisation will provide solutions to the difficulties of a non-performing public sector, service delivery failures, abuse of authority and so on. Chapters 8 and 9 above should provide some cautionary pauses for thought regarding this conviction.

In the meantime, Chapter 19 demonstrates how priorities articulated by ordinary people at local levels do not necessarily match the policies that tend to emerge as PRSP priorities at central level; moreover, PRSP priorities tend to become regarded as the uniform set of poverty reduction instruments that should be 'rolled out' across the country irrespective of local variations in demand and need. Chapter 20 sets outs out a procedure by which poverty estimates resulting from empirical data collection at a point in time can be disaggregated and 'tracked' through time at local levels, thus achieving a dynamic 'macro–micro link' between national poverty indicators and those that are useful to track changes in the spatial incidence of poverty over time. As already mentioned, Chapter 21 provides a synthesis of evidence on the specifically economic macro–micro links for Uganda, Tanzania and Malawi, discovering, as it happens, the widespread tendency for real food prices at farm gate level to have declined in recent history in the LADDER case study countries thus indicating one of the many reasons that farm households have sought, or been forced to seek, more diversified livelihoods in the post-liberalisation phase of their countries' histories.

There are many policy inferences for poverty reduction that may be drawn from the findings and discussion of the chapters of this book. A few of the key ones are summarised briefly here as follows:

1 In the formulation of poverty reduction strategies, a knowledge of how people actually construct their livelihoods, and the blockages they encounter in doing this, is indispensable. Some of this knowledge can be

derived from PPAs; some requires more detailed household level enquiry. While all knowledge is subject to inaccuracy and interpretation, proceeding on the basis of no recent knowledge or 'received wisdom' is not very helpful at all.

2 In low-income countries that have experienced negligible gains in per capita income over many years (i.e. many SSA countries), individuals and households construct complex livelihoods that are diverse, cut across orthodox economic sectors, and rely for their success on mobility, flexibility and adaptability. PRSPs and related poverty reduction frameworks and efforts need to consider carefully what is being done to facilitate and expand rather than disable and close down these attributes. Most PRSPs show little if any understanding of these factors, and some of them are actively antagonistic, exemplified by disparaging remarks on migration found in many PRSPs.

3 Macro–micro links tend to be interpreted by economists solely in terms of price and interest rate effects of macroeconomic and trade policies; however, these effects are mediated by multiple social, institutional and political factors in their transmission from the macro to the micro-level. It is these non-economic factors that are often responsible for placing barriers in the way of individual and family attempts to construct own pathways out of poverty. Some of these barriers are well-documented (for example, gender differences in control over resources and access to labour markets); others much less so (the formal and informal fees and fines and bribes required by local officials in order to start-up small businesses).

4 The donor community places largely untested faith in decentralisation of government as the vehicle to overcome these non-economic barriers, supposing that ineffective public service and petty corruption are attributes of central government that are not reproduced at local government levels when citizens have the power of veto over the actions of their representatives through the ballot box. However, in practice decentralisation tends to reproduce the patrimonial state at local levels. Moreover, it creates new local level bureaucracies and elected representatives with an appetite for revenues to supplement salaries or pay sitting allowances. It also all too readily reproduces factors that demotivate public officers whether they are employed by the central state or by local governments: over-staffing, abysmally low pay, little or no non-salary resources to undertake the functions that posts are meant to perform, and so on. Self-evidently, 'capacity building' does not provide a solution to these particular problems, and is an enormously over-rated device in the donor toolkit of policies supporting poverty reduction.

5 PRSPs need to evolve towards taking non-economic macro–micro links more seriously if they are to move beyond merely being mechanisms to shift donor resources earmarked for education, health and road building. The improving human and infrastructural assets created by the latter

> expenditures will take a generation to result in rising incomes, and even then their beneficial effects will be severely dissipated if inhibiting and disabling institutional environments persist. Local level blockages need tracing upwards to the rules and laws and public sector behaviours that legitimise them from above; and, conversely, central policy decisions that have poverty reduction remits (e.g. changes in land tenure laws) need tracing downwards to discover the effectiveness or otherwise of their implementation in local contexts.

This chapter, and the book, ends on a positive note. Poor rural people everywhere exhibit the most amazing ingenuity in securing viable livelihoods in difficult circumstances. They exhibit agency; and this agency finds ways round the risks and pitfalls and blockages that are thrown at them not only by natural events and adverse trends, but by the way governance operates in its interface with people's livelihoods. It is in harnessing this ingenuity and agency that the true route to rural poverty reduction lies.

References

Abel, N. and Blaikie, P.M. (1989) 'Land degradation, stocking rates and conservation policies in communal range lands of Botswana and Zimbabwe', *Land Degradation and Rehabilitation*, 1 (2): 101–23.

Adamolekun, L. (ed.) (1999a) *Public Administration in Africa*, Boulder: Westview Press.

Adamolekun, L. (1999b) 'Decentralization and inter-governmental relations', in L. Adamolekun, (ed.) *Public Administration in Africa*, Boulder: Westview Press.

Adamolekun, L. and Mvula, A. (1999) 'Malawi', in L. Adamolekun (ed.) *Public Administration in Africa*, Boulder: Westview Press.

Adams, W., Brockington, D., Dixson, J. and Vira, B. (2000) *Common Choices; Policy Options for Common Pool Resources*, DFID Natural Resources Systems Programme Semi-arid production, Project R7973, London: DFID, mimeo.

Adams, W.M. and Hulme, D. (2001) 'If community conservation is the answer in Africa, what is the question?', *Oryx*, 35 (3): 193–200.

Adato, M. and Meinzen-Dick, R. (2002) *Assessing the Impact of Agricultural Research on Poverty Using the Sustainable Livelihoods Framework*, EPTD Discussion Paper, No. 89/FCND Discussion Paper, No. 128, Washington, DC: International Food Policy Research Institute.

Adipala, E., Laker, C., Tizikara, C. and Wadhawan, H. (2003) *Second Joint Government of Uganda – Donors Review (April–May 2003),* Consultants review report, Kampala: National Agricultural Advisory Services (NAADS), Government of Uganda.

Agrawal, A. (2001) 'Common property institutions and sustainable governance of resources', *World Development*, 29 (10): 1649–72.

Agrawal, A. and Gibson, C. (2001) *Communities and the Environment: Ethnicity, Gender, and the State in Community-Based Conservation*, London: Rutgers University Press.

Agrawal, A. and Ribot, J. (1999) 'Accountability in decentralization: a framework with South Asian and West African Cases', *The Journal of Developing Areas*, 33: 473–502.

Ahene, R.A. (2000) *Land Policy of the Republic of Malawi*, Lilongwe: Ministry of Lands, Housing, Physical Planning and Surveys (MLHPPS).

Alan, C. (1999) *Culture and Corruption: The Rise of Civil Society in Promoting Accountability*, Bulawayo: South African Legal Assistance Network, 11 November, mimeo.

Ali, A.A.G. and Thorbecke, E. (2000) 'The state and path of poverty in Sub-Saharan Africa: some preliminary results', *Journal of African Economics*, 9 (1): 9–40.

Aliber, M. (2003) 'Chronic poverty in South Africa: incidence, causes and policies', *World Development*, 31 (3): 473–90.

Allison, E.H. (2001) 'Big laws, small catches: global ocean governance and the fisheries crisis', *Journal of International Development*, 13: 933–50.

Allison, E.H. (2003) 'Linking national fisheries policy to livelihoods on the shores of Lake Kyoga, Uganda', *LADDER Working Paper*, No. 9, Norwich: Overseas Development Group, University of East Anglia. Online. Available HTTP: http://www.uea.ac.uk/dev/odg/ladder/ (accessed 17 January 2004).

Allison, E.H. and Ellis, F. (2001) 'The livelihoods approach and management of small-scale fisheries', *Marine Policy*, 25 (5): 377–88.

Allison, E.H. and McBride, R.J. (2003) 'Educational reform for improved natural resource management: fisheries and aquaculture in Bangladeshi Universities', *Society and Natural Resources*, 16 (3): 249–64.

Allison, E.H. and Mvula, P.M. (2002) 'Fishing livelihoods and fisheries management in Malawi', *LADDER Working Paper*, No. 22, Norwich: Overseas Development Group, University of East Anglia.

Allison, E.H., Mvula, P.M. and Ellis, F. (2002) 'Competing agendas in the development and management of fisheries in Lake Malawi', in K. Geheb and M.-T. Sarch (eds) *Africa's Inland Fisheries: The Management Challenge*, Kampala: Fountain Books.

Amani, H.K.R., Van den Brink, R. and Maro, W.E. (1992) 'Tolerating the private sector', *Working Paper*, No. 32, Ithaca: Cornell Food and Nutritional Policy Program, Cornell University.

Anderson, J. and Van Crowder, L. (2000) 'The present and future of public sector extension in Africa: contracting out or contracting in?', *Public Administration and Development*, 20: 373–84.

Anderson, M. and Grove, R. (1987) 'The scramble for Eden: past, present and future in African conservation', in M. Anderson and R. Grove (eds) *Africa: People, Policies and Practice*, Cambridge: Cambridge University Press.

Appleton, S. (1995) *Woman-Headed Households and Poverty: an Empirical Deconstruction for Uganda*, Oxford: Centre for the Study of African Economies, University of Oxford.

Appleton, S. (1996) 'Women-headed households and household welfare: an empirical deconstruction for Uganda', *World Development*, 4 (12): 1811–27.

Appleton, S. (1998) *Changes in Poverty in Uganda, 1992–1996*, Oxford: Centre for the Study of African Economies, University of Oxford, mimeo.

Appleton, S. (1999) *Changes in Poverty in Uganda, 1992–1997*, Working Paper No. WPS/99/22, Oxford: Centre for the Study of African Economies.

Appleton, S. (2001a) *Poverty Reduction During Growth: The Case of Uganda, 1992–2000*, Nottingham: University of Nottingham, mimeo.

Appleton, S. (2001b) *Poverty in Uganda, 1999/2000: Preliminary Estimates from the UNHS*, Nottingham: University of Nottingham, mimeo.

Apthorpe, R., Chiviya, E. and Kaunda, G. (1995) *Decentralization in Malawi: Local Government and Development*, Report for UNDP and MLGRUD, Lilongwe: UNDP/MLGRUD, May.

Apthorpe, R. and Gasper, D. (1996) *Arguing Development Policy: Names and Discourses*, London: Frank Cass.

Ashley, C. and Maxwell, S. (2001) 'Rethinking rural development', in C. Ashley and S. Maxwell (eds) *Development Policy Review*, 19 (4), London: Overseas Development Institute.

Ashley, S. and Nanyeenya, W. (2002) 'More than income: pro-poor livestock development policy in Uganda', *LADDER Working Paper*, No. 8., Norwich: Overseas Development Group, University of East Anglia.

ASPS (2000) *Irrigation Component. Component Implementation Plan,* Agriculture Sector Programme Support, Dar es Salaam: Ministry of Agriculture and Co-operatives, and DANIDA.

Attwell, C.A.M. and Cotterill, F.P.D. (2000) 'Postmodernism and African conservation science', *Biodiversity Conservation*, 9 (5): 559–77.

Azariadis, C. and Drazen, A. (1990) 'Threshold externalities and economic development', *Quarterly Journal of Economics*, 105 (3): 501–26.

Babirye, D. (1999) *Uganda Participatory Poverty Assessment Progress Report,* Kampala: Ministry of Finance Planning and Economic Development.

Baffes, J. (2001) 'Policy reforms in the cotton markets', in T. Akiyama, J. Baffes, D. Larson and P. Varangis (eds) *Commodity Market Reforms: Lessons from Two Decades*, Regional and Sectoral Studies, Washington, DC: World Bank.

Baffes, J. (2002) *Tanzania's Cotton Sector: Constraints and Challenges in a Global Environment*, Washington, DC: World Bank.

Bailey, C. and Jentoft, S. (1990) 'Hard choices in fisheries development', *Marine Policy*, 14 (4): 333–44.

Bailey, C., Cycon, D. and Morris, M. (1986) 'Fisheries development in the Third World: the role of international agencies', *World Development*, 14 (10/11): 1269–75.

Balihuta, A. and Sen, K. (2001) 'Macroeconomic policies and rural livelihood diversification: a Ugandan case-study', *LADDER Working Paper,* No. 3., Norwich: Overseas Development Group, University of East Anglia.

Bank, L.J. and Qambata, L. (1999) *No Visible Means of Subsistence: Rural Livelihoods, Gender and Deagrarianization in the Eastern Cape, South Africa,* Working Paper, No. 34, Grahamstown: Institute of Social and Economic Research; and Leiden: African Studies Center.

Banturaki, J. (2000) *Cooperatives and Poverty Alleviation*, Dar es Salaam: Tema Publishers.

Bardhan, P.K. and Mookherjee, D. (2000) 'Capture and governance at local and national levels', *American Economic Review*, 90 (2): 135–9.

Barrett, C.B. (1998) 'Immiserized growth in liberalized agriculture', *World Development*, 26 (5): 743–53.

Barrett, C.B. and Carter, M.R. (2001) 'Can't get ahead for falling behind: new directions for development policy to escape poverty and relief traps', *Choices*, 16 (4): 35–8.

Barrett, C.B. and Swallow, B.M. (2003) *Fractal Poverty Traps*, Working Paper, Ithaca: Cornell University.

Barrett, C.B. and Maxwell, D.G. (2004) *Food Aid After Fifty Years: Recasting Its Role,* London: Routledge, forthcoming.

Barrett, C.B., Bezuneh, M., Clay, D.C. and Reardon, T. (2001a) 'Heterogeneous constraints, incentives and income diversification strategies in rural Africa', Cornell University Working Paper, Ithaca: Cornell University.

Barrett, C.B., Reardon, T. and Webb, P. (eds) (2001b) 'Income diversification and livelihoods in rural Africa: cause and consequence of change', *Food Policy,* 26 (4) special issue.

Barrett, B.C., Bezuneh, M. and Aboud, A. (2001c) 'Income diversification, poverty traps and policy shocks in Côte d'Ivoire and Kenya', *Food Policy* 26 (4): 367–84.

Barrett, C.B., Reardon, T. and Webb, P. (2001d) 'Nonfarm income diversification and household livelihood strategies in rural Africa: concepts, dynamics, and policy implications', *Food Policy*, 26 (5): 315–31.

Barrett, C.B., Blume, L.E., McPeak, J.G., Minten, B., Murithi, F., Okumu, B.N., Pell, A., Place, F., Randrianarisoa, J.-C. and Rasambainarivo, J. (2002a) 'Poverty traps and resource degradation', *USAID BASIS CRSP Policy Brief*, No. 6, Washington, DC: USAID.

Barrett, C.B., Place, F. and Aboud, A.A. (eds) (2002b) *Natural Resources Management in African Agriculture: Understanding and Improving Current Practices*, Wallingford: CABI.

Barrett, C.B., Marenya, P.P., McPeak, J., Minten, B., Murithi, F., Oluoch-Kosura, W., Place, F., Randrianarisoa, J.C., Rasambainarivo, J. and Wangila, J. (2003a) 'Welfare dynamics in rural Kenya and Madagascar', Cornell University Working Paper, Ithaca: Cornell University.

Barrett, C.B., Holden, S. and Clay, D.C. (2003b) 'Can food-for-work programs reduce vulnerability?', in S. Dercon (ed.) *Insurance Against Poverty*, Oxford: Oxford University Press.

Bayart, J.-F. (1993) *The Politics of The Belly*, London: Longman.

Bayart, J.-F., Ellis, S. and Hibou, B. (1999) *The Criminalisation of the State in Africa*, Oxford: James Currey.

Bebbington, A. (1999) 'Capitals and capabilities: a framework for analyzing peasant viability, rural livelihoods and poverty', *World Development*, 27 (12): 2021–44.

Behnke, R.H., Scoones, I. and Kerven, C. (1993) *Range Ecology at Disequilibrium: New Models of Natural Variability and Pastoral Adoption in African Savannas*, London: Overseas Development Institute.

Belshaw, D., Lawrence, P. and Hubbard, M. (1999) 'Agricultural tradables and economic recovery in Uganda: the limitations of structural adjustment in practice', *World Development*, 27 (4): 673–90.

Bender, T. (1978) *Community and Social Change in America*, in A. Grawal and C. Gibson (eds) (2001) *Communities and the Environment: Ethnicity, Gender, and the State in Community-Based Conservation*, London: Rutgers University Press.

Béné, C. (2003) 'When fishery rhymes with poverty: a first step beyond the old paradigm on poverty in small-scale fisheries', *World Development*, 31: 949–75.

Berkvens, R.J.A. (1997) *Backing Two Horses: Interaction of Agricultural and Non-Agricultural Household Activities in a Zimbabwean Communal Area*, Working Paper, No. 24, Leiden: African Studies Center.

Bigsten, A. (1986) 'Welfare and economic growth in Kenya 1914–76', *World Development*, 14 (9): 1151–60.

Bigsten, A. and Kayizzi-Mugerula, S. (1995) 'Rural sector responses to economic crisis in Uganda', *Journal of International Development*, 7 (2): 181–209.

Bigsten, A., Collier, P., Fafchamps, M., Gauthier, B., Gunning, J.W., Habarurema, J., Oduro, A., Oostendorp, R., Pattillo, C., Söderbom, M., Teal, F. and Zeufack, A. (2000) 'Tanzania', in *Assessing Aid in Africa*, Washington, DC: World Bank.

Binswanger, H. and Rosenzweig, M. (1993) 'Wealth, weather risk and the composition and profitability of agricultural investments', *Economic Journal*, 103: 56–68.

Bird, K. and Shepherd, A. (2003) 'Livelihoods and chronic poverty in semi-arid Zimbabwe', *World Development*, 31 (3): 591–610.

Black, R., Sabates-Wheeler, R., Skeldon, R., Waddington, C. and Winters, A. (2003) *Mapping Study of Migration Issues*, Brighton: Sussex Centre for Migration Research, March, mimeo.

Blaikie, P. (2004) 'Is small really beautiful? Community-based natural resource management in Malawi and Botswana', *World Development*, forthcoming.

Bolt, V. and Bird, K. (2003) 'The Intra-household Disadvantages Framework: a framework for the analysis of intra-household difference and inequality', *CPRC Working Paper*, No. 32, London: ODI/Chronic Poverty Research Centre.

Booth, D., Holland, J., Hentschel, J., Lanjouw, P. and Herbert, A. (1998) *Participation and Combined Methods in African Poverty Assessment: Renewing the Agenda*, London: Social Development Division, UK Department for International Development (DFID), February, mimeo.

Boserup, E. (1970) *Women's Role in Economic Development*, London: George Allen & Unwin.

Boserup, E. (1990) *Economic and Demographic Relationships in Development*, Baltimore: Johns Hopkins University Press.

Bosworth, J. (2001) *Integrating Land Issues into the Broader Development Agenda: Uganda Country Case Study*, Kampala: DFID.

Bottrall, A. (1985) 'Managing large irrigation schemes: a problem of political economy', Agricultural Administration Unit, *Occasional Paper*, No. 5, London: Overseas Development Institute.

Bratton, M. and Van De Walle, N. (1994) 'Neo-patrimonial regimes and political transition in Africa', *World Politics*: 453–89.

Bromley, D.W. (ed.) (1992) *Making the Commons Work: Theory, Practice and Policy*, San Francisco: ICS Press.

Brown, W. (2002) *Report on a Study of Fisheries Related District Tendering Systems and Implications for Co-management of Lake Resources*, prepared for Department of Fisheries, and Integrated Lake Management Project, Kampala: ILM, draft, April, mimeo.

Bruce, J. and Lloyd, C. (1997) 'Finding the ties that bind: beyond headship and household', in L. Haddad, J. Hoddinott and H. Alderman (eds) *Intrahousehold Resource Allocation in Developing Countries: Methods, Models and Policy*, Baltimore: Johns Hopkins University Press.

Bruce, J.W. (1988) 'A perspective on indigenous land tenure systems and land concentration', in R.E. Downs and S.P. Reyna (eds) *Land and Society in Contemporary Africa*, Paper No. 28, Madison: Land Tenure Centre, University of Wisconsin.

Bruce, J.W. and Migot-Adholla, S.E. (eds) (1994) *Searching For Land Tenure Security in Africa*, Dubuque, la: Kendall/Hunt Publishing Company.

Brummett, R.E. and Williams, M.J. (2000) 'The evolution of aquaculture in African rural and economic development', *Ecological Economics*, 33: 193–203.

Bryceson, D.F. (1993) *Liberalizing Tanzania's Food Trade*, London: James Currey.

Bryceson, D.F. (1996) 'Deagrarianization and rural employment in Sub-Saharan Africa: a sectoral perspective', *World Development*, 24 (1): 97–111.

Bryceson, D.F. (1999) 'African rural labour, income diversification and livelihood approaches: a long-term development perspective', *Review of African Political Economy*, 80: 171–89.

Bryceson, D.F. (2000) 'Rural Africa at the crossroads: livelihood practices and policies', in *Natural Resource Perspectives,* No. 52, London: Overseas Development Institute.

Bryceson, D.F. (2002) 'The scramble in Africa: reorienting rural livelihoods', *World Development*, 30 (5): 725–39.

Bryceson, D.F. and Bank, L. (2001) 'End of an era: Africa's development policy parallax', *Journal of Contemporary African Studies*, 19 (1): 5–23.

Bryceson, D.F., Kay, C. and Mooij, J. (eds) (2000) *Disappearing Peasantries? Rural Labor in Africa, Asia and Latin America*, London: Intermediate Technology Publications.

Buvinic, M. and Gupta, G.R. (1997) 'Female-headed households and female-maintained families: are they worth targeting to reduce poverty in developing countries?', *Economic Development and Cultural Change*, 42 (2): 259–80.

Calaguas, B. and McConnell, M. (2002) 'Poverty reduction strategy papers and water: failing the poor?', WaterAid Discussion Paper, London: WaterAid.

Carney, D. (1998a) 'Implementing the sustainable rural livelihoods approach', in D. Carney (ed.) *Sustainable Rural Livelihoods: What Contribution Can We Make?*, London: Department for International Development.

Carney, D. (1998b) *Changing Public and Private Roles in Agricultural Service Provision,* London: Overseas Development Institute (ODI).

Carter, M.R. (1997) 'Environment, technology, and the social articulation of risk in West African agriculture', *Economic Development and Cultural Change*, 45 (3): 557–91.

Carter, M.R. and May, J. (2001) 'One kind of freedom: the dynamics of poverty in post-apartheid South Africa', *World Development*, 29 (12): 1987–2006.

Chabal, P. (1997) *Apocalypse Now? A Postcolonial Journey Into Africa,* Inaugural Lecture, King's College, London, 12 March, 1997. Online. Available HTTP: http://www.cphrc.org.uk/essays/chabal1.htm (accessed 24 March 2004).

Chabal, P. and Daloz, J.-P. (1999) *Africa Works: Disorder as Political Instrument,* Oxford: James Currey.

Chachage, S. and Nyoni, J. (2001) *Economic Restructuring and the Cashewnut Industry in Tanzania*, Dar es Salaam: Tanzania Agriculture Situation Analysis, September, mimeo.

Chambers, R. (1988) *Managing Canal Irrigation. Practical Analysis from South Asia*, Wye Studies in Agricultural and Rural Development, Cambridge: Cambridge University Press.

Chambers, R. (1989) 'Editorial introduction: vulnerability, coping and policy', *IDS Bulletin*, 20 (2): 1–7.

Chambers, R. and Conway, G. (1992) 'Sustainable rural development: practical concepts for the 21st century', *IDS Discussion Paper Series*, No. 296, Brighton: Institute of Development Studies, University of Sussex.

Chambo, S. and Cooksey, B. (2000) 'The changing form of cooperatives: an analysis of emerging agricultural cooperatives in Tanzania', paper presented at the Fifth REPOA Research Workshop held at the Whitesands Hotel, Dar es Salaam, April 18–19, mimeo.

Chant, S. (1997) *Women-Headed Households: Diversity and Dynamics in the Developing World,* London: Macmillan Press.

Charles, A.T. (2001) *Sustainable Fishery Systems*, Oxford: Blackwell Science.

Chikaonda, M. (2001) *Budget Speech, 22 June 2001*, Malawi News, 23 June 2001.

Chilowa, W., Dzimadzi, D., Chinsinga, B., Kayambazinthu, E. and Mphande, C. (2001) *MASAF Information, Education and Communication (IEC) Impact Assessment: Final Report,* Lilongwe: MASAF, April.

Chukwuezi, B. (1999) *Deagrarianization and Rural Employment in Rural Igboland, Southeastern Nigeria,* Working Paper, No. 37, Kano: Center for Documentation and Research; and Leiden: African Studies Center.

Cleaver, F. (1999) 'Paradoxes of participation: questioning participatory approaches to development', *Journal of International Development*, 11: 597–612.

Cleaver, F. (2002) 'Institutions, agency and the limitations of participatory approaches to development', Chapter 3 in B. Cooke and U. Kothari (eds) *Participation: The New Tyranny?*, London: Zed Books.

Collier, P. and Lal, D. (1980) 'Poverty and growth in Kenya', *World Bank Staff Working Paper*, No. 389, Washington, DC: World Bank.

Collier, P. and Reinikka, R. (2001) 'Reconstruction and liberalization – an overview', in P. Collier and R. Reinikka (eds) *Uganda's Recovery: The Role of Farms, Firms and Government*, Oxford: Oxford University Press.

Compass Tamis (2004) *Success Stories*. Online. Available HTTP: http://tamis.dai.com/compass.nsf (accessed 18 January 2004).

Cooke, B. and Kothari, U. (eds) (2001) *Participation: The New Tyranny?*, London: Zed Books.

Cooksey, B. (2001) 'World Bank assistance to Tanzanian agriculture', in TASA, *Sofrai Project Review, Proceedings, vol. II Annexes, Chapter 3*, Dar es Salaam: TASA, October.

Cooksey, B. (2002) 'Can aid agencies really help combat corruption?' *Forum on Crime and Society*, No. 3, Vienna: Centre for International Crime Prevention, February.

Cooksey, B. (2003) 'Marketing reform? The rise and fall of agricultural liberalisation in Tanzania', *Development Policy Review*, 21 (1): 67–91.

Coomes, O.T. and Burt, G.J. (1997) 'Indigenous market-oriented agroforestry: dissecting local diversity in western Amazonia', *Agroforestry Systems*, 37 (1): 27–44.

Coomes, O.T., Grimard, F. and Burt, G.J. (2000) 'Tropical forests and shifting cultivation: secondary forest fallow dynamics among traditional farmers of the Peruvian Amazon', *Ecological Economics*, 32 (1): 109–24.

Coulson, A. (ed.) (1979) *African Socialism in Practice: the Tanzanian Experience*, Nottingham: Spokesman Books.

Craig, D. and Porter, D. (2003) 'Poverty reduction strategy papers: a new convergence', *World Development*, 31 (1): 53–69.

Crommelynck, A. (2002) 'Bringing together quantitative and qualitative data: findings from the village census and Uganda's participatory poverty assessment process', Kampala: Government Printer, draft, October, mimeo.

Crook, R. and Manor, J. (1998) *Democracy and Decentralisation in South-East Asia and West Africa: Participation, Accountability and Performance*, Cambridge: Cambridge University Press.

Cross, S. (2001) 'Decentralisation and rural livelihoods in Malawi', *LADDER Working Paper*, No. 21, Norwich: Overseas Development Group (ODG), University of East Anglia.

Cross, S. (2002a) 'Customary land tenure, taxes and service delivery in rural Malawi: a review of institutional features of rural livelihoods', *LADDER Working Paper*, No. 21, Norwich: Overseas Development Group (ODG), University of East Anglia.

Cross, S. (2002b) 'A comparative study of land tenure reform in four countries: Uganda, Tanzania, Malawi and Kenya', *LADDER Working Paper*, No. 31, Norwich: Overseas Development Group (ODG), University of East Anglia, December.

Cross, S. and Kutengule, M. (2001) 'Decentralisation and rural livelihoods in Malawi', *LADDER Working Paper*, No. 4, Norwich: Overseas Development Group (ODG), University of East Anglia.

Csaki, C. (2001) 'Reaching the rural poor', in C. Ashley and S. Maxwell (eds) *Development Policy Review*, 19 (4): 563–73, London: Overseas Development Institute.

Cycon, D.E. (1986) 'Managing fisheries in developing nations: A plea for appropriate development', *Natural Resources Journal*, 26 (1): 1–14.

Daily News (2002) *Rural Financial Services Programme, Job Advertisement,* Dar es Salaam: URT/PMO, 2 November.

DANIDA/JICA (2001) 'Proceedings of the 1st National Irrigation Conference, Morogoro, Tanzania, 20th–22nd March 2001', Dar es Salaam: Department of Irrigation, Ministry of Agriculture.

Dasgupta, P. (1997) 'Nutritional status, the capacity for work, and poverty traps', *Journal of Econometrics*, 77 (1): 5–37.

Davidson, A.P., Ahmad, M. and Ali, T. (2001) 'Dilemmas of agricultural extension in Pakistan: food for thought', *Agricultural Administration (Research and Extension) Network Paper,* No. 116, London: Overseas Development Institute.

Davies, S. (1996) *Adaptable Livelihoods: Coping with Food Insecurity in the Malian Sahel,* London: Macmillan Press.

de Janvry, A. and Sadoulet, E. (2000) 'Rural poverty in Latin America, determinants and exit paths', in *Food Policy*, 25 (4): 389–409.

de Haan, A. and Rogaly, B. (eds) (2002) 'Special issue: labour mobility and rural society', *The Journal of Development Studies*, 38 (5), June.

Deininger, K. and Okidi, J. (2002) *Growth and Poverty Reduction in Uganda, 1992–2000: Panel Data Evidence*, Washington, DC: World Bank; and Kampala: Economic Policy Research Council, November 2003, mimeo.

Delgado, C., Liedholm, C., Maynard, M. and Lundberg, D. (1993) 'What is the role of private-sector agriculture and farm linkages to the nonfarm economy?', in D. Seckler (ed.) *Agricultural Transformation in Africa: A round Table Discussion with C. Ackello-Ogutu, M. Carter, K. Cleaver, C. Delgado, E. Gilbert, B.H. Kaestner III, C. Liedholm, M. Maynard, P. Peters, T. Reardon, D. Sahn, A. Shaikh, P. Timmer and Africa specialists of USAID and Winrock International,* Arlington: Winrock International Institute for Agricultural Development.

Delgado, C.L. and Minot, N.W. (2000) *Agriculture in Tanzania Since 1986: Follower or Leader of Growth?*, Washington, DC: World Bank.

Department for International Development (DFID) (1997) 'Priorities for irrigated agriculture', *Water Resources Occasional Paper,* No. 1, Report prepared by H.R. Wallingford, London: DFID, July.

Dercon, S. (1996) 'Risk, crop choice, and savings. Evidence from Tanzania', *Economic Development and Cultural Change,* 44 (3): 485–513.

Dercon, S. (1998) 'Wealth, risk and activity choice: cattle in western Tanzania', *Journal of Development Economics*, 55 (1): 1–42.

Dercon, S. and Krishnan, P. (1996) 'Income portfolios in rural Ethiopia and Tanzania: choices and constraints', *The Journal of Development Studies*, 32 (6): 850–75.

Deshingkar, P., Rao, S., Kulkarni, U., Rao, L., Reddy, R. and Renuka, B. (2004) *Poverty Traps or Opportunity? Changing Rural Livelihoods in Agriculture in Andhra Pradesh*, London: Overseas Development Institute, forthcoming.

Devereux, S. (1993) 'Goats before ploughs: dilemmas of household response sequencing during food shortages', *IDS Bulletin*, 24 (4): 52–9.

Dijkstra, A.G. and Van Donge, J.K. (2001) 'What does the "show case" show? Evidence of and lessons from adjustment in Uganda', *World Development*, 29 (5): 841–63.

Dolan, C. (2002) 'Gender and diverse livelihoods in Uganda', LADDER Working Paper, No. 10, Norwich: Overseas Development Group (ODG), University of East Anglia.

Dolan, C. (2004) 'From farm to packhouse: employment at the bottom of a global commodity chain', *Rural Sociology*, 69 (1): 99–126.

Drèze, J. and Srinivasan, P.V. (1997) 'Widowhood and poverty in rural India: some inferences from household survey data', *Journal of Development Economics,* 54: 217–34.

Dugan, P. (2003) 'Investing in Africa: the WorldFish Center's African strategy in summary', *NAGA (WorldFish Center Quarterly),* 26 (3): 4–8.

Durlauf, S. (1996) 'A theory of persistent income inequality', *Journal of Economic Growth*, 1: 75–93.

Easterly, W. (2001) *The Elusive Quest for Growth*, Cambridge: MIT Press.

EIU (1997) *Country Profile: Uganda, 1997–98*, London: The Economist Intelligence Unit.

Elbers, C., Lanjouw, J. and Lanjouw, P. (2001) 'Welfare in villages and towns: micro-level estimation of inequality and poverty', *Working Paper*, Amsterdam: Free University of Amsterdam.

Ellis, F. (1982) 'Agricultural price policy in Tanzania', *World Development*, 10 (4): 263–83.

Ellis, F. (1983) 'Agricultural marketing and peasant–state transfers in Tanzania', *Journal of Peasant Studies*, 10 (4): 214–42.

Ellis, F. (1988) 'Tanzania', in C. Harvey (ed.) *Agricultural Price Policy in Africa*, London: Macmillan.

Ellis, F. (1998) 'Household strategies and rural livelihood diversification', *The Journal of Development Studies*, 35 (1): 1–38.

Ellis, F. (2000) *Rural Livelihoods and Diversity in Developing Countries,* Oxford: Oxford University Press.

Ellis, F. (2001) 'Rural livelihoods, diversity and poverty reduction policies: Uganda, Tanzania, Malawi and Kenya', *LADDER Working Paper*, No. 1, Norwich: Overseas Development Group (ODG), University of East Anglia, October.

Ellis, F. (2003a) 'Human vulnerability and food insecurity: policy implications', *Forum for Food Security in Southern Africa*, Theme Paper, No. 3, London: Overseas Development Institute, July, mimeo.

Ellis, F. (2003b) *A Livelihoods Approach to Migration and Poverty Reduction*, Paper commissioned by the Department for International Development (DFID), London: DFID, November, mimeo.

Ellis, F. and Bahiigwa, G. (2001) 'Livelihoods and rural poverty reduction in Uganda', *LADDER Working Paper,* No. 5, Norwich: Overseas Development Group (ODG), University of East Anglia.

Ellis, F. and Bahiigwa, G. (2003) 'Livelihoods and rural poverty reduction in Uganda', *World Development*, 31 (6): 997–1013.

Ellis, F. and Freeman, H.A. (2002) 'Rural livelihoods and poverty reduction strategies in four African countries', *LADDER Working Paper*, No. 30, Norwich: Overseas Development Group (ODG), University of East Anglia.

Ellis, F. and Freeman, H.A. (2004) 'Rural livelihoods and poverty reduction strategies in four African countries', *The Journal of Development Studies*, 40 (4), April.

Ellis, F. and Mdoe, N. (2003) 'Livelihoods and rural poverty reduction in Tanzania', *World Development*, 31 (8): 1367–84.

Ellis, F., Kutengule, M. and Nyasulu, A. (2003) 'Livelihoods and rural poverty reduction in Malawi', *World Development*, 31 (9): 1495–510.

Elson, D. and Evers, B. (1997) 'Gender aware country economic reports: Uganda', *Working Paper*, No. 2, Manchester: Genecon Unit, University of Manchester.

Escobar, A. (1995) *Encountering Development: The Making and Unmaking of the Third World*, Princeton: Princeton University Press.

Evans, A. (1992) *A Review of Rural Labour Markets in Uganda*, Washington, DC: World Bank Agricultural Secretariat, World Bank, mimeo.

Evans, H.E. and Ngau, P. (1991) 'Rural–urban relations, household income diversification and agricultural productivity', *Development and Change*, 22: 519–45.

Evans, J., Banda, A. and Seymour, T. (1999) *Opportunities for Better Soil Management*, vol. 2, (Technical Annex), Lilongwe: Government of Malawi, July.

FAO (1995a) *Malawi: Smallholder Irrigation Sub-Sector Programme Socio-Economic and Production Study of Wetland Use*, Rome: Food and Agriculture Organisation. Online. Available HTTP: http://www.fao.org/Gender/static/tci/malawi.htm (accessed 16 January 2004).

FAO (1995b) *The Code of Conduct for Responsible Fisheries*, Rome: Food and Agriculture Organisation.

FAO (2003) Fishery Country Profiles. Online. Available HTTP: http://www.fao.org./fi/fcp/fcp.asp (accessed 17 January 2004).

FAOSTAT Fisheries Data (2003). Online. Available HTTP: http://apps.fao.org/page/collections?subset=fisheries (accessed 17 January 2004).

FAOSTAT Nutrition Data (2003) Online. Available HTTP: http://apps.fao.org/page/collections?subset=nutrition (accessed 17 January 2004).

Feeney, D., Berkes, F., McCay, B. and Acheson, J.M. (1995) 'The tragedy of the commons: twenty-two years later', in K. Conca, M. Alberty and G. Dabelkoa (eds) *Green Planet Blues: Environmental Politics from Stockholm to Rio*, Boulder: Westview Press.

Fields, G.S. (2000) 'The dynamics of poverty, inequality and economic well-being: African economic growth in comparative perspective', *Journal of African Economies*, 9 (1): 45–78.

Floyd, C., Harding, A.H., Paudel, K.C., Rasali, P.D., Subedi, K. and Subedi, P.P. (2003) 'Household adoption and associated impact of multiple agricultural technologies in the western hills of Nepal', *Agricultural Systems*, 76: 715–38.

Foster, J., Greer, J. and Thorbecke, E. (1984) 'A class of decomposable poverty measures', *Econometrica*, 52: 761–5.

Francis, E. (1998) 'Gender and rural livelihoods in Kenya', *The Journal of Development Studies*, 35 (2): 72–95.

Francis, E. (2000) *Making a Living: Changing Livelihoods in Rural Africa*, London: Routledge.

Francis, E. and Hoddinott, J. (1993) 'Migration and differentiation in Western Kenya: a tale of two sub-locations', *The Journal of Development Studies*, 30 (1): 115–45.

Francis, P. and James, R. (2003) 'Balancing rural poverty reduction and citizen participation: the contradictions of Uganda's decentralisation program', *World Development*, 31 (2): 325–37.

Freeman, H.A., Ellis, F. and Allison, E. (2003) 'Livelihoods and rural poverty reduction in Kenya', *LADDER Working Paper*, No. 33, Norwich: Overseas Development Group (ODG), University of East Anglia.

Freeman, H.A., Ellis, F. and Allison, E. (2004) 'Livelihoods and rural poverty reduction in Kenya', *Development Policy Review,* 22 (2): 147–71.

Fujita, M., Krugman, P. and Venables, A.J. (1999) *The Spatial Economy; Cities, Regions and International Trade,* Cambridge: MIT Press.

Fuwa, N. (2000) 'The poverty and heterogeneity among female-headed households revisited: the case of Panama', *World Development,* 28 (8): 1515–42.

Galor, O. and Zeira, J. (1993) 'Income distribution and macroeconomics', *Review of Economic Studies,* 60 (1): 35–52.

Geda, A., de Jong, N., Mwabu, G. and Kimenyi, M.S. (2001) 'Determinants of poverty in Kenya: a household level analysis', Institute of Social Studies Working Paper, The Hague: ISS.

Geheb, K. and Binns, T. (1997) '"Fishing farmers" or "farming fishermen?" The quest for household income and nutritional security on the Kenyan shores of Lake Victoria', *African Affairs*, 96: 73–93.

Geheb, K. and Sarch, M.-T. (eds) (2000) *Africa's Inland Fisheries; The Management Challenge*, Kampala: Fountain Publishers Ltd.

Ghimire, K. and Pimbert, M.P. (eds) (1997) *Social Changes and Conservation*, London: Earthscan; and Geneva: United Nations Research Institute for Social Development (UNRISD).

Gibbon, P. (1999) 'Free competition without sustainable development? Tanzanian cotton sector liberalisation 1994/95 to 1997/98', *The Journal of Development Studies,* 36 (1): 128–50.

Gilling, J., Jones, S. and Duncan, A. (2001) 'Sector approaches, sustainable livelihoods and rural poverty reduction', *Development Policy Review*, 19 (3): 303–19.

Gladwin, C.H., Peterson, J.S., Phiri, D. and Uttaro, R. (2002) 'Agroforestry adoption decisions, structural adjustment and gender in Africa', in C. Barrett, F. Place and A. Aboud (eds) *Natural Resources Management in African Agriculture,* Wallingford: CABI Publishing.

Goetz, A.M. (1995) 'Macro–meso–micro linkages: understanding gendered institutional structures and practices', paper presented at the SAGA Workshop on Gender and Economic Reform in Africa, Ottawa, October 1995, mimeo.

Goetz, A.M., Maxwell, S. and Manyire, H. (1994) *SPA Poverty and Social Policy Working Group Consultancy on Poverty Assessment and Public Expenditure Issues: Uganda Country Study*, Brighton: Institute of Development Studies, University of Sussex, mimeo.

Gonzalez de la Rocha, M. (2000) 'Private adjustments: household responses to the erosion of work', in A. Grinspun (ed.) *SEPED Conference Paper Series*, No. 6, New York: UNDP.

Gordon, A. and Craig, C. (2001) 'Rural non-farm activities and poverty alleviation in Sub-Saharan Africa', *Policy Series*, No. 14, Greenwich: Natural Resources Institute, University of Greenwich.

Gordon, A. and Goodland, A. (2000) 'Production credit for African smallholders: conditions for private provision', *Savings and Development,* 24 (1): 55–83.

Graham-Jolly, H.G. (1995) 'The progress of local government in Nyasaland', *Journal of African Administration*, 8 (4).

Grandin, B.E. (1988) *Wealth Ranking in Smallholder Communities: A Field Manual,* London: Intermediate Technology Publications.

Greer, J. and Thorbecke, E. (1986) 'Food poverty profile applied to Kenyan smallholders', *Economic Development and Cultural Change,* 35 (1): 115–42.

Guijt, I. and Thompson, J. (1994) 'Landscapes and livelihoods. Environmental and socio-economic dimensions of small scale irrigation', *Land Use Policy*, 11 (4): 294–308.

Gunning, J.W. (2001) 'Rethinking aid', in B. Pleskovic and N. Stern (eds) *Annual World Bank Conference on Development Economics 2000*, Washington, DC: World Bank.

Haggblade, S. and Tembo, G. (2003) *Conservation Farming in Zambia*, Lusaka: Michigan State University Food Research Project; and Washington, DC: IFPRI.

Handa, S. (1994) 'Gender, headship and intrahousehold resource allocation', *World Development*, 22 (10): 1535–47.

Hara, M., Donda, S. and Njaya, F.J. (2002) 'Lessons from Malawi's experience with fisheries co-management initiatives', in K. Geheb and M.-T. Sarch (eds) *Africa's Inland Fisheries: The Management Challenge*, Kampala: Fountain Books.

Hardin, G. (1968) 'The tragedy of the commons', *Science*, 162: 1243–8.

Harrigan, J. (2003) 'U-turns and full circles: two decades of agricultural reform in Malawi, 1981–2000', *World Development*, 31 (5): 847–63.

Harriss, J. (ed.) (1997) 'Policy arena: "missing link" or analytically missing?: the concept of social capital', *Journal of International Development*, 9 (7): 919–71.

Haugerud, A. (1983) 'The consequences of land tenure reform among smallholders in the Kenya highlands', *Rural Africana*, 15–16: 65–89.

Havnevik, K.J. and Harsmar, M. (1999) *The Diversified Future: An Institutional Approach to Rural Development in Tanzania*', Stockholm: Swedish Ministry of Foreign Affairs.

Hecky, S. and Moore, K. (2001) 'Chronic poverty in Sub-Saharan Africa and South Asia', *Background Paper*, No. 1, Manchester: Chronic Poverty Research Centre, Manchester University.

Henstridge, M. and Kasekende, L. (2001) 'Exchange reforms, stabilization and fiscal management', in R. Reinikka and P. Collier (eds) *Uganda's Recovery: The Role of Farms, Firms and Governments*, Washington, DC, World Bank.

Hoddinott, J. (1994) 'A model of migration and remittances applied to Western Kenya', *Oxford Economic Papers*, vol. 46: 459–76.

Hoddinott, J. and Kinsey, B.H. (2001) 'Child growth in the time of drought', *Oxford Bulletin of Economics and Statistics*, 63 (4): 409–36.

Holmgren, T., Kasekende, L., Atingi-Ego, M. and Ddamulira, D. (1999) *Aid and Reform in Uganda: Country Case-Study*, Washington, DC: The World Bank.

Holtom, D. (2002) 'Tanzania's PRSP: everyone wants a success story', Swansea: Centre For Development Studies, University of Wales, mimeo.

Howe, J. and Bantje, H. (1995) *Technology Choice in Civil Engineering Practice: Experience in the Road Sector*, Geneva: International Labor Office.

Hulme, D. and Infield, M. (2001) 'Community conservation, reciprocity and park–people relationships: a study of Lake Mburo National Park, Uganda', in D. Hulme and M. Murphee (eds) *African Wildlife and Livelihoods: The Promise and Performance of Community Conservation*, Oxford: James Currey; and New Hampshire: Heinemann.

Hulme, D. and Murphree, M.W. (eds) (2001) *African Wildlife and Livelihoods*, London: James Currey.

Hulme, D. and Shepherd, A. (2003) 'Conceptualising Chronic Poverty', *World Development*, 31 (3): 403–23.

Hussein, K. and Nelson, J. (1998) 'Sustainable livelihoods and livelihoods diversification', *IDS Working Paper Series*, No. 69, Brighton: Institute of Development Studies, University of Sussex.

Hyden, G. (1980) *Beyond Ujamaa in Tanzania: Underdevelopment and an Uncaptured Peasantry*, Berkeley: University of California.

Iliya, M.A. (1999) *Income Diversification in the Semi Arid Zone of Nigeria: Gigane, Sokoto, Northwest Nigeria,* Working Paper, No. 39., Kano: Center for Documentation and Research;, and Leiden: African Studies Center.

Iliya, M.A. and Swindell, K. (1997) 'Winners and losers: household fortunes in the urban peripheries of northern Nigeria', in D.F. Bryceson and V. Jamal (eds) *Farewell to Farms: Deagrarianization and Employment in Africa,* Aldershot: Ashgate.

Illius, A. and O'Connor, T.G. (1999) 'On the relevance of non-equilibrium concepts to arid and semi-arid grazing systems', *Ecological Applications*, 9: 798–813.

ILO (2000) *Safety and Health in the Fishing Industry*, Geneva: International Labour Office.

Inamdar A., de Jode, H., Lindsay, K. and Cobb, S. (1999) 'Capitalising on nature; protected area management', *Science*, 283: 1856–7.

International Federation of the Red Cross and Red Crescent Societies (IFRCRCS) (2002) *World Disasters Report 2002,* Geneva: IFRCRCS.

International Fund for Agricultural Development (IFAD) (2001) *Rural Poverty Report 2001: The Challenge of Ending Rural Poverty*, Oxford: Oxford University Press.

International Fund for Agricultural Development (IFAD) (2002) *Gender and Household Food Security: The Issue Of Poverty Among Female-Headed Households in Africa*, Oxford: Oxford University Press for IFAD. Online. Available HTTP: http://www.ifad.org/gender/learning/challenges/women/60.htm (accessed 15 January 2004).

International Textile Manufacturers Federation (2001) *Survey of Cotton Lint Contamination*, Zurich: ITMF.

Jalan, J. and Ravallion, M. (2001) 'Behavioural responses to risk in rural China', *Journal of Development Economics*, 66 (1): 23–49.

Jamal, V. and Weeks, J. (1993) *Africa Misunderstood or Whatever Happened to the Rural-Urban Gap?*, London: Macmillan.

Jambiya, G. (1998) *The Dynamics of Population, Land Scarcity, Agriculture and Non-Agricultural Activities: West Usambara Mountains, Lushoto District, Tanzania'*, Working Paper, No. 28, Dar es Salaam: Institute of Resource Assessment; and Leiden: African Studies Center.

James, R., Francis, P. and Turiho-Habwe, G. (2001) 'Methods manual for field-work', *LADDER Working Paper*, No. 2, Norwich: Overseas Development Group (ODG), University of East Anglia.

James, R., Mdoe, N. and Mishili, F. (2002) 'Tanzanian rural livelihoods: towards a more enabling institutional environment', *LADDER Working Paper*, No. 13, Norwich: Overseas Development Group (ODG), University of East Anglia, March.

Jayne, T.S., Chapoto, A., Nyoro, J., Mwanaumo, A. and Govereh, J. (2001) 'False promise or false premise? The experience of food and input market reform in Eastern and Southern Africa', in T.S. Jayne, G. Argwings-Kodhek and I. Minde (eds) *Perspectives on Agricultural Transformation: A View from Africa*, New York: Nova Science Publishers.

Jayne, T.S., Govereh, J. and Mwanaumo, A. (2002) 'False promise or false premise? The experience of food and input market reform in eastern and southern Africa', *World Development*, 30 (11): 1967–85.

Jayne, T.S., Yamano, T., Weber, M.T., Tschirley, D., Benfica, R., Chapoto, A. and

Zulu, B. (2003) 'Smallholder income and land distribution in Africa: implications for poverty reduction strategies', *Food Policy*, 28 (2): 253–75.

JICA Japan International Corporation Agency, Ministry of Agriculture and Food Security (2001) *The Study on the National Irrigation Master Plan in the United Republic of Tanzania*, Dar es Salaam: Ministry of Agriculture and Food Security, October.

Jul-Larsen, E., Kolding, J., Overå, R., Nielsen, J.R. and van Zwieten, P.A.M. (2003) 'Management, co-management or no management? Major dilemmas in southern African freshwater fisheries', 1. Synthesis, *FAO Fisheries Technical Report*, No. 426/1, Rome: FAO.

Kabeer, N. and Anh, Tran Thi Van (2000) 'Leaving the ricefields but not the countryside: gender livelihood diversification and pro-poor growth in rural Vietnam', *Occasional Paper Series*, No. 13., Geneva: UNRISD.

Kahkonen, S. and Leathers, H. (1997) *Is there Life after Liberalization? Transaction Cost Analysis of Maize and Cotton Marketing in Zambia and Tanzania*, Washington, DC: USAID.

Kalinga, G., Simba, A.H. and Temu, R.J.M. (2001) 'National irrigation development plan – update', in *Proceedings of the 1st National Irrigation Conference, Morogoro, Tanzania, 20th to 22nd March, 2001. Theme: 'Irrigated Agriculture for Food Security and Poverty Reduction', vols I and II,* Dar es Salaam: Ministry of Agriculture and Food Security.

Kanbur, R. (ed.) (2001) *Qualitative and Quantitative Poverty Appraisal: Complementarities, Tensions and the Way Forward*, Working Paper, No. 2001-05, Ithaca: Department of Applied Economics and Management, Cornell University, May.

Kasente, D., Lockwood, M., Vivian, J. and Whitehead, A. (2000) 'Gender and the expansion of agricultural exports in Uganda', *Occasional Paper Series*, No. 12, Geneva: UNRISD.

Keeley, J. and Scoones, I. (1999) 'Understanding environmental policy process', *IDS Working Paper*, No. 89, Brighton: Institute of Development Studies, University of Sussex.

Kelly, J. (2001) *Improving Revenue Mobilization in Malawi: Study on Property Rates and Business Licencing*, Lilongwe: UNDP/UNCDF, April.

Kenya (1998a) *The First Report on Poverty in Kenya, vol. 1: Incidence and Depth of Poverty*, Nairobi: Central Bureau of Statistics, Ministry of Finance and Planning.

Kenya (1998b) *The First Report on Poverty in Kenya, vol. II: Poverty and Social Indicators*, Nairobi: Central Bureau of Statistics, Ministry of Finance and Planning.

Kenya (1998c) *Economic Survey*, Nairobi: Government Printer.

Kenya (2000a) *Interim Poverty Reduction Strategy Paper*, Nairobi: Government Printer.

Kenya (2000b) Ministry of Finance and Planning (MFP), *Second Report on Poverty in Kenya, vol. III, Welfare Indicators Atlas,* Nairobi: Ministry of Finance and Planning, Government of Kenya.

Kenya (2000c) *Second Report on Poverty in Kenya, vol. I: Incidence and Depth of Poverty*, Nairobi: Government Printer.

Kenya (2001a) Ministry of Finance and Planning (MFP), *Poverty Reduction Strategy Paper for the Period 2001–2003*, Nairobi: Ministry of Finance and Planning, Government of Kenya, June. Online. Available HTTP: www.treasury.go.ke (accessed 18 January 2004).

Kenya (2001b) Ministry of Health (MOH), *AIDS in Kenya: Background, Projects, Impact, Interventions, Policy*, 6th edn, Nairobi: Ministry of Health.

Kenya (2001c) Ministry of Finance and Planning (MFP), *Poverty Reduction Strategy*

Paper for the Period 2001–2004, Nairobi: Ministry of Finance and Planning, Government of Kenya.

Kenya (2001d) Ministry of Finance and Planning (MFP), *Poverty Reduction Strategy Paper for Nyando District,* Nairobi: Ministry of Finance and Planning, Government of Kenya.

Kenya (2002) *Economic Survey*, Nairobi: Government Printer.

Kenya Land Alliance (KLA) (2002) Submission to the Constitution of Kenya Review Commission, *Recommendations from the National Civil Society Conference on Land Reform and the Land Question*, Mbagathi: KLA, May.

Kimalu, P.K., Nafula, N., Manda, D.K., Mwabu, G. and Kimenyi, S.M. (2001) 'A situation analysis of poverty in Kenya', *KIPPRA Working Paper,* No. 6., Nairobi: KIPPRA.

Kinsey, B. (2000) *Mainstays and Sidelines: Temporal Dimensions of Rural Livelihoods with Enhanced Opportunities Provided by Land Reform*, Working Paper, No. 21, Manchester: Institute for Development Policy and Management, University of Manchester.

Kiringai, J. and Manda, D.K. (2002) 'The PRSP process in Kenya', paper presented at the second meeting of the African Learning Group on the Poverty Reduction Strategy Papers (PRSP-LG), Brussels, 18–21 November 2002. Online. Available HTTP: http://www.uneca.org/prsp/docs/kenya_prsp.htm#* (accessed 18 January 2004).

Kobb, D. (2001) 'A Summary of UAPP's experiences in raising revenue in three local authorities', background report for presentation to LGRP, Dar es Salaam: Urban Authorities Partnership Programme, August, mimeo.

Krishna, A., Kristjanson, P., Radeny, M. and Nindo, W. (2003) 'Comparing pathways out of poverty in Kenya and India', *International Livestock Research Institute Working Paper,* Nairobi: ILRI.

Krugman, P. (1991) 'Increasing returns and economic geography', *Journal of Political Economy,* 99 (3): 483–99.

Kydd, J. (2002) 'Agriculture and rural livelihoods: is globalisation opening or blocking paths out of rural poverty?', *Agricultural Research & Extension Network Paper,* No. 121, London: Overseas Development Institute.

Kydd, J. and Christiansen, R. (1982) 'Structural change in Malawi since independence: consequences of a development strategy based on large scale agriculture', *World Development*, 10 (5): 355–75.

LADDER (2001*)* 'Chanzuru-Darajani and Chanzuru-Chekereni Villages', *Ladder Village Reports,* No. 11 and 12, Norwich: Overseas Development Group (ODG), University of East Anglia, December. Online. Available HTTP: http://www.odg.uea.ac.uk/ladder (accessed 24 March 2004).

LADDER Research Team (2001) 'Methods manual for fieldwork', *LADDER Working Paper*, No. 2, Norwich: Overseas Development Group (ODG), University of East Anglia, October.

Lankford, B.A. (2001) 'Red routes on blue rivers: strategic water management for the Ruaha River Basin, Tanzania', *Water Resources Development,* 17 (3): 427–44.

Lankford, B.A. (2003) 'Irrigation-based livelihood trends in river basins: theory and policy implications for irrigation development', *Physics and Chemistry of the Earth*, 28: 817–25.

Lankford, B.A. (2004) 'Resource-centred thinking in river basins: should we revoke the crop water requirement approach to irrigation planning?', *Agricultural Water Management*, Amsterdam: Elsevier Publications.

Lankford, B.A. and Gillingham, P. (2001) 'The impacts of irrigation improvement programmes', in *Proceedings of the 1st National Irrigation Conference, Morogoro, Tanzania, 20th to 22nd March, 2001. Theme: 'Irrigated Agriculture for Food Security and Poverty Reduction', vols I and II,* Dar es Salaam: Department of Irrigation, Ministry of Agriculture.

Larsen, M. (2002) 'Is oligopoly a condition of successful privatization? The case of cotton in Zimbabwe', *Journal of Agrarian Change*, 2 (2): 185–205.

Lind, J. and Cappon, J. (2001) *Realities or Rhetoric? Revisiting the Decentralisation of Natural Resources Management in Uganda and Zambia*, Nairobi: African Centre for Technology Studies, ACTS Press.

Lipton, M. (1984) 'Private interest and the good of all: types of conflict in the development process', paper presented at the British Association for the Advancement of Science, Norwich, 10–14 September 1984, mimeo.

Lipton, M. (2001) 'Escaping poverty: the poor's productive resource needs: a keynote address', paper presented at 2020 Vision; Sustainable Food Security for all by 2020, Bonn, Germany, 4–6 September 2001.

Lipton, M. and Ravallion, M. (1995) 'Poverty and policy', in J. Behrman and T.N. Srinivasan (eds) *Handbook of Development Economics, vol. IIIB*, Amsterdam: Elsevier.

Livestock in Development (LID) (1999) *Livestock in Poverty Focused Development*, Crewkerne: In Development Ltd.

Long, N. and Long, A. (1992) *Battlefields of Knowledge: The Interlocking of Theory and Practice in Social Research and Development*, London: Routledge.

Loury, G.C. (1981) 'Intergenerational transfers and the distribution of earnings', *Econometrica,* 49 (4): 843–67.

Lovell, C. (2000) 'Productive water points in dryland areas: guidelines on integrated planning for rural water supply', London: ITDG.

Lucas, R. (1988) 'On the mechanics of economic development', *Journal of Monetary Economics*, 22 (1): 2–42.

Lugard, F.D. (1922) *The Dual Mandate in British Tropical Africa*, London: Blackwoods.

Lumbanga, M. (2001a) *Coffee Industry Act*, Chief Secretary, Dar es Salaam: Government Printers, 17 September.

Lumbanga, M. (2001b) *Tobacco Industry Act*, Chief Secretary, Dar es Salaam: Government Printers, 17 September.

Lumbanga, M. (2001c) *Sugar Industry Act*, Chief Secretary, Dar es Salaam: Government Printers, 28 February.

Lundbaek, J. (2002) *Privatisation of the Cotton Sector in Uganda: Market Failure and Institutional Mechanisms to Overcome it*, Copenhagen: Department of Economics and Natural Resources, Royal Veterinary and Agricultural University.

Lybbert, T.J., Barrett, C.B. and Narjisse, H. (2002) 'Market-based conservation and local benefits: the case of Argan oil in Morocco', *Ecological Economics*, 41 (1): 125–44.

Lybbert, T.J., Barrett, C.B., Desta, S. and Coppock, D.L. (2004) 'Stochastic wealth dynamics and risk management among a poor population', *Economic Journal*, forthcoming.

Madulu, N.F. (1998) *Changing Lifestyles in Farming Societies of Sukumaland: Kwimba District, Tanzania*, Working Paper, No. 27, Dar es Salaam: Institute of Resource Assessment; and Leiden: African Studies Center.

Maji na Ufanisi (2002) *Poverty Reduction and Water Access in Sub-Saharan Africa: Kenya Case Study*, Nairobi: Water Aid and ODI.

Malawi (1993) *Economic Report 1993*, Lilongwe: Government of Malawi.

Malawi (1998a) *Local Government Act No. 42 of 1998*, Lilongwe: Government of Malawi.

Malawi (1998b) *Final Report: Local Government Financing and Decentralization*, 'The Shroeder Report', Lilongwe: UNDP/UNCDF/IDA, July.

Malawi (1999a) *Final Report: Accountability and Financial Controls in Local Government*, R.A. Kampanje *et al.*, 'The Kampanje Report', Lilongwe: UNDP/UNCDF, September.

Malawi (1999b) Ministry of Natural Resources and Environmental Affairs (MNREA), *The National Fisheries and Aquaculture Policy*, Department of Fisheries, Lilongwe: Government Printer.

Malawi (2000) National Economic Council (NEC), *Profile of Poverty in Malawi, 1998: Poverty Analysis of the Malawi Integrated Household Survey 1997–98*, Lilongwe: NEC, November.

Malawi (2001) *Final Report: Malawi Inter-Governmental Fiscal Transfers Study*, J. Boex *et al.*, 'The Boex Report', Lilongwe: UNCDF/UNDP, April.

Malawi (2002) Ministry of Finance and Economic Planning (MFEP), *Malawi Poverty Reduction Strategy Paper*, Lilongwe: Government of Malawi, April.

Malawi (2003) *Economic Report 2003*, Lilongwe: Government of Malawi.

Malleret-King, D., King, A., Mangubhai, S., Tunje, J., Muturi, J., Mueni, E. and On'ganda, H. (2003) 'Review of marine fisheries resources for Kenya', Annex 1.2 to *Understanding Fisheries Associated Livelihoods and the Constraints to their Development in Kenya and Tanzania*, DFID Fisheries Management Science Programme Project, No. R8196, London: Marine Resources Assessment Group Ltd.

Mamdani, M. (1996) *Citizen and Subject: Contemporary Africa and the Legacy of Late Colonialism*, Princeton: Princeton University Press.

Manda, D.K., Kimenyi, S.M. and Mwabu, G. (2000) 'A review of poverty and antipoverty initiatives in Kenya', *KIPPRA Discussion Paper*, No. 16., Nairobi: KIPPRA.

Manona, C. (1999) *Deagrarianization and the Urbanization of a Rural Economy: Agrarian Patterns in Melani Village in the Eastern Cape, South Africa'*, Working Paper, No. 32., Grahamstown: Institute of Social and Economic Research; and Leiden: African Studies Center.

Manor, J. (1999) *The Political Economy of Democratic Decentralisation*, Washington, DC: World Bank.

Marenya, P.P., Oluoch-Kosura, W., Place, F. and Barrett, C. (2003) 'Education, non-farm income, and farm investment in land-scarce Western Kenya', *BASIS Brief*, No. 14., Madison: University of Wisconsin.

Mayers, J., Ngalande, J., Bird, P. and Sibale, B. (2001) *Forestry Tactics: Lessons from Malawi's National Forestry Programme*, London: International Institute of Environment and Development.

Mazungu, E. (ed.) (2000) *Smallholder Irrigation at Crossroads: A Dialogue on Future Prospects of Smallholder Irrigation in Zimbabwe*, Proceedings of the University of Zimbabwe/ZIMWESI Seminar held at Holiday Inn, Harare, Zimbabwe, 18–20 July 2000.

McAllister, P. (1999) *Agriculture and Co-operative Labor in Shixini, Transkei, South Africa*, Working Paper, No. 33., Grahamstown: Institute of Social and Economic Research; and Leiden: African Studies Center.

McAuslan, P. (2000) 'Only the name of the country changes: the diaspora of "European" land law in Commonwealth Africa', in C. Toulmin and J. Quan (eds) *Evolving Land Rights, Policy and Tenure in Africa*, London: DFID/IIED/NRI.

McCay, A. and Lawon, D. (2003) 'Assessing the extent and nature of chronic poverty in low income countries: issues and evidence', *World Development*, 31 (3): 425–39.

McKean, M.A. (1992) 'Management of traditional common lands (Iriaichi) in Japan', in D.W. Bromley (ed.) *Making the Commons Work: Theory, Practice and Policy*, San Francisco: ICS Press.

Meagher, K. (2000) 'Veiled conflicts: peasant differentiation, gender and structural adjustment in Nigerian Hausaland', in D.F. Bryceson, C. Kay and J. Mooij (eds) *Disappearing Peasantries? Rural Labor in Africa, Asia and Latin America*, London: IT Publications.

Meagher, K. (2001) *The Bargain Sector: Economic Restructuring and the Non-Farm Sector in the Nigerian Savanna*, Aldershot: Ashgate.

Meinzen-Dick, R., Knox, A., Swallow, B. and Place, F. (eds) (2002) *Innovation in Natural Resource Management: The Role of Property Rights and Collective Action in Developing Countries*, Washington, DC: IFPRI, John Hopkins.

Mfanga, M. (1998) 'Govt official, MPs default to re-pay 3bn/- loans', *Sunday Observer*, 27 December 1998.

Migai Akech, J.M. (2001) *Rescuing Indigenous Tenure from the Ghetto of Neglect: Inalienability and the Protection of Customary Land Rights in Kenya*, Nairobi: African Centre for Technology Studies.

Migot-Adholla, S.E., Hazell, P., Blarel, B. and Place, F. (1991) 'Indigenous land rights systems in Sub-Saharan Africa: a constraint on policy?', *World Bank Economic Review*, 5 (1): 133–75.

Mijumbi, P. and Okidi, J. (2001) 'Analysis of poor and vulnerable groups in Uganda', *Occasional Paper*, No. 16, Kampala: Economic Policy Research Centre with support from DFID.

Mims, J. and Mathieu, L. (2002) 'Uganda selected rural livelihoods data tables', *LADDER Working Paper*, No. 25., Norwich: Overseas Development Group (ODG), University of East Anglia.

Mkandiriwe, T. and Soludo, C.C. (1999) *Our Continent, Our Future*, Trenton: Africa World Press, Inc.

Mookherjee, D. and Ray, D. (2002) 'Contractual structure and wealth accumulation', *American Economic Review*, 92 (4): 818–49.

Morduch, J. (1994) 'Poverty and vulnerability', *American Economic Review*, 84 (2): 221–5.

Morduch, J. (1995) 'Income smoothing and consumption smoothing', *Journal of Economic Perspectives*, 9 (3): 103–14.

Moris, J. (1987) 'Irrigation as a privileged solution in African development', *Development Policy Review*, 5: 99–123.

Moser, C.M. and Barrett, C.B. (2003) 'The disappointing adoption dynamics of a yield-increasing, low external input technology: the case of SRI in Madagascar', *Agricultural Systems*, 76: 1085–100.

Moser, C.O.N. (1998) 'The asset vulnerability framework: reassessing urban poverty reduction strategies', *World Development*, 26 (1): 1–19.

Mosse, D. (2002) '"People's knowledge": participation and patronage: operations and representation in rural development', in B. Cooke and U. Kothari (eds) *Participation: The New Tyranny?*, London: Zed Books.

Mukherjee, S. and Benson, T. (2003) 'The determinants of poverty in Malawi, 1998', *World Development,* 31 (2): 339–58.

Mukui, J.T. (1993) *Kenya Poverty Profiles, 1982–1992*, Nairobi: Ministry of Planning and National Development, Government of Kenya.

Mulat Demeke (1997) *Rural Non-Farm Activities in Impoverished Agricultural Communities: The Case of North Shoa, Ethiopia,* Working Paper, No. 25., Addis Ababa: Organization for Social Science Research in Eastern Africa; and Leiden: African Studies Center.

Mule, H.M., Ndii, D. and Opon, C. (2003) *Strategy for Economic Recovery,* Discussion Document, Nairobi: Ministry of Planning.

Mung'ong'o, C.G. (1998) *Coming Full Circle: Agriculture, Non-Farm Activities and the Resurgence of Out-Migration in Njombe District, Tanzania*, Working Paper, No. 26, Dar es Salaam: Institute of Resource Assessment; and Leiden: African Studies Center.

Mustapha, A.R. (1999) *Cocoa Farming and Income Diversification in South-western Nigeria*, Working Paper, No. 42, Kano: Center for Documentation and Research; and Leiden: African Studies Center.

Mwabu, G., Masai, W., Gesani, R., Kirimi, T., Munene, F., Chemengich, M. and Mariara, J. (2000) *Poverty in Kenya: Profiles and Determinants: Final Report to the AERC on the Poverty Project,* Nairobi: University of Nairobi and Ministry of Finance and Planning, mimeo.

Mwabumba, L., Ngulube, M., Kamoto, J. and Milner, J.-M. (2000) *Adaptive Co-management Site Selection Study: Country Report for Malawi*, Lilongwe: Ministry of Natural Resources, Fisheries and Environmental Affairs, Department of Forestry, mimeo.

Mwakalebela, L. (2001) 'In default of Agro-Fund ... 71 businessmen to appear in court', *Business Times*, Dar es Salaam, 16 March 2001.

Mwamfupe, D. (1998) *Changing Village Land, Labor and Livelihoods: Rungwe and Kyela Districts, Tanzania*, Working Paper, No. 29, Dar es Salaam: Institute of Resource Assessment; and Leiden: African Studies Center.

Mwondoshah, M. (1998) 'Govt officials, MPs default to re-pay 3bn/- loans', *Sunday Observer*, 27 December.

Mydral, G. (1957) *Economic Theory and Underdeveloped Regions*, London: G. Duckworth & Co Ltd.

Narayan, D. and Petesch, P. (2002) *Voices of the Poor: From Many Lands,* New York: Published for the World Bank, Oxford University Press. Online. Available HTTP: http://www.worldbank.org/poverty/voices/reports.htm (accessed 21 February 2004).

Narayan, D., Patel, R., Schafft, K., Rademacher, A. and Koch-Schulte, S. (2000a) *Voices of the Poor: Can Anyone Hear Us?*, New York: Published for the World Bank, Oxford University Press. Online. Available HTTP: http://www.worldbank.org/poverty/voices/reports.htm (accessed 21 February 2004).

Narayan, D., Chambers, R., Kaul Shah, M. and Petesch, P. (2000b) *Voices of the Poor: Crying Out for Change,* New York: Published for the World Bank, Oxford University Press. Online. Available HTTP: http://www.worldbank.org/poverty/voices/reports.htm (accessed 21 February 2004).

National Aids and Sexually Transmitted Disease Control Program (NASCOP) (2001) *AIDS in Kenya, Background Projections, Impact, Interventions, Policy,* Nairobi: Ministry of Health.

Neiland, A.E., Jaffry, S., Ladu, B.M.B., Sarch, M.-T. and Madakan, S.P. (2000) 'Inland fisheries of North East Nigeria including the Upper River Benue, Lake Chad and the Nguru-Gashua wetlands. I. Characterisation and analysis of planning suppositions', *Fisheries Research*, 48: 229–43.

Newman, C. and Canagarajah, S. (2000) 'Gender, poverty, and nonfarm employment in Ghana and Uganda', *World Bank Policy Research Paper Series*, No. 2367, Washington, DC: World Bank.

North, D.C. (1990) *Institutions, Institutional Change and Economic Performance*, Cambridge: Cambridge University Press.

Norton, A. and Foster, M. (2000) 'The potential of using sustainable livelihood approaches in poverty reduction strategy papers', A Discussion Paper for DFID, London: ODI, November, mimeo.

Oakerson, R.J. (1985) 'A model for the analysis of common property resources', paper presented at Common Property Resource Management Conference, Annapolis, Maryland, 21–27 April 1985.

Okidi, J. (1999) 'Regional growth disparities and household economic performance in Uganda', *Research Series*, No. 17, Kampala: Economic Policy Research Centre.

Okidi, J.A. and Mugambe, G.K. (2002) 'An overview of chronic poverty and development policy in Uganda', *CPRC Working Paper*, No. 11, Manchester: IDPM, University of Manchester. Online. Available HTTP: http://www.chronicpoverty.org/cp11.htm (accessed 16 January 2004).

Okoth-Ogendo, H.W.O. (2000) 'Legislative approaches to customary tenure and tenure reform in East Africa', in C. Toulmin and J. Quan (eds) *Evolving Land Rights, Policy and Tenure in Africa*, London: DFID/IIED/NRI.

Orr, A. (2000) '"Green gold?" Burley tobacco, smallholder agriculture and poverty alleviation in Malawi', *World Development*, 28 (2): 347–63.

Orr, A. and Orr, S. (2002) 'Agriculture and micro enterprise in Malawi's rural South', *Agricultural Research & Extension Network Paper*, No. 119, London: The Overseas Development Institute.

Ostrom, E. (1990) *Governing the Commons: The Evolution of Institutions for Collective Action*, Cambridge: Cambridge University Press.

Otsuko, K. and Place, F. (eds) (2001) *Land Tenure and Natural Resource Management: A Comparative Study of Agrarian Communities in Africa and Asia*, Washington, DC: IFPRI, Johns Hopkins.

Oxfam International (2002) *Rigged Rules and Double Standards: Trade, Globalisation, and the Fight Against Poverty*, Oxford: Oxfam International, April.

Oyejide, A., Ndulu, B. and Gunning, J.-W. (1999) 'Introduction and overview', in A. Oyejide, B. Ndulu and J.-W. Gunning (eds) *Regional Integration and Trade Liberalization in Sub-Saharan Africa, vol. 2: Country Case-Studies*, London: Macmillan.

Oyugi, N.L., Mwabu, G. and Masai, W. (2000) 'The determinants of poverty in Kenya', *African Journal of Economic Policy*, 8, June.

Pakenham, T. (1991) *The Scramble for Africa*, London: Abacus.

Pauly, D. (1997) 'Small-scale fisheries in the tropics: marginality, marginalisation, and some implications for fisheries management', in E.K. Pikitch, D.D. Huppert and M.P. Sissenwine (eds) *Global Trends: Fisheries Management*, Bethesda: American Fisheries Society.

Pedersen, P. (2002) *The Logistical Revolution and the Changing Structure of Agriculturally Based Commodity Chains in Africa*, Copenhagen: Centre for Development Studies.

Place, F., Franzel, S., DeWolf, J., Rommelse, R., Kwesiga, F., Niang, A. and Jama,

B. (2002) 'Agroforestry for soil fertility replenishment: evidence on adoption processes in Kenya and Zambia', in C. Barrett, F. Place and A. Aboud (eds) *Natural Resources Management in African Agriculture,* Wallingford: CABI Publishing.

Place, F., Ssenteza, J. and Otsuka, K. (2001) 'Customary and private land management in Uganda', in K. Otsuka and F. Place (eds) *Land Tenure and Natural Resource Management: A Comparative Study of Agrarian Communities in Africa and Asia,* Washington, DC: IFPRI, John Hopkins.

Platteau J.-P. (2000) 'Does Africa need land reform?', in C. Toulmin and J. Quan (eds) *Evolving Land Rights, Policy and Tenure in Africa,* London: DFID/IIED/NRI.

Pollnac, R.B., Pomeroy, R.S. and Harkes, I.H.T. (2001) 'Fishery policy and job satisfaction in three southeast Asian fisheries', *Ocean and Coastal Management,* 44: 531–44.

Pomeroy, R.S. and Berkes, F. (1997) 'Two to tango: the role of government in fisheries co-management', *Marine Policy,* 21 (5): 465–80.

Ponte, S. (1998a) 'Fast crops, fast cash: market liberalization and rural livelihoods in Songea and Morogoro Districts, Tanzania', *Canadian Journal of African Studies,* 33 (2): 316–47.

Ponte, S. (1998b) 'The political economy of agricultural input distribution in post-liberalization Tanzania', paper presented at the African Studies Association Meeting, Chicago, 1998, mimeo.

Ponte, S. (2002a) 'The politics of ownership: Tanzanian coffee policy in the age of liberal reformism', paper presented at the African Studies Association of the UK Biennial Conference, University of Birmingham, 9–11 September 2002.

Ponte, S. (2002b) *Farmers and Markets in Tanzania: Policy Reforms and Changing Rural Livelihoods,* Oxford: James Currey Publishers.

Postel, S. (1992) *The Last Oasis: Facing Water Scarcity,* Worldwatch Environmental Alert Series, London: Earthscan Publications.

Poulton, C. (1998) 'Cotton production and marketing in northern Ghana: the dynamics of competition in a system of interlocking transactions', in A. Dorward, J. Kydd and C. Poulton (eds) *Smallholder Cash Crop Production Under Market Liberalisation: A New Institutional Economics Perspectives,* Wallingford: CAB International.

Poulton, C., Kydd, J. and Dorward, A. (1999) *Input Credit for Smallholder Farmers: Can the Private Sector Help?,* Wye: Department of Agricultural Economics and Business Management, Imperial College at Wye.

Poulton, C., Gibbon, P., Hanyani-Mlambo, B., Kydd, J., Maro, W., Nylandsted Larsen, Osorio, A., Tschirley, D. and Zulu, B. (2004) 'Competition and coordination in liberalized African cotton market systems', *World Development,* 32 (3): 519–36.

Pretty, J.N., Guijt, I., Thompson, J. and Scoones, I. (1995) *Participatory Learning and Action: A Trainer's Guide,* London: International Institute for Environment and Development (IIED).

Quisumbing, A.R. (2003) 'Food aid and child nutrition in rural Ethiopia', *World Development,* 31 (7): 1309–24.

Raikes, P. and Gibbon, P. (2000) 'The current restructuring of African export crop agriculture in global context', *Journal of Peasant Studies,* 27 (2): 50–93.

Ranis, G. and Stewart, F. (1993) 'Rural nonagricultural activities in development: theory and application', *Journal of Development Economics,* 40: 75–101.

Ravallion, M. (1994) *Poverty Comparisons,* Chur: Harwood Academic Publishers.

Ravallion, M. (1999) 'Appraising workfare', *World Bank Research Observer,* 14 (1): 31–48.

Reardon, T. (1997) 'Using evidence of household income diversification to inform study of the rural nonfarm labor market in Africa', *World Development*, 25 (5): 735–48.

Reardon, T., Stamoulis, A., Balisacan, M.E., Berdegue, J. and Banks, B. (1998) 'Rural non-farm income in developing countries', in *The State of Food and Agriculture,* Rome: FAO.

Ribot, J.C. (1999) 'Decentralisation, participation and accountability in the Sahelian forestry: legal instruments of political-administrative control', *Africa*, 69 (1): 23–65.

Ribot, J.C. (2001) 'Decentralized natural resource management: nature and democratic decentralization in Sub-Saharan Africa', paper presented at the UNCDF-sponsored Participatory Symposium on Decentralization and Local Governance in Africa, Cape Town, March 2001.

Ribot, J.C. (2002) *Democratic Decentralization of Natural Resources*, Washington, DC: World Resources Institute.

Robert, M. (2002) 'Govt plans new bank for farmers', *The African*, Dar es Salaam, 2 March.

Roe, D., Mayers, J., Grieg-Gran, M., Kothari, A., Fabricius, C. and Hughes, R. (2000) 'Evaluating Eden: exploring the myths and realities of community-based wildlife management', *Evaluating Eden Series*, vol. 8, London: International Institute of Environment and Development.

Rogaly, B., Coppard, D., Rafique, A., Rana, K., Sengupta, A. and Biswas, J. (2002) 'Seasonal migration and welfare/illfare in Eastern India: a social analysis', *The Journal of Development Studies*, 38 (5): 89–114.

Rogers, B. (1980) *The Domestication of Women: Discrimination in Developing Societies*, London: Tavistock Publications.

Romer, P. (1986) 'Increasing returns and long run growth', *Journal of Political Economy,* 94 (4): 1002–37.

Romer, P. (1994) 'New goods, old theory, and the welfare costs of trade restrictions', *Journal of Development Economics,* 43 (1): 5–38.

Rosenhouse, S. (1989) 'Identifying the poor: is headship a useful concept?', *World Bank Living Standards Measurement Study Working Paper,* No. 58., Washington, DC: World Bank.

Rosenstein-Rodan, P. (1943) 'Problems of industrialization of Eastern and South-Eastern Europe', *Economic Journal,* 53: 202–11.

Roumasset, J.A., Boussard, J.-M. and Singh, I. (eds) (1979) *Risk, Uncertainty and Agricultural Development,* New York: Agricultural Development Council.

Rozemeijer, N. and van der Jagt, C. (2000) 'Community-based natural resources management in Botswana: how community-based is community-based natural resources management in Botswana?', in S. Shackleton and B. Campbell (eds) *Empowering Communities to Manage Natural Resources: Case Studies from Southern Africa*, Harare: SADC Natural Resource Management Programme.

Sahn, D. and Arulpragasam, J. (1994) 'Adjustment without structural change: the case of Malawi', in D. Sahn (ed.) *Adjusting to Policy Failure in African Economies*, Ithaca: Cornell University Press.

Saith, A. (1992) *The Rural Non-Farm Economy: Processes and Policies*. Geneva: International Labor Office.

Sandbrook, R. (1985) *The Politics of Africa's Stagnation*, Cambridge: Cambridge University Press.

Sandbrook, R. (1986) 'The state and economic stagnation in tropical Africa', *World Development*, 14 (3): 319–32.

Sandbrook, R. (2000) *Closing the Circle: Democratization and Development in Africa*, London: Zed Books.

Sarch, M.-T. and Allison, E.H. (2000) 'Fluctuating fisheries in Africa's inland waters: well-adapted livelihoods, maladapted management', Proceedings of the 10th International Conference of the Institute of Fisheries Economics and Trade, Corvallis, Oregon, 9–14 July 2000. Online. Available HTTP: http://osu.orst.edu/dept/IIFET/2000/papers/sarch.pdf (accessed 21 February 2004).

Sarch, M.-T. and Birkett, C.M. (2000) 'Fishing and farming at Lake Chad: responses to lake level fluctuations', *The Geographical Journal*, 163: 1–17.

Sarris, A. and Van den Brink, R. (1994) 'Tanzania: from forced modernization to *perestroika*', in D. Sahn (ed.) *Adjusting to policy failure in African economies*, Ithaca: Cornell University Press.

Schuh, G.E. (2000) 'The household: the neglected link in research and programs for poverty alleviation', *Food Policy*, 25: 233–41.

Schultz, B. (2001) 'Irrigation, drainage and flood protection in a rapidly changing world', *Irrigation and Drainage*, 50: 261–77.

Schwartz, L. (1994) 'The role of the private sector in agricultural extension: economic analysis and case studies', *Agricultural Administration (Research and Extension) Network Paper*, No. 48, London: Overseas Development Institute.

Scoones, I. (1998) 'Sustainable rural livelihoods: a framework for analysis', *IDS Working Paper*, No. 72, Brighton: IDS, University of Sussex.

Scoones, I. (ed.) (1995) *Living with Uncertainty: New Directions in Pastoral Development in Africa*, London: Intermediate Technology Publications.

Sen, A. (1996) 'Capability and well-being. The quality of life', in M. Nussbaum and A. Sen (eds) *The Quality of Life*, Oxford: Clarendon.

Sen, K. (2002) 'Economic reforms and rural livelihood diversification in Tanzania', *LADDER Working Paper*, No. 12, Norwich: Overseas Development Group (ODG), University of East Anglia.

Sen, K. and Chinkunda, A. (2002) 'Economic reforms and rural livelihoods in Malawi', *LADDER Working Paper*, No. 20, Norwich: Overseas Development Group (ODG), University of East Anglia.

Sender, J. and Smith, S. (1990) *Poverty, Class and Gender in Rural Africa*, London: Routledge.

SFLP (2002) 'Integrating small-scale fisheries in poverty reduction planning in West Africa – report of the consultation', SFLP/RF/15, Cotonou: Sustainable Fisheries Livelihoods Programme. Online. Available HTTP: http://www.sflp.org/eng/fr/003/doc/rconsuleng.doc (accessed 22 February 2004).

Shackleton, S. and Campbell, B. (2001) *Devolution in Natural Resources Management: Institutional Arrangements and Shifts – a synthesis of case studies for Southern Africa*, June 2001, Report to SADC NRM Project No. 690-0251.12, Harare: SADC Natural Resource Management Programme, mimeo.

Shackleton, S., Campbell, B., Wollenberg, E. and Edmunds, D. (2002) 'Devolution and community-based management: creating space for local people to participate and benefit?', *Natural Resources Perspectives*, vol. 76, London: Overseas Development Institute.

Shah, T. (2000) 'Pedalling out of poverty: livelihood impacts of treadle pump irrigation in South Asia', in *Annual Report 1999–2000,* Colombo: International Water Management Institute.

Shanin, T. (ed.) (1976) *Peasants and Peasant Societies,* Middlesex: Penguin Books.

Shao, F., Mlay, E.E. and Mushi, V. (2003) 'Review of marine fisheries for Tanzania', Annex 1.1 to *Understanding Fisheries Associated Livelihoods and the Constraints to their Development in Kenya and Tanzania,* DFID Fisheries Management Science Programme Project No. R8196, London: Marine Resources Assessment Group Ltd.

Shao, J.R. (2002) *Agriculture and Market Liberalisation in Tanzania: Problems of Cotton Production and Marketing in Bunda District',* Dar es Salaam: TADREG-TASA, June.

Shepherd, A. and Farolfi, S. (1999) 'Export crop liberalization in Africa – a review', *FAO Agricultural Services Bulletin,* No. 135, Rome: FAO.

Shepherd, K.D. and Soule, M.J. (1998) 'Soil fertility management in west Kenya: dynamic simulation of productivity, profitability and sustainability at different resource endowment levels', *Agriculture, Ecosystems and Environment,* 71 (1): 131–45.

Shinyekwa, I. (2002) *Alcohol,* Kampala: EPRC and CPRC, mimeo.

Short, J. (2000) *Impact of Tariff Changes,* Report prepared for the Ministry of Finance, Planning and Economic Development, Kampala: MFPED.

Siegel, S. and Castellan, N.J. (1988) *Nonparametric Statistics for the Behavioural Sciences,* 2nd edn, New York: McGraw-Hill.

Singh, N. and Gilman, J. (1999) 'Making livelihoods more sustainable', *International Social Science Journal,* 51 (4): 539–45.

Skees, J.R. (2000) 'A role for capital markets in natural disasters: a piece of the food security puzzle', *Food Policy,* 25 (3): 365–78.

Songorwa, A., Buhrs, T. and Hughey, K. (2000) 'Community-based wildlife management in Africa: a critical assessment of the literature', *Natural Resources Journal,* 40: 603–43.

Soussan, J., Blaikie, P., Springate-Baginski, O. and Chadwick, M. (2001) 'Understanding livelihood proccesses and dynamics: livelihood-policy relationships in South Asia', Working Paper, No. 7, Leeds: University of Leeds.

SSC Inc and OAFCC Ltd (2002) *The Master Plan Study on Fisheries Development in The United Republic of Tanzania – Summary,* report submitted by System Science Consultants Inc, and Overseas Agro-Fisheries Consultants Co. Ltd, Japan: Japanese Technical Cooperation Agency; and Dar es Salaam: Ministry of Natural Resources and Tourism, Fisheries Division.

Strauss, J. and Thomas, D. (1998) 'Health, nutrition, and economic development', *Journal of Economic Literature,* 36 (2): 766–817.

Sullivan, S. (2001) 'How sustainable is the communalizing discourse of "new" conservation? The masking of difference, inequality and aspiration in the fledgling "conservancies" of Namibia', in D. Chatty and M. Colchester (eds) *Conservation and Mobile Indigenous Peoples: Displacement, Forced Settlement and Sustainable Development,* Oxford: Berghahn Books.

Sullivan, S. (2002) 'On non-equilibrium in arid and semi-arid grazing systems', Guest editorial, *Journal of Biogeography,* 29: 1595–618.

Sundet, G. (1997) 'The politics of land in Tanzania', unpublished D.Phil. thesis, University of Oxford.

Swallow, B.M., Walsh, M., Nyantika, D., Muriithi, S., Noordin, Q., Ong, C. and Shepherd, K. (2002) *Improved Land Management in the Lake Victoria Basin: Annual Technical Report July 2001 to June 2002,* Natural Resource Problems, Priorities and

Policies Programme, Nairobi: International Centre for Research in Agroforestry (ICRAF).

Swynnerton, R.J.M. (1954) *A Plan to Intensify the Development of African Agriculture in Kenya*, Nairobi: Government Printer.

Tanzania (no date) *National Fertilizer Policy*, draft, Dar es Salaam: Government Printer.

Tanzania (1993) *1993 Statistical Abstract*, Dar es Salaam: National Bureau of Statistics (NBS).

Tanzania (1998) *National Poverty Eradication Strategy*, Dar es Salaam: Government Printer.

Tanzania (2000a) *Poverty Reduction Strategy Paper (PRSP)*, Dar es Salaam: Government Printer, October.

Tanzania (2000b) *Tanzania; Agriculture: Performance and Strategies for Sustainable Growth*, Dar es Salaam: Government Printer.

Tanzania (2001a) *Report of the Controller and Auditor General for the Financial Year ended 30th June, 2000*, Dar es Salaam: Government Printer.

Tanzania (2001b) Ministry of Cooperatives and Marketing (MCM), *The Cooperative Development Policy, 2001* (second draft), presented at the stakeholders workshop, Arusha, 17–18 September 2001.

Tanzania (2001c) *PRSP Progress Report 2000/01*, Dar es Salaam: Government Printer.

Tanzania (2001d) Ministry of Agriculture and Food Security (MAFS), *Agricultural Sector Development Strategy*, Draft Final Report, Dar es Salaam: Government Printer, 20 July.

Tanzania (2001e) Ministry of Water and Livestock Development (MWLD), *National Water Policy*, Draft, Dar es Salaam: Ministry of Water and Livestock Development.

Tanzania (2001f) Tanzanian Government Statistics. Online. Available HTTP: http://www.tanzania.go.tz/agriculture.html (accessed 22 February 2004).

Tanzania (2001g) SMUWC, *Final Project Reports*, Dar es Salaam: Directorate of Water Resources, Ministry of Water, Government of Tanzania. Online. Available HTTP: http://www.usangu.org (accessed on 17 January 2004).

Tanzania (2002a) *Household Budget Survey 2000/01: Key Findings*, Dar es Salaam: National Bureau of Statistics, July.

Tanzania (2002b) *Poverty and Human Development Report*, Dar es Salaam: Mkuki na Nyota Publishers.

Tanzania (2003) *2003 Statistical Abstract*, Dar es Salaam: National Bureau of Statistics (NBS).

Tanzania Agriculture Situation Analysis (TASA) (2001) 'Review of SOFRAIP', two vols, Dar es Salaam: TASA, October.

Tanzania Development Research Group (TADREG) (2001) 'CSO statement on environment, rural development and agriculture, 2001/02', Consultative Group Meeting, Karimjee Hall, Dar es Salaam, September 10–11.

Taylor, H. (2002) 'Insights into participation from critical management and labour process perspectives', in B. Cooke and U. Kothari (eds) *Participation: the New Tyranny*, London: Zed Books.

Taylor, M. (2001) 'Whose agenda? Reassessing the role of community-based natural resources management in Botswana', in M. Taylor and C. Twyman (eds) *Community-Based Natural Resources Management in Southern Africa*, Oxford: James Currey.

Teitze, U., Groenewold, G. and Marcoux, A. (2000) 'Demographic change in coastal fishing communities and its implications for the coastal environment', *FAO Fisheries Technical Paper*, No. 403, Rome: FAO.

Tellegen, N. (1997) *Rural Enterprises in Malawi: Necessity or Opportunity?* Aldershot: Ashgate.

Therkildsen, O. (2000) 'Public sector reform in a poor, aid dependent country, Tanzania', *Public Administration and Development*, 20: 61–71.

Thornton, P.K., Kruska, R.L., Henninger, N., Kristjanson, P.M., Reid, R.S., Atieno, F., Odero, F. and Ndegwa, T. (2002) *Mapping Poverty and Livestock in the Developing World*, Nairobi: International Livestock Research Institute (ILRI).

Tiffen, M., Mortimore, M. and Gichuki, F. (1994) *More People, Less Erosion: Environmental Recovery in Kenya*, Chichester: John Wiley.

Toulmin, C. (1992) *Cattle, Women, and Wells: Managing Household Survival in the Sahel*, Oxford: Clarendon Press.

Toulmin, C. and Quan, J. (eds) (2000) *Evolving Land Rights, Policy and Tenure in Africa*, London: DFID/IIED/NRI.

Townsend, R. (1995) 'Consumption insurance: an evaluation of risk bearing systems in low-income economies', *Journal of Economic Perspectives*, 9 (3): 83–102.

Tripp, R. (2001) 'Agricultural technology policies for rural development', in C. Ashley and S. Maxwell (eds) *Development Policy Review, 19 (4)*, London: Overseas Development Institute.

Uganda (1992) Ministry of Finance, Planning and Economic Development (MFPED) *Uganda, 1992 National Integrated Household Survey*, Kampala: MFPED. Online. Available HTTP: http://www4.worldbank.org/afr/poverty/databank/surnav/show_survey.cfm?ID=74 (accessed 24 March 2004).

Uganda (1996) Agricultural Policy Secretariat, *The Impact and Consequences of the Liberalization of Coffee and Cotton Processing and Marketing in Uganda*, Rome: FAO.

Uganda (1997) Ministry of Finance, Planning and Economic Development (MFPED), *Poverty Eradication Action Plan (A National Challenge for Uganda)*, vol. 1, Kampala: MFPED.

Uganda (1999) Ministry of Finance, Planning and Economic Development (MFPED), *Uganda Poverty Status Report, 1999*, Kampala: MFPED.

Uganda (2000a) Ministry of Agriculture, Animal Industry and Fisheries (MAAIF) and Ministry of Finance, Planning and Economic Development (MFPED), *Plan for Modernization of Agriculture (PMA): Eradicating Poverty in Uganda*, Kampala: MAAIF/MFPED.

Uganda (2000b) Ministry of Finance, Planning and Economic Development (MFPED), *Uganda Poverty Profile: What do we Know about the Poor?* Discussion Paper 3, Kampala: MFPED.

Uganda (2000c) Ministry of Finance, Planning and Economic Development (MFPED), *Uganda Participatory Poverty Assessment Report*, Kampala: MFPED.

Uganda (2000d) Ministry of Agriculture, Animal Industry and Fisheries (MAAIF) and Ministry of Finance, Planning and Economic Development (MFPED) *Master Document of the National Agricultural Advisory Services (NAADS) Task Force and Joint Donor Report*, Entebbe: MAAIF; and Kampala: MFPED.

Uganda (2000e) Ministry of Agriculture Animal Industry and Fisheries (MAAIF) *Policy for the Improvement of the Delivery of Veterinary Services in Uganda*, First Draft, May 2000, Kampala: Directorate of Animal Resources, MAAIF.

Uganda (2000f) *Uganda Poverty Reduction Strategy Paper*, Kampala: Government Printer.

Uganda (2001a) Ministry of Finance, Planning and Economic Development (MFPED), *Poverty Eradication Action Plan (2001–2003)*, vol. 1, Kampala: MFPED, February.

Uganda (2001b) Ministry of Local Government, *Statutory Instruments Supplement,* No. 30., Kampala: Government Printer.

Uganda (2001c) *Local Governments Act, 1997*, [With Amendment Act 2001], Kampala: The LDC Publishers Press.

Uganda (2001d) Ministry of Finance Planning and Economic Development (MFPED) *Poverty Eradication Action Plan (PEAP), 2000–2003*, Kampala: MFPED.

Uganda (2002a) Ministry of Finance, Planning and Economic Development (MFPED), *Poverty Reduction Strategy Paper Progress Report 2002,* Kampala: MFPED, April.

Uganda (2002b) Ministry of Local Government, *Statutory Instruments Supplement,* No. 10., Kampala: Government Printer.

Uganda (2002c) Ministry of Agriculture, Animal Industry and Fisheries (MAAIF) *The National Fisheries Policy* (final draft, June 2002), Kampala: Government Printer.

Uganda (2003a) Ministry of Finance, Planning and Economic Development (MFPED), *Uganda Participatory Poverty Assessment Report,* Kampala: MFPED.

Uganda (2003b) Ministry of Finance Planning and Economic Development (MFPED), *Uganda Poverty Status Report, 2003,* Kampala: MFPED.

Uganda (2003c) Uganda Bureau of Statistics, *Uganda National Household Survey 2002/2003: Report on the Socio-Economic Survey,* Kampala: UBOS, November.

Uganda Bureau of Statistics (UBOS) (2003) *The 1993 Statistical Abstract.* Online. Available HTTP: http://www.ubos.org (accessed 25 March 2004).

Uganda Bureau of Statistics (UBOS) (2003) *The 2003 Statistical Abstract.* Online. Available HTTP: http://www.ubos.org (accessed 25 March 2004).

Uganda Investment Authority (2003) Online. Available HTTP: http://www.ugandainvest.com/ (accessed 17 January 2004).

UNDP (United Nations Development Programme) (1994) *Human Development Report, 1994*, Oxford: Oxford University Press.

UNDP (1999) *Human Development Report, 1999,* Oxford: Oxford University Press.

UNDP (2002) *Human Development Report 2002*, Oxford: Oxford University Press for UNDP.

Utne, S., Urasa, S. and Østmo, L. (1994) *Food and Fertilizers in Tanzania*, Report to Norwegian Agency for Development Cooperation (NORAD), Dar es Salaam: NORAD, February, mimeo.

Vandemoortele, J. (1982) 'Income distribution and poverty in Kenya: a statistical analysis', Discussion Paper, No. 275., Nairobi: Institute of Development Studies (IDS), University of Nairobi.

van Koppen, B. (1998) *More Jobs Per Drop: Targeting Irrigation to Poor Women and Men*, Amsterdam: Royal Tropical Institute (KIT).

van Koppen, B., Sokile, C., Lankford, B.A., Mahoo, H., Hatibu, N. and Yanda, P. (2004) 'The failure of formal water rights in rural Tanzania: grafting modern water pricing on colonial water use registration', in F. Molle, R. Barker and J. Berkoff (eds) *Between Prescription and Practice: Irrigation Water Pricing Policies in Context*, Colombo: Comprehensive Assessment of Water Management in Agriculture, International Water Management Institute.

van Vuuren, A. (2000) *Female-headed Households: Their Survival Strategies in Tanzania*, Working Paper, No. 44, Leiden: African Studies Center.

von Braun, J. (ed.) (1995) *Employment for Poverty Reduction and Food Security*, Washington, DC: International Food Policy Research Institute.

Warnock, K. (2002) *Reducing Poverty: is the World Bank's Strategy Working?*, Panos Report No. 45, London: The Panos Institute.

Watkins, K. (1999) *Education Now: Break the Cycle of Poverty*, Oxford: Oxfam International.

Watts, M.J. (2000) 'Contested communities, malignant markets and gilded governance: justice, resource extraction and conservation in the Tropics', in C. Zerner (ed.) *People, Plants and Justices: The Politics of Nature Conservation*, New York: Columbia University Press.

Webb, P., Bistrat, G. and Coppock, D.L. (1991) 'Food sustainability and sustainable growth for pastoral systems in semi-arid Africa', in S.A Vosti, T. Reardon and W. von Urff (eds) *Agricultural Sustainability, Growth and Poverty Alleviation in East and South-East Asia: Issues and Policies*, proceedings of the Conference held in Feldafing on 23–27 September 1991, Feldafing: IFPRI/DSE/ZEL.

White, H. (2002) 'Combining quantitative and qualitative approaches in poverty analysis', *World Development*, 30 (3): 511–22.

Whitehead, A. (2001) 'Trade, trade liberalisation and rural poverty in low-income Africa: a gendered account', background paper for the UNCTAD 2001, *Least Developed Countries Report*, mimeo.

Wiggins, S. (2000) 'Interpreting changes from the 1970s to the 1990s in African agriculture through village studies', *World Development*, 28: 631–62.

Wilkes, A. and Lefrancois, F. (2002) *Blinding with Science or Encouraging Debate? How World Bank Analysis Determines PRSP Policies*, London: Bretton Wood Project and World Vision. Online. Available HTTP: http://www.brettonwoodsproject.org/topic/adjustment/a30blinding.html (accessed 18 January 2004).

Willis, J. (2002) *Potent Brews: A Social History of Alcohol in East Africa 1850–1999*, Kampala: Fountain Publishers.

Wilson, D.C., Nielsen, J.R. and Degnbol, P. (eds) (2003) *The Fisheries Co-management Experience: Accomplishments, Challenges and Prospects*, Dordrecht: Kluwer Academic Publishers.

Wolf, E.R. (1966) *Peasants*, Englewood Cliffs: Prentice-Hall, Inc.

World Bank (1991) *World Bank Development Report 1991: The Challenge of Development*, Washington, DC: World Bank.

World Bank (1994) *World Bank Findings: Africa Region*, No. 23, Washington, DC: World Bank.

World Bank (1995) *Kenya Poverty Assessment*, Report No. 13152-KE, Washington, DC: World Bank.

World Bank (1998) *Malawi Country Assistance Strategy*, Report No. 18349 MAI, Washington, DC: World Bank.

World Bank (1999) *Uganda, 1999 National Household Survey 99/2000*, Washington, DC: World Bank. Online. Available HTTP: http://www4.worldbank.org/afr/poverty/databank/ (accessed 24 March 2004).

World Bank (2000a) *Kenya Country Assistance Evaluation*, Report No. 21409, Washington, DC: World Bank, November.

World Bank (2000b) *Can Africa Claim the 21st Century?*, Washington, DC: The World Bank.

World Bank (2000c) *Tanzania: Country Assistance Strategy*, Washington, DC: World Bank.

World Bank (2000d). *Agriculture in Tanzania Since 1986: Follower or Leader of Growth?* Washington, DC: International Food Policy Research Institute, World Bank.

World Bank (2001a) *World Development Report 2000/2001: Attacking Poverty*, Oxford: Oxford University Press.

World Bank (2001b) *Tanzania at the Turn of the Century: From Reforms to Sustained Growth and Poverty Reduction,* Washington, DC: World Bank.

World Bank (2002a) *World Development Report 2002: Building Institutions for Markets,* Washington, DC: World Bank.

World Bank (2002b) *World Development Indicators 2001*, Washington, DC: World Bank.

World Bank (2002c) *African Development Indicators 2002*, Washington, DC: World Bank.

Wortmann, C.S. and Eledu, C.A. (1999) *Uganda's Agroecological Zones: A Guide for Planners and Policy Makers*, Kampala: Centro Internacional de Agricultura Tropical.

Young, A.A. (1928) 'Increasing returns and economic progress', *Economic Journal*, 38: 527–42.

Yunez-Naude, A. and Taylor, J.E. (2001) 'The determinants of nonfarm activities and incomes of rural households in Mexico, with emphasis on education', *World Development,* 29 (3): 561–72.

Yunusa, M.-B. (1999) *Not Farms Alone: A Study of Rural Livelihoods in the Middle Belt of Nigeria*, Working Paper, No. 38, Kano: Center for Documentation and Research; and Leiden: African Studies Center.

Zeller, M., Schrieder, G., von Braun, J. and Heidhues, F. (1997) *Rural Finance for Food Security for the Poor: Implications for Research and Policy*, Washington: International Food Policy Research Institute.

Zimmerman, F.J. and Carter, M.R. (2003) 'Asset smoothing, consumption smoothing and the reproduction of inequality under risk and subsistence constraints', *Journal of Development Economics,* 71 (2): 233–60.

Zvogu, E. *et al.* (1998) Review and Evaluation of MASAF Safety Net Programme and Assessment of its Impact: Final Report, Lilongwe: MASAF, January.

Index

For Product Safety Concerns and Information please contact our EU
representative GPSR@taylorandfrancis.com
Taylor & Francis Verlag GmbH, Kaufingerstraße 24, 80331 München, Germany

www.ingramcontent.com/pod-product-compliance
Lightning Source LLC
LaVergne TN
LVHW011105300926
849160LV00008B/289

* 9 7 8 0 4 1 5 5 1 1 3 9 1 *